LIBERATION IN ONE LIFETIME

M000287539

Liberation in One Lifetime

Biographies and Teachings of Milarepa

Francis V. Tiso
Foreword by Roberto Vitali

North Atlantic Books
Berkeley, California

Copyright © 2014 by Francis V. Tiso. All rights reserved. No portion of this book, except for brief review, may be reproduced, stored in a retrieval system, or transmitted in any form or by any means—electronic, mechanical, photocopying, recording, or otherwise—without the written permission of the publisher. For information contact North Atlantic Books.

Published by
North Atlantic Books
PO Box 12327
Berkeley, California 94712

Cover photo by Francis V. Tiso
Cover and book design by Susan Quasha
Printed in the United States of America

Liberation in One Lifetime: Biographies and Teachings of Milarepa is sponsored by the Society for the Study of Native Arts and Sciences, a nonprofit educational corporation whose goals are to develop an educational and cross-cultural perspective linking various scientific, social, and artistic fields; to nurture a holistic view of arts, sciences, humanities, and healing; and to publish and distribute literature on the relationship of mind, body, and nature.

North Atlantic Books' publications are available through most bookstores. For further information, visit our website at www.northatlanticbooks.com or call 800-733-3000.

Library of Congress Cataloging-in-Publication Data

Tiso, Francis, author, compiler.
Liberation in one lifetime : biographies and teachings of Milarepa / Francis V. Tiso ; Foreword by Roberto Vitali.
pages cm
Summary: "This book contains translations of early biographies and teachings of Milarepa, one of Tibet's most famous yogis and poets"— Provided by publisher.
Based on the author's thesis (doctoral)—Columbia University, 1989.
Includes bibliographical references and index.
ISBN 978-1-58394-793-7 (paperback) — ISBN 978-1-58394-794-4 (kindle ed.)
1. Mi-la-ras-pa, 1040-1123. 2. Lamas—Tibet Region—Biography—History and criticism. 3. Lamas—Tibet Region—Biography. 4. Spiritual life—Bka'-rgyud-pa (Sect) I. Vitali, Roberto, writer of supplementary textual content. II. Title.
BQ7950.M557T57 2014
294.3'923092—dc23
[B]

2013025876

1 2 3 4 5 6 7 8 9 UNITED 19 18 17 16 15 14

PHOTO BY FRANCIS V. TISO

Lama Khartse of Tarap-Dho, Dolpo, Nepal, recites the life of Milarepa (Spring, 1997).

Contents

Foreword

Roberto Vitali

I wish to open this foreword to the volume of Francis Tiso dedicated to rje btsun Mid la (Milarepa) with a few words concerning where at present the life and activity of the great bKa' brgyud pa master stand in the widening spectrum of the Tibetan studies. While the disciplines concerned with the more concrete expressions of Tibetan culture (from the arts to anthropology and reconnaissance of religious geography) are becoming increasingly popular among upcoming researchers in the present wave of the studies, textual analysis keeps being pursued by the Tibetologists devoted to philology with remarkable developments. Accessibility to the literature, and thus knowledge of it, has allowed them to make a quantum leap forward. It is then quite surprising that a towering personality such as rje btsun Mid la, the most famous ascetic-bard of Tibetan history, has received little attention for the most advanced research in the recent past, despite a few but remarkable exceptions. With his book Francis Tiso provides a much-needed contribution to furthering the knowledge of this seminal personality.

It is possible that the life and deeds of rje btsun Mid la have become a literary *déjà vu,* as Francis Tiso says in his Preface, to the point that the specialists have preferred to deal with more obscure topics urgently requiring their attention. This could be imputed to the wearing out of the initial interest in rje btsun Mid la shown, quite some time ago, by the pioneers in the field of Tibetan studies that I would define as "primordial," since their work leaves much to be desired and has not encouraged scholarly developments. They have engaged in the study of the biography of rje btsun Mid la completed in 1488 by gTsang smyon Heruka, possibly because this text, as Tiso says, was seen as "definitive" in the view of Tibetan savants of the last few centuries.

The *rnam thar* by gTsang smyon thus marginalized other biographical material on him, and it was natural that, at the beginning of the studies, Western authors took it as the source to be used. The personality of Mid la, the embodiment of Tibet's collective mind and aspirations, has thus suffered from a twofold stereotyped process: one created by gTsang smyon Heruka who established orthodoxy and officialdom and the other by the limited perspective of him conveyed by Western authors of the past. Its popularity in cycles outside Tibet and those not devoted to the study of the Tibetan tradition rests on the fact that the west has found in his life story the most consonant token available in Tibetan culture of several themes familiar to its own. His unfortunate childhood, his fall and catharsis, and the role of his guru as demanding father and the latter's wife as worried mother—plus his asceticism and poetical achievements—serve several Western values more than the life examples of other great *bla ma*-s, which share with the biographies of Mid la the complexities and obscurities of a distant culture but do not have those easily recognizable themes typical of his life story.

Avoiding a vision of him as simply a reflection of his true personality, Mid la represents the greatness of self-imposed marginality taking preeminence over the pomp of self-celebrated authoritarianism. Despite the major role played by monastic life, marginality and seclusion never died out in Tibet: they have remained a vibrant undercurrent, which is still resilient despite the many modern changes.

It may seem strange to mention marginality when Milarepa is the most celebrated Tibetan of all times. One needs to brush aside the stereotypes built over his life that led to his transformation into a symbol and reintegrate a fuller perspective. Tiso's work shows Mid la under a different light from the idyllic picture painted by his biographer, gTsang smyon Heruka. It conveys a direct understanding of his personality, digging deep into the sources of earlier times, not yet adulterated by a vision of Mid la as a collective myth given to Tibetan culture for its self-celebration but a man of great personality and significance. It is relieving to see in this book the dismissal of Mid la as a religious counterpart of another great hero of Tibetan imagery, Gling Ge sar. In some ways, the use of the personalities of Mid la and his older contemporary, Gling Ge sar, has run parallel in the course of Tibetan literary history. Both were transformed from personages with a human experience into legends. Tiso also tells the reader how this happened in the case of Mid la.

Tiso aims at showing a master in the classic sense of the Tibetan tradition, in which a guru is not a symbol but a lively presence. Before turning to asceticism, Mid la thoroughly learned the great tradition brought to Tibet by his teacher Mar pa, the tradition of mahāsiddhas of the caliber of Ti lo pa and Nā ro pa (Nāropa). Mid la went one step ahead of his master in the evolution of Buddhist practice in Tibet. Mar pa belonged to the season in which Buddhism was drawn from the Noble Land of India; Mid la inaugurated the season characterized by a local elaboration of the teachings in a way embryonically Tibetan but that also reflected the *mahāsiddha* tradition of India. For instance, his poetical vein was not spontaneous and uncultivated. The Doha tradition of Indian origin and the Tibetan penchant for songs, going back to the earliest historical traces of the culture on the plateau, combined in his person.

Differently from the savants of the later periods of Tibetan culture, Tiso has opted for an approach that considers all the numerous biographies of Mid la as being equally "definitive." In other words, he has espoused an approach that considers it equally crucial to look into the ancient biographies as much as into the one of gTsang smyon to detect two fundamental facts: the traces of rje btsun Mid la's true self for what is possible to reconstruct and the layers of interpretations that have been built up like layers of sediment through the centuries.

Indeed, the life of Mid la offers a unique opportunity to discover how a personality and the context in which it operated have been treated in the literature, which goes from legendary to factual. This wide-ranging attitude is to be credited to the richness of the bKa' brgyud pa biographical genre, which is outstanding in Tibetan literature, for it uniquely concentrates on the lives of his masters and records them in several nuances. For instance, in the fifteenth century, when the life of Mid la was rewritten by gTsang smyon to become a standard of Tibetan asceticism, the slightly earlier *lHo rong chos 'byung* (completed in 1446) was composed with the purpose of collecting as much old biographical material as possible, on the widest number of bKa' brgyud pa of all time.

The biographies of Mid la give an insight into eleventh-century Tibet but also embody values that have become eternal in the eyes of the Tibetan people. The latter relate to signs of his mystical practice and other cults popular in his days and, obviously, poetry and the singing-song genre. The cultural features of this period have required a patient but precious effort to collate this material.

One can draw a picture of the context in which Mid la lived in terms of movements and ideas with remarkable depth and comprehensiveness that include, among others, the composition of the following Mid la gathered around him and thus the transmission that issued from him; his interaction with other masters devoted to hermit life and the scholasticism of his time; and eleventh-century cultural geography, which influenced the behavior of successive generations, for the places he frequented became the destination of future pilgrimage and hermit life. They were located in lands away from the core of everything. The one he initiated was a movement begun at the periphery that traveled in the successive centuries as far as Mongolia, China, and the Ilkhanate of Baghdad.

I wish to close with a brief citation from one of the little known biographies of rje btsun Mid la, which shows how much he was anciently treasured by Tibetans of all walks of life, long before the final process of transformation of his personality into a myth took place. Chos rje Byang chub 'od, *Mid la'i rnam thar* (f.62a),[1] reads,

> While rNgag [*sic*] rDor mo was helping the step-father (*pha yar*) of sgom chen mGon ne in the fields called Wa, Khyal, and sGril, altogether three, at Nya nam Tshar ma because the demarcation of the fields had been mixed up, people

had a conversation, and one asked: "Who is the greatest religious practitioner of our time?" They discussed, and another wondered: "Is Zangs dkar lo tsa ba the best? Or is it Zha ma, the gNyam nam *jo mo*?" At that time, rNga rDor mo said: "The [best] religious practitioner of the present time is the man from our own land called Mid la ras pa."

—Roberto Vitali

author of *The Kingdoms of Gu.ge Pu.hrang According to mNga'.ris rgyal. rabs by Gu.ge khan.chen Ngag.dbang grags.pa*

Preface

More than thirty-five years ago, when I was an undergraduate at Cornell University, I was urged to read a book titled *Tibet's Great Yogi: Milarepa: A Biography from the Tibetan*, edited by W. Y. Evans-Wentz.[2] The book had been a "best seller" already for quite a while. I can still remember the coffee shop in Annabel Taylor Hall, the Commons: antiwar posters on the walls, a small stage and microphones for folk singers, the intensely idealistic conversations, the stray volumes on the old bookshelves, and the atmosphere redolent of flavors and smoke. In a very short time I had read not only the biography but also *The Hundred Thousand Songs of Milarepa,* translated by Garma Chang.[3] I soon came across the other Evans-Wentz volumes: *Tibetan Yoga and Secret Doctrines, The Tibetan Book of the Dead, The Book of the Great Liberation*, and others that were equally hard to resist, hard to understand, and hard to put down. For a generation of young people, these books were the prelude to the actual arrival of the Tibetan lamas in exile from their war-torn Land of Snows. The rest, as the cliché would have it, is history.

Reading the biography of Milarepa was an experience that had the force of a revelation. My previous knowledge of Buddhism was limited to high school readings on the so-called four noble truths and the nature of the Buddhist spiritual path. The way these doctrines had been presented was quite superficial and could not compete with St. Augustine, St. Thomas Aquinas, Teilhard de Chardin, Thomas Merton, and, not least, the documents of the Second Vatican Council, upon which I had begun to feast as a teenager. But in Milarepa's story, I found unexpected elements: a sorcerer converted by a destined encounter with a severe master, Marpa, a practitioner of mysterious tantric rituals and yoga. This form of Buddhism began to challenge my imagination just as I was leaving behind biochemistry to study history and literature to prepare for seminary.

Even the introduction to Evans-Wentz's edition stimulated my fervently Catholic imagination at the time. I was quite annoyed by Evans-Wentz's naïve footnotes praising Gnosticism and denouncing "Church Council Christianity." But in the preface to the second edition, Evans-Wentz acknowledged receiving numerous letters from readers of the first edition. The correspondents, who came from a variety of denominations and religions, recognized in Milarepa those universal characteristics of sanctity "over which no one religion can claim as an exclusive prerogative, but which are held in common among the saints of all religions."[4] Evans-Wentz's convictions about the saints in world religions continued to stimulate my imagination and my research, coming to fruition in my PhD dissertation, "A Study of the Buddhist Saint in Relation to the Biographical Tradition of Milarepa."[5]

The present volume takes the dissertation as a basis, adding on more recent research including fieldwork and refinements of my interpretation of the textual data. In 1997, I undertook a six-month research trip to India and Nepal—funded by the American Academy of Religions and the American Philosophical Society—which considerably advanced my understanding of the Milarepa corpus and confirmed several hypotheses advanced in my dissertation. Further research in Tibet, Nepal, and India during 1999, 2000, 2001, and 2003 contributed to my understanding of the social context of the Milarepa biographies and teachings.

At the heart of this research lies the great collection of biographies (Tibetan: *rnam thar*) that the *bKa' brgyud* masters have composed over the centuries. However I have not neglected the practice instructions given by Milarepa to his disciples in the form of songs of spirituality and in formal didactic prose (*gdams ngag*).[6] The biographical and song materials are in fact greatly clarified by studying the small collections of oral instructions attributed to Milarepa.

So who was Milarepa? Why is he so important? Who were his disciples and biographers? Why did they tell the "same story" over and over again?

We now know that the most widely read biography of Milarepa was written at the end of the fifteenth century by the Mad Yogin of gTsang (gTsang smyon Heruka). This author-complier joined the *Life* to the complete *Songs of Milarepa* (*Mila rnam thar mgur 'bum*), following very early tradition in the lineage. Therefore, there is a 370-year gap between the death of Milarepa (1040–1123? 1055–1128?) and the writing of these biographical texts. Even so, almost no critical work has been done on the older materials on the life, songs, and teachings of this pivotal saint and poet of Tibetan Buddhism. The Tibetans themselves regard gTsang smyon's works as definitive. Only a few of the highest lamas of our own time have expressed a real excitement about serious research on the sources for the biography of Milarepa; most other practitioners could not fathom such a patently alien interest.

In the first place, apart from a critical investigation of the sources, we cannot hope to be informed about the "historical Milarepa." Even the Tibetan sources questioned some of the stories commonly recounted in the Milarepa biographical tradition. For example, Gos Lotsaba, author of the *Blue Annals* (1476), wrote, "I had written the life-story of Mid-la [*sic*] in detail, because I had seen many spurious accounts. I believe that [my compilation] corresponds to actual facts."[7] So where, today, are all these "spurious accounts"? In a relatively short time, I was able to locate about half a dozen older versions of the Milarepa biography in the PL 480 collection in the Lehman Library at Columbia University. There, caged in the deepest caverns of that vast collection, are housed photostatic copies of rare manuscripts and xylographs rescued from the frenzy of the Red Guards. Every generation seems to have made its own contribution to the literary and devotional heritage. These authors were truly remarkable individuals whose own contributions are enhanced by the knowledge they transmit in their lives of Milarepa.

We have discovered that, to some extent, the biography of any Tibetan saint is the literary equivalent of the spontaneous personal songs of the poet-bards of the Himalayan region. The anecdotes are fairly consistent, although the words may vary widely. Each generation recreates the life and songs of Milarepa under the influence of those mysterious *ḍākinī* who dance in the sky and appear only to the best of *yogins* and *yoginīs*.

I would like to conclude this introduction with salutation of respect and gratitude to the many Tibetan masters and lay folk who helped with this research, among whom are His Holiness the Fourteenth Dalai Lama, H. E. Ven. Khandro Rinpoche, H. H. Gyalwa Drukchen, H. H. Drikung Kyabgon Rinpoche (Chetsang Rinpoche), Gen-la Losang Jampal, H. E. Chokyi Nyima Rinpoche, H. E. Tsultrim Gyamtso Rinpoche, H. E. Karma Trinley Rinpoche, H. E. Losang Tharchin Rinpoche, Lama Khartse of Dolpo, Lama Norbu Tsering of Pokhara, Lama Karma Angya of Gakar Gompa, Lama Tsering Tashi of Gakar Lha khang, Lama Namgyal of Ribum Gompa and his late father Lama Pema Wangyal, Ven Khenpo A-Chung of Pokhara, H. E. Trungram Gyaltrul Rinpoche, H. E. Namkhai Norbu Rinpoche, Lama Yeshe of Samye Ling, and Lama Ngawang Chopel of Jampa Lhakhang (Dolpo). I would also like to acknowledge the kindness of many Western scholars: the late Prof. Alex Wayman, E. Gene Smith, Amalia Pezzali, Slava Komarovsky, Franco and Kristin Pizzi, Hubert DeCleer, Michael Saso, Franz Karl Ehrhard, Claus Matthes, Roberto Vitali, Christoph Cüppers, David Germano, John S. Hawley, Toni Huber, David Jackson, Geoffrey Samuel, Per Kvaerne, Todd Lewis, Dan Martin, Glenn Mullin, Giacomella Orofino, Fabrizio Torricelli, Corneliu Cicortas, Peter Alan Roberts, the late Jared Douglas Rhoton, Cyrus Stearns, David Templeman, Robert Thurman, and Serinity Young. Though I have listened to them in earnest, I have not always followed their advice, and I take responsibility for the consequences.

I would like to offer this volume to all who would enter the religious world of medieval Tibet without prejudices or preconceptions. The tradition of Milarepa, as is the case with my own Catholic tradition, knows nothing of a realization that does not, at least in its indispensable initial phases, pass through doctrinal, traditional, ascetical, and literary discipline. Since few of my readers are likely to be highly realized "mahāsiddhas," and since the author, too, must confess his impatience with his lack of gnosis and persistent spiritual sloth, perhaps it behooves us to adhere sincerely to the texts and oral tradition that we have. In the life of Milarepa, we may not only find some reason to admire the humanity and depth of the Vajrayāna but also indeed be inspired to imitate its values and its wisdom.

May we draw near, even if in trepidation, to the holy, and if that encounter should provoke us to desire such realization, so much the better!

SPRING 2007, WASHINGTON, DC

Abbreviations

ADK: *Abhidharmakośa of Vasubandhu*

BA: *Blue Annals*, translated by George N. Roerich

HVT: *Hevajra Tantra*

IsMEO: Istituto Italiano per il Medio ed Estremo Oriente (publisher)

ITB: *Indo Tibetan Buddhism* by David Snellgrove, Shambhala Publications (1997)

LM: *Life of Milarepa*, translated by Lobsang P. Lhalungpa (1984)

LTWA: Library of Tibetan Works and Archives (publisher)

MPPŚ: *Mahāprajñāpāramitā Śāstra*

RTH: rGyal thang pa, *Mila rnam thar*

Songs: *The Hundred Thousand Songs of Milarepa* translated by Garma C. C. Chang (1962) from the Tibetan of gTsang smyon Heruka (the "Mad Yogin of gTsang"). Please note: sometimes this version is referenced; other times, earlier versions of the songs are referenced—this is why in certain places the word is capitalized or italicized and in other places it is not.

Standard Edition: *Mila rnam thar mgur 'bum* by gTsang smyon Heruka (1452–1507). Tibetan edition of this work (1989), published in Lhasa by Mtsho Sngon mi rigs dpe skrun khang.

Takpo: *Mahamudra: The Quintessence of Mind and Meditation* by Takpo Tashi Namgyal, translated by Lobsang P. Lhalungpa (1986)

Timeline. The Life of Milarepa[8]

1. Born around 1050 CE in southwest Tibet.
2. Death of his father around 1057–60. Exploitation of the widow and children by paternal uncle.
3. Milarepa goes to the Yarlung Valley in central Tibet to study sorcery around 1068.
4. He succeeds in killing twenty-five relatives of his uncle; his aunt survives. For nine years, he destroys the barley harvest of his native village with hailstorms (1070–80).
5. He probably works as a sorcerer for another eight years. A conversion experience (1088) leads to his study of *rDzogs chen.*
6. Penitential discipline and study under Marpa the Translator, disciple of Nāropa (himself a disciple of Tilopa, Maitrīpa, and other Indian mahāsiddhas) from 1089 to 1094.
7. He returns to his native village where he meets his sister Peta. He spends three years in solitary retreat until 1097.
8. His retreat at La phyis gang could have been in 1100 or 1110. He attains full enlightenment "in one body, in one lifetime."
9. 1110–23: He instructs disciples and composes numerous Dharma instruction songs.
10. 1123: He dies without leaving bodily relics: his body dissolves into a "rainbow body."

Introduction

1

The Historical Context of the Biographical Tradition

The biographies of Milarepa, without exception, were authored within the *bKa' brgyud pa* order (*chos lugs*) of Tibetan Buddhism. Since not all these biographies were written with the same motivational bearings, it is important for our study of the works of gTsang smyon Heruka and his predecessors that we give some attention to their historical context.

Hagiographical writing is an important instrument for the spiritual formation of practitioners in a religious order. The very identity of the order is embodied in its exemplary founders and their successors. Hymns of praise (*gsol 'debs*) extol these saints with allusions to their marvelous deeds. New disciples would want to know these life stories in detail to understand the allusions. In the case of the bKa' brgyud pa (the "lineage that practices the oral transmission"),[1] we have a set of closely related transmission lines, comparable to (and tangentially linked to) the other three great Tibetan Buddhist orders: *rNying ma pa*, *Sa skya pa*, and *dGe lugs pa*.[2] All the *bKa' brgyud pa* teachings derive from the Indian mahāsiddhas of the seventh to the thirteenth centuries who diffused the Vajrayāna teachings across a wide area of South Asia using spontaneous song and unconventional teaching styles. They are immortalized in *Buddha's Lions: The Lives of the Eighty-Four Siddhas* (*Caturasītisiddhapravṛtti*) by Abhayadatta (ca. late twelfth century).[3]

At least three of these eighty-four extraordinary persons stand out in every historical account of the bKa' brgyud pa: Tilopa, Nāropa, and

Maitrīpa. Tilopa was the guru of Nāropa; Nāropa and Maitrīpa (along with a number of other Indians) were the gurus of Marpa the Translator, who became the guru of Milarepa.[4]

The three main disciples of Milarepa were sGampopa (the Doctor from Lha rje, 1079–1153), Bodhi Radza (i.e., Bodhi Rāja, also known as Ngam rDzong ras pa), and Ras chung pa rDo rje grags (1083–1161). Even though the main lineages of the bKa' brgyud pa in Tibet's Middle Ages passed through sGampopa to his disciples (the Dwags po bKa' brgyud pa), the other two disciples handed on teachings of paramount importance for biographies (*rnam thar*), songs (*mgur*), and oral instructions (*gdams ngag*) traditions. Ras chung transmitted the *Ras chung snyan rgyud*, which he had received from Ti pu pa (Pārāvatapāda) in India. Milarepa knew that these teachings had not been brought to Tibet by Marpa. He therefore sent Ras chung to obtain them. Milarepa received them from Ras chung pa and handed them on to Ngam rDzong ras pa, who compiled the *Ngam rDzong snyan rgyud*. Later, these oral instructions were systematized by gTsang smyon Heruka (1452–1507), the great biographer of Milarepa, in his work the *bDe mchog snyan rgyud*.[5]

The main heirs of sGampopa's teachings came to be known as the "four great" (or "elder") orders and the eight "lesser" (or "younger") orders. The four great orders include the Tshal pa, Kaṁ Tshang (Karma), 'Ba' rom, and Phag mo gru pa lineages. The eight lesser orders spring from the Phag mo gru: 'Bri gung, Stag lung, Khro phu, 'Brug pa, sMarpa, Yel pa, g.Ya' bzang, and Shug gseb.[6]

E. Gene Smith sketches an accurate portrait of the formation of the orders and suborders within the bKa' brgyud pa "family" in his preface to the *Life of the Saint of gTsang*:

> The emphasis on oral transmission, on individual solitary contemplation, on intensely personal bonds between guru and disciple militated against the formation of a dkar-brgyud-pa [*sic*] sect. The very nature of the dkar-brgyud-pa teachings tended to promote constant fission. Gradually,

> however, noted gurus would come to attract large numbers of followers and disciples to their isolated hermitages; and, thus, dkar-brgyud-pa monasteries came into existence. Often a favorite nephew of one of these charismatic teachers would inherit the uncle's meditation hut which was at the center of the clustered huts of the followers. If the nephew were intelligent, he would have an excellent chance of being acknowledged as his uncle's chief disciple and successor. Gradually, the lineage would come to be regarded as blessed and would acquire a share of the prestige and charisma that all of its members had previously commanded. In this way there emerged a hereditary religious nobility in the dkar-brgyud-pa.[7]

This model of development can already be encountered in the lives of Marpa and Milarepa, which were meant by gTsang smyon Heruka as supportive teachings accompanying the transmission of the *snyan brgrud* of *ḍākinī* teachings related to the *Cakrasaṁvara Tantra.* Marpa's dwelling resembles the Indian *gurukula,* in which the family and the circles of disciples share meals and teachings.[8] Marpa's establishment is not far in style from the Newari *bāhāl,* the typical tantric Buddhist community that still survives in the Kathmandu Valley.[9] However, we should note that the *bāhāl* also has many nonresident members who live in the surrounding town, whereas Marpa's role in the community seems to have been mainly that of a landlord, not so much a tantric priest.[10] To the extent that we can glean information from the biographies, Marpa is said to have earned money by doing minor rites, but not in his own hometown.

In the *Life of Milarepa* (part 2, chapter 2), gTsang smyon describes an episode in which Marpa is giving the initiation of the tantric deity Hevajra in his family *gompa* (*dgon pa,* here meaning residential temple rather than monastery). During the rite, Milarepa was menaced by Marpa and leapt to the courtyard below in terror.[11] The initiation would have been held on the second floor in the shrine room reserved for secret rites. Just as in Nepal, the shrine room is opposite the street entrance to a central courtyard, usually just above the main deity shrine that is on the ground floor and is visible to the public. The complex of buildings at Lho brag, which are still extant, confirms the historicity of this reconstruction.[12]

Milarepa himself preferred the solitary caves of the mountain ranges, but even this form of asceticism did not prevent his disciples from living with him for long periods of time, especially toward the end of his life. rGyal thang pa refers to twelve *yogins* and *yoginīs* in Mila's entourage at the time of his death (folio 261 of the rGyal thang pa biography), but neither Ras chung pa nor sGampopa was present. This group of disciples, assiduously practicing tantric yoga, either lived in contiguous caves near that of the great rJe btsun[13] or set themselves up in caves or cabins near one another. In the *Blue Annals*, we read of the meditation caves of great bKa' brgyud masters and the steady growth in the number of their followers. For example, the first Karmapa, Dus gsum mkhyen pa, gathered a flock of more than a thousand monks at Tre bo of Khams.[14]

Through various circumstances and vicissitudes, the principle disciples of Milarepa and of sGampopa attracted large numbers of patrons and disciples. Subgroups proliferated under the direction of numerous recognized masters known for their wisdom and holiness. The several lineages inheriting the spiritual teachings of Marpa and Milarepa began to attract significant aristocratic patronage. With patronage came wealth and political influence. Keith Dowman observes that "the monasteries of Densatil, Tse Gungtang, Tolung, Tsurpu, Drigung, and Taklung were all established by remarkable Kagyu *yogins*" by the end of the twelfth century.[15] These institutions continued to prosper well into the thirteenth century, when two significant challenges may have brought an awareness of the need for reform. The first challenge was spiritual. Sa skya paṇḍita's critique of philosophical and yogic errors among the bKa' brgyud pa appeared in about 1232 in his devastating book, *sDom gsum rab dbye*.[16] The second was the political ascendancy won for the Sa skya order by the same Sa-paṇ from the Mongol (Yuan) dynasty in 1247, ending the menace of an invasion of Tibet but also placing the prosperous bKa' brgyud establishments in a subordinate political position in the new configuration of rapport with the Chinese-Mongol dynasty.[17] This was the historical setting in which a certain rGyal thang pa, a disciple of rGod tshang pa mGon po rdo rje (1189–1258), wrote his "golden rosary" of hagiographies, including the Mila *rnam thar* translated herein. This particular literary effort, with its carefully constructed theoretical framework based on the figure of Vajradhara (the tantric ideal of realization), was one element of a more general response to the challenges of the mid-1200s.

The Sa skya alliance with the Mongols stabilized the political situation in Tibet for a few decades until the decline of the Yuan dynasty. Lacking foreign support, the Sa skya state yielded to the Phag mo gru, whose ascendancy was reinforced by a return to the symbolism of the Tibetan empire of the eighth century. They ruled mainly in central Tibet from the early 1300s to the 1430s. In the 1400s, the major bKa' brgyud centers were again under pressure, this time from the increasingly successful dGe lugs pa reform inaugurated at the turn of the century by rJe Tsong Khapa (1357–1419). By the mid-1400s, the principle bKa' brgyud centers were in a state of crisis despite (or perhaps because of) great economic and political power. The period was turbulent. Gene Smith writes of the "political chaos that plagued Tibet during Yuan and Ming times."[18] The rise of the dGe lugs pa was accompanied by extensive unrest in both dBus and gTsang, taking the form of shifting alignments. The Phag mo gru supported the dGe lugs pa in dBus. The Rin spungs princes of gTsang were allied with the immensely affluent Karma bKa' brgyud hierarchs. These political rivalries took the form of warfare and reprisals. Even though the Rin spungs managed to hold on to part of dBus and most of gTsang in general until 1565, they never fully succeeded in unifying the Tibetan state. The political strategies both of the Phag mo gru in the 1400s and of the Rin spungs in the 1500s came to naught.[19] Only with the help of Mongol allies were the dGe lugs pa able to create a unified state around the figure of the Dalai Lamas. Their strategy reached its apogee in the 1640s with the ascendancy of the great Fifth Dalai Lama at Lhasa.

It is at the very heart of this time of distraction and transition that we encounter the life and work of the great Mad Yogin of gTsang, gTsang smyon Heruka.[20] He was one of a number of tantric practitioners at the turn of the sixteenth century who had acquired the reputation of being *smyon pa*, or "mad" saints. Their madness consisted in unconventional behavior that set them apart from the monks and even from the married tantrics (*sngags pa*) in their hill town gompas (*dgon pa*) and townhouse *bāhāls*. These *yogins* practiced with great freedom in the lonely and terrifying places beyond the margins of society. Their hermitages were caves, cemeteries, forests, and remote parts of the mountains—all places reputed to be infested with dangerous categories of beings. Practicing the most fearsome rites of the several classes of Vajrayāna, they were as strange in appearance as they were provocative in word and deed.[21] In reality, they were anything but mad, since they attained and were recognized for a high degree of holiness. They also produced a considerable body of liturgical and hagiographical literature. The Mad Yogin of gTsang was perhaps the prince of *smyon pa* authors. His immortal *Life of Milarepa* is a masterpiece not only of Tibetan but also of world literature. The Mad Yogin of gTsang was one of a group of *smyon pa* authors: Thang-stong rGyal po,[22] 'Brugpa Kun legs,[23] and a number of gTsang smyon's own disciples who embraced his style of *sādhana*.[24] In effect, this was the special moment of the *smyon pas* in Tibetan religious history. Their influence remains alive today in the living traditions of Himalayan Buddhism. Their writings abound in the libraries of the *sngags pas* of Dolpo, Manang, and the Sherpa country; they appear in *thangkas* and bronze statues in the shrine rooms of remote *gompas*, which still serve as centers of worship for the Bhotia peoples of the Himalayas. Let us review some underlying political developments that also influenced the background for the telling of Mila's life.

Tibet of the late fifteenth century was characterized by a large number of internal tensions, both political and religious. Many members of the old orders and their lay aristocratic patrons were in conflict with the reform movement associated with the *dGe lugs pa.*[25] The latter, founded by the great tantric master and philosopher rJe Tsong Khapa in the early fifteenth century, pursued a course of scholastic training, monastic discipline, and critical revision of the received tantric cycles. They were backed by important aristocratic families around Lhasa in the central province of dBus who were eager for a reform that would enhance Tibet's tradition of state Buddhism.

The earlier orders had already made successful bids for political power. The pro-Mongol Sakyapas were favored under the Yuan dynasty from the 1270s to the early 1300s. In the course of the 1300s, a branch of the bKa' brgyud pa, the Phag mo gru pa, inaugurated a revival of traditional national customs associated with the early Tibetan monarchy. This order seems to have thrown in its lot with Tsong Kha pa's followers in the early 1400s as a struggle with the southwestern province of gTsang began to intensify. By the end of the 1400s, it seemed that dBus was firmly under the control of the dGe lugs and their patrons. Meanwhile, the destiny of the west-central province of gTsang was guided by the Karma bKa' brgyud pa hierarchs, who were the spiritual advisors to the Rin spungs princes. Thus the orders, new and old, found themselves caught up in the struggle for power among aristocratic clans. The reform movements in the religious sphere were inseparable from the violent feudal warfare that characterized the period.[26]

The social disarray inspired a search for new models of religious reform. The impressive group of "mad yogins" represented to many Tibetans what was most essential and authentic in Tibetan Buddhism: a return to the values, practices, and hallowed lifestyles associated with the early Indian mahāsiddhas and their first Tibetan disciples. A reform of the bKa' brgyud orders along these lines gained support from many noble clans, who had an eye to gain territory at the expense of the dGe lugs and their lay backers in the central province of dBus. Only a movement imbued with the religious credibility of real holiness could hope to reconquer the heart of Tibet. The Mad Yogin of gTsang's "allergy" to celibate monasticism seemed poised for a counter attack on the dGe lugs reform program. Smith observes,

> I think that the evidence is fairly conclusive that the *smyon-pa* phenomenon was, at least partly, a reaction against the hereditary lineages with their great prestige and wealth. It was an attempt to reinvest the Dkar-brgyud-pa tradition with some of its former religious fervor, the incandescent spirituality of the early yogis. The chief symbol of this movement was Mi-la-ras-pa who had never been a monk, the mystic poet who had founded no monastery or school, a saint who remained a legend.[27]

It would seem from Smith's comments that the literary and cultural thrust of the *smyon pa* movement was intended to convince the bKa' brgyud hierarchs of the need to initiate a broad reform of their orders based on the traditions of the *siddha*-gurus who were regarded as their "founders" so as to recover lost greatness and authenticity. The *smyon pas'* style of reform was not essentially institutional, as was that of the dGe lugs. Their critique was as much against a new scholastic reform of monasticism as against the unbecoming political ambitions of the older orders. However, it is evident from the text of the *Life of Milarepa* by gTsang smyon Heruka that the Mad Yogin also intended to assail the dGe lugs pa heirs of those earlier bKa' bdams pa monks who had hated Milarepa. He even changed the identity of Milarepa's mortal enemy from a Bon po village sorcerer to a learned *dGe shes!*[28]

The protest of the mad yogins appealed to patrons eclipsed or menaced by the consolidation of power around Lhasa. As we shall see, the great success of the *smyon pa* protest was in the sphere of culture and spirituality. Their visionary program failed as a reversal of the political achievement of the reforming heirs of rJe Tsong Khapa, whose success was due in part to the establishment of an institutional basis. Nothing could stop the rise of the dGe lugs hegemony, consolidated through military victory, extensive institutionalization, and popular devotion.

The biographical writings that are our special area of interest must be seen as products of the conflicted atmosphere in which they were produced. There was good reason for exalting the type of life led by such *siddhas* as Tilopa, Nāropa, Marpa, Milarepa, and others. Their way of life became a model for the reform of Tibet, a nation constructed as a tantric culture. The sublime nature of their *Vajrayāna* teachings and *sādhanas* (ritual and meditation practices) was extolled in the great compilations redacted by gTsang smyon himself (the *Life and Songs of Milarepa* and the *bDe mchog mkha' 'gro snyan rgyud*[29]) and those of his disciple and biographer, rGod tshang ras pa sna tshogs rang grol (the *Ras chung snyan rgyud yig cha*).[30] These texts catalog and transmit the rare esoteric teachings that had in some cases been neglected by the mainstream of even the bKa' brgyud orders, being preserved only in the relatively marginal lineages descending from Ras chung pa and Ngam rDzong ras pa.

In fact, gTsang smyon and his main guru, Shes rab 'byams pa, belonged to the Ras chung lineage,[31] although gTsang smyon had strong ties to the 'Brug pa bKa' brgyud. Today, the main followers of these Ras chung/gTsang smyon teachings are to be found among the "upper" 'Brug pa, who are heirs of Padma dkar po's elucidations of the *bDe mchog mkha' 'gro snyan rgyud sādhanas*.[32] This transmission links up the Ras chung lineage with that of Ngam rDzong ras pa (certainly a principal contributor to the earliest complete biography and songs of Milarepa). The teachings were revived by gTsang smyon and recycled to the 'Brug pa bKa' brgyud, who were able to absorb it all alongside their heritage of sGampopa's *mahāmudrā* teachings.[33]

Among the figures that link the earlier teachings to gTsang smyon, we find the 'Brug pa disciple of rGod Tshang pa (1189–1258), rGyal thang pa, whose work has been translated in this volume. By aligning the three principle heirs of Milarepa's *Bde mchog* (i.e., Cakrasaṁvara) teachings, Ras chung pa, Gampopa, and Ngam rDzong ras pa with later masters, we can see the several strands that bring us to the biography and songs of Milarepa as redacted by gTsang smyon. For the first time, the literary evidence reveals the dynamic phenomenology of tradition in a Tibetan lineage. gTsang smyon identified himself literarily with the figure of Ras chung pa. Through text-critical study, we can show how gTsang smyon interwove what he had inherited from all three lineages of *bDe mchog*, plus some modifications in the structure and devotional content that seem to have originated with rGyal thang pa. The literary tradition passed down from Ras chung pa and Bodhi Radza (Ngam rDzong ras pa) influenced rGyal thang pa's rather free use of received material. In contrast, the Mila biography was treated in a repetitive and at times wooden fashion in imitation of the text attributed to sGampopa. For the former two traditions (Ras chung and Ngam rDzong), the songs are much more important than for the sGampopa "family" of biographies. Since the songs are closely limited to oral initiations on Secret Mantra practice, it would seem that the lineages descending from Ras chung and Ngam rDzong were carried on by masters who persisted in following the Secret Mantra and tantric yoga practices. The other lineages, tied to large institutions, worked effectively with the scholastic and nontantric approach to *mahāmudrā*, leaving such topics as the Six Yogas of Nāropa to specialists—or so it would seem![34] It was not until the great Padma dKar po began to comment on the "hearing lineage" oral teachings in the late sixteenth century that the challenge of the *smyon pas* was integrated into the body of the enormously popular 'Brug pa bKa' brgyud order and beyond.[35]

The political crisis of the old orders, finding themselves embarrassed by the great success of the reformed bKa' gdams pa (i.e., the dGe lugs pa), is further evident in what Smith calls "perhaps the most important development in Tibet during the fifteenth and sixteenth centuries ... the gradual acceptance of the priority of the rebirth (*yang srid*) lineage over familial claims in the transmission of accumulated religious prestige and wealth."[36] Smith asserts that Padma dKar po assigned greater importance to learning and the discernment of authentic signs that a practitioner was an incarnate lama than to family and clan inheritance.[37] Padma dKar po was trying, apparently, to provide an institutional basis for the reforms embodied among the *smyon pas.* His order, allied to the Karma *bKa' brgyud* and the princes of gTsang, was attempting to assert the legitimacy of the older orders against the dGe lugs. In constructing a new, politicized model, rooted in both tantric practice and the system of choosing reincarnate lamas, he was revising a key point in the *smyon pa* program. The mad yogins polemicized against credulity with regard to the reincarnate lamas, the "*sprul skus.*"[38] For Padma dKar po and others who supported him, authentic *sprul sku* lineages guarantee community stability and continuity, thereby liberating the monasteries from the political game strategies of rival clans.

The political advantage of the incarnate-lama system was that it helped the orders' hierarchies to avoid having abbatial appointments manipulated by the aristocratic clans. By selecting promising children to be given a carefully designed spiritual and intellectual formation, the monasteries could provide genuine leadership based on deeply held religious convictions. Historically, the incarnations were often found in families from border areas (Padma dKar po was one of these) or in families on both sides of a power struggle, thus offering a convenient means of peacemaking not unlike political marriages. One should not underestimate the power of religious awe engendered in an encounter with the reincarnation of a great saint of the past. The fact that the incarnation system is still prevalent among all Tibetan orders confirms the (not unchallenged) consensus of its efficacy. As for the *smyon pa* political program, with the triumph of the great Fifth Dalai Lama in the 1640s, it came to naught alongside the hopes of the princes of gTsang and of the Karma bKa' brgyud hierarchy to govern the Tibetan state.

What concrete historical circumstances conditioned the time of the compilation and composition of gTsang smyon's biography of Milarepa? In the course of the 1480s, gTsang smyon collected Milarepa biographies (*rnam thar*) and completed his version by 1488—along with the complete *mgur 'bum* (the *Hundred Thousand Songs of Milarepa*)—at La stod Lho Shel phug in gTsang. The political conditions of the period were highly unstable. In promoting religious reform through literary and teaching activity[39] in this thirty-year period, he would have encountered obstacles produced by the ongoing armed conflict between dBus and gTsang. The location of the retreat place of gTsang smyon in La stod in the western part of gTsang may indicate his need to distance himself from the disorder created by military operations in the eastern part of gTsang. The Tibetan historian Tsepon W. D. Shakabpa suggests that this was a simple question of patronage, indicating nothing of the impact of the conflict on the writing of the *rnam thar.*[40] However, among gTsang smyon's benefactors in this period, we find the myriarch of Byan, the King of Gung Thang, and the Prince of Rin Spungs, clearly indicating connections with aristocratic factions. According to the biography of the Mad Yogin by his disciple rGod tshang ras pa,[41] all these and other patrons were involved in armed conflict at the time of the compilation of these literary classics. It would indeed seem that, had the Mad Yogin been abroad in dBus and gTsang collecting earlier biographies of Milarepa in the period from 1480 to 1500, on many occasions he would have encountered difficulties owing to the unstable political situation.

In spite of the disordered historical times, the works of gTsang smyon evidence a highly developed literary style. The Mad Yogin made use of a great variety of written and oral sources to create a biography that reads like a novel. The impact of this work on the cultural life of Tibet has been comparable to an epic drama. It sets up the life of the homeless *yogin* as the highest ideal for those who seek to attain Buddhahood "in one body, in one lifetime." It elevates the mad yogin to the rank of a universal archetype or exemplar for the serious practitioner and demotes the figure of the scholarly monk from its position of primacy. However, the fact that the sense of nostalgia for the earliest saints of the lineage can be found in the works of rGyal thang pa (thirteenth century) reminds us that the achievements of the late fifteenth-century *smyon pas* had antecedents in earlier periods of bKa' brgyud history.[42] The siddha spirituality and idealism were already part of the worldview of the whole "refuge tree" of the bKa' brgyud order. The eremitical ideal never died out, and the "mad yogin" theme remained alive and was probably not restricted to marginal practitioners, since eremitical practice was a standard feature of the training offered by the monasteries.[43] At the same time, the persistence of the ideal should not diminish our recognition of what the mad yogins did in fact achieve around 1500.

Although the *smyon pa* "protest" failed in the political sphere, there can be no doubt as to its universal triumph in Tibetan culture. *The Life of Milarepa* is a book held dear by members of all the Tibetan orders, with the obvious exception of the Bon pos! Even today, the work of gTsang smyon is recited in many Himalayan Buddhist communities at the New Year festival. The songs of Milarepa are still recited by the fervent practitioners of the yogas transmitted by the masters of his lineage. These sacred songs are in some places (e.g., Dolpo, where I conducted fieldwork) considered "reserved" texts, to be sung and discussed only among experienced tantric practitioners. Currently, Khenpo Tsultrim Gyatso teaches at Bouddhanath in Kathmandu by giving frequent oral commentaries on the *Songs*; he also sends his disciples to the Milarepa "Tiger Cave" at Yolmo, Helambu, Nepal, for contemplative retreats.[44] Numerous copies of the works of Milarepa, Ras Chung pa, gTsang smyon, and rGod tshang ras pa can be found in the libraries of the little gompas of the Bhotia regions of northern Nepal. In these border areas, it seems that the disciples of the mad yogins found refuge in the course of the conflicts between dBus and gTsang—between the Karma bKa' brgyud and the dGe lugs—from 1480 to 1680 and perhaps even later than the triumph of the great Fifth Dalai Lama. The ongoing search for "hidden valleys" on the part of bKa' brgyud and rNyingma practitioners is part of the phenomenon of the cultural persistence of the mad yogin ideal.[45] The same ideal seems to have animated the richly complex *ris med* (unbiased) movement in nineteenth-century Eastern Tibet in its fierce effort to preserve precarious pre–dGe lugs and even Bon po teachings. Our present work owes much to the twentieth-century heirs of the *ris med* masters, who were willing to learn from all the lineages and put the teachings to the test in rigorous retreat environments.[46]

Part One

Literary Aspects of the Biographies of Milarepa

2

Hagiography and Tradition

Scholarly research on the biographical literature associated with holy founders, spiritual masters, and saints has made considerable progress thanks to advances in literary criticism and hermeneutics in the course of the twentieth century. It is not my intention to repeat the theories and discoveries of others in this chapter, although I will be making use of critical hermeneutical methods at several key points of the presentation. What I would like to emphasize from the start is a conviction that our literary analysis of the texts of those religions that make use of texts will be flawed to the extent that we fail to ally anthropological data with text-based hermeneutics. There is the text, and there is the social context. For our purposes, there is a tradition of writing biographies of Milarepa, and there is a living tradition of religious practices inseparable from those biographies. The "author" cannot be dissociated from the text produced and from the tradition being practiced. I would also assert that the act of producing the text and the reading of that text by a succession of disciples is a spiritual practice in itself. As a spiritual practice, writing and reading biographies define the boundaries and the ethos of the community in question, in this case the several bKa' brgyud orders of Tibetan Vajrayāna. The power of the literary form is ensconced in the aura of holiness associated with Milarepa and with the tradition that carries on his teachings. Clarifying what we mean by the notion of holiness in general and of holy persons in particular requires a brief excursus on phenomenology.

The Tibetan word *dam* is used to translate the Sanskrit terms *sat* or *parama*. A classic example would be the Sanskrit term *saddharma*, translated in Tibetan as *dam chos*, and in English as holy doctrine.

There is also a resonance with the Sanskrit term *gāḍ*, which means "immersed in, bathed in, intense." So one could speak of "saturated in being" or "immersed in that which truly *is*." The logical consequence of this concept would be its application to a person who has attained the absolute truth in a verifiable way. Similarly, any teaching or practice that conduces to the attainment of enlightenment would be "holy" as well.

Taking this a step further, it is possible to imagine a holy person as someone who is truly "enlightened," who is not recognized as such by the general public, and who perhaps does not wish to have such recognition. The classic example of this from Buddhist tradition would be the *pratyekabuddha*, someone who attains enlightenment in solitude but does not teach the Dharma. Traditionally, such a person is not necessarily lacking in compassion, for his or her attainment is believed to have in any case a virtuous effect on sentient beings. The Dharma, whether verbalized or not, is always good, always true. It would be the lack of merit present in the world at the time of a *pratyekabuddha* that would impede the manifestation of teachings, texts, monuments, institutions, and the like.

More typically, however, a person who has attained holiness by following the path of Buddha Dharma will be recognized by other holy persons and even by the general public as someone worthy of veneration. Inner attainment can be distinguished from external cult, but usually they go together. South Asian cultures seem to have the capacity to recognize the holy person with a kind of collective intuition. In fact, at times it is the general public that first adheres to the saint, even before the representatives of institutional religion do so. The biographies of Milarepa assert this phenomenon by recounting the spontaneous devotion of humble villagers in contrast to the hostility and envy of monks. Strange as it may seem, the beliefs, practices, and teachings of a particular saint have less persuasive power over the public imagination than the simple, nonverbal fact of the presence of the holy person, who presumably attained realization as a result of fidelity to those beliefs and practices! The public seems to "know," regardless of the contents of the respective paths to holiness. One could even speak of an "interreligious instinct" in India and the Himalayas. Ramakrishna, Ananda Mayee Ma, Mother Teresa of Calcutta, and Ramana Maharshi all received that kind of recognition long before institutions were constructed around their presence.

The task of hagiography in relation to the phenomenon of the recognition and cult of a saint is the task of any narrative genre: an attempt to translate that collective, spontaneous "knowing" into *telling*.[1] Narrative may take on the task of imposing a kind of literary order on reality, or it may function as a way of unleashing a more or less healthy disorder. The latter is the explicit intent of such mad-*yogin* singers of tales as 'Brug pa kun legs or gTsang smyon Heruka.[2] 'Brug pa kun legs has the temerity and wit to point out the pride and spiritual materialism of those saintly biographies that read like account books of teachings given and offerings received. gTsang smyon's madness is evident in his willingness to rewrite the biography of Milarepa (and of Marpa); to retell it in his own way; and to risk exposing his own personality defects to the point of identifying himself with the erratic, recalcitrant, and prideful Ras chung pa.

The way narratives are constructed to tell the tale of a saint reveals much about what a particular author and his culture understand to be "holiness." We must keep in mind, however, the aspect of mystery, of the nonverbal and inexpressible when recounting the presence of the holy in a sanctified human being. No narrative can fully convey that aspect of "knowing" or intuiting the presence of the saint. That is the case within a particular cultural context, and it is even more so cross-culturally. A careful blending of the historic, the mythic, and the literary (i.e., style, structure, and genre) attempts to create a climate within which readers *may* find themselves persuaded that here, indeed, holiness was made manifest, and to that suggestion, readers *may* find themselves moved to true faith and devotion. As rGyal thang pa says at the end of his narrative, "I bow down to the Saint (*rje btsun*) … who is completely liberated (*rnam thar*) [Tibetan: *rje btsun rnam thar rdzogs la gus phyag 'tshal*]."[3] This phrase can equally be translated as "I bow down to the completed biography of the Saint," for the text merits veneration if it achieves the sacred purpose of its author.

Texts that merit veneration are generally classified as canonical or scriptural. In their widely quoted work, *The Biographical Process,* Reynolds and Capps make a distinction between sacred biography and hagiography. Just as the "ideal type" of a religious founder (Buddha, Jesus, Muhammad) can be distinguished from the saint, who is the exemplary follower, so too, the literary forms applicable to founder (sacred biography) and saint (hagiography) may be distinguished. The biography of a founder participates in and, especially, gives shape to the formation of the first communities of believers; such accounts become scripture, that is, canonical, and hence "sacred" biography. The accounts of a founder are in fact better read as proclamation (*kerygma*) than as biography, for they focus more on the events of the founder's life as they bear upon and disclose his religious message.[4] The New Testament Gospels are a good example of this process. In the case of the life of the Buddha, the biographical process is nuanced by a different view of history and soteriology. Buddha Śakyamuni is understood to be carrying out a pattern for this world-cycle that was already manifest in numerous previous Buddhas. Typically, biographical episodes were worked into etiological accounts in the *Vinaya* (monastic legislation), thus legitimating and reinforcing the structures of monastic life. The Buddha's cosmo-mythic "Twelve Deeds" also function not as historic biography but as a sort of ritual by which each and every great world renouncer saves the world. The distinction drawn by Reynolds and Capps between sacred biography and hagiography tends to blur because the Buddha himself is understood to be carrying out a pattern for this world-cycle that was already manifest in numerous previous Buddhas.[5] The Buddha is not unique and his biography is not "foundational." Rather, it is a dharmic soteriological pattern, working itself out in the lives of the fortunate beings who encounter it either in person or in the form of a sacred text. However, it is also true that in the early Buddhist scriptures, the biographies of Arhats make distinctions between the realization of the saints and that of the Buddha; the former are dependent on encounter with the latter.[6]

In Mahāyāna Buddhism, the matter has evolved such that the biographies of Buddhist saints can also take on the status of canonical scripture. The Sixth Ch'an patriarch's biography is a well-known example in Chinese Buddhism.[7] Certainly the life of Milarepa takes on the aura of sacred scripture.[8] In the *rnam thar* of Milarepa by rGyal thang pa, we see an attitude of devotional practice ("I bow down ..."), verse after verse. Today one may use the biography of Milarepa (i.e., the one by gTsang smyon Heruka) as a spiritual practice in the bKa' brgyud pa by receiving reading permission and empowerment, showing that it is recognized as a tantric practice text. The biography of Milarepa, along with the iconography that can be observed in thangka representations of his life, constitutes a tantric contemplative cycle of practice in its own right. The same pattern can be observed in the cult of Padmasambhava (Guru Rinpoche), Yeshe Tsogyal, Ma gcig Labdron, Je Tsong Khapa, and literally hundreds of other Tibetan sanctified persons. One might draw the conclusion that, since the attainment of Buddhahood is the goal of tantric practice, such attainment necessarily constitutes the attainer as an object of veneration. By generating the triple body of a Buddha, the fully realized *yogin* manifests as a unique tantric deity. Meditation on the form of such a saint constitutes a path by which the practitioner attains complete enlightenment. The text of the biography thus comes to be seen as a physical manifestation of the process by which a human being can attain Buddhahood "in one lifetime, in one body"; the "book" becomes "canonical" because of its results.

Closely allied with the process by which a text becomes canonical is the principle of lineage (Tibetan: *brgyud*). The *Blue Annals*, for example, is predominantly a collection of the biographies of saints and lineage-holding gurus who practiced and transmitted various cycles of Mahāyāna and Vajrayāna teachings. In this fifteenth-century work, the controlling principle of lineage (*brgyud*) relates the hagiographical accounts of individual saints to the life, attainment, and doctrine of various lineage founders. In the thirteenth-century *bKa' brgyud gser 'phreng* of rGyal thang pa, the *rnam thar* of Vajradhara comes first as a theoretical account of primordial Buddhahood to which the specific details of the hagiographical accounts to follow adhere. The human beings who become saints in the bKa' brgyud system realized the "state" of Vajradhara—that is, the tantric form of Buddhahood—while manifesting outwardly the distinctive characteristics by which they are known in iconography. Thus Vajradhara's rather schematic "biography" occupies the functional role of a lineage founder, upon whose teachings saints attain realization.

In most religious traditions, the biographies of saints confirm the sacred power and efficacy of the founder's vision to continue to transform other human lives. The function of hagiography is essentially conversion: to attract attention to an ideal and to provoke a response of faith that gives rise to a desire to imitate the practices and beliefs of the holy person.[9]

Thus the *Songs* (*mgur 'bum*) states, "Having heard this song ... they had all heard the Jetsun's life story and with great faith, they came this time to learn the Dharma. They asked Milarepa how he had managed to undergo the trials of probationship and had exerted himself in ascetic practice, and to recount the way through which he had finally obtained his Enlightenment."[10]

Another aspect of awakened faith at this stage is the suggestion that the patrons touched by the literary account believe that previous meritorious actions are now bearing fruit. To encounter a living Buddha indicates that one has accumulated enough merit to undertake the spiritual life in earnest, with hope of success.[11] This is what signifies the exaggerated numbers of persons—easily liberated by various Buddhas and Bodhisattvas—in Mahāyāna literature. Buddhist eschatology has a definite perception that, in the appearance of a "World Honored One," the time is at hand for deliverance. Early Buddhism's biographical accounts of the enlightenment of the Buddha tell us that he was at that time implored by the gods to teach in the human realm, for there he would find beings endowed with merit and on the verge of awakening. The tales of the mahāsiddhas also refer to this phenomenon, with King Indrabhūti being said to have emptied his kingdom by disseminating the tantric doctrines and enlightening thousands of persons.[12]

That the appearance of a saint coincides with presence of many beings on the verge of enlightenment is a persistent feature of the Milarepa *rnam thars*. *The Life of Milarepa* says, "Those disciples who achieved complete enlightenment were as numerous as the stars in the night; those who achieved non-return to samsara were also many, as particles of dust on the face of the earth. Those men and women who had entered the path of liberation were too numerous to be counted."[13]

The "Grey Rock" account in the *Songs* (episode 23) gives the most advanced teachings on *Mahāmudrā* last, after one *yogin* in particular has begun to experience the fruits not only of having heard the biography but also of having put into practice the teachings of the *rJe bTsun* under his guidance, for devotion to the guru and engaging in the rigors of the master-disciple relationship tends to cause the convergence of the roles of "saint" and guru:[14] one encounters the holy in a saint, who in the role of the guru sustains the disciple on the path until enlightenment is reached. It is the sanctity of the guru that makes the verbal teachings efficacious in practice.

The *rnam thar* itself, functioning as the guru in book form, has the power to lead persons to the spiritual path. Just before the colophon, gTsang smyon concludes the biography by saying, "This story of liberation, the *Life of Milarepa*, leads to the path of emancipation and supreme knowledge."[15] In the preface, the narrator sets up for himself a sort of literary identity as Ras chung pa, who is bidden by celestial beings to supplicate the master for his life story: "Venerable and precious master, … for the sake of guiding other sentient beings on the way to liberation, tell us, O Compassionate Master, the origin of your family, tell us your story and works."[16]

Although both Victoria E. Urubshurow and Janice Willis have insisted that the *rnam thars* are a form of in-depth instruction on spiritual practice,[17] it is undeniable that these biographies do not give the kind of detail that we find, for example, in the First Panchen Lama's *Great Seal of Voidness* or in *The Six Yogas of Nāropā* with Tsong Kha pa's commentary.[18] The *rnam thars* function to inspire potential practitioners and to sustain the practice of those advanced disciples already initiated in the same way as Christian hagiography does. A child may find the biography of St. Francis, for example, sufficiently fascinating to want to learn more about that saint's devotion to the Crucified Christ, but in order to learn how to meditate on Christ's passion and death, one has to make use of devotional manuals for the five sorrowful mysteries of the rosary or for the *Via Crucis.* These instructions are not found in saints' lives any more than detailed comments on the practice of heat yoga[19] are found in any biography of Milarepa. However, one of the attractive features of rGyal thang pa's version of the biography is the description of some of the difficulties in *gtum mo* practice that would be helpful to an advanced bKa' brgyud pa practitioner (see folios 220–21, 232) and perhaps bear witness to the experience of the author himself.

Studies of hagiography and sacred biography have tended to focus either on a quest for the historical figure "behind" the legend or have sought to correlate mythic elements found cross-culturally. The Tibetan *rnam thars* present us with special challenges since they do show a concern for historicity, and they seem to delight in bluntness when it comes to some apparent faults in their subjects.[20] At the same time, the mythological and marvelous abound, under the influence of Indian and Central Asian epic, tantric symbolism, and the antecedents handed down in the *sūtras.* Some of these marvelous events may have actually happened, too. Sorting all this out requires numerous sources. Nevertheless, situated as they are in the self-conscious identity of Tibetan lineages and religious orders, the *rnam thar* is a recognizable literary form.

The *rnam thar* is meant to be an account of the "liberation" of a human being from the delusions of cyclic existence. Even if the term *rnam thar* has come to mean simply "a biographical account," the classical meaning (Sanskrit: *vimukti*) continues to resonate in the literary form. There is a traditional threefold typology of the *rnam thar*: outer, inner, and secret. Outer *rnam thar*s describe events in a person's life, a record of things said, persons encountered, initiations received, and journeys undertaken in the outer world. The inner *rnam thar* describes the spiritual practices undertaken and the attainments acquired. The secret *rnam thar*, corresponding to "Buddha activity," can mean visionary experience but is more likely to mean external behavior that manifests Buddha-nature in an unconventional way, as in the biography of 'Brug pa kun legs, for example.[21] Regardless of these distinctions, the Tibetan *rnam thar* intensifies the reader's interest and faith in the formative presence of the sacred. This is a literature of spiritual practice and experience par excellence.

The encounter of guru and disciple, absolutely crucial to the bKa' brgyud biographical tradition, is characterized by a spontaneous and unerring awakening of faith and devotion. *Dad pa*, or faith, is characterized as *dang pa'i dad pa so ma*, or spontaneous faith at the first encounter with one's lama.[22] This reaction, though auspicious, requires further discernment on the part of the disciple. Thus Mila seeks Bre ston lha dga' for the *rdzogs chen* teaching in good faith but finds that this guru cannot help him overcome the grave obstacles he has acquired by the use of destructive magic. Indeed, in the sGampopa version, Bre ston admits that even he has been unable to make progress in the system he expounds (folio A.30; see chapter 22). Thus true awakened faith is a long way from blind, uncritical faith without understanding (*rgyu mtshan med pa'i dad pa*). A solid faith based on understanding is *rgyu mtshan yod pa'i dad pa*. Milarepa shows his disciples how to come to this kind of faith when he warns of the difficulties of the life of serious contemplative practice.[23] An initial enthusiasm is not enough; one must undergo trials and must know that a radical commitment is indispensable to the attainment of *siddhi* through reliance on a guru. The rGyal thang account seems to suggest a gradual disclosure of the identity of the true guru—from the first experiences with the sorcerers; to the *rdzogs chen* master; to a glimmer of experience under rNgog, a main disciple of Marpa;[24] to full awakening under the guidance of Marpa.

In the bKa' brgyud pa biographies, there is a heightened sense of drama and destiny in the frequent references to promises and vows made in previous lives or the forming of a votary bonding in the present life in anticipation of a better future rebirth in the presence of the guru. Disciples beg the guru to be with them always, even in future lives, until enlightenment is attained; thus the guru fulfills his Bodhisattva vow to remain in cyclic existence until all have attained enlightenment. There is also the use of prophecy to foretell the moment of enlightenment or the path appropriate to particular disciples. The past ripens in the present and the destined disciple is thrilled to discover the teacher and the practice for which his previous vows and merits have destined him.

These bKa' brgyud biographies have Indian antecedents in early Pali and later Sanskrit works.[25] Milarepa himself, in a moment of discouragement, read the story of rTag tu ngu (Bodhisattva Sadāprarudita), in the *Perfection of Wisdom Sūtra in Eight Thousand Lines,*[26] and was thus inspired to return to Marpa and continue the rigorous penances he had imposed.[27] We know of a Sanskrit biography of Śāntideva[28] and of other Mahāyāna figures such as Candragomin, Nāgārjuna, and so on. Significantly, the *Lives of the Eighty-Four Mahāsiddhas* was translated from Sanskrit into Tibetan.[29] The highly repetitive pattern of these biographies, combining a narrative introduction, conversion experience, initiatic *dohā*, and concluding narrative indicating successful spiritual practice and Bodhisattva activity, suggests the existence of a wider oral tradition and should not delude us into believing that this is all that is known of the siddhas. In fact, the Tibetan *Tanjur* (transliterated as *bstan 'gyur*) is full of works written by or commented upon by these very siddhas, who were far more learned and literate than these popular biographies would lead us to believe. There is evidence to suggest that these tales, which arose in the period from about the ninth to the thirteenth centuries, influenced the growth of saints' biographies among the Hindu sects, a hagiographical tradition that was emerging in the same historical period and geographical location.[30] It is quite possible that the concept of a saint who manifests amoral or unconventional behavior, which is such a striking characteristic of siddha biographies, decisively shaped medieval Hindu exegesis of the epic and *purāṇic* heroes such as Kṛṣṇa, with all their ambiguity, in order to find the holiness that tradition posited for these figures. Soon this allegorization of the sanctity of the behavior of heroes came to be applied to any holy man whose strange behavior could thereby be read in transcendental terms as a disclosure of holiness. As late as Tāranātha (the end of sixteenth century), we find connections between the siddha biographies and the north Indian religious traditions; for example, his life of the siddha Śāntigupta has many points of contact with the lives of Nāropa, Marpa, and Milarepa that are known to have come from the circle of gTsang smyon Heruka a century earlier.[31] In his study of the life and teachings of the *sant* mystic Dādū, Giuseppe Calia presents a representative of the originally Vajrayāna *sahaja* practice recycled as a Hindu practice that seems to be a radically simplified kind of Mahāmudrā. The connection between Hindu and Buddhist siddhas among the followers of Gorakhnāth is also well known.[32]

In these late biographies, narrative, symbol, and imagery are so intermingled that narration for the purpose of edification and religious guidance prevails over commitment to historicity. One cannot but wonder if it will ever be possible to show the historical process by which a distinctly biographical tradition emerged from the religious "soup" of the siddha environment.[33] Certainly the early Buddhist siddha biographies, both Sanskrit and Tibetan, are among the first efforts to disclose the holy in tantric categories both mythic and at least partially historical.

Our problem is similar to that of the historian of late Roman antiquity who is no longer so sanguine about denying the existence of semilegendary characters such as St. Anthony of Egypt, thanks to the dying of old polemics and the discovery of numerous literary sources.[34] We may now approach the Milarepa *rnam thar* by gTsang smyon Heruka asking to what extent this work gives us the historic Milarepa's life and doctrine and to what extent it represents an interpretation of the context of the bKa' brgyud pa in the late fifteenth century. The same question occupied Charles Van Tuyl in his 1972 dissertation[35] in which he attempted to identify an early source for the Tse ring ma chapters of the *mila mgur 'bum* and to demonstrate Bon po influence in the early, possibly historical, Milarepan corpus. In any case, the gap of three hundred and sixty years between the death of Milarepa and the writing of the *rnam thar* and *mgur 'bum* by gTsang smyon only increases our suspicions and compounds our difficulties in tracing the strands of literary and oral tradition adhering to the life and songs of this extremely popular saint and folk hero. In fact, we have a multiplicity of sources and themes in the redactions accomplished by gTsang smyon, reflecting not only literary embellishment but also historical controversy within the lineage, some of which we have already discussed in our review of bKa' brgyud pa history.

3

Redaction Critical Study of the Milarepa Biographies

By working in detail on the important death episode in several *Mila rnam thars*, I have been able to elucidate several key aspects of the redaction process by which gTsang smyon reconstructed the figure of Milarepa for his time.

In his *rnam thar* of Milarepa, rGyal thang pa, a disciple of rGod Tshang pa of the 'Brug pa bKa' brgyud pa, gives us a short verse on the death and realization of the great rJe btsun:

> Thus the *rje btsun*-guru, possessing the six perfections
> And defeating the four Māras,
> Having completed all his enlightened activity,
> Manifested the way to pass out of suffering;
> I bow down to the completion of the biography
> (*rnam thar*) of the Saint. (verse 26, folio 259)

Not only in his death, but also throughout his life, Milarepa has death as a frequent, if not constant, companion. The death of his father when he was a seven-year-old child, the deaths of relatives caused by his own practice of black magic, his mother's threat of suicide, his extreme penitential suffering under Marpa leading him to the brink of suicide, the discovery of the bones of his mother in the ruins of the family home, and even his experience at La phyis Gang (a victory over death and the attainment of the "charism" of immortality) give rise to a whole body of very remarkable teachings on death, transmitted largely in the *mgur 'bum* traditions, notably but not exclusively in that of gTsang smyon Heruka.

In several episodes of gTsang smyon's version of the *mgur 'bum*, there are instructions on death, dying, and the intermediate state after death (*bardo*). In chapter 48, Milarepa instructs an elderly couple, Shindormo and Lesebum, on how to prepare for death. In chapter 30 ("On the Bardo"), Milarepa sings of the body as a mandala and says, "Oh, whenever death may come, I shall feel naught but joy." Death is the topic of the chapter on the salvation of the dead and in the account of the conversion of a dying Bonpo. Even the dramatic encounter (in chapter 53) with the Indian tantric siddha Dam pa Sangs rgyas reveals the centrality of one's readiness for death as a sign of the authenticity of one's realization.

These fundamental values are summed up remarkably in the various accounts of Milarepa's death, which is consistently mentioned as a *teaching*, a manifestation of what Mila has practiced, realized, and transmitted, and not solely as a historical event that one necessarily mentions when one writes a biography. And as a teaching, it is subject to the modifications introduced by successive authors in a process of editing and rewriting—that is, *redaction.*

Anyone who has been trained in biblical exegesis who reads the biography of Milarepa inevitably begins to see similarities between the Gospel narratives and those of the Tibetan authors, who themselves claim to be "inspired." The predictions of the passion and death that we find in the Synoptic Gospels function as teachings on death and discipleship, seeking to contextualize the meaning of Christ's death as a symbolic teaching that must be taken to heart daily by the believer (and to all He said, "If anyone would come after me, let him . . . take up his cross daily and follow me" [Luke 9:23]). The relation between the passion narrative itself (the longest and final part of all four Gospels) and the rest of the Gospel narrative has been studied in considerable detail by numerous commentators over the centuries. Recent scholarship has been able to show how complex these texts are, particularly in their use of oral and literary sources. Similarly, some of the *Mila rnam thars* have an exceptionally long chapter on his death, which takes the form of an elaborate funerary pageant in which ordinary humans, disciples, and celestial beings each have a part to play.

In the light of these fertile similarities, we introduce the methodology of what biblical studies calls "*redaktionsgeschichte*" to the biographical tradition of the *Mila rnam thar* and *mgur 'bum*. Here we will begin to address the issue of redaction, making use of the very important Milarepa "passion narrative," but there is abundant material to continue this line of research on the entire tradition, as we have indicated elsewhere.

What is *redaktionsgeschichte* and how is it useful for a study of *rnam thar*? In his introductory study, Norman Perrin points out that Willi Marxen invented the term for New Testament studies in 1956:

> It is concerned with studying the theological motivation of an author as this is revealed in the collection, arrangement, editing, and modification of traditional material, and in the composition of new material or the creation of new forms within the traditions of early Christianity. Although the discipline is called redaction criticism, it could equally be called "composition criticism" (*Kompositionsgeschichte*) because it is concerned with the composition of new material and the arrangements of redacted or freshly created material into new units and patterns, as well as with the redaction of existing material.[1]

One of the things that is certainly evident in the Mila biographical tradition is the active role of the author. E. Gene Smith's indispensable introduction to the *Life of the Saint of gTsang* brings this out quite clearly. Also, sGampopa in his *rnam thar* of Marpa and Milarepa is aware of an ongoing "oral tradition." In the *Blue Annals*, there is a criticism of "spurious sources," and in rGyal thang pa, we find the use of first lines or stanzas of an existing *mgur 'bum*, with the implication that the reciter of the text should continue to sing (i.e., re-create in the manner of the epic bard) the rest of the song. The fact is that each generation of disciples rewrote the biography, introducing new elements and amplifying older material in accordance with the interests and problems of that particular moment in the history of the various branches of the bKa' brgyud order. As Perrin tells us, "The prime requisite for redaction criticism is the ability to trace the *form* and *content* of material used by the author concerned or in some way to *determine the nature and extent of his activity* in collecting and creating, as well as in arranging, editing and composing."

There are many variations among the more than twenty-five versions of the life of Milarepa that are still extant, which suggests a tendency to re-create, as would be expected of oral tradition. The actual decision on the part of the authors to write down the biography and songs suggests a more complex interplay of influences. One primary motive for writing a biography is to make available to disciples a consistent source of inspiration. Another reason seems to be to clarify lineage relationships in the "*guruparampara*" relevant to each branch of the "four great and eight lesser" subdivisions of the bKa' brgyud. There is also the question of political crisis and persecution, which tend to create a climate in which sponsored literary production can play an important role. The production of a biographical text is seldom detached from some degree of historical pressure. It is possible that rGyal thang pa's version (late 1250s), for example, appears as part of a response to criticism of the siddha element in the bKa' brgyud order.

The most popular versions, the *rnam thar* and the *mgur 'bum*, assembled and redacted by gTsang smyon Heruka at the end of the fifteenth century, show all the evidence of reworking in the context of a program of religious reform, the so-called *smyon pa* movement among bKa' brgyud *yogins* such as gTsang smyon, 'Brug pa Kun dga' Legs, and so on. In fact, the Mila tradition is probably more accessible to this type of study precisely because we know a great deal more about Milarepa, his biographers, and the history of the lineage over a much longer period (1125–1500) than we do about Jesus and his disciples (30–100) during the period of the redaction of the Gospels.

In the earlier versions, such as that of rGyal thang pa, as well as in the works of gTsang smyon, there is a noticeable flavor of "epic" style. Geoffrey Samuels has pointed out that the written versions of the epic of Gesar are several centuries later than the Mila biographical corpus.[2] Without committing ourselves to demonstrating a relationship between the *Mila rnam thar* and the epic of Gesar, clear suggestions of the literary world of the inspired bards can be seen in the self-introductions, the delight in tales of combat of all kinds, the interweaving of prose and poetry, the way the character of Milarepa is developed in the course of his life, and the pageantry of the account of his death. Our texts are not far removed from oral sources and the influence of the oral style of tale telling, all of which any attempt at redaction criticism must take into account.

There is also the problem of the transmission of the texts themselves. We have the gTsang smyon "original xylograph" (which is nearly identical to J. W. De Jong's manuscript "C"), but we apparently do not have "original" manuscripts or xylographs of earlier versions. Only in the case of the works of sGampopa are there several extant versions with which to make a critical edition. Nevertheless, in texts such as those of sGampopa, rGyal thang pa, and others, one does not see a tendency for later scribes to make major changes. The variants are the usual ones of copyists' errors and not of redaction per se. One exception is the Ras chung *mila rnam thar*, which turns up reinserted word for word in the gTsang smyon version of the *rnam thar*; this *mila rnam thar* by Ras chung pa can be found gTsang smyon's edition of the *smran rtsi shes rigs spen mdzod*. There is another related but significantly different version attributed to Ras chung pa in the *Bde mchog snyan brgyud*. Thus even the written texts collected by gTsang smyon in the process of writing the biography and songs of Milarepa show evidence of a history of prior redaction.

Actual work with the texts that have come down to us becomes simpler when we choose one episode or pericope, in this case the death of Milarepa. Limiting ourselves to eight versions of this pericope, we have selected eight analytical categories that should reveal relationships among the variant accounts. Once we have established what the variations are, it becomes quite easy to arrive at family relationships among the versions. The variations within a family suggest input from one or more oral traditions or parallel texts that are not included in this study. Major variations suggest more profound dislocations and challenges in the history of the lineage of transmission. The two tables show the versions and the analytical categories. Table 3.2, following the letter and number code of Table 3.1, gives the relevant details from each of the biographical versions.

TABLE 3.1. THE DEATH OF MILAREPA

Versions	**Analytical topics**
1. sGampopa (1100s)	A. Place names/pilgrimage
2. Dorje Dze Od (late 1500s)	B. Year
3. 'Brug pa'i Chos 'byung (1600)	C. Persons named
4. *Blue Annals* (1476)	D. Relics and possessions
5. *Smran rtsi shes rigs spen mdzod* (1200?)	E. Siddhis
6. Ras chung snyan rgyud (1100s)	F. Titles of Milarepa
7. rGyal thang pa (1260)	G. Songs
8. gTsang smyon (1488)	H. The Murder Story

TABLE 3.2. ANALYTICAL BREAKDOWN OF THE DEATH ACCOUNTS

A.	1. Brin, Ti se	2. Ti se, Brin, India
	3. Abhirati	4. No place names
	5. Heavenly pure realm	6. gNya Nang of Drin
	7. India, Tibet, Chu, dbar hermitage, sNye nam, realm of the Clear light, Brin, Mang Khung, White Rock ta po, Lo ro	8. Trode Tashi gang, Nyanang Dingri, Chuwar, Pure Land, Rekpa Dukchen of Drin, Driche Cave, Dahkhar, Eagle's Egg, Loro Dol in South Tibet, a temple in Chuwar
B.	1. None	2. Eighth day of the fourth month, year of the bird; age eighty-two
	3. 1123; age eighty-three	4. Age eighty-four; water female hare year 1123
	5. None	6. None
	7. Age seventy-three; year of the monkey (1116? 1128?); evening of the full moon day of the last of the three spring months; at dawn	8. Age eighty-four; sunrise, fourteenth day of the twelfth month of the year of the wood hare (1136) under the ninth lunar constellation (or water female hare year, 1123, age eighty-three!)
C.	1. Lama Milarepa	2. Milarepa, Tashi Tseringma
	3. Milarepa, Akṣobhya	4. rJe btsun, followers, Ma gcig zha ma, Buddha
	5. Sentient beings, Ras chung pa, Ngam rDzong ras pa, others	6. Lord Yama, Lama Milarepa, a certain Bon po, a beautiful lady, six disciples, *ḍākinīs*, Ras chung pa.

	7. *rje btsun bla ma* Milarepa, four Māras, sentient beings, twelve *yogins* and *yoginis*, guru, siddhas, the people, followers, Teacher Byang 'bar, the Blessed One/ Mighty sage/Buddha, bKa' brgyud gurus, demon Yama 'Bri sgom g.yang legs, lCam me, "the Six Lords of Light," Ras pa zhi ba skyong, patroness Legs se, Bonpo Tsan dar 'bum, a beautiful woman, gShen chung pa, Ras chung pa, people of Bring and sNye nam, rGya gar bya ba of Brin, *ḍākinīs*, *pha bos* and *ma mos*, rGyal thang pa bde chen rdo rje	8. Geshe Tsak puh wa, Milarepa, a concubine, disciples, a *naga* demon at Rekpa Dukchen, demon of illness, devotees of Mila, Ras Chung pa, Maitrīpa, sGam po pa, Shi wa 'od repa, Ngam rDzong ton pa Seba Repa, Repa hermit of Di, people of Nyanang and Drin, a celestial youth, a second body at Nyanang, *ḍākinīs*, monks at the cremation, *yidams*, list of disciples and their *siddhis*
D.	1. Relics not mentioned	2. Not mentioned
	3. Not mentioned	4. "Not even a small amount of bones or relics was left."
	5. Rainbow body	6. The relics were taken up by the *ḍākinīs*. Before the eyes of the six disciples, there was not even a trace of the corpse. A package of molasses was found behind the wall.

	7. Rainbow body. gShen chung pa asked to take the hat and staff to Ras chung pa. A mirror adorned with a flame, a piece of flame-colored silk, a rusty knife, a pouch of flour, some cotton garments, a white under-garment, ritual headdress with mirror, small samaya texts. Of the relics, not even a bit of finger or toenails was left; they had been taken away by the *pha bos* and *ḍākinīs.* The aggregates passed away without remainder.	8. Staff and robe bequeathed to Ras chung pa. To sGam po pa, the hat of Maitrīpa and the staff of black aloe wood. To Shi wa 'od repa, the wooden bowl. To Ngam rDzong Ton pa, the tinder box. To Hermit Repa of Di, the bone spoon. Strips of cotton cloth were given to other disciples. A last will. No relics will be left. The *ḍākinīs* carry off the relics in a globe of white light. An egg-shaped object appears. A reliquary stupa appears. A marble slab under the cremation cell is left, inscribed with four sacred syllables. Under the hearth there was a square piece of white cloth, a knife, raw sugar, and instructions to cut up the sugar and the cloth and give them to all; poem: "The Good of a *Yogin*" and "On the Cotton Cloth," a rain of celestial flowers.
E.	1. Deeds and virtues	2. Mila was never separate from the state of *samādhi,* and he experienced no duality between meditation and post-meditation; he achieved the absolute truth of *dharmatā,* the manifestation of *dharmakāya.* He appeared in three different places after his dual cremation.
	3. He went to the Buddha field of Akṣobhya	4. Ma gcig Zha ma said, "Since his perseverance was greater than that of others, he surely should be considered to be a Buddha."

5. Deeds without limit for sentient beings. Rainbow body went to the heavenly pure realm.	6. *bla ma rnal 'byor, rje btsun, rje btsun chen po Mi la*. At the time of his passing away, he attained the Bliss of Yoga without entering the Intermediate State; a self-arisen fire blazed up from the corpse; victory banners and parasols appeared; swastikas and *srivatsas* all around; rainbow-colored smoke; sounds of musical instruments; *yidams*, heroes, and *ḍākinīs* made offerings; the saint dissolved into voidness.
7. *bla ma rje btsun, rnal 'byor gyi dbang phyung…* The six perfections attained; defeated the four Māras; completed enlightened activities, his body disappeared even before his death, like an apparition; clairvoyance with regard to the fact of the plan to murder him; his consciousness went to the realm of the Clear Light. Sounds of music at the moment of death. White ray of light from the top of his head, which remained in the sky. Corpse would not burn. Self-arisen flame from the heart cakra consumed the corpses. Eight auspicious symbols appeared. A sparkling light in the sky. Songs of sky-beings heard by all. No relics: sign of a completely perfect Buddha. Emanations: at least two; one went to help a mortal enemy.	8. *rje btsun Mi la ras pa, grub thob rnal 'byor, rje btsun rin po che, rje btsun chen po, rje dus gsum sangs rgyas 'gro ba'i mgon. thugs mkhyen rtse chen po'i ngang nyid. bla ma rje. dang po bla ma. pha yi mkhyen brtses. pha thugs rje. rje bla ma. rje yid bshin nor bu. rje grub thob. thugs rje can. 'gyur ba med pa'i rnal 'byor pa. 'jigs pa bral* (and many other titles in Shi wa Od Repa's invocation). At the end of the text: *rnal 'byor gyi dbang phyug chen po Mi la ras pa; rnal 'byor gyi dbang phyug chen po Mi la ras pa; rnal 'byor gyi dbang phyug chen dpal Mi la ras pa*. Mila knew about the poison. Celestial manifestation at a ritual feast. Transference of illness and conversion of the Geshe. Present at the same time in more than five places. Shrinking of the body at Chu war. A second body at Nya nang. Appearances to Ras chung pa. Self-arisen fire. Appearance of *yidams* at the pyre. The cremation cell undergoes transformation. *Ḍākinīs*, songs, egg-like object, stupa. A mass of light in the sky. A rain of celestial flowers that recurs annually.

F.	1. Lama Mi la	2. ?
	3. ?	4. *rje btsun, sangs rgyas*
	5. None	6. *bla ma, rnal 'byor, rje btsun, rje btsun chen po Mi la.*
	7. *bla ma rje btsun, rnal 'byor gyi dbang phyug* Mid la raspa, *bla ma grub thob, rje btsun gyi rgyal po* Mid la ras pa	8. *rje btsun* Mi la ras pa, *grub thob, rnal 'byor, rje btsun rin po che, rje btsun chen po, rje dus gsum sangs rgyas 'gro ba'i mgon. Thugs mkhyen rtse chen po'i ngang nyid nas bla ma rje. Dang po bla ma. Pha yi mkhyen bsteses. Pha thugs rje. Rje bla ma. rje yid bshin nor bu. rje grub thob. rje. thugs rje can. 'gyur ba med pa'i mal 'byor pa. 'jigs pa bral* (and many others in the invocation by Shi wa Od Repa). At the end of the text: mal '*byor gyi dbang phyug chen po* Mila ras pa *rnal 'byor gyi dbang phyug chen po* Mila ras pa *rnal 'byor gyi dbang phyug chen dpal* Mi la ras pa.
G.	1. None	2. None
	3. None	4. None
	5. None	6. A song of the *ḍākinīs*: *nor bu rin gshegs dus so 'o // … rje btsun skye med stong par thim//*

	7. Apparitions of death: *rnal 'byor mid la ras pa nga // 'chi bdag bdud kyi ba mo yis // ... 'ja' lus gyur nas dbyings gshegs zer // de ltar snang ba gnyis kar bden //*; a song of mourning by celestials: *bla ma rin cheng gshegs dus 'dir... mkha' 'gro'i dbang phyug bla ma rje // pur sbyongs mkha' spyod gnas su gshegs //*; Introductory verse: *de lta'i bla ma rje btsun de nyid kyis // bdud bzhi bcom nas yon tang drug dang ldan // phrin las rdzogs nas mya nga 'da' tshul stan // rje btsun rnam thar dzogs la gus phyag 'tshal //* See pp. 233–34	8. Song of forgetfulness to the Geshe; how to see the gods; promise to bless the regions of his journeys; song of spiritual gain; song of the great seal of voidness; song of the Geshe's conversion; song of authentic spiritual practice and its perils; the verdict on the relics; song of the six essential principles (sung from the cremation cell); a song of liberation from attachments (with comments on the funeral rites by *ḍākinīs*); Ras chung's "seven limbs" invocation; Ras chung's invocation on the basis of example; *ḍākinīs* instruct on how to invoke Mila; invocation of Shi wa od asking for a reliquary stupa; Mila's reply from the stupa on the need for discernment; the food of a *yogin* (about the relics found in a cave); a song by *ḍākinīs* on mourning
H.	1. None	2. None
	3. None	4. None
	5. None	6. A Bon po bribed a lady with a turquoise to feed Mila some poisoned yogurt. Clairvoyance and forgiveness.
	7. A Bon po of sNye nam, Tsan dar 'bum. He sends his girlfriend, having promised her a turquoise. Mila displays clairvoyance and forgives. Mila interprets the meaning of his death for his disciples and refuses remedies. Visits another enemy after his death.	8. Geshe Tsakpūhwa is a culprit, motivated by jealousy. The girlfriend, the turquoise, the poisoned yoghurt, the clairvoyance, and the forgiveness scene. The Geshe pays for an annual commemoration.

These tables provide evidence for two distinct "families" or transmissions of the biographies. Versions 1–5 represent materials that cluster around the tradition of sGampopa, since they most closely resemble his very brief and discrete account "in outline form." Versions 6, 7, and 8 seem to give freer voice to the narrative process and have closer ties to the Ras chung pa tradition. This is especially evident in the account of the murder of Milarepa by poisoning. The developmental process of redaction is extremely clear in the song of the *ḍākinīs*. In the *Ras chung snyan rgyud*, likely a very early version, it is a short hymn that celebrates the mourning and tells of the self-arisen fire, the auspicious symbols, and the disappearance of the relics. The same material and vocabulary may be found in the rGyal thang pa's and gTsang smyon's versions but with the expansions attributable to oral composition and literary manipulation.

Why the "Ras chung family" places such emphasis on these events whereas the sGampopa family almost completely ignores them can only in part be ascribed to the absence of the latter during the last days of the *rje btsun*. It does seem that rGyal thang and gTsang smyon knew of and were strongly influenced by the *Bu chen bcu gnyis* version of the songs of Milarepa, which includes a lengthy funerary pageant with invocations (this work is rich in liturgical allusions), preceded by an account of the poisoning, which concurs in identifying the guilty party as a Bon po (folios 234–43). The increased use of place names and "etiological" tales, especially in gTsang smyon, suggests the use of guidebooks and oral tradition associated with pilgrimage to the places of the life of Milarepa. The sources deriving from what we are calling the "Ras chung" tradition seem to have been produced in the places of pilgrimage; the more detached works derive from Central Tibetan communities, which would have had little direct interest in promoting place-name etiologies associated with pilgrimage sites.

gTsang smyon, perhaps influenced by his own experience of persecution by scholars from Se ra and 'Bras spungs, changed the assassin from a Bon po to a geshe. Part of the "art" of his own life was the self-identification with Ras chung pa and even with Milarepa himself, so that in a sense, Milarepa lives again in the poetry and adventures of the life of his greatest biographer. Thus the "Ras chung" family shows its own peculiar concerns through narrativity strongly influenced by epic style.

Given what we now know of the Milarepa biographical tradition, we could say the following (substituting "*Mila rnam thar*" for Gospel and "*lineage*" for "early Church" in the original text of Perrin):[3]

1. The *Mila rnam thar*s as we now have them are not simple creations out of a whole cloth but consist of collections of material, the final selection and arrangement of which we owe to the *sacred authors* themselves.
2. The material now presented in the *Mila rnam thar*s has a previous history of use in the *bKa' brgyud* lineage—largely a history of oral transmission. It circulated in the *lineage* in the form of individual units or collections of related material, and in this form it served definite functions in the life and liturgy of the *lineage* in doctrinal exposition and apologetic, in exhortation and instruction.
3. The smallest units of tradition—the individual story, saying, dialogue, song, and so on—have definite forms that can be defined and studied. Each of these forms served a definite function in a concrete situation in the life of the *bKa' brgyud* lineage. This situation is what is referred to as the *Sitz im Leben* of the material. The main purpose for the creation, the circulation, and the use of these forms was not to present the history of *Milarepa* but to strengthen the life of the *lineage.*

4

Survey of Sources

The past thirty years have been generous in providing the Western scholar with numerous previously unavailable sources for the life and teachings of Milarepa.[1] None of these would fall into the category of primary sources,[2] since none exist as autograph manuscripts of Mila or his immediate disciples. All represent the transmission of early texts and oral accounts more or less redacted. A thorough investigation of each source (along with the collection and evaluation of additional sources) for its relative historic value will one day give us the material necessary to write a reasonably coherent history of the life and times of Milarepa. The present work attempts to show some of the problems and to suggest methods for evaluating the sources as we now have them.

4.1. The Biographies of Marpa and Milarepa by sGampopa

I have worked with three editions of this text:

1. *Collected Works of sGampopa*, vol. 1. (I-Tib-82-902155). Reproduced from a manuscript reflecting the tradition of the Dwags lha sGam po redaction prepared through the efforts of Spyan snga Bsod nams lhun grub from the Hemis Monastery in Ladakh. (Darjeeling, West Bengal: Kargyud Sungrab Nyamso Khang, 1982), folios 23–42.
2. *Collected Works (gSung 'bum) of sGampopa bSod nams rin chen*, vol. 1. Reproduced from a manuscript from the Bkra shis chos rDzong Monastery in Miyad Lahul by Khasdrub Gyatsho Shashin. (Delhi: 1975), folios 16–26.

3. *Selected Writings of sGam po pa bSod nams rin chen (Dwags po Lha rje) with the Biography Written by His Descendant sGam po pa bSod nms Lhun Grub.* Reproduced from a rare manuscript collection from the Gemur Monastery in Lahul by Topden Tshering. (Ballimaran, Delhi: Jayyed, 1974), folios 18–30.

An extensive study could be done on this text, which probably represents one of the oldest accounts of the lives of Marpa and Milarepa. It is substantially in accord with later versions but tends to be fragmentary and has some episodes that do not appear in other versions. The following are some examples: Lha dga's admission that he himself made no progress in *rdzogs chen* practice; Mila's false appraisal of his own progress when he mistook the light from the butter lamp on his head for "luminosity"; his escape from the devotional clutches of a crowd of *tantrikas*; his veneration by three monk-scholars of La stod; his dwelling in a forest, where a prospective patron found his appearance unworthy; Mila's explanation of what "doing nothing" means using an example from the life of Atiśa; his transformation into a crystal stūpa that flies; his flight on the back of a lion near Rong Kha bzhi, a town near the contemporary Tibet-Nepal border; his demonstration of foresight by telling the relatives of Dar ma brTen, a traveler, that he is not dead and is on his way home; and the claim that his funeral rites were performed at Brin and at Mount Ti se.

In common with other accounts, he went to dBus to learn magical power (but no description of his deeds or penances is given); he served both Marpa and rNgog; he returned to his ruined home after study with Marpa; he ate nettles and turned green; his sister helped feed him; some lamas were envious of him and tried to dishonor him; he spent the winter miraculously at La phyi gangs (spelling is the same as the gTsang smyon version; rGyal thang pa gives La Phyis); he sang the "Song of the Staff" to a merchant on the way to Nepal; and he fell down a precipice and survived.

The biography is given "in outline form" and is attached integrally to that of Marpa. Gampopa's text refers to "many other accounts" of, for example, his life as a disciple under Marpa. There are some hints of encounters with *ḍākinīs* and of his struggles with interior practice. The *mgur* are mentioned but not quoted (perhaps the lama telling the tale is supposed to sing them from memory?). There is no account of a murder attempt and the author asserts that Milarepa was an "emanation" (i.e., of a transcendent Bodhisattva).[3]

4.2. A Description of the Twelve Great Sons' Life and Songs of Milarepa

In spring 1997, I was able to investigate the Newark Museum manuscript in a photocopy with Norbu Tsering, a lay lama from Western Tibet, and with Slava Komarovsky, a talented Russian scholar of Tibetan dialects.

The Newark Museum manuscript is a *dbu chen* copy of the complete text of the *Bu chen bcu gnyis* version of the life and songs of Milarepa. This text seems to have been compiled by Bodhi Radza (alias Ngam rDzong Ras pa) in the mid-twelfth century, bringing together accounts of episodes from the life of Milarepa gathered from the great disciples who were alive at that time. The colophon lists these disciples: Ras chung pa, Se ban ras pa, Ngam rDzongs ras pa, 'Bri sgom ras pa (the four "Balancers"), Zhi ba 'od, Sangs rgyas Skyabs, rDo rJe dBang phyug, gShen sgom Ras pa, Drong sog, mKhar Chung, sNyen sgom, Khyi gra (the eight close disciples), Dwags po lha rje, Li skor Chags Ri ba, Lo ston dGe 'dun, sKyo Ston shag dgu, Dam pa brgyag phu ba, Bro ban bkara shis (the six disciples close by at the time of death), Legs se 'bum me, dPa' dar sbum, gSal le 'od, and Ras chung ma (the four "sisters"; folio 243 verso). It is therefore a text of immense importance. The Newark manuscript contains a large number of errors of spelling[4] and grammar; even so, it is possible to identify the language of the account as Central Tibetan. Because of the archaic constructions and the grammatical errors made by the copyist, we were at first working with the hypothesis that this was possibly a western Tibetan account, but after many days of translation and interpretation, we concluded that Milarepa and Ngam rDzong wrote in excellent Central Tibetan.

This early version is, not surprisingly, a source for significantly different versions of the episodes later redacted by gTsang smyon Heruka. For example, the "Song of the Four Pillars" (folios 13–14) is a dream not of Milarepa, but of Marpa. Marpa interprets his own dream and prophesies that Milarepa will be his sole lineage holder. This version is actually more coherent with the facts since, were the dream Milarepa's, it would have occurred before his full enlightenment and would therefore have had less authority. It is interesting that the Twelve Great Disciples version is also closer in some details to our rGyal thang pa version, further confirming our convictions that the Mad Yogin took the traditional material and redacted it very freely in the manner of an oral reciter of the epic.

The Twelve Great Disciples version devotes only the first fifteen folios to an account of Milarepa's childhood, misdeeds with black magic, and conversion under Marpa's tutelage. On the fifteenth folio, the author gives the list of the seventeen virtuous qualities that we have reproduced below, section 4.3. Each of these qualities is illustrated by a series of seventeen episodes, many of which correspond to the Mad Yogin's *Hundred Thousand Songs of Milarepa* (*mila mgur 'bum*). It is significant that the early version presents itself as a *rnam thar* and *mgur* collection (the exact wording of the title is badly damaged on the first folio of the manuscript: *rje btsun chen po mid la ras pa'i rnam thar ... ng ... mo ... bzhugs* so// ... *mgur*//) and that this collection is referred to as a *mgur 'bum* in both the Ras chung pa version in the *bDe mChog snyan rgyud* biographies and in the sGampopa version. From this we should infer that Ngam rDzong ras pa was in some special way entrusted with the task of collecting the *mgur* of Milarepa, probably from the recollection of the great disciples listed at the end of the manuscript. Therefore, any attempt to establish the authentic songs of Milarepa will have to make use of the Twelve Great Sons text.

In view of the importance of this work, we offer the following outline of its contents with folio numbers based on the Newark manuscript:

1. Folio 11: Marpa gives instructions and initiations.
2. Folio 12: Marpa gives Milarepa instructions about further *ḍākinī* teachings to be obtained in India and bestows a scroll with written instructions for removing obstacles at a later time.
3. Folio 16: Milarepa sings the song about all things being without substance (*snying po med*) in the ruins of his family home.
4. Folio 19: Milarepa's intention to attain Buddhahood in the present incarnation (one body).
5. Folio 36: The La phyis gang episode.
6. Folio 38: First encounter with Ras chung pa.
7. Folio 43: Shin dor mo at Yolmo in Nepal.
8. Folios 44–45: Encounter with five monks.
9. Folio 49: Mila encounters an ogress and illusory apparitions.
10. Folio 54: Retinue of five goddesses.
11. Folio 55: Song of Definitive Meaning to the Tse ring ma goddesses.
12. Folio 57: His sister Peta and his aunt make a visit; conversion of the aunt.
13. Folio 59: Admonition to Ras chung pa to meditate and not waste time on begging.
14. Folio 60: A debate with Dar lo.
15. Folio 62: Dar lo is converted.
16. Folio 63: An angry debate between Lo Ston and Ras chung pa; Lo Ston is converted (folio 65) and becomes one of the six great monastic teacher-disciples.
17. Folios 66–67: Ras chung goes to India and Nepal with some rDzogs chen practitioners.
18. Folios 68–73: Ras chung meets Prince Ti pu pa and receives *ḍākinī* teachings.

19. Folios 73–74: Milarepa and Ras chung pa meet again; Ras chung's pride; staff and books from India.
20. Folio 78: The Tale of the Yak Horn; Ras chung is unyielding before his guru (interesting drawings of the episode; cf. the statue of Milarepa in the Gyantse Stupa, in which the saint is portrayed with a yak horn, based on this episode).
21. Folio 82: Ras chung pa's repentance as Milarepa manifests supranormal powers.
22. Folios 83–84: Levitation and passing through rocks.
23. Folio 86: A debate with 'Bri sgom, a prospective disciple.
24. Folio 87: The story of a dying Bon po who is devoted to Milarepa; Milarepa liberates his own parents from cyclic existence at the insistence of Peta (Folio 89–90).
25. Folio 92: Questions and answers from *ras pa* disciples; a mandala is shown; sufferings of the Six Realms.
26. Folio 93: The lower realms. Rich and poor both suffer.
27. Folio 94: Why do you sing songs? Mila replies, Because the deities like it, and *I* like it!
28. Folio 95: Meditation on the elements, colors, space, and limitless consciousness in a series of ten *samādhis.*
29. Folio 96: Sponsors fight over water during a drought.
30. Folios 98–99: Milarepa meets with a group of four siddhas; he is attended by forty disciples.
31. Folio 101: Milarepa preaches to a flock of miraculous birds; they are eight *ḍākinīs*.
32. Folio 103: Further tales of Ras chung pa; meeting with Ron chon ras pa.
33. Folio 108: Good places for spiritual practice.
34. Folio 111: The hunter, his dog, and the deer (The story of Hunting Ras pa).
35. Folio 115: Meeting with Geshe gYag ru thang pa; he falls asleep during the scholarly debate, but soon the Geshe is converted and becomes a *ras pa.*

36. Folio 116: Se ban ras pa becomes a disciple.
37. Folio 117–18: Demons are subdued.
38. Folio 119: Vase initiation and the consecration of a *thangka.*
39. Folio 121: A mother, A phyi snang ma, offers her son to Milarepa as a disciple.
40. Folio 122: The story of Shi ba 'od (very similar to the Mad Yogin's version).
41. Folio 132: Shi ba 'od visits Bari Lotsawa with Milarepa and another disciple; the superiority of meditation practice over study.
42. Folio 134: Female disciples ask Milarepa for his life story.
43. Folio 135: The story of Pal Dar 'bum; female disciples.
44. Folio 141: Story about Skyir rong rab chad rgar and Shin dor mo; her final liberation (folio 143).
45. Folio 144: Mang yul and Gung Thang; Se ban ras pa's story. The story of Ngam rDzong ras pa.
46. Folio 145: The Song of the Staff, as in the Mad Yogin's.
47. Folio 151: A woman *yoginī,* Tog den Ras Chung ma. Milarepa "sleeps."
48. Folios 154–63: The story of the eighteen great demons on the attack.
49. Folio 163: Bodhi Radza concludes his special section (corresponding to "The Pearl Rosary," chapter 28 in the Mad Yogin's *Songs*) with a poem on how he faithfully wrote everything down in accordance with the guru's instructions.
50. Folio 164: Five ladies come making offerings in the counterclockwise direction.
51. Folio 184: Offerings to the five mandala deities.
52. Folio 188: End of the second part of the biography based on Bodhi Radza and Shi wa 'od; meditation on light, sound, and fragrance. The Tse ring ma goddesses appear.
53. Folio 190: Song of the Great Snows.
54. Folios 192ff.: Milarepa tells his life story.

55. Folio 195: Patrons prefer Ras chung pa to Milarepa. Milarepa sings admonitory songs to Ras chung pa.
56. Folio 200: Ras chung pa wishes to go to Central Tibet; Mila puts his faith to the test. Milarepa manifests as seven people (Folio 201); Milarepa acknowledges Ras chung pa's faith in the guru and his attainment of compassion but warns him to be free of desires.
57. Folio 206: Songs of Ras chung pa.
58. Folio 207: Ras chung pa's affair with a princess.
59. Folio 210: Ras chung escapes from the princess and returns to Milarepa.
60. Folio 213: A cycle of prophecy related to sGam po pa.
61. Folio 214: Teachings to sGam po pa: radicality of *mahāmudrā* practice.
62. Folio 216: Dream interpretation. Through Folio 221: Questions and answers between sGampo pa and Milarepa.
63. Folio 221: The story of bKra shis Legs se brtsegs.
64. Folio 222: Arrival of patroness Lha cig lcam me. A quarrel over a bride is calmed.
65. Folio 224: Ras chung asks about definitive meditation experience.
66. Folio 226: Complete transmission of the oral lineage to Ras chung pa. Milarepa exposes his rear end as a reminder to practice.
67. Folios 227ff.: Patrons and offerings.
68. Folio 232: End of the *mgur 'bum* cycle of stories and beginning of the chapter on the Death of Milarepa.

4.3. The Seventeen Virtuous Qualities in Early Biographies of Milarepa

One of the features that occurs in three early Milarepa biographies is a list of seventeen "*yon tan*"—that is, virtuous qualities. The earliest biography that has this list is by Ras chung pa. The text can be found in the *Bde mchog snyan brgyud Biographies: Reproduction of a Collection of Rare Manuscripts from the Stag-sna Monastery in Ladakh* folios 133–89.[5] Also from the first generation of Milarepa's disciples, the *yogin* Ngam rDzong ras pa (also known as Bodhi Radza) composed a biography of the Milarepa in which the seventeen virtuous qualities are illustrated with narrative episodes. This extremely rare text, which includes the *rnam thar* and the collected songs (*mgur 'bum*), is in the Newark, New Jersey, Museum Tibetan Collection, 36.280, the "*Biography of Milarepa.*" It is said to have been composed by the "Twelve Great Disciples" (*Bu chen bcu gnyis*), but the living tradition states that it was composed by Bodhi Radza, the third of Milarepa's disciples to have received the complete *Cakrasaṁvara Hearing Lineage* instructions.[6] The third biography to build a sequence of narrative episodes on this list of *yon tan* is by Grub Thob O-rgyan pa Rin chen dpal, the *Bka' brgyud yid bzhin nor bu yi 'phreng ba* (*A Precious Rosary of Lives of Eminent Masters of the 'Bri gung pa dkar brgyud pa tradition*), from the library of the Ven. Kangyur Rinpoche (Leh, 1972). This realized siddha of the 'Bri gung pa order was a close contemporary of the 'Brug pa master rGyal thang pa bde chen dorje, author of the *rnam thar* of Milarepa that we translate in the following list.

Ras Chung pa's List of Virtuous Qualities

1. Practical experience of samādhi involving a direct awareness of *saṁsāra* as being without essence. Episode: Milarepa's return to his home village.
2. Dreams arising as signs.
3. Bliss-heat (*gtum mo*). Episode: At Brag dkar.
4. Being spontaneously free of the need for food. Episode: La phyis gang.

5. Experience arises as bliss. Episode: Encounter with Ston pa Dar lo.
6. Realization arises as the basis of the path. Episode: The lamp of gnosis.
7. Appearances arise as favorable conditions of the Path. Episode: Five mahāsiddhas' practices.
8. Self-liberation of the eight worldly dharmas. Episode: Story of enmity with his aunt; an interview is conducted through a curtain.
9. Same?
10. Repaying the kindness of parents. Episode: The death of a Bon po; his soul is guided by Milarepa.
11. Transforming into a supreme deity, a "god of gods." Episode: Milarepa goes to Kathmandu and is recognized as a supreme master.
12. Not being harmed by obstacles. Episode: With Ston pa Dar lo.
13. The birth of the torch of wisdom. Episode: Ras chung comes back from India full of pride.
14. Qualities of greatness due to great activities and practices. Episode: Locked up in a temple, he easily escapes.
15. Great ability. Episode: Combat with demonic forces.
16. Greatness of blessings. Episode: consecration of a *thangka* (Cakrasaṁvara?).
17. *Samādhi*: Greatness through potentiality. Episode: Se ban ras pa and Ngam rDzong are present as Milarepa demonstrates great contemplative absorption.

The List in the ***Bu chen bcu gnyis Mila rnam thar/mgur 'bum***

1. Absence of true substance in cyclic existence
2. Dreams arising as signs
3. Recognizing bliss-heat
4. Being free from craving for food and clothing

5. Experience arises as bliss
6. Realization arises as the basis of the path
7. Appearances arise as favorable conditions of the path
8. The eight worldly dharmas arise as self-liberated
9. No harm from quarrels or debate
10. Repaying kindness (of parents)
11. Great actions
12. Becoming a god among gods
13. Igniting the lamp of gnosis
14. Ability of great power
15. Great blessings
16. *Samādhi*: Fulfillment of one's potentiality
17. *Mahāmudrā*: Introducing others into the great seal

The List in Grub Thob Orgyan pa's *Mila rnam thar, Bka' brgyud yid bzhin nor bu yi 'phreng ba (A Precious Rosary of Lives of Eminent Masters of the 'Bri gung pa dkar brgyud pa tradition)*

1. Cyclic existence is without essence
2. Dawning of dreams as signs
3. ?
4. Free of need for food
5. Contemplative experience arises as bliss
6. ?
7. ?
8. Self-liberation of the eight worldly dharmas
9. No harm from debate
10. Repaying kindness of parents
11. Great actions
12. Becoming a god among gods
13. ?
14. Great power
15. ?
16. Great contemplative absorption
17. Bestowing (teachings) of *mahāmudrā*

Evidently, the Ras chung pa and Ngam rDzong ras pa lineages considered these virtuous qualities to be noteworthy. Their versions of the life of Milarepa use the list of seventeen to group his enlightened activities. In fact, the whole narrative of Milarepa as a saint depends on these episodes. sGampopa does not refer to these virtuous qualities at all. However, the 'Bri gung biography by O rgyan pa reproduces the list with exactitude as late as the end of the thirteenth century. Just a few decades earlier, rGyal thang pa had excluded this set of episodes from his version, which was constructed around twenty-six visualized verse episodes, fifteen of which occur after Milarepa leaves his Guru Marpa. Few of these episodes correspond to the narratives that accompany the seventeen virtuous qualities in the other versions. Clearly, rGyal thang pa invented his own narrative structure. After O rgyan pa, none of the biographies returns to this pattern as far as we can tell with one possible exception: the *Black Treasury* version attributed to the Third Karmapa Rang 'Byung rDo rJe. However, there is little evidence to support the claim that this biography of Milarepa comes from the pen of the Third Karmapa. According to Franz-Karl Erhardt, the text was found near Ding ri (southern Tibet) under a statue at the beginning of the nineteenth century. Cyrus Stearns did a cursory study of the text and found it to be the same as the *Bu chen bcu gnyis* version, with a few additional otherwise unknown biographical episodes.[7] Knowing that the *Black Treasury* contains the same material as the Twelve Great Sons version, we can rely on the two texts to construct a better version of the original. The Twelve Great Sons manuscript contains many scribal errors; the *Black Treasury* is in highly abbreviated *dbu-med* script. Fragments of the Twelve Great Sons text can be found in disparate places. Partial manuscripts are said to be in Sweden (not confirmed). There is an excellent copy in the Oxford Bodleian Library, which confirms our observations about the errors in the Newark manuscript. Apparently, this book was sent to England by a member of the 1904 Younghusband expedition in Central Tibet.[8] In addition, portions of the liturgical text, the *Rain of Wisdom*, contain Milarepa sacred songs in a form identical to that in the Twelve Great Sons version.

4.4. The *rnam thar* of Milarepa from the *dkar brgyud gser 'phreng:* A Thirteenth-Century Collection of Verse Hagiographies of the Succession of Eminent Masters of the 'Brug-pa dKar-brgyud pa Tradition by rGyal thang pa bDe Chen rDo rJe[9]

I have located only this one edition of the text, which is in *dbu med* script. On the basis of internal evidence, the collection is from the middle of the thirteenth century; the last master whose biography is given is rGod tshang pa mGon po rdo rje (1189–1258). rGyal thang pa is not among the bKa' brgyud masters in Khetsung Zangpo's encyclopedic collection; he must have been a codisciple of rGod tshang pa mGon po rdo rje along with O rgyan pa and the others mentioned in the *Blue Annals*,[10] but his name does not appear there.

The manuscript is probably from the sixteenth century and is written in calligraphy used in the region of sNye nam, according to the late Lama Pema Wangyal.[11] The structure of the work is of verses with "commentary"; however, the commentary consists of narrative sections, which also include excerpts from the songs of Mila himself and of other beings. The format is reminiscent of the epic rather than of the scholastic commentaries of the Indo-Tibetan tradition. The verse amounts to a sort of devotional pause along the way, as the reader is invited to join the author in a "bow" to a scene in the life of the saint. Such *thangkas* as that of the life of Milarepa in the Los Angeles County Museum of Art show episodes from his life around a large central figure of the saint; rGyal thang pa has written a biography that could easily be arranged as a *thangka* with twenty-six verses illustrated by various narrative episodes.[12]

rGyal thang pa also assumes that the reader or reciter of this *rnam thar* knows other sources. For example, the songs are usually cited with a group of initial lines, with an indication that the reciter is to continue the song to its conclusion from memory.[13] One exception is the song to the scholar Dar blo. rGyal thang pa uses this eccentric format to gather together the oral traditions that have come down to him, creating a devotional epic narrative. The approach to hagiography adopted by rGyal thang pa was not lost to the lineages that were to give rise to gTsang smyon Heruka. As Peter Alan Roberts observes, "[The *bDe-mchog sNyan-brgyud Biographies*] use of rGya-ldang-pa as the source for its biography of Ras-chung-pa indicates the convergence between the Ras-chung-pa lineages and the 'Brug-pa bKa' brgyud, a convergence that at the end of the fifteenth century would serve as the milieu for Tibet's greatest biographical literature."[14]

4.5. The *Blue Annals* as a Source for the Life of Milarepa

The *Blue Annals* was written by 'Gos lo tsa ba gZon nu dpal (1392–1481) between 1476 and 1478.[15] It is considered by later Tibetan historians as the principal authority among works of its kind. It is a *chos 'byung*—that is, a history of religious matters—and it consists almost entirely of the biographies of the most important saints and lineage holders of Tibetan Buddhism. The accounts include data of the "outer" type and also of the "inner" with occasional references to the "secret" to the extent that the saints being described engaged in enlightened activity. Each "book" is sorted out in relation to the spiritual lineages that can be grouped together. If a particular figure is associated with more than one lineage, we often find collateral references to him or her in the several collections. Usually, however, a single figure's *rnam thar* is given in the context of a particular lineage.

'Gos lo was abbot of the Karma rnying Monastery[16] and was eclectic in his contacts with diverse lineages and orders. It is particularly fascinating to see that Book 8, "The Spiritual Lineage of the Lord Translator Mar pa which was known as Dwags po bKa' brgyud" is more than three hundred pages long; pages 728–53 cover the Shangs pa bKa' brgyud teachings transmitted by Nāropa's consort Niguma, and pages 839–67 present the *mahāmudrā* lineages. Thus of a work of more than one thousand pages, four hundred are devoted to lineages and doctrines associated with bKa' brgyud pa spirituality.

Folios 11b-16a (Book 8) of the Tibetan text[17] give the biography of Milarepa ("the *yogeśvara* Mid la ras pa," 427–36). This account, it should be remembered, is ten years older than the version by gTsang smyon Heruka. 'Gos lo writes, "Up to this, I had written the life story of (Mid-la[18]) in detail, because I had seen many spurious accounts. I believe that the above account by myself corresponds to actual facts."[19] He then proceeds to summarize another biography that includes material that we find in the *mila mgur 'bum* and in rGyal thang pa. Of particular interest is 'Gos lo's version of the autobiographical song presented to Zi ba 'od (see BA, 431–32 and cf. *Songs*, 160–61).[20] Thus from the *Blue Annals*, we know that there were many biographies in existence by the end of the fifteenth century, some of which are still extant. Some accounts were associated with transmissions to particular disciples such as Ras chung pa and Zi ba 'od. Evidently, 'Gos lo considered some of the accounts of the deeds of Milarepa "spurious" and possibly harmful, because they do not give a reliably "factual" account.

4.6. The Work of gTsang Smyon Heruka

One of the problems that has contributed to a lack of attention to the earlier biographies of Milarepa has been the mistaken idea that gTsang smyon was a direct disciple of Ras chung pa. If such were the case, the biographies by other bKa' brgyud pa masters would presumably be of lesser historical value. It turns out that the biography that has become so well known is actually the culmination of a long history of literary activity.

H. Guenther says that gTsang smyon Heruka "according to tradition was one of the disciples of dPal Phag mo gru pa (CE 1110–70) who in turn was a disciple of sGam po pa (CE 1079–1153)."[21] This version is perpetuated as recently as the third volume of Mircea Eliade's *History of Religious Ideas*.[22] However, in 1969, E. Gene Smith had solved the puzzle of the identity of the author of this masterpiece (i.e., the *mila rnam thar*), of *The Hundred Thousand Songs of Milarepa* (the *mila mgur 'bum*), and of the biography of Marpa in his preface to the *Life of the Saint of gTsang*, edited by Lokesh Chandra. In their respective dissertations, Victoria Urubshurow and Charles Van Tuyl used the discoveries of Gene Smith to enter the literary world of Milarepa.[23]

The name gTsang smyon Heruka requires some exegesis of its own. gTsang refers to the province of origin of this eccentric tantric *yogin*. *Smyon* pa refers to his reputation as a "mad" spiritual genius. Gene Smith observes that the *smyon pa* (mad holy man) "is the antithesis of the scholastic monk; yet to view the phenomenon simply as a reaction against monastic reforms and dGe lungs pa rationalism misses much of the point. The *smyon pa*, too, represented a force of reform ... an attempt to rededicate the dKar [*sic*] brgyud pa sects to old truths and insights that were being forgotten."[24] Finally, Heruka is a reference to the male deity in the Cakrasaṁvara tantric cycle (and others), who is semiwrathful, in union with a female consort (Vajrayoginī) and indigo blue in color. This deity would have been gTsang smyon's personal *yidam*, the tutelary deity through whom the *yogin* attained realization.

In addition to authoring the biographies and song collections, gTsang smyon was responsible for a massive doctrinal collection, the *Bde mchog mkha' 'gro snyan rgyud* in twelve volumes.[25] This work, completed toward the end of his life, systematizes the special transmissions from Milarepa to Ras chung pa, *The Ḍākinī Hearing-Lineage Teachings on the Tantric Cycle of Cakrasaṁvara*. The fact that gTsang smyon identified himself with the Ras chung lineage is significant for his work on the biographical tradition of Milarepa, since authentic material on Mila was transmitted by Ras chung. We now have *Bde mchog mkha' 'gro snyan rgyud* biographies of Milarepa attributed to Ras chung pa and edited by gTsang smyon in two editions.[26] Of course, in the biography of Milarepa by gTsang smyon, the "prologue in heaven" that justifies the whole enterprise is a visionary experience of Ras chung pa who visits the land of Urgyen (*'o rgyan*) where the Buddha Mi bskyod pa (Akṣobya) was discoursing on the lives of Tilopa, Nāropa, and Marpa.[27]

Victoria Urubshurow summarizes the account of the production of the life of Milarepa from the *rnam thar* of gTsang smyon by his disciple, rGod tshang ras pa sna tshogs rang grol:

> The Mad Yogin was visited, as was Rechung before him, by female celestial beings ... and was invested with a mission to bring into print the life and songs of Milarepa. Thence, Tsangnyon Heruka commissioned a search of the central provinces for stories of the great saint and his songs. In the course of this project, the mad *yogin* became ill and went into retreat for the duration. While in retreat the five sisters of long life, Tseringma, appeared in [his] contemplation, and pledged to help extend Kagyu teaching. The encounter with dakinis offered Tsangnyon Heruka sufficient confidence to testify that the extraordinary biographical texts composed were just as though "coming from the lama's mouth" and that his helpers "accomplished the block printings without thinking about worldly things and enjoyments."[28]

It was my hope that one of the older sources would prove to be a literary source for the works of gTsang smyon. I was looking for a text that would match all or at least a significant portion of a song, tale, or episode in the works of gTsang smyon. In the *rnam thar* neither by sGam po pa nor by rGyal thang pa did I find such a source. We do have such a source in the *Ras chung mila rnam thar* from the *mkha' 'gro snyan rgyud* copied word for word in some passages of the *rnam thar* by gTsang smyon.[29] The following facts have surfaced in this research:

1. There are a few *lines* in common between rGyal thang pa's songs and those of the gTsang smyon version of the *Mila mgur 'bum.*
2. There are "parallels of meaning" in the sense that the same general stories are told but with different vocabulary and prosody; the common vocabulary is relatively small.
3. In general, each account shows considerable independence rather than dependence on the earlier versions. Some kind of creative retelling is in process.

gTsang smyon elaborates, extends, and embroiders the texts he has received from tradition. I am led to suspect that the Mila corpus was for a very long time an oral tradition handed down by storytellers who did not memorize it. Rather, these poets were creative the way a bard is creative and only in the late fifteenth century were the oral tales collected and organized by a literary genius into a coherent but highly redacted romance. This genius, gTsang smyon Heruka, though thoroughly literate, must have also possessed the unique charisma of the entranced bards of the oral tradition of Tibetan epic and hagiography.

4.7. Oral and Literary Interface

Before claiming these conclusions to be established, it seems appropriate to investigate oral forms of poetic transmission and to suggest the mechanism for the oral aspect of the biographical process that produced the *Mila rnam thar.*

R. A. Stein has studied the oral tradition in Tibet in depth. His observations take us into the native Tibetan milieu in which Milarepa himself lived and composed his folk balladry combining Dharma teaching in the tradition of the Indian mahāsiddhas with the imagery, prosody, and native genius of the Tibetan *glu* and *mgur.*[30] Stein describes the epic (*Gesar*) in his introduction to the Bhutanese edition:

> The oral versions are spread by professional singers or bards (*sgrung mkhan*) who wander all over the country. Some may know the whole or a great many chapters of the epic, others only some of them. If invited for recitation, they can recite and sing for days and weeks. They are said to be inspired when singing, or even in a kind of rapture or trance (*sgrung 'bab*). In any case their attitude at the moment has largely a religious tint. They wear a special hat, the parts of which are explained in a special song (*zhra-bshad*) in the same way as do other specialists on other occasions. The recitation resembles that of the theatre. The main story is quickly

> told in prose in a kind of psalmody. It is frequently interrupted by dialogue between the persons who appear in the story. These are in reality an exchange of long songs (*glu*) chanted in various melodies.... in which each person first presents himself as well as his weapons, his horse, etc. This is done, as in the theatre, by means of a stereotyped formula like: "Do you know me? If you don't, I am so and so ..." As we know it now in all of its available versions, the epic has certainly been composed by a clerical author belonging to the type of inspired poet-saint or *yogin* (especially in the bKa' brgyud pa and the rNying ma pa orders).[31]

The last sentence in particular indicates that it is a *literate yogin* who is able to make the transition from a purely oral recitation to a written compilation. In Khams during July 2000, I was able to observe a pageant performance of the Gesar epic, enacted by the young monks of the Ya chas Gompa and sung by Lama A-chos, abbot of this large community of two thousand monastics. The abbot is an accomplished *yogin*, a master of ritual, and a scholar, fitting exactly our description of the ideal bard.

In order to establish the process of transmission from the oral poet Milarepa to his biographers, we need to know something about oral composition: the art of the bard or "singer of tales." For this we turn to the work of A. B. Lord on the Yugoslav epic cycles:

> Oral epic song is narrative poetry composed in a manner evolved over many generations by singers of tales who did not know how to write; it consists of the building of metrical lines and half lines by means of formulas and formulaic expressions and of the building of songs by the use of themes... . By formula I mean "a group of words which is regularly employed under the same metrical conditions to express a given essential idea." ... We shall see that the formulas ... are capable of change and are indeed frequently

> highly productive of other and new formulas ... we shall see that in a very real sense every performance is a separate song; for every performance is unique, and every performance bears the signature of its poet singer... . The singer of tales is at once the tradition and an individual creator. His manner of composition differs from that used by a writer in that the oral poet makes no conscious effort to break the traditional phrases and incidents; he is forced by the rapidity of composition in performance to use the traditional elements... . His art consists not so much in learning through repetition of the time worn formulas as in the ability to compose and recompose the phrases for the idea of the moment on the pattern established by the basic formulas.[32]

What Lord has given us is an insight into the process of oral composition during performances. "Each performance is more than a performance; it is a re-creation."[33] So the song is, in a sense, "generic," a concept, a known quantity in the context of a particular cultural tradition; the singer of tales has to create a work of art in relation to the tale that is in some sense already on the threshold of consciousness of his audience.

Returning to Stein, we can situate this oral process in its Tibetan milieu by looking more closely at the state of mind of the singer of tales. In Yugoslav culture, the state of mind of the bard is tacitly assumed; he must be in a state of ease, of relaxation, a "natural" frame of mind, in tune with his art and with his audience. He must be recollected but ever ready to act and to respond. This is not all that different from the frame of mind that one may observe in a Newari *vajrācārya* as he performs a *homa* (fire) offering at Swayambunath. As I observed in the case of the lamas of Dolpo and of Khams, any good ritual specialist carries the flow of the rite in his psychosomatic habits. To perform well, he or she must have mastered the art of relaxing within the natural tension of carrying out a complex procedure under the scrutiny of a public that is, to put it bluntly, paying for the rite to be performed. Stein perhaps exaggerates or romanticizes the bard's recollection as a kind of "trance."[34] Perhaps it would be better to use the term "concentration" or "recollection" (the French term *recueillement* is appropriate here and is used by De La Vallée Poussin in his translation of the *Abhidharmakośa*). Recollection accompanied by extraordinary force of character typified the performance of Gesar that we observed in Khams on July 18, 2000, by Lama A-chos of Ya chas Gompa (Chung T'ai City, western Sichuan Province, People's Republic of China).

The religious character of the epic in Tibet is stronger than that of the epic in the Balkans, though in the latter a religious element (Christian or Muslim) is not absent. "For its efficacy, the epic must be recited exactly and completely. Thus a bard is necessary. The manner of the recitation is rather a delicate matter. It brings on the real presence of the god or hero—considered to be a god."[35] The bard wears a hat that has a mirror on it that symbolizes the presence of rDo rje 'Chang (*Vajradhara*). In the folk idiom, such a symbol represents the bard's "entrancement" by the deity. Gesar, for example, is believed to be an emanation of the great Guru Padmasambhava, in whose headgear was a mirror that also represented Vajradhara. Like Vajradhara in the typology of saint, hierophant, and guru, the bard by the very nature of his inspiration tends to assimilate roles. Stein shows how the bard shares in the identity of psychopomp, Mad Yogin, warrior, athlete, sorcerer, and hero.[36] "If the recitation of the epic is a religious and magical act, he who is its specialist, the bard, is a person characterized by inspiration in every sense of the word—poet, singer, and musician, but also medium, diviner, shaman. Also his behavior and his vesture present numerous resemblances to those of various specialists of the magico-religious domain."[37] Milarepa is presented as a participant in this identity; as a siddha, he is disconcertingly capable of assimilating diverse societal roles. Even in the sGam po pa biography, we find references to Milarepa as a disconcerting presence and a bard. In rGyal thang pa's version, we find full-scale songs and a structure that resembles the pattern of the epic. In the *rnam thar* and *mgur 'bum* created by gTsang smyon, we find a combination of genres similar to the work of rGyal thang pa: *dohā,* narrative, *mgur,* and even drama (the ninth chapter, the *Parinirvāṇa,* is an elaborate liturgical pageant), such as one might expect in the assimilative environment of the epic.

Epic themes found in the sources for the life of Milarepa include the following:

1. Demon attacks, which place us in the milieu not only of Gesar but also of the *Ramāyana* and the *Mahābhārata.* Magical weapons, vast arrays of demonic enemies, the aspect of illusion and deception, the boastful threat-songs, and the tendency to project the psychomachia outward onto natural phenomena situate us in the world of the South Asian epic.[38]
2. Mila himself is presented as a bard, as an inspired and even "entranced" instrument of the Dharma. Some aspects of his costume and behavior resemble those of the bard.[39] As a Buddhist proclaiming the Dharma, Milarepa was able to integrate his native ability as a singer of *glu*[40] with his illumination as a lineage holder of highest yoga tantra transmitted from Nāropa to Marpa and of the mahāsiddha *dohā* tradition transmitted by Maitrīpa to Marpa. The *smyon pas* and siddhas claimed to despise learning and books (or rather learning that merely involved verbalization and quibbling). Perhaps this was their strategy for maintaining sympathy with the people; certainly the assimilation of the identity of a folk bard was a brilliant move toward situating Buddhism firmly at the center of the indigenous cultural amalgam.[41]
3. The important pre-Buddhist phenomenon of shamanic or oracular possession in Tibet gave a communicable shape to the message of the Mad Yogin (*smyon pa rnal 'byor pa*). In chapter 53 of the *mgur 'bum,* Mila encounters the accomplished *yogin* Dampa Sangye and proclaims himself crazy in a lineage of crazy ones, starting with the great rDo rJe 'Chang (i.e., Vajradhara)—crazy like a sick man or one

possessed by a demon, which suggests that to the popular imagination, the hierophant/saint is a "Varjadhara" because he is "entranced" by Vajradhara. This is sacred madness, which puts the saint in constant touch with absolute reality. One has to be both mad and divine to be adequate to the permanent vision of truth.[42]

4. Mila is the type of hero that we find in Gesar. As a boy, under the name of Jo ru, Gesar is ugly and mischievous. He plays very bad practical jokes, making use of his supernatural powers. Only after a series of initiatic trials is he installed as king of gLing with the name of Gesar[43]—a *cakravartin* (wheel-turning world sovereign) subduing demons and villains in the surrounding territories.[44] As a boy, Milarepa is presented as powerless and a bit spoiled. His mother thinks he has no will power, so she tells the youths who accompany him to dBus to watch over him so he will persevere in his study of magic. His mother sees the son as an insult to his father's memory, unable to avenge himself on their enemies and barely able to help provide for their needs. Mila undertakes the practice of destructive magic, which proves to be an initiatic trial by which he triumphs over his enemies; his remorse over his sinful vengeance gives rise to higher aspirations. Just as *glu* (folk songs) are characteristic of human life in the course of cyclic existence, so too are the deeds of sorcery merely the playing out of samsaric themes—that is, nasty practical jokes. However, once the karmic connection between evil doing and future consequences has become apparent, Milarepa is ready to take the right path, leading to Buddhahood, the realization of which will be manifest in his mastery of the art of *mgur* (sacred song). First he must pass through the trials of probationship under Marpa and of ascetic practices in the snow ranges. His combat with demons,[45] with the elements, with his human

> despisers, and with himself solidifies his achievement and makes permanent the realization that he initially glimpsed in the cave of Lho Brag. Along with his title *rje btsun*—"the one worthy of veneration" (i.e., saint)—rGyal thang pa regularly attaches the term *rgyal po* (victor; Sanskrit: *jina, narapati, rājan*; thus we have *rje btsun gyi rgyal po mid la ras pa*), suggesting that the saint is both world conqueror and world renouncer, a theme going back to the earliest conceptions of the Buddha.[46]

Additional contrasts between rGyal thang pa and gTsang smyon suggest that the former is following an independent approach distinct from those of sGampopa, Ras chung pa, and Bodhi Radza:

1. rGyal thang makes little mention of Indian sources for the doctrines of Milarepa and the training of Marpa, whereas gTsang smyon devotes considerable space in the *rnam thar*s of Marpa and Milarepa to the transmission of the doctrines and practices of the mahāsiddhas to their Tibetan disciples. This concern for authenticity and for Indian origins was meant to dispel the criticism of bKa' brgyud pa practices, especially *Mahāmudrā*, as being a veiled survival of the Chinese "quietism" of Hwa shang.[47]
2. In the biographies of rGyal thang pa and by sGam po pa, the errors of Milarepa in the early stages of practice are frankly recounted (see rGyal thang pa, folio 230, for an error in the use of mystic winds and folio 231 for an emotional reaction to Marpa's death; in the sGampopa version, see folio B.20/A.31 for his mistaken appraisal of an experience of "luminosity"), but no such errors are mentioned in gTsang smyon's accounts.
3. In the bitter antischolastic polemic in gTsang smyon's chapter 34 ("The Challenge from the Logicians") in the *mgur 'bum*, the scholar Dar blo is turned into a demon.[48] In the version by rGyal thang pa, Dar blo is converted; this account

goes so far as to claim that his merits were equal to those of Milarepa himself (folio 245).

4. In the rGyal thang pa version, Milarepa is positively cruel to his aunt when she wishes to repent; it is Peta, Mila's sister, who intercedes for the aunt. In gTsang smyon's version, it is Peta who wishes to prevent the aunt from seeing the *rje btsun*.[49] This bears out the often-repeated observation that, over time, hagiographical accounts tend to diminish the imperfections of the saint and that in earlier versions one may find occasional "flaws" that the devotional values tradition has not yet suppressed.[50]

The idea that hagiographical literature in Tibet might undergo these kinds of transformation is confirmed when we turn our attention to the history of the genre itself. Chung Tsering,[51] a contemporary scholar of Tibetan literature, has pointed out that the *rnam thar* as a literary form is heir to two earlier types of literature. The first is the canonical form *skyes rabs*, the life of the Buddha and in particular the previous lives of the Buddha as recounted in the *Jātaka* tales. The second is the *rtogs brjod*, the epic, based on the celebration and understanding of heroic deeds. The epic of Gesar makes its appearance in written form in the fourteenth and fifteenth centuries in accounts of famous people and their deeds, but one must also keep in mind that the great Sanskrit epics (*Mahābhārata, Ramāyana*) were known in Himalayan cultures. The *Ramāyana* was already translated into Tibetan by the ninth century. Epic of this kind is a mixture of oral history and fictional embellishment. The latter depends on the canons of literary taste imported from India with the translation, in 1277, of key Sanskrit works on poetics by Sakya Paṇḍita. Other Tibetan scholars contributed to this phase of "sanskritization"—for example, Shong dun Lotsawa and Dorje Khentzen, who translated the works of the Indian poet Daṇḍin. Thus there was an actual theoretical basis for the transformation of epic types of literature into poetic compositions such as that of rGyal thang pa and, later, of gTsang smyon Heruka.

gTsang smyon's achievement was to write Tibetan with finesse and to make the *rnam thar* form universally understandable. His literary promotion succeeded in popularizing the siddha ideal throughout Tibet, even in circles that did not follow his lead in contemplative and liturgical matters. His version of the *Mila rnam thar* did make the claim of being based on the "uncommon transmission" of Milarepa's teachings (*thung mong ma yin pa*), but this was more a matter of the Mad Yogin's own personal myth as mystic and as author; his way of recasting the songs of Milarepa is technically based on the Tibetan translations of Sanskrit works on poetics.

5

Toward Identifying the "Voice" of Milarepa

My research on the biographical tradition of Milarepa has brought to light a large number of hagiographical texts demonstrably older than the well-known *rnam thar* and *mgur 'bum* in part authored and in part redacted by gTsang smyon Heruka around 1500. Fieldwork in Nepal and India has confirmed the hypotheses previously advanced in my 1988 dissertation. In addition, we now have a clearer picture of the transmissions descending from Milarepa to sGampopa, Ras chung pa, and Ngam rDzong ras pa ("Bodhi Radza"), each of whom developed a characteristic approach to the biographical, song, and yogic traditions of the bKa' brgyud pa. It is now possible to attempt to locate the authentic voice of Milarepa within these textual traditions. I hope that some points of contact between the oral teachings (*gdams ngag*) and the songs (*mgur*) tradition may increase our understanding of the literary and spiritual processes that are involved.

In order to disclose the *redaktionsgeschichte* of this large literary corpus, we will attempt to identify the criteria and the methodology for establishing the *ipsissima vox* (i.e., his "very own voice") of Milarepa as evidenced in the texts attributed to him. Prime candidates for Milarepa's teaching voice may be found in the older versions of the *mgur 'bum* (such as the *Bu chen bcu gnyis* and the work of rGyal thang pa) and in the various Milarepa *gdams ngag*. Several of the latter are to be found in the *gDams ngag mdzod*, volume 5, compiled by Jamgon Kongtrul Lodro Thaye the Great (1813–99). Further examples from the isolated *dgon pas* of the central Himalayas are preserved in the microfilm collections of the National Archives of Nepal and turn out to be excerpts from the *bDe mchog snyan brgyud* collection. These materials make possible a study of the transition from the original oral compositions of the master to a series of redactions by disciples leading to a standardized body of teaching vocabulary characteristic of the lineage. In addition, we may look forward to further refinements of a redaction-critical approach to the works of gTsang smyon Heruka and his school based on this research methodology.

To begin with, I would like to identify the body of material attributed to Milarepa and then examine it for authenticity. This material has been redacted, which simply means "transmitted along with accumulated editorial modifications." That means that the reader will want to get involved in unraveling the editorial modifications to find out more about Milarepa himself, if possible. Can we still hear the actual voice of a twelfth-century Tibetan *yogin* in these texts, or are we locked into the issues and editorial decisions of later centuries? Do we really have anything of the early twelfth century? He lived only 875 years ago, and the literary culture and spiritual practices are still alive to some degree. There is therefore good reason to hope that we can find a way back to this interesting and pivotal religious figure of Tibetan Buddhism.

What we have today in the Tibetan milieu (which now includes Tibet/Himalayan Bhotia communities, exile communities in South Asia, and exile communities in the rest of the world) would be the following:

1. The Tibetan cultural community manifests widespread familiarity with the *Life of Milarepa* and *The Hundred Thousand Songs of Milarepa* [1] (*rnam thar mgur 'bum*), both of which were redacted, compiled, and recreated by the Mad Yogin of Tsang around 1500.
2. The *gDams ngag mdzod* collected by Jamgon Kongtrul the Great in the nineteenth century is chiefly known among the heirs of the *ris med* practice traditions.
3. The various editions of the *bde mchog snyan brgyud*, originally assembled by Ngam rDzong ston pa (Bodhirāja/Bodhi radza),[2] a direct disciple of Milarepa, contain his teachings.

I located some manuscript versions of these materials in the National Archives of Nepal. A clear edition with brief commentary by Padma dKar po has been studied by Fabrizio Torricelli.[3]

4. The *Ras chung snyan brgyud* also contains Milarepa materials.
5. The *sGam po pa sum 'bum* and other collected works of early bKa' brgyud pa masters should also contain these materials.
6. There are many biographies of Milarepa, dating from the twelfth to the eighteenth centuries, containing a great variety of episodes and materials, according to the interests and the received traditions reported by their authors. These texts seem to be little known in the contemporary Tibetan community and their variance from the gTsang smyon version tends to provoke negative judgments on their value and authenticity, even though they are more ancient.

The biography by the Mad Yogin[4] is of course very well known. In Himalayan Bhotia communities, it is publicly recited during Losar, the reciter pointing out episodes on a *thangka* as he sings (see frontispiece).

However, the *mgur 'bum* is considered inappropriate for public recitation;[5] the episodes, which look to us like expansions of the episodes of the *rnam thar*, are considered restricted teachings that are recited and discussed within the circle of initiated *yogins*; the songs themselves are often cited by masters when they instruct disciples. This text has had a long history, including extensive redaction by the Mad Yogin. There is now evidence that the core collection of the *mgur 'bum* is actually the so-called *rnam thar/mgur 'bum* attributed to the "Twelve Great Disciples" (*Bu chen bcu gnyis*) but in which the oral tradition links with the name of Bodhi Radza, the third of Milarepa's disciples entrusted with the *bde mchog snyan brgyud*.

The *gDams ngag mdzod* collection is formally transmitted to advanced practitioners. Jamgon Kongtrul the Great wanted to preserve all these oral teachings (*upadeṣa*) in the nineteenth century, when many of the living transmissions were in danger of dying out. The idea was to put everything in a complete set of volumes that could be formally read out loud (*lung*) to the new generation of masters. Upon receiving specific practice instructions (*khrid*), they would proceed to train in these teachings in retreat. Only those who have the *lung* and *khrid* can do the practice, only those who have the blessing of the lineage can achieve success (*grub*) in the practices, and only those who have attained can legitimately transmit these teachings in the future.[6]

The same holds for the oral teachings related to the *yidam Cakrasaṁvara*, collected in the *bde mchog snyan brgyud*. The reason for orality and for secrecy is related to the most fundamental principle of tantric practice: through assiduous practice under the guidance of one's destined (*rten 'brel*) guru, one actually attains the lesser siddhis and, hopefully, in "one body, in one lifetime," the supreme siddhi, which is nothing less than perfect enlightenment, *samyaksaṁbodhi*.

Focusing specifically on the texts attributed to Milarepa himself, we hope to be able to uncover something in the *Songs* collections that is also authentically by Milarepa. Because these songs are essentially a form of didactic poetry, in the course of research, I attempted to find parallel expressions across several genres in the works of Milarepa. The oral instructions seem to be taken down as notes by the disciple (often Ras chung pa) who has been given the teaching. In one case, a later editor has added a "frame story" to introduce the material.[7] The text on the intermediate state translated later in this book is another example of a concluding frame story attributed to Milarepa. Here, Milarepa instructs Ras chung pa on the way to hand on the instructions he has received.[8] There is even a reference to Ras chung's dalliance with a noble lady. This "frame" could, of course, have been added by a disciple of Ras chung pa, or even by a much later biographer. A clue might be in comparing this text to the same account in the *Ras chung rnam thar* by a disciple of the Mad Yogin, either Lha btsun rin chen rnam rgyal (1473–1557) or rGod tshang ras pa brtsams sna tshogs rang grol.[9]

Segregating the body of the instruction from such frame stories, we are in a good position to start collecting oral expressions that have been transmitted within the written materials. What happens in oral composition or performance (this is true for oral didactic poetry as well as for oral performance epic poetry) is that the speaker does not recite word for word from memory but rather re-creates anew in every performance, making use of his overall knowledge of the material, whether didactic or narrative, and of his specific knowledge of the terminology traditionally applied to the topic. This means that the reciter repeats certain expressions over and over, recombining them with the phraseology that is employed to round out the teaching or narrative. On the basis of the phenomenology of oral performance, we can expect to find certain expressions repeated in Milarepa's didactic poetry in the various *mgur 'bum* collections and also in the notes taken by his disciples during the bestowal of oral instructions. Both are orally based and both make use of standard expressions many times repeated.[10]

The *mgur 'bum* preserves a song that Milarepa is said to have sung to a group of pigeons, who turn out to be disguised *ḍākinī*:[11]

> O gracious ["remembered with affection"] Marpa of Lhobrag!
> I meditate on what is recollected in my heart,
> I pray that I might never be separated from you.
> Such joy comes from mingling one's own mind with the Guru!
> Such joy, this natural character of appearances!
> Having realized the non-arisen *(skye med)* as the *Dharmakāya*,
> Having mingled the non-artificial within the *Dharmakāya*,
> Therefore I am not interested in such distinctions as "high" or "low" views.
> The mind in this non-artificial state is a source of bliss [corrected from *Bu chen* manuscript: *bde 'byung*].
> Clarity-Voidness-Awareness: having set forth (*ngo sprod nas*) these,
> The natural is dissolved into the primordial.

It matters not to me whether I have a good or bad meditation experience,
This non-artificial mind is a source of Bliss.
The six senses [and their objects dissolve] into their own brightness.
Setting forth the non-duality of the grasper and that which is grasped [subject and object],
Thus, happiness and sorrow dissolve into one.
Passing away (*'das*, corrected from the *Bu chen* ms.) into the non-artificial state,
I pass no judgment on what ought or not ought to be done.
This non-artificial mind is a source of bliss.
The nature of the *Dharmakāya* is to be fruitful;
Once it has been set forth as the variegated *Nirmāṇakāya*,
Right to the end, they are mingled in liberated recollection.
I have no desire to succeed at anything in particular,
This non-artificial mind is a source of bliss.

In this text we can see that the few variations introduced by gTsang smyon are significant. I sense in the *Bu chen bcu gnyis* text of the same song a "rugged" sound that has been normalized by the Mad Yogin. Boldface is used in these tables to highlight the variants.

1. *Bu chen:* Ā **ma'i** drin lan mar pa lho brag pa // (the long A may suggest a *rdzogs chen* milieu. Note also the irregular meter, with nine beats).

   gTsang smyon: **e ma ho** // drin can mar pa lho brag pa // (*e ma ho* suggests the milieu of the *Cakrasamvara tantra.* Note the division into a poetic/hymnic introduction and a seven-beat line, which remains relentlessly consistent).

2. *Bu chen:* sems ma bcos pa 'di bde **mo na gda'** // abiding in this "easy" *(bde mo)* natural [state of the] mind (nine-beat line).

ye shes stong gsal sems kyi rang bzhin 'di // *this* is the nature of the mind: wisdom, voidness, and clarity (nine beats).

gTsang smyon: sems ma bcos pa 'di bde **mor gda' //** (says the same thing in seven beats) **stong gsal** sems kyi rang bzhin 'di // What happened to the term for gnosis (Tibetan: *ye shes;* Sanskrit: *jñāna*)? Seems it was cut just to keep to seven beats!

3. *Bu chen:* tshogs drug rang sar **dwangs** pa la // The six sensorial mechanisms self-arise *radiantly*. Here we have seven beats!

   gTsang smyon: tshogs drug rang sar **dag** pa la// The six ... self-arise in *purity*.

4. *Bu chen:* **thug phrad dran grol gyi** ngang du 'dres // mingling within, memory is liberated from "touching and meeting." Or "right to the end," they are mingled in liberated recollection. Note that there are eight beats here.

   gTsang smyon: **goms pa 'dris 'dzag gis** ngang las 'dres // for the meditator, external familiarity subtly (*'dzag gis:* dripping) mingles with that which is within (eight beats).

Another example of this can be found in the *snying po med* song that Milarepa sings upon his return to the ruined family house in the village of rTsa of Gung Thang. There is a marked contrast between the litanic simplicity of the *Bu chen* version and the literary sophistication (and complete reworking) of this material by gTsang smyon, who has turned the earlier composition into two songs linked by his own expansion of the narrative known to the earlier tradition, as witnessed by the Bu chen text and the identical material preserved in the *bKa' brgyud mgur mtsho.*[12] One song is sung over the dust/bones of his mother and another to his late teacher's son. The *Bu chen* version is a listing of the causes of sorrow, each followed by a "responsory"—that is, the word "essenceless" (*snying po med*). The version by rGyal thang pa is quite close to the *Bu chen* litanic form but represents an independent tradition with signs of oral recomposition:

1. *Bu chen bcu gnyis:*

Folio 16.5:

kye ma 'khor ba'i chos la snying po med//
mi rtag mi rtag snying po med//
'gyur zhing 'gyur zhing snying po med//
mi nges mi nges snying po med//
yul yod bdag med snying po med//
bdag yod yul med snying po med//
bdag dang yul gnyis 'dzom yang snying po med// (9 beats)
'khor ba'i chos la snying po med//
pha yod bu med snying po med//

Folio 17.1:

bu yod pha med snying po med//
pha bu gnyis ka 'dzom yang snying po med//
'khor ba'i chos la snying po med//
ma yod pha med snying po med//
pha yod ma med snying po med//
pha ma gnyis ka 'dzom yang snying po med//
'khor ba'i chos la snying po med//
[pha ma bu gsum 'dzom yang snying po med//
'khor ba'i chos la snying po med//][13]
mi yod nor med snying po med//
nor yod mi med snying po med//
mi nor gnyis ka 'dzom yang snying po med//

Folio 17.2:

bde skyid long spyod 'dzom yang snying po med//
'khor ba'i chos la snying po med//
ci byas sdug bsgnal snying po med//
ci bsag mi rtag snying po med//

ci bsgrub sgyu mar snying po med//
thams cad 'dzom yang snying po med//
'khor ba'i chos la snying po med//
snying po med pa'i rang bzhin la//
nga ni rnal 'byor bdag cag gi//
snying po'i don cig cug bsdu āng//
rje mi bskyod ngo bo rdo rje 'chang//
sprang [sprung?] ri khrod zin par byin gyi brlob//

2. Same song from the *mila rnam thar* in the *Ras chung snyan brgyud*//I-Tib-73-902914, vol. 1. 97–125ff.

Folio 111.7 (from the episode illustrating the first of 17 *"yon tan"* [virtuous qualities]):

mgur bzhes pa/
kye ma 'khor ba snying po med//
mi rtag mi rtag snying po med//
'gyur zhing ma gnes snying po med//
nor yod mi med snying po med//
mi yod nor med snying po med//
ma yod bu med snying po med//
bu yod ma med snying po med//
thams cad yod kyang snying po med//
snying po med pa'i dus 'di rdu [?] [sdu = "also"]//
snying po dam pa btsal bar bya// ces sung/

3. Mila rnam thar in the *bde mchog snyan brgyud* biographies, I-Tib-84-900297, 133–89ff., again from the episode illustrating the first of 17 *"yon tan":*

Folio 155.3:

dgos mi la'i 'khor ba la snying po mi 'dug pas snying po ci blang dgos snyam nas mgur gsungs pa/
kye ma 'khor ba snying po med//
mi rtag mi brtan snying po med//

gyur zhing nges med snying po med//
mi yod nor med snying po med//
nor med me yod snying po med//
ma yod bu med snying po med//
bu yod ma med snying po med//
gnyis ka mdzom kyang snying po med//
thams cad mdzom kyang snying po med//
snying po med pa'i dus 'di rdu [rdu]//
rnal 'byor snying po cis mi btsal// zhes gsungs so/

4. From the *Standard Edition* of the *rnam thar/mgur 'bum*, p. 137:

kye ma kye ma kyi hud kyi hud āng/
'khor ba'i chos la blo gtad byed pa rnams//
bsams shing bsams shing yi mug yang yang ldan/

5. From the *bka' brgyud gser 'phreng* by rGyal thang pa (thirteenth century), folio 219:

rje bla ma rnams la phyag 'tshal//
kye ma kye ma snying po med//
spyir 'khor ba'i chos la snying po med//
rtags shing rtags shing snying po med//
'gyur gyin 'gyur gyin snying po med//
yul dang ma dang sring mo gsum//
gsum kar yod kyang snying po med//
da snying po med pa'i dus di tu // (rdu?)
rnal 'byor snying po cis mi tshol//

For such a simple, litanic song, there is considerable evidence of redactional transformation. This only makes it more difficult to identify the actual voice of Milarepa, except perhaps in the use of *snying po med* as the responsory half-verse.

Another example of this editorial process is the song based on Mila's premonitory dream on progress in spiritual practice, "On the Primordial

Ground."[14] gTsang smyon's version shows him at work with a lighter redactional hand. As a control over this process of recomposition in the later literary tradition, we can compare the *Bu chen* version with that of the Mad Yogin alongside that given in the version of the same song given by rGyal thang pa in the mid-thirteenth century. gTsang smyon follows the *Bu chen* rather closely, whereas rGyal thang pa's excerpt (he does not give us the complete text) is a sort of scrambling of the material. Three lines are clearly related to the tradition; three lines are entirely original. It begins to look like a different oral transmission at work here. Ras chung received the *bDe mchog snyan brgyud*, but so did Bodhi radza (Ngam rDzong), and in this case gTsang smyon clearly borrows from the latter. It seems that rGyal thang pa is working with the Ras chung pa transmission in this particular case (which we demonstrate by the following comparisons, which show three lines in common between the Ras chung pa version and the rGyal thang pa version, with tenuous connections with the Bu chen tradition followed by gTsang smyon).

1. Here is rGyal thang pa's version (folio 220):

Tibetan text	Observations
gzhi mnyam pa nyid kyi sa gzhi la //	= line 3 of gTsang smyon
zung 'dzug glang chen gnyis sdebs nas //	In neither Bu chen nor gTsang smyon.
thabs dang shes rab bshol btags te //	= approx. line 9 of gTsang smyon
blo dang ldan pa'i thong mkhan gyis //	Not in either.
brtson 'grus drag po'i smos [rmos] byas nas //	Like line 12 of gTsang smyon
tha ba sra yang phed te mchi //	Not in either.

2. Here is the passage in the *Ras chung snyan brgyud mila rnam thar* (folio 156.1–4):

Tibetan text	Observations
mnyam pa nyid kyi sa gzhi la //	= rGyal thang pa's version.
dad pa sngon 'gro'i chu gyur ste //	Unique to Ras chung pa.
bdud rtsi lnga'i yi rlan gyis sbangs //	Unique to Ras chung pa.
'khrul rtog med pa'i sa bon btab //	Unique to Ras chung pa.
gnyis med glang chen zung ltebs nas //	Close to rGyal thang pa.
thabs dang shes rab bshol btags nas //	= rGyal thang and gTsang smyon.
blo dang ldan pa'i thong mkhan gyis //	= rGyal thang alone.
brtson 'grus myur ba lcag gis bzhur //	Close to rGyal and gTsang smyon.
tha ba sra yang phed de mchi //	= rGyal thang; not found in others
tha ba sra yang phed de mchi //	Same as rGyal thang; not found in the others.

These lines from Ras chung's version were "left to the imagination" by rGyal thang pa:

'brus dus su smin de mchi//
zhing pa'i dpe dang sbyar ba 'di//
rnal 'byor pa mi rmi lam lags//
tshig tham don la skyes pa med//
slad kyi byub bsgrub pa rnams//
nyams su len na de ni mdzod// ces so

This technical excursus on Milarepa's poetry gives us direct access to the redactional process that occurred over the centuries as the biographical tradition evolved. It seems clear that oral composition, which lies at the root of the process in Milarepa's own creativity, continued to influence the way his songs were received and transmitted, with only key phrases or concepts remaining constant over time.

Now that we have examined some examples of redactional technique, we can touch upon the technical terminology of yogic experience to attempt another approach the actual voice of Milarepa.[15] Here we will work with didactic materials to mine the "gems" of yogic vocabulary.

To begin with, the yogic terminology is a problem. Precise use of it requires resolving the problem of the transmission of these concepts[16] from India to Tibet. To what extent did the translation collaboration between Nāropa and Marpa bring new terminology into Tibetan? To what extent did Marpa adhere to the rules established by his predecessors? Did Milarepa adhere to this extant body of terminology? He certainly knew it and used it. In searching for "dialect" expressions in the *Bu chen* text, which I am taking provisionally to be the oldest extensive version, very few regional expressions where found, but there is abundant evidence for the old language of dBus, indicating that Milarepa and his disciples probably adhered to the language and style of the Yar lung valley, where Milarepa had already studied magic and where it seems he was well-established even before his penitential experiences under Marpa. With Marpa, he was in an intense milieu of both study and practice, as we can see from his philosophically precise discussions of such difficult topics as voidness and *karmamudrā* (i.e., sexual yoga) practice. Milarepa's presentation of the great seal (*mahāmudrā*; *phyag rgya chen po*) adheres to what we know of the terminology adopted by Tilopa, Nāropa, Marpa, and Maitrīpa for expressing the inexpressible.

Milarepa's teachings are from the *gDams ngag mdzod*, folios 109–20: *mdzad pa'i snyan brgyud gsal ba skor gsum*, the "Explanation of the Three Cycles." The first term that merits clarification is on folio 111, *srog rtsol*: "vital force."

The text states,

Tibetan text	Translation
srog dang rtsol ba *'dzin dus su //*	[Use] breath/vital force and effort at the time of holding the breath;
mi rtog don la dmigs kyang rung //	Keep the mind in nonconceptuality,
thig le nyag ngag cig la dmigs kyang rung //	Visualize the full droplet in the form of the moon,
phyag rgya mtshan ldan zhig la dmigs kyang rung //	Contemplate the wisdom-endowed consort,
gtum mo me khab tsam la dmigs kyang rung //	Meditate on yogic heat, like a fine candle flame [at the navel]
yar 'dren mar 'dren bzhu btul byed kyang rung //	Or [on the drops] ascending and descending, uniting and melting.
shes pa rnam rtog yul la ma 'phros na //	[all can be done] if you know how to keep mental constructs from spreading out toward their objects.

These lines refer to the mental and physical energies of the body, which are channeled into the central channel. "*Srog*" refers to the central channel itself and the contemplative act of placing the guru's instructions ("kindness") into it, and "*rtsol*" means the inserting into the channel of the subtle breath energies, whether pure or impure, whether material or subtle, so that they become "wisdom" fluxes of energy. Milarepa advises the *yogin* to keep the mind in a nonconceptual state at this time.[17]

Another *yogic* term is found on folio 112.5 et passim: *'debs, btab, thebs*: "Planting, placing."

The text states,

Tibetan text	Translation
snying po don 'di gdod nas gnas //	This essential goal (Buddhahood) abides primordially;
des na sems can sangs rgyas rgyu //	Thus sentient beings [merely create] the cause [of the manifestation of] Buddhahood;
rgyu las 'bras bu ***btab pa*** *la //*	In fact, the result was implanted in the cause.
gdod nas thebs kyis da ltar min //	Abiding there, having been there [primordially], it [cannot be said to be] implanted now;
da ltar ***'debs*** *byed rnam rtog yin //*	Now the implanting is done by conceptual mind [but only insofar as concepts may tend toward the goal]
rnam rtog don du ***'debs*** *byed pa //*	Only thus does the conceptual mind implant causes and conditions tending toward the goal.

In the ultimate sense, there is no one to plant or purify anything; no one creates and no one acts to bring about perfection in the ultimate sense. In the relative sense, however, there are practices that clean off the "adventitious defilements" that obscure the primordial, innate, ultimately pure Buddha nature. These practices, such as working with the drops, winds, and channels to arrive at an experiential knowledge of the essentially void nature of all phenomena, are themselves participants in the nature of conceptuality. Thus a plethora of extant spiritual practices are made possible by the conceptual mind itself. So the "problem" also has mechanisms for resolving its own problematic aspects. Of course, when one attains the stabile breakthrough that recognizes all conceptuality and conceptualization as such, all the concepts and mental constructs (even the purest) fall away of themselves, as Tilopa taught in the *Mahāmudropadeśa*. What distinguishes the path of method from the usual training course in debate and Buddhist logic is the application of tantric meditation practices to the direction perception of the true nature of reality.

The next yogic term, found on folio 119, is *nyams rtogs*: "experiential realization." The text 119.1–2 is as follows:

> *stong pa'i go chag gtsigs su che* // The armor of voidness is of great importance.

[Comment by Lodro Tharchin Rinpoche: Meditation on voidness shields us from conceptualizations; rely on voidness rather than on the fear generated by confusion deriving from conceptualization.]

> *nges pa'i shes pa mi skye bar* // Unless you gain certainty [on the teaching of voidness],
> *nyams rtogs 'byung bar ga la rigs* // how could you possibly attain experiential realization?

[Comment: *nyams rtogs*, experiential realization, can be understood in two ways:

1. *nyams*:
   a. Realization of the deities through habitual pure vision
   b. Seeing the void nature of all phenomena
2. *rtogs*: direct understanding]

One of the challenges of research on yogic terminology in Tibetan is the fact that different lineages introduce subtle variations in their interpretation of key vocabulary. These comments by Lodro Tharchin Rinpoche illustrate the way the living tradition understands the terms typically used by Milarepa at the fountainhead of the lineage.

6

Conclusions on the Literary and Teaching Voice of Milarepa

From the materials examined, a few observations may be ventured to guide further research. The voice of Milarepa is more likely to be found in the poetic material, particularly in those didactic poems that are, of their very nature, easy to memorize after a single hearing. A good example of this would be the *snying po med* song; other good examples are those songs that work with the device of threes:[1]

May I be blessed by the Guru to dwell in a cave!
In the cave of meeting (*brag sprad*) is the place of blessings.
Faith, intellect, and morality, these three
Are the Life Tree of the mind;
If you plant this tree firmly, you'll be happy.
That's how to make your Life Tree a treasure;
These three: non-attachment, non-desire, non-ignorance:
These are the mind's armor;
If you wear it, it is light, but resists weapons;
If you make armor, make it like that!
These three: meditation, effort, perseverance;
These three are the good stallion of the mind;
When it runs, it's quick; when it escapes, it gets to freedom;
If you get a stallion, get one like that.
These three: self-awareness, self-clarity, self-bliss;
These three are the fruit of the mind;
If you plant it, it grows; if you eat it, it's juicy;
If you want fruit, get that kind.

These are the twelve aspects of the meaning of mind
Arising in the mind of a *yogin*.
Thus I respond to you, faithful sponsor.

[Then on the following line, Milarepa tries again, since the listener is not getting the point:]

The blessing of the Guru abides in the mind,
The blessing that makes it possible to realize Voidness in the mind;
As a gift to my faithful sponsor,
I'll sing a song that pleases the tutelary deity;
Appearance, voidness and inseparability:
These three are the View, in brief.
Clarity, non-conceptuality, and non-wavering:
These three are Meditation, in brief.
Non-attachment, non-desire, and absence of error:
These three are Action, in brief.
No hopes, no doubts, detachment (indifference):
These three are the Result, in brief.
No deception, no hiding out, no cheating:
These three are the tantric vows (*samaya*) in brief.

This kind of poetry is easy to remember and can be jotted down by the disciple in the course of a meditation retreat undertaken shortly after having received the oral teachings.

Another example of Milarepa's voice can be found when he uses metaphors that have the ring of originality—for example, "like throwing stones at the footprints of a thief." There are so many of these that Jäschke and Candra Das are full of these references to the "proverbs" of Milarepa. In the *gDams ngag mdzod*, vol. 5, folios 344–61, in an instruction on the *bardo* to Ras chung pa, he gives a fivefold discussion of the metaphor of sky that has some traditional resonances but also a touch of originality:

1. The sky, with clouds melting away, appearing blue in color; the sky becoming cloudy; the sky streaked by narrow images: this is not the sky of Dharmatā.
2. Shapes in the sky that exemplify space, such as rocks, caves, windows, and the like.
3. ... If I could show the sun in mid-winter early in the morning of the day of the full moon, from its rising over the mountain peaks up to [noon], feeling its warmth, in this time span, in this realm of the appearance of light in the middle of the sky, bright and clean, there is [to be found] a [valid exemplification of *Dharmatā*]; there one sees the naturally existent presence in its place, dependent on [causes and conditions] of the three times. At that time, in all the six families, there is the stabile, self-arisen *Dharmatā*. For the best, it lasts on an average three meditation sessions [seventy-two minutes]; for the middling ones, two sessions; and for the least capable, one session. If one had not received this instruction, then one would be unable to understand it: that *Dharmatā* is in all sentient beings experientially.
4. As the rain of summer washes down the dust [from the atmosphere].
5. If the sky becomes clear of clouds, before the winter storms rise up, there is a naturally pure sky that occurs. At that time there is no appearance, no non-appearance; whatever is a basis is not linked to color, form, or measure. This would exemplify the intermediate state of *Dharmatā*.

Another example, with traditional roots, is the following, again from the *gDams ngag mdzod* texts:

> When the body has become firm and steady there appear various types of signs. Gradually, the Four Blisses occur. Then one can endure external heat and cold. There will be few worms on the body, a glowing complexion, a stainless

> body, light as cotton, ease in stretching or contracting the limbs, there will be little mucus in the mouth and nose, a fragrant body, little interest in food and drink, hearing pleasant sounds, sleeping little and few dreams, skillful in answering questions, one speaks pleasantly on all topics, skillful in composing verse, one overcomes one's faults, what one says accords with the meaning, one helps others to overcome their faults, one is satisfied with what one has, there is a feeling of sadness toward cyclic existence, one prefers remote solitary places, one's heart desires solitude, one wants to meditate again and again, one does not feel the oppression of the body, one has no definite abode, and one does not stay constantly in one place, 115.1 Around him gather the assemblies of the *ḍākinīs*; he obtains prophecies in dreams, he obtains expertise in all teachings, gradually clairvoyance occurs, even in his sense of smell; he is able to blend the "inner" and the "outer"; his promises suffer no breaches; but when the time is right he can let go of promises. But if it's not the right time, it is as hard as killing a god to get him to violate his promises.
>
> Now, it is not suitable to "believe in" such a person, because in that case you succumb to the demon of conceptualization. It's like this: "Almost, but not quite." "The tree trunk, but not the fruit." These are the virtues, but not nonconceptuality. But when experience corresponds to the view, [then it] cannot be destroyed by that enemy, the Four Demons. Appearances definitely "hit home" and astonish. And then one cannot conceptualize about apparently external objects! One's own self-clarity is clear within.[2]

In the *gDams ngag mdzod*, an aside of Milarepa illuminates his way of thinking, which glides smoothly between the Indian Buddhist tantric tradition, the erotic tradition, and his own experience:

As for those who have exhausted the Path of Accumulation, there is the actual and imaginary [practice with consort]. When you use the imaginary one, have in your mind whatever you like. When you are enjoying being together, think of whatever you like. This is where mind functions as object. Now when you actually rely on a genuine partner, the qualifications of such a consort are explained in all the tantras. Now in my own opinion, as a *yogin*, whatever suits your mind is a qualified consort. If you share a lot of Accumulation [of Merit], if her actions are lovely, if she performs secret actions free from hurry. Now go to a solitary place together and perform actions without fear/shame. Even one's own mother, daughter or sister may become a special basis and the virtues will arise without faults [?]. But if it has to do with instructions lacking the virtuous qualities, don't even think about that!

In all the tantras it is said that quotations such as "relying on mother or sister" are Buddha-word subject to non-literal interpretation. But some people think these quotations are [literally] true. So, without practicing in accordance with the Meaning, they do it [that way] with individuals. Don't even sit on the same seat as a *yogin* who [does this] without knowing the way of union; his actions, like those of ordinary beings, bring no benefit and are faulty. Therefore, one should rely on this instruction of one who is skilled in the way of union. These practices are only for the few and not the practice for everybody. Otherwise, secret mantra practices, instead of being the Path of Method, become just confusion without control. They don't produce the virtues and become instead the Path of Blame. So practice in secrecy. 116.7 This profound instruction of Secret Mantra, in my opinion, is superior from the point of view of the Path of Method rather than (*'khags*) from the perspective of the View.[3]

It is typical of Milarepa's teachings that the *thabs lam* (path of method) is considered superior to the path of knowing, since the existential quality of the gnosis obtainable through method (which in his teachings *always* refers to the Six Dharmas of Nāropa) is superior to that attained through study and debate. One obtains the "best of voidnesses" through method and not through exclusively relying on study. It is obvious from the way he formulates his arguments that Milarepa really studied—there should be no mistake about this.

Based on the foregoing observations, the best way to determine the voice of Milarepa is to study what are likely the earliest versions of his didactic poems and, in his oral teachings, those "asides" of his that were taken down as notes during the time of formal transmission.

7

Final Remarks on the Literary Tradition

Why was Milarepa's story a great success? Why did a saint and poet emerge as a captivating and popular folk hero? Evidently, the transmission of tantric Buddhism from late medieval India to Tibet was not easy. The new perspective was not universally accepted. There was resistance from the followers of Bon, there was the inertia of the "unnamed religion" of folk tradition (*mi chos*), and there were the locked-in attitudes and habits of isolated mountain people. In addition, there was always some penetration by other cultures and civilizations—most emphatically that of China—to limit any strictly Indian cultural monopoly. The task before tantric Buddhism was to undertake effective translation of texts, enculturation of religious values, and dissemination of persuasive propaganda (especially via the practice of thaumaturgy) that would undermine the existing antagonisms.

The Buddhist Vajrayāna itself underwent transformations in the process of its historical diffusion in Tibet. The First Diffusion, whose design was determined by a fusion of the scholasticism of Abbot Śāntarakṣita with the tantric attainments of Padmasambhava, encountered conflict with Chinese Buddhism and with the Bon po tradition, which had previously been the religion of the Tibetan state. The realities of life in the remote villages and towns of Tibet made possible an almost imperceptible synthesis of Bon, Ch'an, and even Taoist elements in what eventually became the religion of the "Land of the Snows." Syncretism was a fact of life in Tibet, both as a result of the spontaneous sociogeographic factors that shape every aspect of Himalayan life and at times as a deliberate strategy of rival sects. Of course, syncretism was already a well-developed characteristic of the Buddhism of medieval India.

In the Second Diffusion period, newer lineages with equally clear Indian origins constructed a reform movement to some extent imitative of the earlier model devised under King Trisong Detsen by Abbot Śāntarakṣita and Tantric master Padmasambhava. Among the bKa' brgyud pa, we see sGam popa presented as the principal heir of Milarepa precisely because he unites the two streams: that of tantric scholasticism received from Ātiśa in the bKa' gdams pa order and that of tantric realization received through the lineage of Marpa and Milarepa. In the biographical tradition, Milarepa seems to come across as the Padmasambhava of the Second Diffusion!

When we come to the time of gTsang smyon Heruka, however, the Second Diffusion and its concerns with reform and syncretism are matters of the past. Now other conflicts, such as the rise of Mongol influence, the Gelug pa reform, and proliferating sectarianism, have stimulated new ways of retelling the story of the archetypal saint.

The ongoing literary process that we observe in successive biographies of Milarepa discloses the dynamism at the heart of Tibetan Buddhist Vajrayāna. In the bKa' brgyud pa, whose very name signifies the transmission of sacred word and precept (*bka'*), historical circumstances provoked and conditioned the singing of new tales, and new problems gave rise to new "answers" that came in the form of hagiographical models. By means of an ongoing dialectic between oral and written narrative, the essential values embodied in Milarepa resurfaced in each generation of sacred transmission (*brgyud*) and stimulated reforms such as that of the mad yogins (*smyon pa*).

The biographical tradition, studied alongside the songs and oral teachings, proves useful for tracing these historical dynamics in that the subject remains the same: Milarepa the poet, *yogin*, siddha, and saint. What changes over time depends on the following narrative elements:

1. The narrative is being retold by new singers to new audiences.
2. The singer of the tale is himself an embodiment of the ascetical spirituality of the lineage; in his written narrative we are in contact with a dialogue between more or less known

historical forces and the tradition of literary activity among practitioners of Buddhist tantricism.

3. That same tantric tradition provides a rationale for ongoing change, brought in via the *ḍākinī* dimension of literary activity; these spiritual forces are perceived to create a revelatory mythos that permits the singer of the tale to say, "It is time now to disclose an aspect of the saint's life that was bound in secrecy before." Here we see the influence of the rNying ma pa *ter ton* (empowered discoverers of hidden literary treasures) movement in shaping the literary and religious imagination.
4. Continuity is assured by the fact that transmission depends on deeply felt interpersonal connections between master and disciple. The Dharma is perceived as an indispensable set of orally transmitted teachings that are acquired with difficulty, interiorized, practiced, and brought to fruition entirely on the basis of the strength of the disciple's faithfulness and devotion to the guru. The right guru is encountered on the basis of causal connections deriving from virtuous deeds and vows made in previous incarnations.
5. Another element of continuity in the biographical tradition is that although *Chos* (*Dharma*), Bon, and the "religion of the people" (*mi chos*) are distinguished, they are not unambiguously separated in practice. The earlier biographies argue that none of the religious folkways of Tibet was adequate to the circumstances of the Second Diffusion. Thus Milarepa's biographers tended to crystallize the essentially attractive elements of these three folkways in the saint, showing how Tibetans could live well with all three if Buddhism were seen as the ordering principle. Hence the importance of Milarepa's syncretistic origins: beneficiary of the primordial symbolism of his mother's dream experiences during pregnancy, heir of rNying ma pa spirituality on the paternal side of the family,

> experienced in village cults and folk singing, trained in the black arts and in *rDzogs chen*, Milarepa becomes a saint and culture bearer.[1] He refounds Tibetan culture, using the elements of the past in a structure determined by the Indian tantric Buddhist masters. The literary achievement is brilliant: the saint as a religious type becomes the cornerstone of a new social vision that embraces a sublime interior life, making possible an exuberant popular cult[2] and giving rise to a prolific religious order that came for a time to dominate much of Tibetan political life.

At first it may seem strange that a hermit bard should become a viable model for a vast social vision and the renewal of an entire civilization. As a hermit, however, he is a thaumaturge—a focus of sacred power. As a bard, he is a creative nexus, a voice fertile with the spontaneity revered in the Himalayan milieu. Buddhist thought was already well adapted to the role of cultural architect; the tantric siddhas of medieval India were poets and wonder workers, whose approach was distinctly "popular" but whose influence reached up from the smoking charnel grounds into the royal courts. Since every encounter with a truly realized saint was a sign of one's own good karma and accumulation of sacred merit, the very act of venerating a saint was a sign that the devotee, too, will soon attain the same status. It is understood that one's own Buddha nature recognizes the attainment of Buddha nature in a saint. As the *Vajrapañcara Tantra* states, "Even appearing as ice, he accomplishes the aims of sentient beings; even appearing as a lion … and as a woman who sells beer … as a prostitute … even appearing as an ordinary person in an inferior caste."[3] And as the *Vajraśekhara Tantra* affirms, "Even if he appears as an ordinary person … all *yogins* who realize the meaning of wisdom as Vajradhara are thereby made into the unexcelled Vajradhara—so great, therefore, is the number of Vajradharas!"[4] As the one who holds the Vajra of skillful salvific means, the saint creates "an oasis of a pure land in the midst of an impure land"[5] in which all aspects of life may occasion full and unexcelled enlightenment.

Part Two

bKa' brGyud pa Spirituality

8

The Theme of Tradition in Anthropological and Historical Perspective

In the introduction to his translation of the *Life of Milarepa*, the distinguished Tibetan scholar Lobsang P. Lhalungpa makes the following observation about the notion of "tradition":

> It is not possible for any book, however great, to communicate the entire atmosphere of a tradition, including the thousand and one impulses that the teacher sets in motion by interacting with individual who in their turn may succeed or fail in the outer expression of their understanding. It is easy to accept intellectually that a tradition is a world, but not so easy to feel what this means, especially when the very core and heart of a tradition, in this case the practice of meditation, is presented with such intuitive force. A tradition is a world. In that world, the essence of the tradition, the single movement that created it from the beginning and that continues to maintain it in the lives of all who follow it, permeates and suffuses all the forms and details of life and perhaps may never be spoken of explicitly. But when it is spoken of explicitly, and in a language that seems familiar (such as the language of psychology) it is a mistake to appropriate it as one's own without asking why all these other forms are also part of the tradition.[1]

Lhalungpa's comments are an open window to the environmental nature of the transmission of sacred teachings. It is the transmission's continuum (which is the relevant meaning of the Tibetan word *brgyud*)[2] that interests us as we examine bKa' brgyud pa spirituality.

The process of transmission within a culture takes its ongoing nourishment from the day-to-day exchanges and communications among people who have nearly everything in common. The daily rhythms of a Himalayan village are built up out of the textures of expression, movement, and restraint, creating a sense of presence that endures for generations. Beyond these visible, audible, and tactile features, the sensitive observer may be intuitively aware of a certain degree of nonverbal communion and delicately gestured understandings among, for example, fellow disciples of the same lama.

When it comes to translating these gestures of rituality and of human communion, the outsider is at a distinct and largely insuperable disadvantage. This disadvantage merits the methodological critiques of Edward Said's *Orientalism* and Donald S. Lopez Jr.'s *Curators of the Buddha.* The problem is now manifesting in the current academic style of discourse directed to the study even of the traditions of Western society. A post-enlightenment tradition that effectively "colonializes" the traditional religious matrices of Western civilization still awaits significant revision.

The fragmentation that the post-enlightenment mainstream has created as its own ethos constitutes a *tradition of antitraditionalism* that has been imposed on its own process of assimilating Asian thought. This is why the translation of texts and ideas involves both the reader and the translator in a labyrinth of limits about what is permitted to be published. It also requires the author to make explicit or implicit assumptions about what may or may not be compared so as to approximate an understanding of the materials of Asian civilizations. When we come to speak of spirituality, we must classify the beliefs and practices of a particular religious tradition for the sake of clarity and accessibility. Beyond that, we begin to ask our informants and their texts about the goals of those practices. We would like to know what happens to a human being who dedicates time and talent to a given set of traditional practices. This is by no means an easy question to answer, because the totality of any person's life even as sheer information is, at present, inaccessible. We must be led on by our own curiosity, empowered by an implicit faith in the old Stoic proverb, "Nothing human is alien to me." Nothing, that is, except that which our cultural formation forbids us to see and to recognize![3] Fortunately, scholars in the field of tantric studies have recently taken some bold steps to remedy the deficiencies of research by inviting practitioners, both Asian and Western, to speak at conferences and colloquia.[4] In the field of cultural anthropology, a more autobiographical approach has also broken down barriers between the researcher and the persons whose spirituality is the object of research.[5]

This part of our chapter attempts to link the contemplative praxis of the bKa' brgyud with the biographical, song, and oral instruction traditions associated with Milarepa. The structure of the chapter is complex and therefore merits a methodological introduction. There are thirteen parts, which repeat some of the same material in greater and or lesser detail, enabling the reader to gain a familiarity with the elements of spiritual praxis from a number of perspectives:

1. A review of the roots of Buddhist tantrism
2. A general discussion of liberation in the Vajrayāna
3. A more developed discussion of the attainment of Buddhahood as the ground of praxis
4. The features of the path
5. The goal as understood in this form of Vajrayāna
6. The religious character of Vajrayāna
7. The archetypal concept of Vajrayāna
8. The general pattern of tantric practice among the bKa' brgyud pa
9. A presentation of deity yoga as *skye rim* (stage of generation) for Vajravārāhī
10. Presentation of the deity yoga for Cakrasaṁvara
11. A discussion of *rdzogs rim* (stage of completion) in the form of the Six Yogas of Nāropa

12. A discussion of *mahāmudrā* based on teachings of Milarepa and authentic traditions of the lineage
13. The enlightenment of Milarepa based on the biographical accounts and related literature
14. Tables summarizing the key theoretical material of this chapter

The material being presented here has its own definite historical and textual track record, which is currently being elucidated by scholars of tantric studies. The *rnam thar*s that we are examining seem to have been written in order to illustrate the theoretical path to liberation in an exemplary fashion, based as far as possible on the deeds of these remarkable individuals. The theoretical basis, path, and fruition are described schematically in the account of the archetypal figure of Vajradhara, which we discuss later and in the notes to our translation of the *rdo rje 'chang rnam thar* from the rGyal thang pa *bKa' brgyud gser 'phreng*. The biographies of lineage saints puts "flesh" (however illusory) on this grand account that seeks to harmonize Mahāyāna and Vajrayāna ideals.

There is, moreover, the very serious problem of comprehensibility in these accounts, something often linked to the pledge of secrecy by which tantric initiates are bound. The main reason for writing about spiritual matters is for the author to address an informed readership that to some degree possesses the prerequisites for understanding such material. In the case of mystical systems in general and tantrism in particular, it should be clear that persons lacking basic intuitive gifts and the rudiments of a disciplined practice of meditation will be unlikely to grasp the meaning of the phenomena being described. This becomes very serious when we present the material related to the practice of the Six Yogas of Nāropa. It is not every reader who will automatically know what "channels, winds, and drops" (*rtsa, rlung, tig le*) might mean psychologically or physiologically; certainly these topics are less accessible than ordinary matters of human anatomy, for example. This is the reason the direct oral instructions of a qualified spiritual preceptor are considered by the tradition to be indispensable. There is a very lively need for both preceptor (i.e., guru/bla ma) and student to be gifted in quite subtle forms of spiritual discernment. Otherwise, one can easily confuse coarse biological phenomena with fluxes of energy in the psychosomatic anatomy of the "subtle body" of the *yogin*. Moreover, there are ethical presuppositions governing the motivation for undertaking such transformative practices. The tradition strongly emphasizes that the altruistic attitude of a Bodhisattva (i.e., *bodhicitta*) is the only correct basis for undertaking this arduous path of spiritual training.

The spirituality of the bKa' brgyud pa order is essentially a form of yoga because of its historic contact with the content and heritage of classical Indian forms of spiritual practice. The influences of Vedic theism, *Upaniṣadic* esotericism, Atharvavedic rites and magic, haṭha yoga, and the tantric practices of the Śaiva schools are very much present as direct borrowings or as contrapuntal themes. The insistence on mental stasis (*citta vṛtti nirodha*) in Patañjali's *Yoga Sutras* is contested: first in Kaśmiri Śaivism's dynamic theism[6] and later by the appropriation of tantric ritual and practice by the Buddhist-oriented mahāsiddhas.

Deriving from the latter by direct transmission, the bKa' brgyud pa orders evolved a coherent Buddhist program of practice for its own *yogins*. This meant assimilating the three yānas[7] of Buddha Dharma and grounding the practitioners in highly evolved forms of meditation training based on the perennial śamatha and vipaśyanā meditative methods of early Buddhism.

9

Liberation in the Vajrayāna

A Survey of Tantric Practice in Indian and Tibetan Buddhism

The historical and spiritual continuity of the Vajrayāna, a central concern of the living tradition, can be approached by means of an evocation of the basic religious experience of practitioners of this form of Buddhism in places of pilgrimage. Following the classic presentation of the ground, path, and goal of tantric practice, we are able to examine the nature of the liberation sought in the Vajrayāna, both in India among the mahāsiddhas and in Tibet among the various religious orders. The means by which practitioners attain the goal will be addressed along the way.

Within the wider experience of historic Buddhism, there is the esoteric tradition known as "tantra" or Vajrayāna. Alex Wayman observes, "We should first distinguish between a sūtra and a tantra, since both words mean a kind of cord or thread. A sūtra was believed to have been proclaimed by the Buddha but is normally received by its form in the canon; it has contents of doctrine and practice, which need to be understood as stated in such scriptures. A tantra also means a text preserved in the canon, but is susceptible of multiple interpretations, and, as something to be practiced, must be heard directly from a guru."[1] The word tantra in fact comes from the use of a pair of cords to tie together the decorative boards that serve as covers for the long, narrow strips of paper or palm leaf used in traditional Indian and Tibetan book manufacture. Metaphorically, tantra refers to continuity in the transmission of teachings from guru to disciple and from one guru to the next; it also refers to the overall goal of the practice of tantric yoga:

direct perception of the interconnectedness of all phenomena as "voidness" and as the eternal play of the guru (in Tibetan: *snang srid kun kyang bla ma'i rol pa ste//* "All appearances and all existence are the play of the guru."). Tantra also refers specifically to the liturgical text of the ritual (*sādhana*) celebrated by the practitioner (*sādhaka*). The expression "esoteric Buddhism" refers to the fact that these practices are to be undertaken and studied only under the direction and with the permission of the guru.[2] In Tibet, the same idea is found in the generic expression for tantric practice, "Secret Mantra," which refers to the fact that the "words of power" are transmitted under a bond of secrecy from guru to disciple.

Historically, the Buddhist tantras have antecedents in the *Chaṇḍogya Upaniṣad* (where we find the use of mantras related to specific deities), in the early use of *mudrā* (ritual hand gestures) in Vedic Brahmanism, and in early speculations on the *samādhis* (states of contemplative absorption) and on the three *nāḍīs* (channels paralleling the spinal column and carrying the life-energy or "*prāṇa*") as found in the *Yoga Upaniṣads.* Within the Buddhist ritual world, we already find protective spells (*dharaṇī*) incorporated in the first centuries CE. Archeological evidence at Gandhara indicates that the Brahmanical fire sacrifice (*homa*) was accepted as a part of Buddhist ritual as early as the late second century BCE.[3] In the *Mañjuśrī mūlakalpa Tantra* (first three centuries CE), we find the fire sacrifice highly developed for the celebration of vigorous magical rites, including exorcism. In the *Mahāyāna sūtras,* such as the *Laṅkāvatāra, Mahāmāyuri,* and *Saddharmapuṇḍarika,* we find chapters on the *dharaṇī*—protective spells to be recited orally. By the sixth century, we have the *Guhyagarbha Tantra,* part of a family of ritual texts that emphasize the cult of Vajrapāṇi ("He who holds the thunderbolt scepter in his hand"). Tantras of this kind were transmitted to Tibet from India during the so-called First Diffusion of Buddhism from the eighth to the ninth centuries CE.[4]

The later tantras[5] from the seventh to the tenth centuries are associated with the eighty-four mahāsiddhas who promoted tantric yogic practice extensively in India. Early examples include the cult of the savioress Tārā and the *Tattvasaṁgraha*, a yoga tantra requiring extensive explanation from other texts and from the guru, to be understood and practiced.[6]

The *Mañjuśrīnāmasaṁgīti*, probably from the seventh century, is one of the ritualized compendia of practice texts typical of the period that remains an important liturgical text in Tibet to the present day. From about the eighth century, we have further developments of the "highest yoga tantra" (*anuttarayogatantra*)[7] class, such as the *Cakrasaṁvara* and *Hevajra* "mother" tantras, probably representing the oral syncretism of Buddhism with Kaśmiri Śaivism[8] (with noteworthy continuity in the practice of meditation on the interior energy centers, cakras, and the fluxes of energy, or prāṇa). These practice cycles were probably written down in Bengal in the mahāsiddha milieu and transmitted shortly thereafter to Tibet along with commentarial traditions deriving from such masters as Kaṅha, Nāropa, Maitrīpa, Śāntipa, Padmasambhava, Buddhaguhya, Abhayakaragupta, Vāgīśvarakīrti, and others.[9] The abilities of these realized masters (siddha means "accomplished") guaranteed the authenticity of both the practices and the style of transmission from guru to trusted and tried disciple.[10]

When we speak of the milieu of the mahāsiddhas, we are quite literally speaking of places of pilgrimage (*pīṭha*) venerated by both Buddhists and Hindus.[11] These were and are "power points" in the South Asian landscape at which pilgrims could encounter divine presences in all their transformative forcefulness.[12] In June 1995, I made a pilgrimage to several of these traditional "*tīrtha*" (holy place along a river ford) in Nepal. At Pharping, eighteen kilometers southeast of Kathmandu, there are at least three holy sites, all of which are increasingly popular today. There is Dakṣinkālī, a place of animal sacrifice to the Mother Goddess; there is Bajrayoginī, originally a Buddhist shrine where the Goddess manifested to a Nepali siddha named Pham thing pa in the form of sky-dancing Vajrayoginī; and there is a pool and sacred cave where Padmasambhava meditated in the eighth century.

When I arrived at 7:00 a.m. at Dakṣinkālī, there were already crowds of people, and the ritual slaughter had begun. This is a place of incense, anointing, ritual bathing, sadhus and beggars, chanting piped in over loudspeakers and sung by Brahman *pūjaris*, and dozens of sales booths providing food and ritual plates to enable the pilgrims to perform the traditional ceremonies. Scores of people arrive continually on the days of sacrifice. Goats and hens seem to be the principal victims offered up for the usual worldly concerns: prosperity, health, and protection from evil—propitious conditions for any undertaking. This is a weekly festival of popular religious action in which little has changed since the days of the great siddhas, with the emphasis here on the wrathful and Śaivite traditions of the Mother Goddess.

Bajrayoginī is a place of syncretism between tantric Buddhism and popular Hinduism. The devotees recite prayers before her temple, which is constructed in two stories. The upper story contains the gilded bronze statue of the dancing feminine form seen in a vision by Pham thing pa in the early eleventh century; this, her secret form, is draped in brocade. The ground level contains her more modest image in bas-relief, available to the devotees who apply colored powders and sing her *bhajans* (devotional songs). The yogic practices associated with this form of Vajrayoginī have been handed down, according to our informants, to the present day among the Sa skyapa Tibetan Buddhists.

The Padmasambhava (Guru Rinpoche) sites are guarded today by newly arrived Tibetan monastic communities and retain an atmosphere of silence, meditation, and devotion, thus rounding out the range of religious experience within the tantric spectrum. Who could resist the temptation to sound the fossil conch shell in the solid rock alongside the stairs that ascend to the gompa?

Another site in the landscape of tantric pilgrimage is just north of the Annapurṇa Mountain Sanctuary in Lower Mustang. It is in the heart of the Himalayas at an altitude of 3,600 meters, at the source of a refreshing sacred stream. This is where the shrine known as Muktināth is found. Also known as *Muktikṣetra*, the "field of liberation," it is a quiet place most of the year. At the time of the full-moon festival in late August, it becomes the goal of thousands of pilgrims and the site of a festival and horse fair.[13] Unlike many other famous shrines around the world, Muktināth is a remarkably unassuming place. Not until one arrives at the cluster of tiny inns below the sacred precinct does one recognize that a holy place is at hand. All the temples are rather small and low; there are groves of poplar trees among which are strung innumerable Tibetan Buddhist prayer flags of many colors. The entire *fanum* (sacred space) is demarcated by a low stone wall, not more than two meters high. There are numerous, unsteady-looking stone cairns, some of which can be dignified with the term "chorten" (*chos rten*, Tibetan for stūpa, or reliquary mound).

Above all, there is the sound of flowing water. On all sides of the central Viṣṇu /Lokeśvara temple, there are 108 boar-shaped spouts sprinkling fresh spring water in a three-sided bathing area. The spouts symbolize the Boar Avatāra of Viṣṇu; one of the principal ritual activities for the pilgrims is to bathe under these spouts and take some of the sacred water home. The monsoon rains on the afternoon of my visit competed with the rivulets all around to produce a continuous rush of sound. After a long meditation on that sound, the rains having halted, I went out and stood on the banks of the most ebullient of the torrential creeks to soak in the beauty of the moment. Seized by a deep awe that passed through my entire body as a physical sensation coming to a focus in my skull, I remained for a long time in silence and contemplative peace without effort, without deliberate concentration, calling to mind the Tibetan Buddhist prayer, *Dorje Chang Tungma*:

> Non-distraction is taught to be the actual meditation,
> Thus, whatever arises, the true meditator simply rests within
> the uncontrived,
> In the very freshness of the essence of thought:
> Grant your blessing that he may be free from the idea of
> something to meditate on![14]

No wonder this was a place of meditation for Guru Rinpoche and the eighty-four mahāsiddhas, who are said to have planted their *yogin*-staves here, beside these sweet waters, to see them grow into the poplar grove that stands there today. Here is a holy place where all the mechanisms of religiosity of the high and low traditions drop away of their own accord, giving the vivid sense that "*saṁsāra* is indeed not-other than *nirvāṇa*," that "thou art non-different from That," that being alive is the best of *sādhanas*, that the environment itself is the best of gurus, and that there is no more striving once one has had the *darśana* (seeing) of the truth—all this existentially present in a flash, in the splash of waters in that precarious Himalayan grove behind mighty Annapurṇa.

Such insights, I believe, will dawn upon even the humblest of pilgrims to such places of power. Not just the *yogin* who has prepared himself with millions of mantras, prostrations, and maṇḍala offerings, not just the Brahman pilgrim who has come on foot from the south of India, but even the ordinary man or woman of little faith may be granted that glimpse of something sublime, a ray of divine truth in such a holy place. As the Dorje Chang Tungma states,

> The essence of the mind stream (*rgyud*: continuity, and
> therefore, tantra)
> Is taught to be the *dharmakāya* (the totality of phenomena);
> Nothing whatsoever, yet it manifests as anything whatsoever,
> Appearing in unhindered play to the true meditator:
> Grant your blessing that he may realize the indivisibility of
> saṁsāra and nirvāṇa.

Therefore, with this specifically religious and universal symbolism, rooted in pilgrimage and in the encounter with a sacred environment in the great book of this world, the "cosmic revelation" of holiness, one may dare to speak of liberation in the Vajrayāna.

10

The Buddha Within

Ground or Basis of the Path

The theoretical basis of tantric Buddhism is built out of the preexisting elements of early Buddhism and Mahāyāna Buddhism. In particular, with the theory of the *tathāgatagarbha*, it was understood that Buddha-nature is innate in all beings. As Milarepa taught, "This essential goal [Buddhahood] abides primordially."[1] All ritual and contemplative methods have been devised to disclose that fundamental nature of reality. In the tantric systems, a plethora of skillful means (*upāya*) identified with the enlightened state of mind is employed to liberate and empower the manifestation of Buddha-nature in the form of a human being. In particular, tantric Buddhism makes use of the symbolism of religion for this purpose.

The *Guhyasamāja Tantra* explains the word tantra as "*prabandha*," "continuous series," and as "threefold":

1. The cause (*hetu*), meaning the disciple, trainee, or candidate.
2. The means (*upāya*), meaning the tantric path of actual spiritual practice.
3. The result (*phala*), meaning in that tantric system, the "rank" of Vajradhara (the deity-form who holds the thunderbolt scepter). Hence, a tantra establishes the continuity of master and disciple along a specific path of practice, and, in addition, it intends to establish in the practitioner a spiritual continuity in the stream of consciousness from cause to fruition.[2] This approach recognizes that every sentient being has Buddha-nature as the basis of the continuity of mind.

> The *Hevajra Tantra* asserts, in harmony with the general Mahāyāna view, that "all beings are Buddhas, though they may be burdened by defilements."

Practices along the path refer to the cultivation of this primordially liberated nature such that there is a full manifestation of Buddhahood in a multitude of possible forms. The symbol of the Vajrayāna is the "thunderbolt scepter," indestructible like diamond, which stands for the spectrum of skillful soteriological means, which abound in this form of Buddhism.

The Dalai Lama confirms this interpretation: "Because the vajra vehicle has more skillful means than that of the Perfections (Mahāyāna), it is called the method-vehicle."[3] The basis of the tantric method of progress on the spiritual path is precisely the inherent Buddha-nature of beings; by performing sacramental acts and yogic disciplines as if one were already a fully liberated being, one accelerates the time of realization. The cause, the result, and the path are thus, in practice, indivisible. The key to this kind of courageous haste is the Mahāyāna vow of the Bodhisattva: everything one does is consecrated to the liberation not only of oneself but also of all sentient beings. One undertakes the Vajrayāna because of the immense sorrow and compassion that one feels when one contemplates innumerable suffering beings who one is at present unable to help concretely. The Vajrayāna practices develop in one the capacity to devise and apply an ever-increasing variety of means to benefit others; by the fundamental Buddhist principle of nonself, such generosity stops the tendency to evaluate choices in terms of self-interest. Self-interest and the welfare of others are seen as inseparable.

The ground of the spiritual life is this "Buddha of one's own mind" (*rang sems sangs rgyas*), and the goal is Buddhahood (*sangs rgyas*), which consists of that perfect and complete enlightenment that entails abiding permanently in neither saṁsāra nor nirvāṇa.[4]

The main hindrances to achieving the basic liberation from cyclic existence and thereupon to attain complete enlightenment are the two obscurations:

1. The obscuration of disturbing emotions
2. The obscuration of dualistic ways of knowing

These are the two "clouds" that seem to obscure the purity of the sky of the Buddha of one's own mind. Of course, even the thickest monsoon clouds are still illuminated by the sunlight behind them. So in Buddhism we have a view of defilement that is basically optimistic; there is here no doctrine of "total depravity."[5]

The obscuration of disturbing emotions is that which obstructs liberation and is purified through the practices of calm abiding and meditative insight (*śamatha* and *vipaśyanā*). This entails the "right meditation" aspect of the Eightfold Path. Even more persistent is the obscuration of dualistic knowledge, which refers to a habitual attachment to the threefold conceptualization of subject, object, and action (the grasper, the object grasped and the act of grasping). The practice of "right philosophical view" is designed to suppress this obscuration. A contemporary Tibetan master, Thrangu Rinpoche, observes that "merely holding these three concepts, however subtle, in mind constitutes what is commonly called the obscuration of dualistic knowledge. It obstructs omniscience, which is insight into the real nature of things (as in the case of Buddha, who is omniscient in this precise sense)."[6]

In effect both purifications involve sweeping away two types of ignorance. Buddhahood is complete freedom and compassion unobstructed by ignorance of things as they are. Buddhahood would be inaccessible were there not already in every being the germ or essence that is capable of such a state of perfection. Buddhahood would be inaccessible were there not the germ of the state of perfect enlightenment present in every sentient being. When a spiritual pilgrim glimpses this insubstantial germ in an experience of contemplation, the conceptual trap of subject, object, and comprehension is destroyed. This glimpse allows the pilgrim a degree of understanding of voidness or emptiness. According to Mahāyāna doctrine, this is the real nature of every phenomenon.

Thrangu Rinpoche observes, "When we say empty, we usually mean 'without any concrete substance or matter.' When I strike the table with my hand it makes a sound. That means it has some substance or concreteness. But the enlightened nature, the Buddha nature, has no concrete substance whatsoever. Its essence is empty."[7] We could also say its essence is like space, or "openness." Thrangu Rinpoche advises, "When we practice, we should look into the mind wondering, 'How is the mind? What is it like?' Our mind gives rise to an inconceivable number of different thoughts and emotions. Most of what we see around us are constructs fabricated by the mind, but still when we sit down and look into the mind asking ourselves, 'Where is my mind?' we discover that it is impossible to find it anywhere. There's not a 'thing' to be seen or found. That is why it is said that the essence is empty, but is it only empty? No, it's not. Its nature is luminous. Clarity and wakefulness are present because it is possible to know, perceive, and think. *At the final stages of enlightenment, inconceivably great virtues and wisdoms manifest.* These aspects of being empty, luminous, and having certain qualities are completely inter-related. . . . Therefore, when we say that the essence is empty, it doesn't mean there is no essence!"[8]

This position has a long history in the debates between the Mādhyamika and the Yogācāra philosophers of classical Buddhist India. The Yogācāra master Dharmapāla, the topic of mental elaborations (Sanskrit: *prapañca*), says that when we claim that any natural phenomenon is or is not, we cause the proliferation of more elaborations. Instead, Dharmapāla insists that the true nature of reality can be conceptualized neither as existence nor as voidness. Thusness, or authentic Buddha-nature, completely transcends all kinds of conceptualization.[9]

As can be observed in Chinese vegetarian cooking, one type of food (tofu or seaweed) can be skillfully arranged so as to give us the idea that we are eating another food, such as fish or sausage. The mind, subject to restricted sense data, lets itself be deceived by color, texture, flavor, and shape. In daily life, this is going on all the time. Conceptualization, a result of ignorance, is the root of the bondage of all sentient beings in cyclic existence. Thus *prapañca*, the mental elaboration of phenomena and the creation of difference is a feature of all conceptualization. The result of this essentially erroneous process is the constitution of objects with distinct character corresponding to the concepts we have previously created.

The true nature of the mind and of consciousness is openness and Buddhahood; realization of this "brings about the calming of the dynamic elaboration (*prapañca*) of co-dependent origination," as the great Nāgārjuna taught.[10] For Nāgārjuna, the realization of *śūnyatā* by the aspirant moving toward full enlightenment is none other than the awakening to the twelve-member chain of dependent origination that we find in the early Buddhist scriptures. This is the chain that holds beings illusorily in the cycle of continuous becoming. A fully enlightened Buddha *sees*—that is, has a profound and irreversible intuitive penetration of dependent origination, sees deeply the void nature of the causes and conditions of each link in the twelve-member chain and, spontaneously, by means of this seeing, experiences the falling away of "elaboration" and the collapse of the defilement of ignorance.[11]

Tilopa says the same in his "Teaching on the Great Seal" (*Mahāmudropadeśa*): "One's own mental activity (of fabrication) is cut off at the root (*rang sems rtsad chod*), And intrinsic Awareness (*rig pa /vidyā*) is disclosed."[12] The message is optimistic. Primordial awareness—which is the Buddha-nature, is the germ of the *tathāgata*, and can be called the great seal (*mahāmudrā*)—is a real human experience. This teaching is at the basis of the tantric practice of the bKa' brgyud pa orders in Tibet, descended from Tilopa, Nāropa, Marpa, Milarepa, sGampopa, and Ras chung pa.

11

The Path to Liberation and Its Features

The human person, as opposed to other types of sentient beings, is in a privileged position with regard to the realization of Buddhahood. Humans can enter upon and pursue the spiritual path. Hence the masters speak of learning to appreciate the "precious human birth." It is a great loss and a sign of the fierce grip of ignorance that afflict most humans who do not practice the path that cultivates intuitive wisdom and merit. Why do we need wisdom and merit? First of all, we should realize that to sweep away the defilements of ignorance, we need exceptionally flexible minds, and we must feel very much at home with matters accessible mainly to the intuitive mental faculty; this is not to exclude the intellect, but in the end, intellectual analysis is too much involved with the fabrication of concepts and categories that have only a limited usefulness in realizing liberation. Only the intuition, arduously trained, can see "things as they truly are," in accordance with "right philosophical view" as we have stated earlier.

In Mahāyāna Buddhism, wisdom always relates to the doctrine of voidness; the perfection of wisdom (*Prajñāpāramitā*) is precisely intuitive cognition of the metaphysical impermanence of all conditioned phenomena. According to Nāgārjuna, only the "Mother"—that is, that nonconceptual wisdom (*prajñā*) that realizes that phenomena do not "inherently exist"—is the path of liberation for all. Nāgārjuna is also said to have taught (*Mūlamadhyamakaśāstra* 18, 4–5, a Chinese text attributed to Nāgārjuna) that "when actions and afflictions cease, there is liberation; they arise from false conceptions; these in turn arise from the elaborations (*prapañca)* of false views on inherent existence."

These elaborations cease in the realization of voidness. There are many ways of describing voidness or emptiness. For example, it can mean that no phenomenon is intrinsically valid or convincing; nothing "here below" is eternal, unchanging, and "true" in any absolute sense. No experience should knock us off balance, convincing us of the truth content of otherwise unexamined assertions. This means that even religious ecstasy, various degrees of yogic absorption (i.e., *samādhi*), and so forth should not convince us that any a view is final and absolute. This is in fact the basis of the Buddhist critique of yoga as the "suppression of the vibrations of the mind" (*citta-vṛtti-nirodha*). Nothing conditioned really stops "vibrating"! And the following is the idea of Iśvara (the Lord God as Creator): experience of God is not necessarily experience of the Absolute. Voidness also refers to the nonpresence of any underlying "*substratum*" to material natures; this enters the classical philosophical contest on the vexed question of the nature of change in things. There are no *substantia*, there are only *accidentia* arising from *śūnyatā*—that is, "openness," a field of unlimited possibilities both of form and nonform; anything can become anything else, since all phenomena are radically conditioned, impermanent, and resultants of prior causes and effects.

Merit is a warmer notion, more familiar to the religious pilgrim who seeks to acquire merit by performing religious actions. For Mahāyāna Buddhism, merit can be accumulated in such a way as to give relative shape to the future manifestation of one's own Buddha-nature. Thus in the *Origin of the Tārā Tantra*, Jo nang Tāranātha tells us that, long ago, a princess resolved to become a Buddha in the form of a woman and, to that end, performed innumerable prostrations, penances, and maṇḍala offerings. Her acquired merit, continually rededicated for the "benefit of all beings," expresses the perfect Mahāyāna spirit.[1] "Thanks to this merit, may all beings as numerous as space itself is vast rapidly attain the state of Vajradhara."

The merit gained by spiritual practice is shared universally in the classic formulae of dedication. The basis of sharing merit is the fourth *brahmavihāra*, common to all forms of Buddhism: that all beings abandon their attachments toward their dear ones, no longer discriminating between friends and enemies, thus attaining universal, impartial compassion (*upekṣa*). The merit of a Bodhisattva (a being on the path toward the full enlightenment of a Buddha) is dedicated to all sentient beings without difference or preference.

12

The Fruition

Fully Enlightened Buddhahood

It should be apparent that these practices give rise not only to a "mind" that is flexible but to a type of person. Historically, Buddhist traditions have recognized three different manifestations of sanctified personhood:

1. The Arhat of early Buddhism, who has conquered the defilements and passions that obstruct liberation.
2. The Bodhisattva, who actively cultivates wisdom and merit toward the perfection of universal compassion, vowing to attain complete Buddhahood for the benefit of all beings.
3. The mahāsiddha, who fearlessly accelerates the Bodhisattva path by means of esoteric practices that transform the body, speech, and mind manifestations of one's humanity by means of physical postures and gestures, mantra, and visualizations that take the goal as the path. This is the realized being of the Vajrayāna, also referred to as a "Vajradhara"—one who bears the thunderbolt scepter.

Vajradhara is precisely the primordial Buddha-nature fully liberated and developed within the Mahāyāna path with the intention of acquiring a plethora of skillful means with which to assist in the liberation of all sentient beings. In the multiplicity of the biographies of various mahāsiddhas or tantric "saints," the transcendental qualities of Vajradhara as a universal archetype are rendered entirely immanent when the spiritual alchemy of Vajrayāna attains its objective (i.e., siddha-artha).

The masters become "Vajradhara" and their life stories (*rnam thar* = *vimukti*, or "completely liberated") are meant to authenticate that attainment. Our thirteenth-century master,[1] rGyal thang pa, describes the *yogin* as Vajradhara:

> The esoteric meaning of Vajradhara Buddha is as follows: Vajradhara Buddha is all those who hold in their mental continua the realization of Dharmakāya as Voidness, as the highest truth of nature (*dharmatā*) ... whoever is firm in the compassionate thought of Enlightenment and in the wisdom of all the Buddhas is the Victor Vajradhara, the Lord of all the Tathāgatas. This means that whatever altruistic attitude (*bodhicitta*) there is, is the wisdom of the Buddhas. Vajradhara Buddha is what the enlightened attitude is.... All *yogins* who realize the meaning of wisdom to be Vajradhara become thereby the unexcelled Vajradhara. So great is the number of Vajradharas.[2]

Thus the figure of Vajradhara is the key to tantric Buddhist teachings on transformation and sanctity as manifested in the mahāsiddhas and great lineage holders. So it should be no surprise that the eighty-four mahāsiddhas frequented a place of "popular" piety known as Muktināth, where they are said to have left their staves to spring up into poplar trees at the Himalayan headwaters of the Mukti (liberation) River.

Since we are speaking specifically of Vajrayāna liberation, we should look at those features of tantric Buddhism that sum up the goal of practice. Here we find the "seven limbs or features of the kiss" in a work of Vāgīśvarakīrti, the Nepali master who had a vision of Vajrayoginī at Pharping nine hundred years ago. The seven features are:

1. He possesses the perfect enjoyment body (*saṃbhogakāya*) with the thirty-two major and eighty minor marks, along with knowledge.
2. He possesses the union (kiss) of wisdom and compassion. He perceives clearly that voidness and compassion are not a

dichotomy but constitute an indivisible reality in the way of seeing of a Buddha.

3. He possesses the four blisses as supreme bliss. These are the ecstatic experiences associated with the four principal tantric consecrations:
   a. *The vase.* Sound: Oṃ, at the forehead cakra.
   b. *The secret.* Sound: Aḥ, at the throat cakra.
   c. *The knowledge of wisdom.* Sound: Huṅ, at the heart cakra.
   d. *The fourth consecration.* Sound: all three, at the navel cakra.
4. He has direct realization of the absence of intrinsic substratum (*niḥsvabhāva*) both of self and of all the phenomena of nature.
5. He has the altruistic attitude (*bodhicitta*) in both the relative and absolute sense in the form of great compassion. In spite of his realization of voidness, he abandons no one and knows how to help beings without limits.
6. The unbroken continuity of his compassion remains forever. His every action is a manifestation of compassion for all beings.
7. He possesses noncessation (*anirodha*), never dissolving permanently into nirvāṇa.[3]

The beauty of these seven features is that they put a name and a teaching on what we have seen at Pharping, eighteen kilometers south of Kathmandu. There the *yogin* and guru Vāgīśvarakīrti has left the legacy of his teachings and has blessed the temple of Bajrayogini where even today something of the visionary atmosphere of the eleventh century remains alive. His text, the *Saptāṅga*, tells us how to bring the experiences of sexuality and death to the path of liberation. He teaches us how to recognize when desire and its fruition finally drop away from our stream of awareness. At that very moment, one attains the self-arisen state of pure, unmediated perception, in which all discursive thinking is exhausted. This is the glimpse of the sublime Buddha-nature that the humble pilgrim longs to make a permanent way of seeing, unafraid of either being or nonbeing, of form or of formlessness, and wise in the ways of applying these discoveries to the human condition.

The Vajrayāna challenges us to see convergences and divergences as a continuous play "of the guru"—that is, reality continually calling us back to the home from which we thought we had wandered. The whole of reality, even our errors, even our historical background, cannot be separated from the total experience of reality, which the Buddhist tantras call the great seal, or *mahāmudrā*. If anything is excluded from the ultimate view, such a view cannot be ultimate! The religious person matures as he or she struggles for integrity and purity, only to find that the pilgrimage itself teaches us, like a gentle mother, to be grateful even to our own faults and childlike missteps. So whether we return in memory to the butchery of hens and goats at blood-soaked Dākṣinkālī or to the cool sweet waters of unassuming Muktināth, we are ever in that wide and open field of liberation. It is here that we approach the depth and the wider application of the bKa' brgyud path.

13

The *rDo rJe 'Chang rnam thar* in bKa' brgyud Spirituality

The term *rnam thar* is applied in some of the *gser 'phreng* collections to what would seem to be a scholastic outline of the characteristics of Buddhahood. Among the several branches of the bKa' brgyud pa, we have identified several examples, one of which is translated in this volume.[1] Followers of the tradition of Tilopa, Nāropa, Maitrīpa, Marpa, and Milarepa wrote cycles or collections of *rnam thars* of the principal lineage holders; such cycles were called *gser 'phreng*, a "golden rosary"[2] of sacred biographies that would stimulate the devotion of present and subsequent generations of practitioners, disciples, and lay followers.

At the start of some collections of saints' lives, there is a *rnam thar* of the primordial or archetypal tantric form of the Buddha: Vajradhara (Tibetan: *rdo rje 'chang*), or the "holder of the thunderbolt." These texts, which are not biographies at all, function as a theoretical introduction to the collection of "historical" biographies to follow. The introductory *rnam thar* of *rdo rje 'chang* provides a convenient summary of the characteristics of a Buddhist saint from the point of view of the Mahāyāna in general and of the Vajrayāna in particular.

Judith and Mervin Hanson[3] presented a preliminary study of the *rdo rje 'chang* material in their article "The Mediating Buddha" in 1985. They made use of a Shangs pa bKa' brgyud *rnam thar* of *rdo rje 'chang.* I was able to study a more precise *rdo rje 'chang rnam thar* in the *gser 'phreng* authored by our 'Brug pa bKa' brgyud master, rGyal thang pa, in the mid-thirteenth century. Both the Shangs pa author and rGyal thang pa develop portraits of Vajradhara in outline form based on the relevant theories about the emergence of Buddhahood in the personal continuum of a sentient being. Thus in the words of the Hansons, "A fairly consistent role for Vajradhara begins to emerge. Very simply, it is one of mediation, transmission or linkage."[4]

There is more, however. Vajradhara represents the archetype of the tantric Buddhist saint, the fully realized being who has surpassed the "liberation state of the Arhats" to serve as a nexus for the energies of primordial compassion and voidness. As Lhalungpa observes, "Vajradhara is the highest *manifestation* of enlightenment, the visual presentation of the *Dharmakāya*... being the highest cosmic force arising from the *Dharmakāya*'s expanse, Vajradhara represents the supreme integrating force and the source of unfolding compassion. In Vajradhara all Saṁbhogakāya forms, their qualities and functions are unified. Hence Vajradhara is described as the all-pervasive sovereign of the attributes of Enlightenment."[5]

As the study of the *rdo rje 'chang rnam thar* indicates with greater and greater clarity, especially as one explores the other biographies of the collection, the apparently transcendent characteristics of Vajradhara are rendered entirely immanent in the completed process of spiritual transformation evidenced in the lives of the lineage-holding masters and *yogins*. As rGyal thang pa tells us,

> The esoteric meaning of Vajradhara Buddha is as follows: Vajradhara Buddha is all those who hold in their mental continua the realization of *Dharmakāya* as Voidness, being the highest truth of Nature (*dharmatā*) ... "Whoever is firm in the compassionate thought of Enlightenment and in the wisdom of all Buddhas is the Victor, Vajradhara, the Lord of all the Tathāgatas." This means that whatever altruistic attitude (*bodhicitta*) exists is the wisdom of the Buddhas. Vajradhara Buddha is what the enlightened attitude is... . This means that a *yogin* can cognize the meaning of the wisdom *Dharmakāya* by his meditation. If one were to contemplate in that way, he would become like Vajradhara. Yes, we

> accept this teaching! As the [*Vajraśekhara*] tantra states: "All *yogins* who realize the meaning of wisdom to be Vajradhara become thereby the unexcelled Vajradhara. So great is the number of Vajradharas!"[6]

Thus *Vajradhara* is the very key to tantric Buddhist notions of sanctity as manifested in the mahāsiddhas and lineage holders. The archetype is realized in the historic *rnam thars*; in fact *Vajradhara* is the *means* that must be employed to attain the supreme goal.

The basic structure of the *rdo rje 'chang rnam thar* is quite simple:

1. There is a four-verse root text that summarizes the entire work.
2. Vajradhara is a teacher of sūtra and tantra who benefits sentient beings.
3. He possesses classic Mahāyāna and Vajrayāna qualities, perfections, and virtues:
   a. The five certainties
   b. The five gnoses (Tibetan: *ye shes*)
   c. The five bodies
   d. The seven features (literally, seven limbs; in Sanskrit: *saptāṅga*; in Tibetan: *yan lag bdun*)
   e. The eight sovereignties (i.e., of a *saṃbhogakāya*)
   f. The thirteen stages (*bhūmi*)
   g. He is the sixth Buddha of the maṇḍala
4. Esoterically, he holds the *Vajra* and is assimilated to the realized *yogin*.

Perhaps the most unusual numerical grouping in the *rnam thar* is the tantric set of the "seven features of the *saṁpuṭa*," or the *yan lag bdun*. We must state immediately that these seven are not the seven limbs of enlightenment (*sapta-bodhi-aṅga*), nor are they the seven "branches" or standard parts of a liturgical service. This seven has some features in common with the "seven grandeurs of the Mahāyāna" from the *Mahāyānasūtrālaṃkāra*, with the order completely rearranged.

The seven limbs or features of the *saṁpuṭa* are a "seven" that turns up in relatively rare and isolated instances.[7] mKhas grub rje mentions this seven in the context of summarizing the "tantra of effect" in relation to the highest tantra class.[8] For rGyal thang pa, the seven features are as follows:

1. He possesses the Saṁbhogakāya with the thirty-two major and eighty minor marks along with knowledge.
2. He possesses the union (or the kiss; Tibetan: *kha sbyor*) of wisdom and compassion.
3. He possesses the four blisses as *mahāsukha.*
4. He has direct realization of *niḥsvabhāva* for both self and dharmas.
5. He has the altruistic attitude (*bodhicitta*) in both the relative and the absolute sense.
6. His compassion remains in unbroken continuity.
7. He possesses noncessation (*anirodha*), never dissolving permanently into nirvāṇa.

The importance of these seven features is apparent in the work of mKhas grub rje, who states, "At the time of the third initiation, ... the mind simultaneously experienced bliss void and the symbolic Clear-Light.... The attainment in that way of the consubstantial coupling (*ngo bo gcig pa'i zung 'jug sku dang thugs*) of body and mind is called 'coupling in the realm of learning' (*śaikṣayuganaddha*). The fruit ... resulting from the continuous contemplation of the affiliation of that [coupling] is explained as the 'coupling beyond learning' (*aśaikṣayuganaddha*) or the means of accomplishing the rank of 'having the seven members of the saṁpuṭa' (*kha sbyor yan lag bdun ldan gyi*)."[9]

The pivotal Sanskrit source for this concept in relation to the fourth consecration turns out to be the *Saptāṅga* (*yan lag bdun*)[10] of Vāgīśvarakīrti, who was probably the Nepali scholar-*yogin* Pham thing pa (eleventh century), the most famous member of a family of gurus, a gatekeeper at Vikramaśīla who taught the "Father" class tantras (Guhyasamāja) and yogic breathing. He was a disciple and attendant of Nāropa for nine years, taught the *Hevajra Tantra* in accordance with the system of Nāropa, and was one of Marpa Lho brag pa's gurus. He has a number of works in the *bsTan 'gyur* and was active in producing translations from Indian languages that eventually found their place in the Tibetan canon.[11]

The following is an outline of his *Saptāṅga,* a work that is of sufficient value to be presented here. It has never been translated previously into a Western language.

Part 1. Salutations to Mañjuśrī:

— The book is presented as a colored *maṇḍala* that looks like a tree with seven branches.

Part 2. The seven features are described:

— The thirty-two signs and the eighty minor marks of a *saṃbhogakāya* (folio 381.1–3)

— The kiss (*kha sbyor*) as a union of two "faculties" (folio 381.4–5; i.e., senses and sense organs)

— Natural and supreme pleasure: *mahāsukha* (folios 381.5–382.3)

— *Niḥsvabāva* (folios 382.3–391.4): A long argument to demonstrate that the metaphysical doctrine of "no intrinsic substratum" really gives access to the absolute: Buddhahood, the highest realization. It cannot be reduced to the assertion of the nonexistence of fantasies and illusions. He discusses the nature of voidness; sameness and difference; the apparent nature of "becoming"; the limits of language in the face of ultimate reality; the correct use of the doctrine of the two truths; how to perform the erotic visualization of the goddess correctly; how to meditate on the mind itself and on mental activity; the concepts of *sahaja*, yoga, and *Mahāmudrā*; distinctions between *Cittamātra* and *Madhyamaka*; and perception and states of consciousness. He teaches a mantra of voidness.

— *Mahākaruṇā*: Great compassion (folios 391.4–391.6). How to fulfill the aspirations of sentient beings; the nature of suffering
— The uninterrupted practice of compassion (*rgyun ma chad pa*) (folios 393.6–394.5)
— No cessation (*'gog pa med*) (folios 394.6–395.4)—that is, the nonabiding (*apratiṣṭhita*) nirvāṇa

Part 3. The praise of one who possesses the stage of the seven features (folios 394.6–401.3):
— Causality: the arising of the seven features and their relation to the four consecrations: the vase, the secret, the knowledge of wisdom, and the fourth
— The fourth consecration is expounded in the light of tantric ritual and yogic experience (folios 395–401.3); we offer a selection of the twenty-one laudatory verses:

The various qualities of the Fourth Consecration come to be fully cognized when there is sexual union with the *Karmamudrā* when the tip of the *vajra* is in the place of pleasure; whoever experiences this attains the [Third] Consecration of the Knowledge of Wisdom!

Whoever, going forth from that [sexual union], but maintaining the Altruistic motivation (*bodhicitta*), attains the Fourth Consecration ...

Thus also, it is the Knowledge of Wisdom when a Vajradhara finally expels the very essence of the Life Breath; and that too is the Fourth!

Thus also when Desire and its Fruit finally pass away from the Mind and one attains *Sahaja*, which is when all thinking is exhausted and abandoned, [but] Perception [remains], that is the Fourth.

Thus when one immediately perceives all there is in the Three Realms as Self-Arising Gnosis (*rig pa*), that is the Fourth.

And when one perceives right away in the Consecration of the Knowledge of Wisdom that all the Three Realms are essentially a lie, that is the Fourth.

And, immediately upon drinking a bit of the Nectar upon one's tongue, that is the Fourth ...

And just whatever a *Karmamudrā*, a woman who is a Holder of Gnosis (*vidyādhariṇī*) teaches, is the Fourth.

A *Karmamudrā* who is continuously wrathful is said to eliminate attachment very quickly!

And whoever completely abandons the *Karmamudrā* to partake of the *Mudrā* of Insight, right away, that one attains the Fourth.

And whoever completely abandons the *Mudrā* to meditate only on the *Mahāmudrā* as the essence of Voidness, that one attains the Fourth ...

Therefore, perceiving the Self and thoroughly enjoying it skillfully in various aspects constitutes the Fourth [Consecration]. And yet, [the one so consecrated] is lacking in any attachment to a Self! (f. 400.1–400.3)

Part 4. On characteristics of Buddhahood and its fruits:

— The qualities of one who possesses the seven features are only distinct from the point of view of conventional language; thus they are distinct signs and sounds that are, in reality, not distinct at all.

Part 5. On meditation (folios 402.6–405.1):

— Faith is an indispensable prerequisite for acquiring higher gnosis. In six months, if one practices meditation three, four, or six times a day, one can attain realization—even someone who does not have the thirty-two signs and eighty marks of a bodhisattva on his body can attain Buddhahood in one lifetime (folio 403.3–6).

— Meditation practice is essential because of the certainty and imminence of death. Without meditation, one "dries out"; by means of meditation, one churns the mind like the gods churn the ocean of milk to obtain the nectar of *Tathāgata.*

Beginning with research on Tibetan *rnam thars* from the eleventh to the sixteenth centuries, we have found ourselves inevitably drawn to the period of the Second Diffusion of Buddhism, or the early eleventh century. Here, in northern India and Nepal, circles of Buddhist *yogins* and scholars were propagating a radical spirituality centered on the sacredness of the human body, disclosed as a means of liberation from ignorance, rage, and desire. In this environment, the scholar-*yogin* Vāgīśvarakīrti expounded a harmonious synthesis of the concepts of the *yoginī tantras* with earlier strata of Mahāyāna Buddhist systems. As a disciple of Nāropa and a guru of Marpa, he is a link to the lineages that gave rise in Tibet to the *dwags po bKa' brgyud* schools. Vāgiśvarakīrti's little outline in five parts on the seven features of one who holds the rank of a Vajradhara presents yogic experience vividly and enthusiastically, especially in describing the "fourth consecration," as can be seen in his twenty-one laudatory verses.

Our thirteenth-century author rGyal thang pa is deeply indebted to him:

1. He explicitly follows his system in describing the state of Vajradhara.
2. His account of rituals performed by Milarepa (e.g., a miraculous vase initiation, an invocation of Tārā, an evocation of the eighty-four mahāsiddhas, etc.) in his *mi la rnam thar* reflects Vāgiśvara's manner of discussing the four consecrations in the context of mahāsiddha yogic practice.
3. He concurs in the possibility of realizing Buddhahood in one body, in one lifetime through intense faith and meditation practice just as the *Saptāṅga* asserts, presenting itself as an authoritative Sanskrit (Indo-Nepali) commentary for the claims that all *bKa' brgyud pa* biographers later advanced in

their *rnam thars* of Marpa and Milarepa as the cornerstone of *bKa' brgyud* pa spirituality and sanctity.

Vāgīśvarakīrti is unaware of a contrast between practice and philosophical theory; in his *Saptāṅga,* ritual is not repudiated in favor of presumably "pure" or "spontaneous realization." Instead, tantric rites are shown to give rise to a realization that may subsequently embrace all human experience without exception. In following him, rGyal thang pa seems to be asserting the faithful adherence of his own lineage to a pre-Sa-paṇ style of yogic practice. rGyal thang pa, taking an irenic position, describes scholarly opponents of Milarepa as full of merit; they are eventually liberated,[12] in contrast to the account in the *mila mgur 'bum* by gTsang smyon Heruka, in which Dar blo, a master of scholastic debate, becomes a demon.

14

Tantric Practice in the bKa' brgyud

In order to enter into and practice according to the Vajrayāna, one makes a connection with a guru. Thus begins the indispensable relationship that will lead to realization, exemplified in all the *rnam thars* of the lineage. We do not know what preliminary practices were required in the earliest bKa' brgyud communities. Elizabeth English observes, "Sādhana texts also say little of the previous spiritual practice that has prepared the practitioner for taking up the sādhana or of the initiations that have qualified him to do so. Such preliminaries are so fundamental to the tantric system that they are usually taken for granted by the author of a sādhana ... the practitioner should be someone 'who has an undivided attitude of devotion toward his teacher and the Buddha, who has firmly seized the will to enlightenment, [and] who has correctly obtained initiation.'"[1] It seems from the evidence of the *rnam thars* that formal preliminary practices were not systematized in the time of Marpa and Milarepa. Nevertheless, it is of some value to summarize the practice in the form that seems to have evolved in the course of the twelfth century.[2] The preliminaries were apparently systematized in the course of the institutionalization of the tantric communities and monastic orders in the decades following the death of Milarepa.

Typically, two sets of preliminary practices are presented to the aspirant. The *general* preliminary practices, inculcated by Atiśa and permanently ensconced in Tibetan tantric literature, consist of reflecting and acting upon four main topics related to the First Truth of the Holy Ones (*āryasatya*) of early Buddhism, *duḥkhaḥ*:

1. The difficulty of being and becoming a human being; the "precious human birth."

2. The transitory nature of everything: impermanence.
3. The relation between our actions in the past and our present situation in life: *karman*, or "cause and result."
4. The general unsatisfactory character of cyclic existence: it is easy to fall into undesirable future existences if we commit harmful actions. Continuing in *saṃsāra*, subject to the law of *karman*, we do not attain happiness, nor do we accomplish beneficial deeds for our own good or for the good of others.

Then there are the *special* preliminaries,[3] which are actual ritual practices one undertakes to repeat a very large number of times (more than 100,000) in order to interiorize in the stream of consciousness that which would be otherwise merely external. These repetitions are believed to accumulate a very large store of the merit indispensable for serene progress on the path of tantra, and they have the effect of spiritualizing the way of life of the practitioner to a very high degree.

The first of the special preliminaries is that of Taking Refuge, a practice that Vajrayāna Buddhism has in common with the other forms of Buddhism. One verbally "takes refuge" in the three jewels: Buddha, Dharma, and Saṅgha, simultaneously making a full prostration while visualizing a "refuge tree" that portrays the great saints, tantric deities, protectors, and masters of the lineage. Then recited as one single formula with the Refuge is the Bodhisattva Vow, or "awakening *bodhicitta*," the thought of attaining enlightenment for the benefit of all beings: "By the merit of practicing generosity and the other virtues, may Buddhahood be realized for the benefit of all beings." Thus in the words of the contemporary head of the 'Brug pa bKa' brgyud Order, H. H. Gyalwa Drukchen, "Whatever I do now is no longer for myself, but for the benefit of all beings without exception."[4]

The second special preliminary is the recitation of the Hundred Syllable Mantra of Vajrasattva for inner purification. The deity-bodhisattva Vajrasattva, having the face of one's guru and holding a thunderbolt scepter and bell in each hand, is visualized above one's head; a purifying nectar descends from the deity into the practitioner to wash away negative ***karman***, infractions of sacred vows and promises, conflicting emotions, illnesses, negative occult influences, obstacles, ignorance, and all the "veils" to true knowledge. The nectar, now slightly darkened, is visualized to flow out below the body of the practitioner into the golden earth.

The third special preliminary is the ritual of the Maṇḍala Offering, which is directed to one's gurus and which accumulates the merit needed to "fuel" the higher practices. Based on the first of the six perfections of the Mahāyāna, *Dāna* (generosity), one offers a rice or jewel maṇḍala of the symbolic universe on a plate of precious metal. The idea is that generosity diminishes the habit of attachment, egocentrism, and self-serving and makes possible the realization of nonself and voidness.

The fourth special preliminary is that of guru yoga, in the form of devotional recitation of hymns or mantras centering on the guru as the source of the teachings and guidance that make liberation possible. rGod tshang pa, guru of the thirteenth-century biographer rGyal thang pa, taught, "The attainment of Buddhahood in a single lifetime can only be granted and can in no other way be guaranteed, except through devotion and veneration of the Guru."[5] More recently, the late Dudjom Rinpoche, head of the rNyingmapa Order, said, "Devotion and fervent prayer that comes from the heart unceasingly, and even if only for an instant, to perceive the Guru as the Buddha himself, this is the universal remedy, superior to all others, for dissipating the obstacles and making progress."

Having completed the special preliminaries to the satisfaction of the guru, one may begin the main "highest tantra" (*yoganiruttaratantra*)[6] practices, based on the "yidam" (tutelary deity) practices that we will describe in greater detail later. These are in two steps—"generation" or creation (*utpattikrama*) and completion or perfection (*niṣpannakrama/saṃpannakrama*). The first of these depends on the visualized recreation of the world as a maṇḍala and the accomplishment of rites through which the enlightenment of all who dwell within the maṇḍala realm (ultimately all sentient beings) can be secured. Abiding in the maṇḍala and palace of the deity also entails acquiring for oneself the visualized body of the deity, making possible the arduous practices of completion stage yoga. The latter focuses on the *yogin*'s actualization of his or her own enlightenment through the yogic transmutation of mind and body into embodied enlightenment. The stage of creation is meant to generate pure images mentally in order to purify negative habitual tendencies. Once purified, the body, speech, and mind continua of the practitioner become capable of undertaking the arduous interior yoga of the transformation of the channels, winds, and drops (Sanskrit: *nāḍī, prāṇa, bindu*). Once this transmutation has advanced sufficiently, the practitioner is able to make use of anything at all to manifest Buddha-nature. This stage is explained by Tilopa in his teaching to Nāropa on the banks of the Ganges:

> Like space, who can find its position?
> So too is your own thinking activity:
> The Great Seal is not to be localized.
> Be relaxed in its unmodified and primal essentiality.
> Once the bonds are released, liberation is beyond
>   questioning.
> When thinking activity has no objects, that is the Great Seal.
> Practicing it, you will attain enlightenment.
> Beyond meditation, enlightenment is attained.
> Beyond object and subject, it is the best of views.
> Not characterized by agitation, it is the best of
>   contemplations.
> Not characterized by effort, it is the best of actions.
> Without hope or fear, the goal simply appears.
> Freed from all limits, it is the best of views.
> Limitless, deep and wide, it is the best of contemplations.
> Just reposing in non-action is the best of actions.
> Just keeping free of longing is the best of goals.
> Free from all desires, if you do not adhere to any extreme,
> You will realize all the doctrines of the scriptures.[7]

15

bKa' brgyud pa Tantric Practice

Enlightenment "in One Lifetime, in One Body"

We have already discussed the ordinary and extraordinary preliminary practices; these are also discussed widely in the Tibetan dharma literature now available in translation.[1] Comparatively fewer studies have been directed to the deity practices called "*utpattikrama*," or "stage of creation." Basing ourselves for the sake of completeness on Sarah Harding's study of the teachings of Jamgon Kongtrul the Great,[2] we will examine the theory behind stage of creation practice. With a view to relating the theory to the practice of two of Milarepa's principal tutelary deities, we will describe some key features of the Cakrasaṃvara and Vajravārāhī tantric cycles. Outside of the texts gathered by Jamgon Kongtrul in his great compilation of oral teachings, the *gDams ngag mdzod*, little can be known of the practice instructions as they would have been given in Milarepa's lifetime.

Vajrayāna spirituality centers around devotional and meditation techniques directed toward particular tutelary deities (*yidam*) and their maṇḍalas.[3] In effect, tantric practice makes use of the intrinsic attractiveness of religious and magical practice to engage the embodied imagination of the *yogin* in an alchemical process. The philosophical basis for incorporating overt religiosity within a Buddhist path is the realization of voidness. This voidness (*śūnyatā*) is experienced in meditation as "radiance-awareness [and] ... is the primordially pure basis of all manifestation and perception, the Buddha-nature [itself]."[4] It is stated, time after time, by the lamas that Buddha is not found anywhere outside of the intrinsic state of one's own mind. Thus in the scheme we will discover in Milarepa's own oral teachings, the ground of realization is one's own true nature; the path is whatever it takes to discover that nature; the fruition is the disclosure of one's own true nature to consciousness.

Thus whatever brings the awareness back to its true nature constitutes a form of *upāya*, or skillful salvific means. The use of a variety of techniques reflects the development within Buddhist meditation traditions of a vast body of experience with bringing the mind to subtle states of consciousness. The Vajrayāna pioneers recognized that deity forms are nothing more and nothing less than a manifestation of the primordial purity of Buddha-nature. By developing elaborate ritual cycles of practice, it becomes possible to transform the mind's habitual patterns of attachment and aversion into an instrument of visionary intuition that recognizes the world as an enlightened realm—the maṇḍala of a vast array of powerful beings. "The practice of deity meditation is a skillful way of undermining our ordinary mistaken sense of solid reality and moving closer to a true mode of perception."[5]

Jamgon Kongtrul taught, "The basis of purification, which is this very Buddha-nature, abides as the Body with its clear and complete vajra signs and marks. A similar form is used as the path and leads to the fruition of purification: that very divine form which existed as the basis."[6] One will notice immediately in Jamgon Kongtrul's comment a reference to the *saṃbhogakāya* form of Buddha with the thirty-two signs and eighty minor marks; we have already indicated in our comments on Vajradhara how the Vajrayāna appropriates this concept and applies it to the variety of deity forms used in the tantric liturgical cycles. By meditating on a form that resembles the glorified human body, visualized in creation stage meditation, the *yogin* comes to an existential realization of that divine form as it abides within the true nature of the mind itself. The deity can be perceived as a form to which the *yogin* relates in liturgical action and meditation or as dissolving into formlessness and luminosity. By identifying oneself with such a form, the *yogin* also is divinized and experiences dissolution into light and voidness. It is also understood that these forms were mystically revealed to highly realized masters in their contemplative experiences; they are not mere randomly generated deity forms. The *yogin* or *sādhaka* (practitioner) visualizes these forms according to the iconographical canon and performs the appropriate deity *pūjā* leading to a more contemplative meditation session in which the *sādhaka* identifies with the tutelary deity.

Vajrayāna conceives of such identification not only as a means for realizing voidness but also as a way of preparing the mind stream of the *yogin* for later manifestation—at the time of enlightenment—as a variety of compassionate and efficacious forms that take on the task of benefiting beings in accordance with the vows of a Bodhisattva.[7] The skillful identification of a practitioner with the deity also creates conditions in his or her own subtle body at its interface with the material body that allow for a fruitful practice of the stage of completion yogas, making use of the visualized channels, winds, and droplets. Without such identification, the material and subtle body confluence would be unable to sustain itself during the release of the powerful energies (cf. *kuṇḍalinī*) that lie dormant in the subtle body and are aroused by completion stage practices. This is why the result of creation stage practice is supposed to be a deity-like "Vajra body." This is the manner in which the saints are depicted on the scroll paintings (*thang ka*).

A key sign of such attainment would be an abiding relationship with the tutelary deity, whose presence arises effortlessly for some advanced *sādhakas* at all times.[8] This should not be too surprising in view of the large number of mantra repetitions involved in deity practice, often done in lengthy retreat settings in which a habitual state of recollection is maintained. The extension of such depth contemplative experience to one's daily life is facilitated by the guidance of the guru, who enables the *sādhakas* to recognize the relationship between the stages of practice and realization to the stages of human life itself. The normal stages of a life cycle are conceived of as "*bardos*"—intermediate states analogous to that between death and rebirth in which enlightening energies can be awakened and rapid spiritual progress achieved.[9]

In addition, the different classes of tantras cultivate different degrees of relationship with the tutelary deities.[10] In his retreat manual, Jamgon Kongtrul gave detailed instructions for a very vigorous training in these *sādhanas*, building the daily schedule around four major sessions of ritual and contemplative practice.[11]

There are a number of published descriptions of deity yoga now available in translation, such as Stephan Beyer's *The Cult of Tārā: Magic and Ritual in Tibet*; Khenpo Könchog Gyaltsen and Katherine Rogers's *The Garland of Mahāmudrā Practices*; and Geshe Kelsang Gyatso's *Guide to Ḍākinī Land: A Commentary to the Highest Yoga Tantra Practice of Vajrayoginī.* A very useful manual on empowerment and deity practice is given in the work of Tsele Natsok Rangdröl previously cited. Many of the Vajrayāna centers around the world now have the tantric ritual texts available to practitioners in translation.

It seems that Milarepa's principal yidams were Vajravārāhī (Vajrayoginī) and Cakrasaṃvāra, but he also practiced Hevajra, Guhyasamāja, Tārā, and possibly Kālacakra;[12] of course, in his early years, he had initiations in rNyingma pa practices related to the nāgas and the infamous initiations into the practices of destructive magic.

Nāropa and Marpa were closely associated with the *yoginī* tantra deities. In the biography of Marpa, quite a number of such cycles are mentioned, including *Mahāmāyā*, the *Caturpiṭha Tantra*, and so forth. Scholarship in *Vajrayāna* Buddhism has not been able to trace in detail all the texts, transmissions, and practices that were a vital part of the spirituality of the earliest bKa' brgyud pa masters. We present here a brief introduction to the *Vajravārāhī* (*Vajrayoginī*) system and iconography and a brief synopsis of the *Cakrasaṁvara* iconography to give the reader a glimpse of these cycles that so profoundly transformed Milarepa during his years of discipleship with Marpa.

16

Oral Teachings of Khandro Rinpoche on the Stage of Creation for the Practice of Vajravārāhī[1]

Khandro Rinpoche is one of the leading contemporary lamas; she lives primarily in Mussorie, near Dehra Dun, in North India. She has been recognized as the tulku of the late consort of the Fifteenth Karmapa. Coming from the distinguished family of the present holder of the Mindroling lineage, she is a lineage holder in both the rNyingma pa and Karma bKa' brgyud pa orders. These teachings were given in 1994 in connection with the Vajravārāhī initiation she gave in the south of France. Khandro Rinpoche urged me to publish this study of Milarepa in order to benefit not only scholars but also practitioners, and it is in that spirit that I reproduce these exceptional teachings as an example of the living tradition of oral teachings on the stage of creation:

> We take time from mundane activities to perform sacred activity, a purified activity. You sit down, you calm down, you recite, you visualize the deity, the light is generated from the deity, the deity is dissolved in light and is absorbed into ourselves. Nothing here is from outside: it is all from within ourselves. If you think the deity is going to do everything for you or if the ritual is in itself going to give you liberation, you're going backwards. And if you cannot do the whole visualization, that may be ok, but you need to get the mind to be more flexible. The idea here is not mechanics, but to tame and develop the mind. We have to get rid of self-created obstacles and really deal with our own mind and not our fabrications. As one does the practice, one begins

to notice specific personal problems that come up from our own mind. When we notice this, we must begin to work on those thoughts [that arise] as obstacles. It depends on us; this is of course a non-theistic system entirely focused on interiority. There are no shortcuts. You have to do the practice over time to get the benefits on the level of interiority. As you get rid of attachments to concepts and problems, you acquire that flexibility that is the interior Vajra nature, that is the Vajra master, that is the deity, the Vajra-being.

So the Yidam, the innate deity, is not a deity existing outside oneself. It is a reality within us. One comes, through the practice of deity-yoga, face to face with our inner true nature. There are many yidams in the bKa' brgyud pa lineage. All the qualities of Buddhahood are associated with yidams. Vajrayoginī is the first yidam given to a bKa' brgyud practitioner and she represents egolessness, the state of non-ego and the cutting off of ego. She is the first yidam because egolessness [and surrender of ego] is the basis of the path. Later on, as one gains knowledge, one may discover one's true personal yidam, but one always starts with Vajrayoginī.[2]

Initiation into Vajrayoginī means entering into the maṇḍala of her essence, taking on the qualities of Vajrayoginī, and becoming that more and more. In this way, we are looking into our own mind and checking what we find there. We are also looking upon the guru and forming dharma connections.

There are five "families" within the maṇḍala of the yidam. Vajrayoginī manifests as the five ḍākinīs: Padma-ḍākinī, Vajra-ḍākinī, Buddha-ḍākinī, Ratna-ḍākinī; and Karma-ḍākinī. In the maṇḍala the ḍākinīs are arranged as five squares in the form of a cross. In a thangka, the ḍākinīs are arranged around the central figure of the yidam.

The two forms of this yidam come from two lineages. The one transmitted in this initiation is used within the Karma bKa' brgyud and comes from Tilopa who received it from Vajrayoginī herself; he passed it on to Nāropa who gave it to Marpa; Marpa's transmission via Milarepa went to sGampopa. Dus sum mkhyen pa received it from sGampopa and handed it on in the lineage he founded (Karma bKa' brgyud); the third Karmapa, Rang 'Byung rDo-rje, compiled the *sādhana* we are using. Another form, transmitted to Ras chung pa by Tiphupa, comes down through the 'Brug pa bKa' brgyud and the dGe lugs pa. Vajrayoginī is a Mother Tantra of the highest tantra class.

The goal of the iconography is to go beyond extremes and concepts. This would be termed "pure perception" of things as they are, and not as we project them to be. We should not screen out what we don't find appealing; we need to see the whole of things. Iconography is designed to bring us to that attitude.

Iconography of Vajravārāhī (Vajrayoginī)

Each iconographical detail in the visualization has a meaning associated with Dharma categories.

1. Hooked knife: Cutting through evil.
2. Skull cup (kapāla): manifestation of wisdom (*prajñā*).
3. Khatvāṅga on the left (staff): this is her consort/also: skillful means; also: Eightfold Path.
4. Scarf on shoulder: twofold, indicating the inseparability of Mahāyāna and Vajrayāna.
5. Three skulls on the *khatvāṅga*: the three *kāyas*.
6. The head of a sow coming out of her head: cutting through ignorance.

Iconography of Vajravarahi according to the Karma Kagyu tradition

7. Hair is half up and half down. Up means manifesting vajra wrath for taming ignorance (*avidyā*); down means compassion.
8. Crown of five skulls: the five Buddha families.
9. Three eyes: Vajrayoginī is a knower of the three times (*dus sum mkhyen*).

10. Wrathful expression: tames obstacles to the Dharma and to practice of Dharma.
11. Fifty-one severed heads: conquer the fifty-one types of fabricated concepts.
12. One face: means *sama-rasa* in the *dharmakāya*, that is, the "one existential taste" mystical experience.
13. Head ornaments, earring, waist belt, bracelet, girdle, necklace: The six pāramitās (perfections).
14. Two arms: wisdom and skillful means in union.
15. Two feet: (standing): not dwelling in the two saṃsāric extremes of eternalism and nihilism.
16. Corpse beneath feet: Overpowering the ego.
17. Sun-disk: Wisdom//moon: compassion.
18. Lotus: spontaneous birth of enlightenment from saṃsāra without defilement.
19. Full form of the body: Red with White Light: *prajñāpāramitā* (The perfection of wisdom, visualized as a female deity form); the union of wisdom and compassion.
20. Necklace of red flowers: Total non-attachment.

The *samaya* of this practice, the covenant binding Guru and Disciple, consists of performing these twenty actions and embodying these attitudes at all times. Vajrayoginī is the symbol of that egolessness that knows how to *Be* without *Being Attached.* This is getting out of the mental glue that keeps us bound to *saṃsāra*, in spite of our spontaneous attraction to Enlightenment. It takes a lot of courage to cut away our attachment to saṃsāra; that is why we should do the practices of all three "vehicles" (*yānas*). These practices give us the necessary courage to face what Enlightenment really is. Every practice is an approach to a mind that is fearless, vast, open, and non-manipulative in confrontation with that which is.

17

Oral Teachings of H. H. Gyalwa Drukchen on Cakrasamvara[1]

H. H. Gyalwa Drukchen is another major *sprul sku* born in the Tibetan exile community of a distinguished family. He is the head of the 'Brug pa bKa' brgyud order. These teachings were given at his center in Plouray, Brittany, in France and at Namkhai Norbu Rinpoche's center, Merigar, in Arcidosso, Italy. I was His Holiness's translator at the latter initiation (English to Italian). His Holiness is believed to be the incarnation of the great sixteenth-century master Padma dKar po; these teachings reflect a profound comprehension of Padma dKar po's own studies and commentaries on the Cakrasaṃvara oral transmission (*bDe mChog snyan rgyud*), both in relation to the stage of creation and the stage of completion.

Cakrasaṃvara[2] is a vast and profound teaching that centers on the experience of great bliss (Sanskrit: *mahāsukha*). The male deity is Heruka; the female consort deity is Vajrayoginī and represents the realization of wisdom, which is the same as saying the realization of emptiness. The union of the two deities is itself great bliss, which we also call *mahāmudrā*, or the great seal. In terms of the salvific methods used in the Vajrayāna, the sharpest and the greatest is the use of the respective energies of male and female. It is important to understand the meaning of these two energies in union. Their energy is the essential energy of the universe. To realize the universal truth, which we call mahāmudrā, you must make use of these two fundamental energies. Since we, along with all sentient beings, are in a saṃsāric condition, we make use of these two marvelous energies that are basic to our fundamental state in life; on the relative level of existence, everything in us is based on that pair of energies. This pairing of energies can be found in men and women, in water held in a container, in sound arising from the striking of two objects, in a house containing its inhabitants, and in thunder as the result of the clash of hot and cold air masses. Thus the basic functioning of the world as we know it is based on the pairing of energies. This is a natural law exists whether you know it or not, whether you use it or not, and whether you use it rightly or wrongly. No one made it and no one can avoid it. Now the Vajrayāna teaches that beings, if they knew how to use this energy correctly, could be enlightened in one second with no difficulty. These two fundamental energies are so strong that there would be no problem at all in attaining instant enlightenment. Most of the time we abuse these energies, using them unskillfully. The Vajrayāna trains us to use them correctly so that we can realize our own true nature: Buddhahood, or *Tathāgata.* This is how *yogins* such as Milarepa attained Buddhahood in one lifetime: by using these energies skillfully. If we are eager to attain enlightenment we are going to want to understand and make use of the union known as great bliss.

No matter how much one might say about this union, the fact remains that it is present at all times and all our commentaries should serve only to point this out as concretely as possible. Just think of colors, emotions, and so many things in nature and in our minds that are driven by these dual energies! If we allow these two energies to drive us the wrong way, the habitual saṃsāric way that is all but out of control for us, then we will be struggling endlessly with our bondage to saṃsāra in the form of mental fabrications and illusory attachments. This gives rise to suffering. But used correctly, these same energies can give enlightenment in a second; we have to be very careful with this.

Cakrasaṃvara is one of the practices given by the Buddha to utilize our energies in an enlightened, nirvāṇic way. In fact, Cakrasaṃvara is a practice that engages the two primal energies of the universe through skillful use of the five defilements that normally afflict us. Vajrayāna is different from Hīnayāna and Mahāyāna because it actually appreciates the defilements without rejecting or renouncing. Instead, we practice by working with the defilements. The method here is definitely different. All the Buddhas have been born in this desire realm and were enlightened at the place known as Bodhgāya. This desire realm is the realm of strong emotions that engage us in a lifelong struggle. But according to the Vajrayāna, the Buddhas are born in this realm precisely because it is in the midst of desires and defilements that it is possible to be enlightened. Somehow we need these strong emotions to realize wisdom: "There is no wisdom if there is no emotion," it is said.[3] Without defilement, there is no basis for establishing the experience of wisdom. Therefore, the realm in which we find ourselves is perfect for the purpose of attaining Buddhahood: ups and downs, defilements, and emotions constitute a wonderful set of favorable circumstances. All the Vajrayāna texts praise those beings who can practice within the Kāmadhātu, the dimension of desire, but one has to be careful. The defilements are understood to be not different from the wisdoms; they are the *Tathāgatas*, the great union, and the wisdom of the realization of our true nature. Since male and female energies are coordinated by desire, the practice of Cakrasaṃvara depends on working with desire. It is obvious that desire handled in a worldly manner leads to great harm; the Vajrayāna trains us to handle emotion with appreciation. That is the way.

The term Cakrasaṃvara (i.e., Cakrasaṁbhāva) literally means the "embodiment of the wheel [of desire's energy]." The wheel represents the flow of energy and its function. The embodiment or "compression" aspect is related to the fact that the universe arises and is held together by the union of male and female energies. Cakrasaṃvara is the universe, and the universe is Cakrasaṃvara! So when we practice in this system, the energies of the universe flow around us with the help of desire. We are moved by these energies, and so is the universe. Eventually, as we gain experience with the practice, we will discover how to become aware of these energies in ourselves and how to slow them down. This will become clearer when we learn the channel-and-wind practices of the stage of completion, in which the subtle body channels are identified as carriers of the male and female energies. Now in order to work with our awareness, we have to have mastered śamatha practice, because without excellent calm abiding and concentration, it is impossible to observe and slow down the flow of energies. In fact, our defilements such as anger tend to slow down when we are aware of them in a state of calm abiding, and gradually we learn to master desire and the energy of the emotions. At a further stage of practice, instead of wanting to slow down the circulation of energy, we will actually want to speed things up in order to gain the skill to recognize Cakrasaṃvara mindfully under all the circumstances of life and be able at that point to accelerate our attainment of enlightenment. This is why even Vajrayāna practitioners practice renunciation at first, in order to slow things down and concentrate. Later, having laid a good foundation, they engage in such activities as sex, consumption of meat and alcohol, and dwelling in fearsome locales in order to heighten emotions and accelerate realization. This requires a great deal of flexibility and skill. A beginner has to be careful not to accelerate the energies too rapidly. Also, it becomes quite clear that flexibility and skill can only be developed through an ongoing relationship with a qualified master or guru.

This lineage of Cakrasaṃvara comes through the 'Brug pa bKa' brgyud transmission: Vajradhara to Tilopa, to Nāropa, to Marpa, to Milarepa, to sGampopa, to Phag mo gru pa, to Ling chen ras pa, and to gTsang pa rgya ras (founder of the 'Brug pa order). gTsang pa rgya ras passed the lineage on to Wan chen ras pa, who handed it on over several generations until Padma dKar po, the fourth lineage holder in this series, who wrote commentaries on the tantra and on the stage of completion practice texts going back to Milarepa. At Padma dKar po's cremation, his heart was not burnt and a bone relic manifested an image of Cakrasaṃvara, showing the degree to which Padma Karpo had perfectly identified himself with this yidam.[4]

Iconography of Cakrasamvara according to the Drukpa Kagyu Tradition

Iconography of Cakrasaṃvara

1. Blue color of body: voidness.
2. Two arms and one face: the self-arisen nature of the mind.
3. Medium form: "Four truths" means the "four truths of the āryas."
4. Twelve arms: the twelve *bhūmis* (levels of Bodhisattva attainment).

5. Two legs: The left is bent and presses on a male deity, destroying anger. The right left is straight and stamps on a female deity, destroying worldly desires. Thus the deity destroys the two causes of saṃsāra. The third cause of saṃsāra, ignorance, is represented by the head of the male deity and is also crushed.
6. The three eyes: knower of the three times: wisdom, all seeing, and clairvoyant.
7. Jewel ornament: accomplishment of the result of practice.
8. Crossed vajra: how the path is accomplished through activity and understanding.
9. Slice of the moon over deity's head: the great blessing of great union.
10. Hair of the deity tied up: going up means he is entirely out of saṃsāra; going down means benefiting beings.
11. Five skulls: great union has none of the five defilements, five emotions, five thoughts, or five skandhas.
12. Vajrayoginī's *mālā* of skulls: the fifty-one *saṃskāras* (the conditioned factors of existent phenomena as conceptualized in the *Abhidharma* literature).
13. She is naked: free of fabrication; uncontrived.
14. Six ornaments on the deity: bone ornaments, ash, and *tilaka* (forehead paste ornament)—symbols of impermanence.
15. Wrathful faces: overcome the four Māras, which include the skandhas, death, *devaputra*-pleasures (sensual pleasures enjoyed by the deities of the desire realms), and the defilements.
16. Tiger skin: impeccability.
17. Nine heads on his *mālā* of fresh heads: power, qualities of action with the body, and speech and mind; the nine *rasas* (aesthetic savors) of Indian literature.[5]
18. Sun disk: luminosity.
19. Moon disk *mahāsukha*, supreme pleasure.

20. Lotus: great compassion, *mahākaruṇā.*
21. Scarf: ethics.
22. The first two of Cakrasaṃvara twelve arms (the right hand holding a vajra and the left a bell) are embracing his consort Vajrayoginī/Vajravārāhī. This represents great union.
23. The next two lower arms hold a stretched-out, blood-stained elephant hide as a cloak hanging down his back. This gesture represents the mind relaxing into the natural state.
24. In his third right hand is a *ḍamaru* (ritual drum), representing bliss.
25. The fourth hand holds an axe, representing wrathful wisdom.
26. The fifth hand holds a cleaver, representing cutting off the ego.
27. The sixth hand holds a trident held pointing upward to represent destruction of the three poisons (ignorance, anger, and desire).
28. In the third left hand is a *katvāṅga*, representing the *maṇḍala* of the deity and the three *kāyas.*
29. The fourth hand holds a skull cup filled with blood, symbolizing freedom from *saṃsāra* and attainment of siddhis.
30. Hand number 5 holds the vajra lasso, which represents compassion.
31. Hand number 6 holds a four-faced head representing freedom from the four signs of impermanence (birth, sickness, old age, and death).
32. Vajrayoginī's legs are around Cakrasaṁvara, reiterating the meaning of great union.
33. Her vajra-knife symbolizes cutting off the ego.
34. Her hand holds a skull behind the male deity to symbolize the rejection of extreme views. [6]

18

The Six Yogas of Nāropa, *Mahāmudrā*, and the bKa' brgyud Teachings on the Stage of Completion

Milarepa received the teachings on the six yogic practices of Nāropa from Marpa. These six practices were culled from the esoteric systems of several of the "highest yoga tantra," Vajrayāna practices in vogue among the mahāsiddha *yogins* and their circles in India. Basically, the Six Yogas are related to the broader category of tantric practices known as *rtsa rlung* (channels and winds, or sometimes *rtsa rlung tig le* practices—that is, channels, winds, and droplets of consciousness). They are superficially quite similar to haṭha yoga āsanas but in fact are based on different principles. First of all, they presuppose the attainment of a "vajra body" through identification with the yidam as we have discussed in relation to the stage of creation and deity yoga. Second, they involve a variety of movements united to breath control that are called "yantra yoga" (Tibetan: *khyil khor rnal 'byor*) and do not rely as heavily as haṭha yoga on static postures. Third, they involve visualizations of the subtle body and its components in a way that is similar to but distinct from what we find in the classic works on haṭha yoga such as Patañjali's *Yoga Sutras*, the *Haṭhayogapradīpikā*, and the *Śiva Saṁhita*. In spite of these significant differences, there was still a great deal of cross-fertilization between classic Indian yogic practice and the Vajrayāna, mediated to a large degree by Śaivite tantrism.

From the point of view of bKa' brgyud yogic practice, however, the stage of completion is of paramount importance and received a high degree of subtlety in the course of its transmission. It is the stage of completion that generates the three bodies of a fully liberated Buddha, thus transforming the *yogin* into an Enlightened One "in one body, in one lifetime." The practices that bring about this result are divided into those with form and those without form. The Six Yogas constitute the set of practices "with form." They work with subtle energies within the body (the "*rlung*" or winds), employing these forces to purify the channels and energy centers (*cakra*) while at the same time developing the intensity of consciousness itself (*tig le*) as it moves ever more freely among the channels of the subtle body. Successful practice of the Six Yogas gives the *yogin* control over the five elements of which the body and the world consist and open the door to the formless practice known as the great seal, or *mahāmudrā*.

Once the *yogin* has advanced in the practice of even one of the Six Yogas (Milarepa seems in particular to have favored the *caṇḍālī* or *gtum mo* heat practice), a flood of insight into the nature of reality itself arises spontaneously. There is a sense of spaciousness, of openness, that allows the habitual subject-object dualism to diminish. In fact, the ordinary awareness of such a *yogin* begins to take on the habit of perceiving that there is no reality to the subject-object distinction. As a result, every fleeting element of experience occasions an ever more intense recognition of the unicity of perception and phenomena, which the tradition calls *samarasa*, or *ro-gcig*—"one taste," which can also be translated "an experience of oneness." Living habitually in such a state is the perfection of the attainment of the great seal, or *mahāmudrā*, the "formless" practice that rounds out the stage of completion.

If one were to read Milarepa's own discussion of *mahāmudrā* in his simple, two folio work *The Clarification of Mahāmudrā,* it would be easy to see that he himself understood the connection between the Six Yogas and *mahāmudrā*. He pays homage to Marpa, the guru who compassionately gave him the transmission, and identifies himself as one in whom the *gtum mo*, the yogic heat, "blazed up" so that he could remain warm though dressed only in cotton cloth, from which derives his sobriquet, "*ras pa.*" He also notes that he has received incomparably valuable tantric initiations. Milarepa then proceeds in extremely terse and schematic remarks to comment on the three aspects of *mahāmudrā* practice: the ground or basis, the path, and the fruition. There is nothing in this text that suggests a direct connection between the previously mentioned tantric initiations and *gtum mo* practice and the attainment of *mahāmudrā.* If one were to examine later works from the lineage of Gampopa, similarly, one might come to the conclusion that *mahāmudrā* is the result, not of tantric practice, but of traditional Buddhist śamatha and vipaśyanā meditation. What is missing here is the oral instruction of an experienced *yogin* who can point out to the disciple at the appropriate moment when there has to be a realignment of the interior frame of reference such that what was previously associated with the coarser aspects of the five skandhas can now be recognized on ever more subtle levels of meditative awareness. Without this connection, one might easily miss the extraordinary subtlety of the consciousness that goes along with the attainment of *mahāmudrā.* With all the language of "force" and "energy," it is very easy for the inexperienced reader to imagine that the texts are proposing rather coarse movements and extreme pressure on the bodily organs. It is true that some of the movements preliminary to these attainments are forced and violent. For example, the yogic maneuver known as "*babs*" ("falling") involves all the rigor of breath retention in the manner of "pot breathing and retention" (*kumbhaka*) coupled with the extremely difficult maneuver of using the legs locked in *padmāsana* to propel the body upwards into the air, returning to *padmāsana* in the split second during which the body falls back to the ground. However, the real power of these completion stage practices is encountered when the mind settles into a deep contemplative absorption (*samādhi*) in which microscopic fluxes of energy in the channels can be observed. Only when this ability has been mastered can the intense degree of awareness that is *mahāmudrā* be experienced from moment to moment.

In the biography of Gampopa in the *Blue Annals*, there is an account of Milarepa's manner of guiding his greatest disciple in this very direction. In the first place, Milarepa hands Gampopa a skull cup of wine to drink, thus creating a context in which the rigorous bKa' gdams pa monk-physician is challenged to break his *Vinaya* vows; Gampopa's mind hesitates for a moment, just long enough to notice the hesitation and to recognize the risks involved with holding back as well as with going forward. Gampopa then seizes the skull cup and drains it completely, symbolically embracing nonduality without reservations. Milarepa then warns him that his meditation training has so far been seriously lacking in efficacy and might even give rise to disastrous rebirths in the *rūpa-dhātu* or *arūpyadhātu* deity realms, where his ultimate enlightenment would be impeded for eons. "Sand," says Milarepa, "when pressed, will not become liquid butter." In other words, attachment to monastic precepts and to elementary meditation practices (particularly śamatha concentration) actually tends to undermine the energetic processes that give rise to full enlightenment. These practices lack "*bodhicitta*" in the full sense of that word: there is a lack of right motivation based on compassion for all sentient beings such that they might all attain Buddhahood, and there is a lack of skill in the use of sexual fluids and the subtler but related bodily energies in the manner of highest tantra. Milarepa goes on to say that it was the fault of 'Brom ston, who prevented Atiśa from teaching the Vajrayāna *dohākośa* in Tibet, that has thus impoverished the bKa' gdams pa spiritual practice. "Had he been allowed to do it, by now Tibet would have been filled with saints!"[1] And should there be any doubt that Milarepa is concerned about the right use of sexual imagery, he goes on to say, "The bKa' gdams pa stage of generation consists only of meditation on the yidams in the form of solitary heroes (*lha po reng po*)"—that is, without their female consorts. If that were not bad enough, "their Stage of Completion consists only of meditation on the merging of the world and its inhabitants into the sphere of Voidness," which would preclude the necessary development of the subtle body that only the Six Yogas can achieve. Milarepa then instructs Gampopa to meditate using the Ā-*thung* heat yoga visualization that places consciousness delicately and firmly in the central channel while causing the yogic heat, itself based on subtle sexual energy, to spread throughout the body.[2]

Milarepa couples this completion stage practice, so dear to him as we have said earlier, with initiation into the tantric cycle of Vajravārāhī, the female solitary yidam who empowers realization of voidness in the manner of highest tantra. All the signs of success appeared in Gampopa in the following sequence:

1. The subtle energy (*prāṇa*) entered the cakras and made them function properly.
2. Gampopa gained preliminary control over his breathing so that he could complete one breath cycle in an entire day; he also gained the ability to breathe through his fingertips, indicating that he had access to all the channels in the body.
3. He had a visionary experience of the sun and moon being seized by Rahu, the eclipse demon, as the side channels were purified and the male and female elements of both coarse and subtle body were united. This kind of visionary experience indicates that the essential shift in the spiritual frame of reference from a coarse to a subtle level of perception of the phenomena of the five skandhas is taking place.[3] This is why Milarepa exclaimed, "Now, now, now," when Gampopa reported this phenomenon to him. The vision was the sign that success would be imminent, so Milarepa sent Gampopa to meditate in solitude for three years. Milarepa warned Gampopa to avoid worldly people, saying, "Their breath will cause your practice to deteriorate." By following the tantric practice regimen indicated by Milarepa, Gampopa was undergoing a subtle process of transformation that would be at risk in certain environments. Later, Gampopa ran into spiritual difficulties when he returned among the monks of his own order (the bKa' gdams pa) for a three-year period.[4]
4. In spite of the obstacles, after three years, he "perceived the nature of his mind and the ultimate nature of the elements of phenomenal existence."[5] This is in effect the realization

of *mahāmudrā*, which presupposes the attainment of an extraordinary degree of meditative acumen (*ye shes ngos zin*, or penetration of the nature of mind) and the habitual recognition of the unicity of perceiver and perceived (*rang ngo zin pa*, or seeing into one's own face).

5. Gampopa was then able to recognize that Milarepa is indistinguishable from the *dharmakāya* itself and that it would be an error to think of him as "merely" a great siddha; he thus attained the perfection of guru yoga, which predisposed him to become himself a great founder of teaching lineages.[6]

This account illustrates the way Milarepa would have guided his disciples in accordance with his own realization that the best way to attain a direct experience of voidness is by means of the "path of skillful means" (*thabs lam*), by which he specifically meant the practice of the Six Yogas. The tantric "technology" is appropriated in such a way as to produce a direct awareness of the primordial state of mind. That awareness is then cultivated (*bhāvanā*) in retreat in order to become the constant state of the body-mind continuum.

Looking into the texts attributed to Milarepa that directly concern the *thabs lam*, we can gain even greater insight into his teaching methods and the way of appropriating the yogic traditions he received. In *The Clarification of the Three Cycles*, he alludes to four bodily practices for working with the winds or prāṇic energies:

1. Knots in a Fibula. The metaphor refers to a button or cloth tie made up of loosely interwoven knotted threads. It means to keep all the five elemental winds or fluxes gathered together rather than allowing them to become extended or scattered. Thus what would otherwise be mundane fluxes of vital energy become channeled for yogic purposes.
2. Bent like a Hook. This refers to the primary wind of the body, which, through the power of inhalation, draws in all the elemental winds.

3. Shooting an Arrow Upward. The steps of this practice are to inhale and to hold the breath in the lower abdomen to the count of twenty-one of the following maneuvers: slap the right knee, the left knee, and forehead once and then snap the fingers; revolve the breath within the abdomen by moving the abdominal muscles; and exhale swiftly and vigorously through the nostrils.
4. Milking the Sky Cow. This refers to the meditation on the red and white drops (female and male subtle elements within the body): at the crown of the head, there is a white droplet containing the syllable Haṁ; at the navel there is a reddish droplet with the syllable Raṁ or E; gradually the meditator causes the two to unite, filling the body with great bliss.

Having gained proficiency in these four bodily methods, it becomes possible to proceed with the visualization of the subtle body as four cakras (at the swelling at the top of the head, at the throat, at the heart, and at the navel) and the empty cylinder of the central channel. In this type of practice, the subsidiary channels are intertwined within the cakras rather than visualized as spokes extending from a wheel. Since the body of the *yogin* has already been assimilated to the "void" body of the yidam deity in the stage of creation, it is easy to imagine the translucent central channel as equally "void" or open and cylindrical. Milarepa considers this visualization the most practical way to encounter the primordial openness of all being; the visualized "open" central channel is very effective and precise, unlike the more general Mahāyāna style of meditation on all phenomena as generically "void."

If there were any doubts about the *karmamudrā* practices being part of the Six Yogas, they would be dispelled by Milarepa's comments in this work and in the related work *The Clarification of Ignorance.* Here, he gives the traditional teachings on the characteristics of the female yogic partner. This practice involves the use of yogic sexual intercourse to make the union of the "white and red droplets" more effective and vivid.[7] However, the usual way to do this is by means of visualization in solitary retreat. The mental and physical energies of the body are channeled into the central channel such that the energies are no longer mundane but yogic or "wisdom" energies. The mind is maintained in a nonconceptual state of tensile strength. One visualizes a luminous droplet in the form of the full moon and the flame of yogic heat is visualized as sharply pointed at the top and rounded at the bottom, the male white droplet at the crown of the head and the female red droplet at the navel. The red ascends to the head and unites with the male; the two melt and descend through the body spreading blissful sensations at the throat, heart, and navel cakras, producing great bliss (*mahāsukha*). Under the guidance of the guru, these blisses lend themselves to the attainment of perfect one-pointed meditative stabilization. Such stabilization effectively discloses the primordially present awakened state of mind; thus the result, Buddhahood, is already present in sentient beings. For Milarepa's system, the path of method is identified with the practices of the stage of perfection—that is, the Six Yogas—that work with winds, droplets, and channels as a means by which the disciple learns personally and directly about the essentially open ("void") nature of all phenomena. This realization of nonconceptual unity abides in the embodied state of the *yogin* but is not produced by the body;[8] in fact, it is primordially self-arisen and not produced at all.

Next, Milarepa explains the arising of the three bodies of Buddha in the course of practice along this path of method in his work *The Purification of the Stains of Mental Elaboration* (folios 118.3–120.1).

Mullin's works on the Six Yogas have brought a great deal of clarity to an area not always accessible to the scholar of the tantras. Following Lama Pal Pakmo Drupa's lineage (one of the Four Older bKa' brgyud lineages, descending from sGampopa), he writes,

> The Six Yogas are listed as follows: inner heat yoga; illusory body yoga; clear light yoga; yoga for the transference of consciousness to a higher realm; transference of consciousness to another body; bardo yoga.[9] In this arrangement of the six, the inner heat is the foundation of all the yogas; the

> illusory body and clear light yogas are grouped together as the actual practices for inducing the experience of enlightenment and the yogas of consciousness transference ... are auxiliary or branch applications... . [T]he sixth, or bardo yoga, is regarded as both a branch of the illusory body yoga and as a third auxiliary practice. In other words, the first three yogas, inner heat, illusory body, and clear light, are the real methods for accomplishing enlightenment in one lifetime. The last three yogas ... are only required if one fails to accomplish enlightenment before death draws near, and a forceful last-minute method of self-projection is required.[10]

This is clear in Milarepa's own teaching in the Cakrasaṃvara oral transmission in the *gDams ngag mdzod* text (folios 344–61), *bDe mchog snyan brgyud kyi lam blo nas gcod pa bar do ngo sprod kyi gdams ngag zab mo.*[11] More recent bKa' brgyud teachings drop the transference of consciousness into another body and divide the dream yoga from the illusory body yoga to make up a set of six.[12] The original name for the Six Yogas was perhaps "the oral instruction transmission for achieving liberation in the bardo," at least according to both Marpa and Milarepa. Mullin points out that this was known to rJe Tsong Khapa. Mila uses the term "the three blendings" in these works, which Mullin relates convincingly to the Six Yogas system.

19

The Enlightenment of Milarepa

Wishing to tie together these extraordinary teachings with their basis in Milarepa's own enlightenment, we now examine the key moment of attainment in detail. The attainment of enlightenment and the other siddhas, the so-called supreme or lesser spiritual achievements, seems to be inseparably linked to the *yogin*'s diet. In the biographical tradition of Milarepa, food is not a topic easily ignored. In the life of Milarepa by gTsang smyon, food is an important topic, most especially the practice of eating nettles, from which Milarepa's body turned green. The topic is even more important in the rGyal thang pa version of Milarepa's life because here it relates to Milarepa's attainment of enlightenment.

Upon his return to his native region to practice austerities in the mountains, Mila was provided with food by his sister Peta. Peta, left an orphan by the deaths of both mother and father and abandoned for many years by her brother (known then as a fearsome sorcerer), wandered about as a beggar. She shared her meager gatherings with Milarepa, much as even today in the Himalayas the family will provide food to a relative who is making a long retreat. As Peta saw it, Mila was in precarious health as a result of his austerities—he had become anorexic. Mila was already completely detached from any preoccupations he might have had about material nourishment and was serenely following the teachings of Ācārya Asaṅga (late fourth century CE) in the *Yogācārabhūmi* about food, being content with the minimum necessary (folios 223–24) as an indispensable material precondition for meditative attainment. In reply, Peta repeated the ancient canonical arguments on preferring moderation in all things, the Buddha's "middle way" veering neither toward self-indulgent gluttony and sensuality nor toward sterile, self-destructive asceticism. Yielding to his sister's insistence, Mila ate a bit more food than usual. The results were good: he partially experienced the illusory body and concluded, "A little food in the belly gives rise to spiritual experience" (folio 225).[1] Then Mila sang a *mgur* (sacred song) of gratitude and happiness upon having drunk some *chang*, or Tibetan barley beer.[2]

It is important to recognize in this reference linking food to the illusory body an allusion to that dimension of realization that was lacking to the primordial beings who tasted of the "sweet earth" in the "Buddhist Genesis" found in the Pali Canon and discussed in the *Abhidharmakośa* of Vasubandhu (see Table 20.1).[3] Only with the illusory body can the *yogin* experience deeply rebirth, death, and the intermediate state (*bardo*) between death and rebirth. The illusory body can only be generated by the practice of the highest class of tantras, which the Vajrayāna insists are indispensable for attaining the state of a Buddha. The goal of Mahāyāna Buddhism is to become a Buddha through traversing the path of a Bodhisattva, but the actual attainment of complete, perfect enlightenment requires the illusory body. According to rJe Tsong Khapa, commenting on the correspondence between stages of the life journey and the stages of tantric realization in such practice, "Meditation on the Dharmakāya constitutes the purification of death, because the Dharmakāya is equivalent to the experience of the primordial beings of the Clear Light of death. Meditation on the sambhogakāya enables the purification of the intermediate state ... and meditation on the Nirmāṇakāya is the purification of birth."[4] Thus the three bodies (*trikāya*) of a perfect Buddha are acquired by meditating in the illusory body, in the Illusory Samādhi, which, alone for a human being, allows an interior experience of death, rebirth, and of the state between death and rebirth. This illusory body, with its corresponding contemplative absorption (*samādhi*) is reached exclusively through the practice of the two stages of Yoga Tantra: the phase of creation (*utpatti-krama*) and the phase of completion (*sampanna-krama*).[5]

Only in this way may a human being bring about the Reversal of Energies[6] that maintain us in cyclic existence. Now let us see how rGyal thang pa explains Milarepa's experience of this process.

In the first place, the phase of creation refers to the practices of liturgical rites and interior visualizations empowered by the great initiations (*abhiṣekha*) that Marpa conferred on Milarepa upon the completion of years of labor, penance, and humiliation. Having perfected these practices, Mila acquired the "divine body" from the yidams, enabling him to undertake the subtler yogic processes of the phase of completion, which in his tradition is essentially the Nāro Chos Drug, or the Six Doctrines (or Yogas) of Nāropa, guru of Marpa. Milarepa's focus in practice was on the first of the six—namely, the yogic heat or "*gtum mo*" (*caṇḍālī*).

In the system of Asaṅga, heat together with perception is the basis for the vital force that transports a being from one existence to another and sustains life itself. Thus *gtum mo* is not merely a magical heat useful for yogic practice in cold climates; it is in itself a tantric practice that can actually bring the *yogin* to perfect enlightenment. It was through this practice, once he perfected it, that Mila merited the title "*ras pa*"—that is, one who wears only light cotton cloth in the cold of the Himalayas (folio 230). However, even more spectacular than *gtum mo* is the attainment realized during Mila's winter retreat at La Phyis Gang (folio 232–36, corresponding to chapter 2 in *The Hundred Thousand Songs of Milarepa*).

Traveling to Lho Brag, Mila stopped at Tsar ma of sNye nam in southern Tibet, not far from the present-day border of Nepal. There, the devout sponsor rNgog dor mo offered him some food for his retreat. The saint only accepted nine measures of cereals and then left for La Phyis mountain (near Everest). That very morning there was a terrific snowstorm that went on for eighteen days. There was so much snow that neither man nor beast could go out for seven months. Thinking that Mila was dead, the inhabitants of Tsar wept bitterly.

Milarepa was well aware of the seriousness of his situation in the hermitage and considered performing *'pho ba*—that is, the yogic expulsion of the aggregate of perception, *vijñāna*, from the body, in this way accepting his own inevitable death as a spiritual practice. In the light of what we have said about the connection between *dharmakāya* meditation and death, this decision was quite objectively correct and might have brought about perfect enlightenment in the intermediate state. However, a woman dressed in leaves suddenly appeared and said, "Do not perform expulsion (*'pho ba*)! You must eat contemplative absorption (*samādhi*). Day and night, you must only do the practices of creation and completion! We Dharma-master *ḍākinīs* will bless you. You will not die! We will take care of you"[7] (folio 232).

> Setting all worries aside, Mila meditated day and night in states of *samādhi*, experiencing various sensations: Now and then there was a feeling of cold; of snow blindness; of deafness, and so forth. There were many kinds of difficulty. Since he had nothing to eat, there was a feeling of weightlessness. He was stirred by the rush of interior energies and was stunned. Little by little, the clear light dawned and increased. In those seven months, having hardly enough food to fill the end of a spoon, meditating in a state of *samādhi*, taking his contemplation as food, the body was not overcome by death. From within, numerous signs of virtue arose (folio 232). At that time, immortality was achieved, the *siddhi* of life immortal (*tse'i dngos grub bgyi ba*); though sentient beings are impermanent, he manifested the opposite quality.[8] The apparition body is not dominated by death when one accomplishes this *siddhi*. He would now no longer need food ... he would now always be free of hunger. In this way, he realized the supreme attainment (folio 237). Manifesting the teachings for his disciples, he attained the dharmakāya, which is described as being unchanging, immovable, and fully accomplished. In short, he attained both the ordinary and the supreme *siddhi*.[9]

In the meantime, the disciples believed that Mila was dead and therefore celebrated the funeral rites in accordance with the *Bardo Thodol* (*Tibetan Book of the Dead*).[10] But as soon as it was possible to ascend to the hermitage, they came to find the saint near his cave, sitting amid the snow, with most of his food still uneaten (folio 234). He even offered to prepare it for them in compensation for the inconvenience they experienced in looking for his "corpse."

rNgog dor mo asked him how it was possible for him to survive such an experience. The saint replied, "The reason that I did not die is that I wear the clothing of yogic heat (*gtum-mo*); I eat the food of contemplative absorption,[11] I meditate on Guru-yoga and practice the creation and completion phases of meditation. With the help of deities (Tib.: *yidam,* Skt.: *iṣṭadevatā*, which are the divinities visualized in the Creation Phase of their respective tantric cycles) and of the *ḍākinīs*, I did not die" (folio 234).

In this account of the enlightenment of Milarepa, we have much that is allusive of the "Buddhist Genesis" and of Asaṅga's teaching on Reversal of Energies. Asaṅga explains that the body, the "dwelling of sentient beings," is necessarily constructed of four kinds of food in conjunction with what he calls the vital organ (*jīvitendriya*), or "vital force."[12] In order to reacquire the freedom and subtlety that beings have lost in this world cycle, it is necessary to "reverse" in stepwise fashion the stages of degeneration that sentient beings have undergone since they fell from the status of mind-made embodiment. Beings must now become detached from both the material food and the psychological nourishment that, far from sustaining them, only impedes their spiritual transformation. Therefore, Milarepa reverses his attachments to all kinds of food:

1. Material and morsel food—that is, barley, nettles, beer, and so on
2. The food of physical contact—that is, sensory experience
3. The food of the will—that is, the act that carries the vital force from one life to the next, related to yogic heat (*gtum mo*)

4. The food of perception—that is, the germ that becomes new life, informed by the will and sustained by vital force

Instead of eating material food, Milarepa ate the *samādhi* associated with the practice of deity and guru yoga. The senses, deprived of stimulation, were purified and manifested a series of symptoms indicating their complete reversal. Practicing the Six Yogas and making the fire of *gtum mo* to blaze up, he attained mastery over the will associated with the urge to be reborn from lifetime to lifetime. In the rush of interior energies, the clear light dawned as the very germ of consciousness itself became liberated from the residual stains of ignorance and attachment. No longer fixated on the "purity of things perceived as external objects" nor on the "freedom of the nature of the mind perceived as the inner subject," the *yogin* recognizes the "true face of utter lucidity" (*'od gsal; rang ngo shes pa ru*), the enduring and dynamic clear light. He is now free from hopes and fears, unlimited and unconditioned, and attains the supreme perfect enlightenment, in which one does not remain fixated in nirvāṇa (so that a true Buddha is neither confined to nirvāṇa nor forcibly reborn within saṁsāra), enjoying both perfect liberation and remaining available in infinite ways to assist those whose perceptions are yet limited to aspects of cyclic existence.[13]

In this state, Mila sang to his disciples, "Happy in equilibrium is the kingdom of the *yogin*'s body!"—that is, neither absorbed in worldliness nor extinguished in absolute liberation, the perfected *yogin* (as Vajradhara) identifies himself with the *dharmakāya* (all the reality that is), with the perceptive faculty (*vijñāna*), perfectly free like a mirror, untarnished by impurity, egoism, rage, desire, or ignorance. At that point in his realization, Milarepa "gave a significant teaching to his disciples on the non-duality of self and others (folio 236), having transcended even that fixation himself."[14]

Milarepa saw the Clear Light that winter at La Phyis Gang, which our authors are identifying as the self-luminosity that characterized the state of the primordial conscious beings who lived on ecstasy at the beginning of the cosmic cycle. They had that same luminosity, but, lacking the yogic illusory body (which can only be developed through the practice of the Six Yogas), they could not control, direct, or transform luminosity for the benefit of others. Thus they fell into attachments and distractions, yearning for the "tasty earth" and so forth, as shown in the "Buddhist Genesis" (*Aggañña Sutta*). Material bodies, sexuality, shame, theft, violence, and the caste system arose as a consequence of the corruption of those primordial luminous, motile beings.[15] Milarepa's rigorous asceticism coupled with the tantric practices of the lineage of Tilopa, Nāropa, and Marpa brought about a reversal of the energies of corruption, as predicted in Asaṅga's system seven hundred years earlier.

The *Mahāmudrā* (Great-Seal[16]) realization that Milarepa attained is in perfect harmony with the view that he received from the lineage, especially in the *Mahāmudropadeśa* of Tilopa.[17] The state of perfect enlightenment, according to Tilopa, goes beyond practices and thoughts (stanzas 3 and 5); when you have gone beyond rejecting and accepting, you are free in the great seal (stanza 6). The essence of your mental activity, the Clear Light, cannot be obscured by centuries of cyclic existence (stanza 13). Even the term "the clear light of mental activity" requires discretion, for authentic realization cannot be compassed by any verbal expressions. In his oral teachings (*gdams ngag*), Milarepa himself advises his disciples that it is better to realize voidness directly through yogic practice focusing on the central channel (*avadhūtī*) than to debate about ultimate reality using words (e.g., *Clarification of the Three Cycles*, folio 110). It is not that he himself is inept with words that he says this. In fact, he is quite skillful in articulating all the classic philosophical propositions of Madhyamaka, in addition to being able to guide others through the labyrinth of spiritual development with sacred songs (*mgur*). Milarepa shows how a truly realized Buddha can make use of verbal concepts, practices, and sharp-edged encounters to bring others compassionately toward realization. Taking matters along a gradual path determined above all by the needs of the persons to be liberated, Milarepa was able to catalyze an irreversible transformation of ground perception in others. Thus he was able to heal the faculty most wounded by the primordial degeneration upon which *saṁsāric* perception is based. His biography illustrates the following for us who are still "en route":

> Ordinary people possess erroneous perception,
> The Saints are the opposite: they perceive the truth.
> And the Buddhas, having a perfectly correct perception,
> Are detached from dualistic opinions.[18]

20

Tables

Spiritual Transformation

TABLE 20.1. THE STAGES IN THE EVOLUTION OF THIS WORLD-AGE[1]

A. The World of Radiant Light
   1. Beings
      a. are created out of mind,
      b. are nourished on ecstasy,
      c. are self-luminous,
      d. journey through space, and
      e. abide in glory.
   2. The primordial beings become human beings who are endowed with all the same characteristics.

B. There is a tasty earth on the surface of the waters, sweet as honey.

C. The primordial humans begin to eat the tasty earth.
   1. They lose their self-luminosity.
   2. The cycles of time begin.

D. Humans begin to know envy and lament the disappearance of the tasty earth.

E. Vegetation in the form of sweet mushrooms appears; then bamboo shoots appear.

F. Humans, having eaten greedily, lament the disappearance of these foods.

G. The ideal rice emerges:
   1. Eating it gives rise to male-female differentiation.
   2. Knowledge of the physical distinction produces the following:
      a. Passion
      b. Heat
      c. The first sex acts
   3. Society condemns sexual relations as shameful.

H. The first shelters are erected in order to hide the sex act.

I. Laziness causes people to gather rice for more than one meal:
   1. Rise loses its perfection.
   2. Fields are divided up among owners.

J. Persons begin to steal rice; as a consequence, people fall into the practices of censure, lying, and punishment.

K. Because of criminality, society agrees to select leaders and police. This gives rise to the *Kṣatriya varṇa,* the warrior caste.

L. The origin of *Brahmana varṇa* (Brahmin caste) is attributed to a return to idealism.

TABLE 20.2. THE FOUR TYPES OF FOOD: PRODUCTION AND SUSTENANCE OF THE DWELLING PLACE OF BEINGS IN THE SYSTEM OF ASAṄGA

A. Material food in the form of mouthfuls

B. The food of physical (sensory) contact (the bodily senses are believed to extend themselves to gather input)

C. The food of the will

D. The food of (simple) perception (which lies behind the operation of the physical senses)

TABLE 20.2. EACH OF THESE FOUR FORMS OF NUTRITION BRINGS ABOUT THE FOLLOWING FOUR CORRESPONDING RESULTS

A. The mouthfuls are the basic sustenance of a body composed of organs.

B. Sensory contact nurtures the sense-bases to sustain the personality.

C. The will is constitutive of the act that launches a new existence from the intermediate state between birth and death.

D. Perception (pure or simple consciousness) is the seed launched from the intermediate state, propelled by the will, which becomes a new existence.

E. Vital force is that which sustains heat and perception.

TABLE 20.3. THE TWO PHASES OF TANTRIC PRACTICE

A. The phase of creation (or of generation; Sanskrit: *utpatti-krama;* Tibetan: *skye rim*)
   1. is constitutive of the path,
   2. generates the illusory body of the yidam deity within the *yogin,* and
   3. generates an interior state in which the yogin is able to contemplate efficaciously the following:
      a. birth
      b. the intermediate state
      c. death

B. The phase of completion (or perfection; Sanskrit: *sampanna-krama;* Tibetan: *rdzogs rim*)
   1. constitutes the fruition and consists of two stages:
      a. the practices executed with form (e.g., the six yogas) and
      b. the practices executed without form (i.e., formless *mahāmudrā*), whereupon

2. the yogin, abiding in the illusory *samādhi* of the formless *mahāmudrā,* completes the accumulations of merit and wisdom and
3. by the force of this merit, is empowered to manifest the three bodies of the Buddha *(trikāya)* as follows:
   a. *Nirmāṇakāya,* the appearance body of a Buddha
   b. *Sambhogakāya,* the perfect enjoyment body
   c. *Dharmakāya,* the body of that-which-is

TABLE 20.4. THE SIX YOGAS OF NĀROPA (FROM *VAJRA VERSES OF THE WHISPERED TRADITION* BY THE MAHĀSIDDHA NĀROPA)[2]

1. Inner heat yoga
2. Illusory body yoga
3. Dream yoga
4. Clear light yoga
5. Consciousness transference yoga
6. Forceful projection yoga

EXTRA TOPICS

- *Karmamudrā*
- Yoga of cultivating the correct view (advanced *mahāmudrā* meditation)
- *Bardo* (intermediate state) yogas: apply all previous methods to the experiences of daily life, dreams, and death

TABLE 20.6. THE SPECIAL PRELIMINARY PRACTICES

1. Refuge and awakening the enlightened altruistic motivation (*bodhicitta*)
2. Offering the maṇḍala
3. Vajrasattva purification practice
4. Guru yoga practice (hymns, mantras)

Part Three

Texts in Translation

21

The Biography of Milarepa by rGyal thang pa bDe chen rDo rJe

Folio 189: This is the biography of the Saint (*rje btsun*)[1] Victor Milarepa (*mid la*[2] *ras pa*).

Folio 190: Honor to the guru!

For this purpose, I have written the biography of one called Saint Milarepa in which there are two categories: there is the presentation of the root-text and the explanation of its meaning in a commentary. First, there is the root verse giving the doctrine:

Honor to the Lord
Guru Victory Banner!
The Saint-Guru, Lord Milarepa
Who emanates an excellent illusory body,
By which one may be spiritually disciplined,
Which took on ordinary guise, and performed
Various types of austerities;
Thus I bow down to the Lord who attained the virtues. (1)
In order to bring to fruition the causal connections with previously established aspirations[3]
He was born in rTsa ba'i lung (Grassy Valley), one of the five small towns
In the border region of South Tibet, in the human realm;
I bow down to the place of birth of the Saint (2)
As for the family in which Mila was born,—the lineage of his father's ancestors—
The clan was not great

Folio 191:

He was a son of a low-caste clan[4]
In a family of no great repute, with few members, and without a genealogy;
I bow down to the family from which the Saint came. (3)
Into that setting, the Saint Milarepa
Entered the womb of his mother when she was tired;
During sleep, in a dream, she foresaw great difficulties;
I bow down to the Saint's entry into the womb. (4).
Thus, having entered the womb, when the ninth month was going on to the tenth,
On the fifteenth day of the lunar month,
There were auspicious planets and stars,
With omens and signs signifying that the Lord was to be born;
I bow down to the time of birth of the Saint. (5)
The Lord was carefully and affectionately cared for by his father:
When his father died, he was harmed and injured by all;
Mother and children being impoverished,
[He] learned to sing songs and received fees from everyone;
I bow down to the Saint's time of troubles. (6)
The Saint, having learned to sing songs,
Was able to care for his mother and sister as well,
By means of the fees earned by his excellent recitation.
But they were despised by all who stole from them, robbed them and afflicted them;
I bow down to the disheartening sorrows of the Saint. (7)
Being admonished by his mother, he went east to the province of dBus,
Where he sought for the knowledge of magical power and received the skill of producing magical hailstorms;

By means of magic he unleashed hailstorms upon the land of his enemies;
I bow down to the Saint, great in magic power. (8)
The magical power of hailstorms caused him dismay,
And renunciation arose in him;
True and reverent faith having arisen,
He became mindful of the divine Dharma of the Holy One;
He relied upon the holy Lama G.yu Thog Lha dGa';

Folio 192:

I bow down to the prophecy about Saint Marpa (given to Mila by Lha dGa'). (9)
He went before Marpa, requesting provisions and the Dharma;
The Saint (Mila) was well cared for by the Lady's kindness;
The Saint (Marpa) told him that the Dharma is difficult to practice and imposed the service of heavy labor upon him;
I bow down to the difficult labor performed by the Saint. (10)
Even though he revered and served Marpa,
The Lady could not persuade him to bestow the Holy Dharma;
She said: "Lama rNgog will bestow the profound Dharma practices."
I bow down to the Saint's success in obtaining the Dharma. (11)
Accompanying this master and his disciples,
He went before Marpa;
Having exhausted karmic obscurations,
He was now a vessel worthy of instructions;
He mastered all the teachings and spiritual advice;
I bow down to the prophecy[5] of the Saint's future success in Dharma practice. (12)

Possessing the essential oral instructions, Saint Milarepa,
Having obtained all the teachings, became mindful of his
mother and sister;
He went before the Lama (Marpa) asking to return to his own
region;
I bow down to the Saint's receiving permission. (13)
Having thus obtained permission, at the point of departure,
He bowed to the father and mother and received their
blessing;
Out of devotion to the Lady he placed his head beneath her
feet seven times;
I bow down to the Saint, overcome by the force of sincere
faith. (14)
From there he went up to rTsa in Gung Thang.
His mother was dead; the field was dried out; the house had
fallen down;
His sister had been expelled from her land;
Immeasurable sorrow (*ngen-shes*) arose (in him);
I bow down to the song of the arising of the thought of
renunciation of the Saint. (15).
His sister Peta heard that the Saint had returned;
At the White Rock meditation cave,
His sister came to meet him;
The sister, having embraced him, weeping in torment,
Fell down in a faint;
I bow down to the Saint and his sister at their meeting. (16)
He practiced renunciation at Ling ra and other places;
He practiced meditation and severe asceticism in the six
cliff-caves;
Without a companion, in solitude, he erected the
Victory Banner of striving for attainment;

Folio 193:

I bow down to the culmination of the Saint's ascetic practice. (17)
At that time he went to Snye-nam;
He begged from a householder-patron who provided him with supplies,
But he did not reside there; he went to the snow-mountain La Phyis;
I bow down to the Saint, meditating in the snowy ranges. (18)
After passing seven months there, the Saint was thought to have died;
Some people went to see what happened to the Saint;
Since they found that the Saint had not died,
They invited him to their town;
I bow down to the Saint who inspires wonder. (19)
He, the Lord, then went to meditate
In the solitude of Seng ge gling of Mon gyi kha dod;
Even there he attained immeasurable virtue;
To you, o Holy Saint, I bow down. (20)
Then, when he resided in sNye nam brod bu;
His aunt and sister heard about his reputation;
They went to see the Saint to invite him to both households;
I bow down to the song of meeting with the Saint. (21)
He dwelt between Brin and Chu-bar;
Innumerable signs, omens, wonders, and warnings were made
By Tshe ring ma and innumerable attendant goddesses and demons,
I bow down to the kindness[6] of the Lama that entirely destroyed them. (22)
The Lord went to the Valley of the Land of Snye-nam,

To liberate a Bon-po of Snye-nam who was wandering in the intermediate state.[7]
The learned scholar Dar Blo achieved true faith by his kindness;
I bow down to the One who subdued the assembly[8] of the monks. (23)
Thus for the male and female patrons in Brin,
Spiritual understanding arose
When he flew down a precipice [*nams rtogs shar dang cong la 'phur ba dang*]:
The Saint Lama Bhagavān was seen as Tārā[9] [*sgrol mar mthong*]
I bow down to the Saint who possesses virtue. (24)
Thus the Saint Mila the *yogin*,
Not abiding in that land, went to the three provinces of Western Tibet;
In southern g.Yas Ru, north of a part of the land of gTsang; and so on;
I bow down to the wandering [of the Saint]
Who was without attachment to any hermitage.[10] (25)
In the same way the Saint Lama subdued the Four Demons

Folio 194:

And possessed the six perfections;
Having brought his labors to completion,
He showed the way to pass away.[11]
I bow down to the Saint who is completely liberated (26).[12]
Thus the verses of praise were composed.
This is the biography of the Saint-Victor Milarepa written in words of praise, prepared by rGyal thang pa bde chen rdo rje.
Lord Milarepa, who has emanated an excellent illusory body (*mchog gi skus*),[13]

Who took an ordinary appearance,
I bow down to him, who has acquired immeasurable virtue
by various ascetical practices. (1)

This is the meaning:[14]

Thus the Saint-Victor named Milarepa did this: In general, he is only an illusory manifestation (Tibetan: *rnam par 'phrul ba*; Sanskrit: *vikurvāṇa*) of a Buddha. So he has come in an ordinary manner in this era of the spread of the five corruptions (*snyigs ma lnga; kaṣāya*). Thus he also served the aims of the ordinary sentient beings.

From a *Sūtra*:
The Blessed One, a perfect Buddha,
In the era of the spreading of the Five Corruptions,
By his illusory manifestation in which every means for forming [disciples] is [found],
Accomplishes the aims of beings;
Sometimes he practices asceticism;
Sometimes he goes about in an ordinary manner, etc.
Also, it is stated in the *Vajra-pañjara Tantra*:
Even appearing as ice, he accomplishes the aims of sentient beings;
Even appearing as a lion, he accomplishes the aims of sentient beings;
And as a woman who sells beer,
Even appearing as a prostitute, he accomplishes the aims of sentient beings;
Even as an ordinary person and appearing in an inferior caste,
He accomplishes the aims of sentient beings.
Thus, a perfect Buddha, manifesting as an ordinary person in an impure caste, accomplishes the aims of sentient beings, so it is said.[15]
Even the Saint-Victor Milarepa, in accordance with the capacity of ordinary persons, manifested as the body of an ordinary person.

Folio 195:

Thus it is to be concluded that he came so as to achieve the aims of ordinary persons. The Saint himself said to Lama Ras chung pa and Zhi ba 'od: "In your opinion, who am I?" He [further] inquired: "What is your understanding?" Zhi ba 'od replied: "According to my capacity for understanding, I think that you are no less than a Buddha." The Lama said to him: "This you are doing out of devotion, at this moment of time. This one ('I') was foretold by Buddha himself; I came as an illusory manifestation of Buddha himself, I was once Ācārya Ārya Nāgārjunagarbha;[16] I am an illusory manifestation of him in this birth." Then, the Saint Victor Milarepa said: "This is an illusory manifestation of Buddhahood, a true Nāgārjuna-garbha:[17] and according to the capacity of ordinary persons, I have now emanated as the body of an ordinary person; I have come for the welfare of ordinary persons."

Thus, the Saint Victor Milarepa was born in the ordinary Mid-la family; having been born, his ordinary body went without eating and without putting on clothes.[18] He acquired virtues through the practice of various kinds of asceticism. In this time of the spread of the five corruptions, he came for the sake of ordinary sentient beings.

By the force[19] of aspirations co-dependently arisen in former times.
He was born in rTsa-ba'i Lung, one of the Five Small Towns,
In a border territory, in the south of Tibet, in the human realm.
I bow down to the birthplace of the Saint. (2)

This is the meaning:

Then the Saint Victor Milarepa, whose ancestors were generally of the Yas

Folio 196:

Cod clan according to human pedigree, in general were workers in Bar Phug. During the time of his ancestors, the land was lost. Thereupon, his forefather set out alone as a trader. Having made a sizable (*tshad*) bet (*thebs*) at dice (*cho lo*), he exhausted all his wealth, being burdened with many debts. He could not endure remaining in that place. At that time, many merchants from the northern region came down to rTsa of Gung Thang.[20] This ancestor provided a kind of inn for the traders. The family did business with the traders. Thus they set themselves up in rTsa of Gung Thang. That country, in general, was called the Five Small Towns. These were called Ron pa, dMungs, Shag pa, dGun pa, and rTsa pa.[21] The Saint's birthplace was called rTsa; his father went there first and having acquired (land) he founded a house on the land. These facts about the place of his birth enable one to recognize it.

The paternal family lineage of Mila family shows
That he was the child of low caste commoners;
It was not a great family; his family was of no
Great repute, with few members and without even a
genealogy;
I bow down to the family in which took place the advent of
the Saint. (3)

This is the meaning:

This is the family heritage of the Mid la clan of the Saint Victor Milarepa. His grandfather was Mid la Vajra Victory Banner; his father was called Mid la Wisdom Banner. His mental continuum was good; he was friendly to all; also, he knew a small amount of the doctrines of the rNying ma pa. When he attained the age of twenty, he laid claim to, acquired, and settled in the place called rTsa of Gung Thang. On that occasion, in what was called the Five Small Towns, there were but few who owned little portions of the land.

Folio 197:

There were only one or two family dwellings on the land. They thought: "Should the fire die out, from where shall we obtain it? If our provisions give out, from whom shall we borrow?" It was a very sad place. Mila's father married a woman of that place named Myang tsha dkar rgyan ma. They dwelt happily. There were not many people in the human lineage of Milarepa. There was only a single son from each father; therefore, they were an object of contempt to all. The burden of taxes and compulsory labor (*corvée*) was very great on them. Very great difficulties arose; they were at the point of giving up their land. It was then that the mother was going to abandon the father. One morning when the mother was dreaming, a woman appeared who had the signs of ugliness.

Well, now, Listen! Lady White-Ornament (dKar legs man);
Your true husband is Wisdom Banner;
The Mid la family is not good,
Their lineage is not great—it is ordinary,
He himself is in bad shape;
However a son will soon be born to you,
Bearing auspicious signs;
Therefore, do not give up; stay and be happy;
Having said this and having patted her on the head, she disappeared. This is an account of the paternal family heritage of the Saint.[22]

Thus, the Saint, Milarepa,
Entered the womb of his mother when she herself was exhausted;
During sleep, in a dream, she foresaw great difficulties;
I bow down to the Saint's entry into the womb. (4)

This is the meaning:

Then the Saint, Milarepa, in the womb of the [woman] who was called Nang lam dkar legs ma,[23] on the eighth day of the month Stag-pa,[24] while he was abiding in the womb of his mother, she herself became very tired and while she

Folio 198:

slept she had a particular dream; the dream occurred just like this: One evening, with faith, the mother was fording a river both wide and pure. During her crossing of the river, she was blocked; hardship and difficulty[25] without measure arose. Afterwards, however, she managed just barely to escape; thus, a dream-omen occurred.

Another evening, the mother dreamt that she ascended a great mountain. The ascent of that mountain was accompanied by great hardship and difficulty so that she could not [proceed]; finally, she just barely managed to ascend. Another evening, she dreamt of a ladder going upward into the atmosphere—a long ladder that she was ascending.[26] She felt trapped on the ladder by great hardship and difficulty but finally she just barely managed to get free ... [In another dream], the cub of a lioness was being brought up and nourished, great hardship and difficulty necessarily occurred, etc. [i.e., but finally things turned out well]. It was in just this way that dream omens came to his mother during her pregnancy. Even her experiences during the daytime such as spinning, carrying burdens, etc., in every way whatever, she had hardships and ceaseless difficulties. But afterwards, when the labor was done, very pure things were produced. Such things involving hardship and difficulty came about during the time of her pregnancy.

In this way, the ninth month having passed,
In the first half of the tenth month of pregnancy,
On the fifteenth day of the month there were good stars and
planets.
The Lord was born accompanied by signs and portents;
I praise and revere the time of the birth of the saint. (5)

This is the meaning:

The Saint, in the first half of the tenth lunar month, in the sheep year (*lug-gi lo*),[27] in the month of the Pleiades (*kārtika*; November–December, under the sign of Scorpio), on the fifteenth day of the month, at sunrise, a cow was giving birth to a calf; as soon as it was born

Folio 199:

that cow produced two and one-half gallons of creamy milk (in Gung Thang?). This, being churned, produced two and one half gallons of butter of Gung Thang. [?]

Inside [the house?] they had two and one-half gallons of barley and thought of fermenting beer for the invocation of the deities at the birth of the little boy. They brought out the barley, which increased to 500 gallons.[28]

The mountain of butter produced filled up ten scales; happiness arose together with good omen when the 500 gallons of butter were produced.

At the time of the birth, his father, Shes rab rGyal mtshan, had gone to undertake business in the land of dGun. Someone was sent out to that place to tell the father that he had a son. They told the father: "Yesterday your wife gave birth to a son; you are requested to come up for the naming ceremony." Having smiled, the father said: "Hearing the news now [makes] this a happy report! Thus, I will name the boy right away!" So his son was given the name Happy Report (*thos pa dga'*). These good omens and happy events occurred at the birth of the Saint.

His father protected and cherished him very much;
When his father died, he suffered, being harmed by all;
The mother and children were bereft of everything;
He learned singing so as to obtain alms from all.
I bow down and praise the Saint's time of troubles. (6)

This is the meaning:

The Lord Mila Happy Report, since he was the only son of his father, was very much protected and cherished. He dwelt in great happiness. After three years, a daughter was also born. She was adorned with the name Peta. Thus, parents and children all dwelt together in happiness and even some enjoyment.

Folio 200:

After some years, the father was stricken by a disease of the lungs. It could not be expelled by any means, so he died. All the property was taken on behalf of the father's side of the family; nothing whatever remained for the mother and the two children. Some relatives and neighbors criticized [his] faults to the mother and children. They even carried off much of the mother's property (she had a copy of the *Ratnakuṭa Sūtra*) (*dkon rtsegs gcig*). There was no inheritance for them! The mother and two children lived this way. At that time, the mother raised the brother and sister by working at the loom, weaving and spinning. After the father's death, their wealth exhausted, they were looked upon with contempt by all the people. They were short of food and clothing and they were emaciated.

At that time in the town there was a teacher who was a tantrika. He knew how to read and to teach reading. Mila served him as an assistant in the rituals. He provided for his mother and sister with the leftover food from the rituals, received as an offering for his reading. Even by this, they were not much benefited.

The Saint learned to sing a song from a bard (*glu mkhan*). He provided for his mother and sister with the fees from singing, but even this was not enough.[29]

All the neighbors and relatives were continuously stealing from them, making use of their property, and beating them for no reason. The mother and her two children were not at all happy. These things awakened an immeasurable sense of renunciation in the Saint as well as compassion for the misery experienced by sentient beings.

> Admonished by his mother, he set out east for dBus,[30] there
> to learn from a magician all about the magic power of
> producing hailstorms,
> So as to bring down hail on the land of his foes:
> I bow down to the Saint, possessor of great magical power. (8)

This is the meaning:

Folio 201:

At that time, the so-called Mila "Happy Report" was trying to obtain fees for his singing on a street in the village. It happened that his mother met her son there with tears pouring from her eyes. She said: "So this was the son I bore! You are unable to harm your hated enemies even with the point of a needle! You cannot benefit your beloved family with so much as the tip of a hair! What a rotten son has been born to Mid la Shes rab rGyal mtshan! I, your mother, and you my children are beaten up. We have been deprived of whatever we had in the house. What good is there in this singing of yours?" Saying this, she tossed about rocks and dirt. Mila Happy Report fled inside. Along with the fees he got from reading and from singing, and a sack of roasted barley and a sack of some barley, etc., he gathered up what few things he had. He was beaten by his mother and sister. They pulled the hairs on the back of his head.[31]

On that occasion, the mother and children consulted. The mother said: "Now, there is no hope for us, mother and children,[32] in this life we are living in this place. We have no alternatives. My son, hasten to dBus to learn magic. I would like to pay back these people with sickness of heart," so she said. Having made this speech, she resolved on a course of action. Accompanied by a few friends, she sold the field that was her property and she bought a sorrel-colored horse named Te la grags. Furthermore, she made up a sack of the fees and goods they had managed to earn. Mila went off carrying the sack to dBus. His mother and sister went to see him off; they arrived at Pal ma Glorious-Plain. She offered her son her love; she gave him much advice. He went off, together with many traders who had come from Khams. Then he arrived in dBus and asked around for a great magician.

Folio 202:

Near Yar Lung sgur po, there was no one greater than G.yu ston Khro rgyal ba the sorcerer.[33] [Mila] went from Kha rag to Yar Lung. He met G.yu ston Khro rgyal and came before him. He offered the dark brown horse and its burden of goods. He gave an exact account of his former sufferings, requesting the sorcerer to be so kind as to take an interest in him and provide him with both provisions and the teachings of magic power. The sorcerer replied: "Other suppliants have offered vast amounts such as the *Perfection of Wisdom in One Hundred Thousand Lines* (*mdo sde 'bum*), but you alone have offered all you have.

You have tasted affliction, therefore you must abide here one year, whereupon I will quickly bestow the teachings of magic. I will provide whatever you need to succeed in the sorcery of hailstorms, etc."

Then Mila Happy-Report shed tears, having again given a full account of the afflictions that had occurred to his mother and her children; his heart was seized with much grief! G.yu ston also shed tears; "Alas, no one more pitiable than you has previously come before me; you really need magic power—I speak from my heart. I have a friend named sNying Khro rgyal who is a greater sorcerer than I; he is a Bon po. This Bon po and I have exchanged magical teachings for we are friends.[34] I obtained the teachings on the magical production of hailstorms from him without difficulty. I have an oath not to pass this knowledge on to others. Therefore, go to request this from him."

He gave [Mila] a white mare loaded with roots used for dyeing; Mila went before the Bon po, offered the horse and pigment and re-told the story of his many afflictions.

Folio 203:

Then he asked him, out of compassion, to transmit (*btag 'tshal*) the teachings of magic. The Bon po said: "Among the many people who have come before me for this technique, no one has come who has previously suffered as much as you have." And he, too, began to weep. Then he transmitted the technique of magic to Mila Happy-Report and to his own son.

They were enclosed so as to perform the [fearsome] rites of propitiation.[35] They recited mantras [*zlas pa*] for a month; signs that the magic had taken effect completely began to appear. At the same time, in his native village, having directed his power against the enemies who had hated his mother and sister, within three days this power was unleashed on them. Among those who hated them, the son of his uncle, G.yu rGyal, was about to be married. A group of people was gathered for the feast and the house suddenly fell on them unaware. Twenty-five (*nyi shu rtsa lnga*) of those who had shown hatred for mother and children, the inimical fathers and sons died. Those who did not die were possessed by demons.

"It was I, Mila Happy-Report, who unleashed this! You have become food suitable for the demons! All those possessed by demons are to die!"

In summary, all this was done to the family of his enemies; it came about that one old lady did not die. Thus it came about that the story was passed along and reached dBus. Then the Bon po said: "My son, it was good for you to compel me; offer a goat in thanks to my deity. There only remains one old lady; so we are satisfied. It would be easy to kill her too!"

Then the people of rTsa and Ron pa villages deliberated, saying, "It is not worth it to kill these two, mother and daughter, but it is expedient to kill him!" To do this, they hired three men. After making preparations, they sent them to kill Mila Happy Report.

Folio 204:

Then a *yogin* arrived at the home of the mother and the sister; he offered to convey a message to Mila. The news they sent in a letter was: "Son, you are successful. By the force of your power, all our enemies have died. We obtained a small parcel of things and also a small quantity of provisions. We are now (*da rung*) sending you the provisions thus obtained. Do not come back to our town. Make hail against the townsfolk! Men have gone to kill you. Be attentive to that also!" This was the message they sent. Then the *yogin* went quickly to dBus, where he met Mila Happy Report and passed on the aforementioned messages. Mila Happy Report was satisfied. He rewarded the *yogin* with more food, who returned. On the road he met the men who were sent to kill Mila. He engaged them in conversation and persuaded them that Mila had escaped from their plan to kill him [by foreseeing it]; knowing (*rig nas*) this, they returned to the village.

Then Mila Happy Report went to see the Bon po. He requested him to be so kind as to help him unleash a hailstorm on the town of his enemies. The Bon po said: "I have a technique for doing it. Entrust yourself to me. I will show you."

Thus, the technique of causing hailstorms was taught. It took a month to accomplish. They recited mantras and inserted a powder into a boiling substance.[36] This gave rise to violent thunder, etc.—all the omens. Hail arrived at the town of rTsa pa in Gung Thang. The entire harvest of nearly ripe ears of barley—all of it—was smashed by the fall of hail. The hail was sent to pass over the other mountains and streams. In fact, this kind of destructive hail fell for many years and all the enemies were overthrown. In brief, by these deeds, Mila Happy Report,

Folio 205:
having gone to dBus, learned the techniques of destructive magic.

A sense of revulsion and of renunciation arose in him,
because of his use
Of the magic power of destruction and hail.
He remembered the sacred Dharma of the Holy One [*dam pa'i*]
And devout faith grew within him;
He relied upon a holy lama, 'Bre ston Lha dGa';
I bow down to the prophecy about Saint Marpa. (9)

And this is the explication:

The Lord Mila Happy Report destroyed many people by his magic and destroyed fields with hail, thus causing great misery and harm to beings. Immeasurable grief and penitence grew within him. He went before Lama g.Yu ston Khro rgyal, saying, "On my own, I asked you, my Guru, for the two teachings on hail and sorcery, in which I have succeeded. By relying on that power, I have heaped up an immense negative karma by having caused the death of sentient beings. At dawn this morning, immeasurable grief arose in me. Now I offer a confession of all my sins. Please, holy Lama, consider granting me a Doctrine [*chos*] giving rise to sacred Buddhahood in one body, in one lifetime."[37] Thus he supplicated. The Lama said: "Very well! I have many teachings by which you can become a Buddha in one life in one body, but I cannot be your Guru.[38] In Upper Nyang there resides a holy, perfected Lama named 'Bre ston Lha dGa'. Go there to request the holy Doctrine."

Both he and the Bon po furnished Mila with many provisions for Dharma practice. He went to Upper Nyang and met Lama 'Bre ston Lha dGa', telling him all that he had previously done. The Lama said: "My son, you are a very great sinner. Practicing the method of rDzogs-chen[39] under my guidance in the morning, you can realize Buddhahood that morning; learning it in the evening, you become a Buddha that evening. Overcoming all sin,

Folio 206:

you can become a Buddha in one body, in one lifetime; I will teach you this holy Dharma practice."

Mila was very delighted with that. He listened to the Teaching and [tried] to practice. But the power descending through the Lineage had no effect.[40] He therefore supplicated the Lama, who said: "How many sins have you heaped up?" Mila replied: "Previously I have sinned using magic power, hail, etc." He retold the story in detail.

The Lama said: "I had no idea that you had so much sin! How can I be your spiritual guide?"[41] And he, too, shed many tears. "Now, my son, the Lama who is going to be your spiritual guide is a direct disciple of the great Saint Nāropa, named Marpa Lotsawa,[42] who dwells in Lho Brag. Go to him and ask for Dharma teachings. He is capable (*thub pa*) of being your spiritual guide. I too will go to him for Dharma; I will take you to him." Thus the teacher and the disciple set out together.

Then, on the way, Mila Happy Report asked Lama 'Bre ston: "What is Lama Marpa like? What Doctrine does he know? What Guru did he serve? What virtues does he possess?" The Lama expounded the virtues and biography (*rnam par thar pa*) of Lama Marpa in detail. Mila Happy Report, hearing such virtue on the part of the Lama, and trusting in it (*rten nas*), experienced limitless inner devotion and made many prostrations toward the place where Marpa dwelt. He also bowed to Lama 'Bre ston, placing his feet on his own head.[43] "Holy Lama, please consider accepting me and acting as my spiritual guide. It would be very kind of you!" Thus he supplicated.

By these deeds, Mila Happy Report, burdened by the accumulated karma of evil deeds done by the power of sorcery and hail, experienced renunciation

Folio 207:

and generated immense devotion toward his guru.

He came before Marpa to ask for the Dharma along with
provisions;
The Saint was cared for by the compassionate Lady;
For the sake of Dharma, which is hard to acquire,
The Saint performed labors:
I bow down to the Saint as he performs hard labor! (10)

This is the explication:

Then Lord Mila Happy Report, having shown reverence to 'Bre ston, with whom he intended to go on, but Lama 'Bre ston completely fainted, and remained stupefied. Thus, Mila Happy Report set out for the presence of Lama Marpa on his own. He arrived at Lho Brag and went up toward Marpa's dwelling place. He met three *tantrikas* (*sngags pa*), the master (*dpon*) and two servants (*g.yos gnyis*), plowing a hard, dried-out field. He asked them: "In this territory there is a Lama named Marpa bLo gros, a genuine heart-son disciple of the Holy Guru Glorious Nāropa. Where is his dwelling place?"

The elder *tantrika* replied: "I am going to seek an audience with him. You yourself should finish this plowing." He then went off to a nearby house.

Mila carefully plowed the field. After a little while, having finished the plowing, he sat down and waited. From inside the house, he was invited to come up, so he went in. There the *tantrika* who had been plowing was sitting on a rug, clothed in a yellow gown. He was cleaning the dirt from his face. When they met, he was seated with a rather serious look on his face. Mila pondered: "A little while ago, this was the very same one who was doing the plowing."[44] As he reflected, he did many prostrations. Having offered something as a kind of present,

Folio 208:

he recounted in detail his former deeds. "I heard of your fame, o Lama, and I come before you supplicating your kind consideration. Please grant me both the Dharma and provisions for study, in your kindness, since I yearn to know." Marpa said: "If you want provisions, no teachings; if you want teachings, no provisions. I bestow only one, not both! You yourself must choose."[45]

Mila replied, "In that case, please, in your compassion, grant me the Dharma. I will provide whatever is necessary by gathering alms."

Marpa said: "In that case you need to perform labor as a fee for the Dharma. Go gather provisions and come right back."

Mila Happy Report went off into the neighborhood that morning, sometimes offering a song (*glu*); thus he performed his alms rounds. In that neighborhood he obtained much barley so he came back carrying a full sack. He offered the barley to the Lama's wife, saying: "I will perform whatever service you need, o Lady. Please give me a little of this barley to eat." Thus he supplicated the kind Lady. He exerted himself in the service of the Lady and she cherished him and took care of him.

Then the Lama said: "You are called Mila Happy Report. It is said that you have performed mighty sorcery. If my enemy came against me in the morning you are to slay him that morning with sorcery."[46]

"Great Sorcerer, now I am going to build a fort named Srog mkhar skya bo. You are to carry all the stones as your fee for the Dharma."

For this project, Mila went down in the morning

Folio 209:

and exerted himself for a long time, carrying stones. A sore appeared on his back. Then, the Lady went before Marpa and asked: "Let him rest until the sore on his back is healed." The Lama said: "Let him now carry the load of stones on his right shoulder." And so he did, for a long time.

And a sore appeared on the right shoulder also. The Lady made the same request as before, but the Lama said: "Let him now carry the load on the left shoulder." So he exerted himself at this labor for a long time and wore out a sore on the left shoulder. From carrying rocks, three sores broke out. But not one word of Dharma teaching was bestowed.

The Lady furnished him with a round lump of butter and a carcass of meat. She said: "Use this as an initiation fee. This evening someone is going to be initiated. You, too, should go in to the rite of initiation."

Lama Mila entered to be initiated and offered the two items. Marpa looked over them carefully. Then he said: "This is the very meat that was given to me as a gift by a devout patron; and this butter is the same butter offered by the patroness Tho pe mo! Having stolen my meat and butter, you have dared to ask for an initiation!" He dragged Mila Happy Report by the hair and threw him out. He was not admitted to the initiation.

The Lady said: "He suffered immensely doing that work for you; he carried rock on his back until sores broke out. Who would have done such a thing—to produce a sore on a man?[47] He is not a beast of burden. Bestow the Dharma on him now, at this time. It would be better to let him leave to go wherever he may go if the Dharma is not to be completely transmitted at this time. It is not he who is asking you; it is I myself. You should know that I provided him with the meat and butter and advised him to come to you for the Dharma,

Folio 210:

but you would not bestow it."

The Lama said: "If he desires the Dharma, let him quickly build this fort."

"How can he do it? Now there are many sores!"

"Just as one makes a sore-ring for a beast of burden, make a sore-ring on his back so he can carry rocks. Then I will consider his request." This is what the Lama ordered.

"He desires the holy Dharma, but he needs to clean away the defilements of karma; thus he is useful to me."

So, the Lady made a sore-ring and Mila transported the rock with effort. His hands and feet became very weak[48] because of the sores and the flesh of his body was exhausted with pain. He completed the fort with nine stories named sKu mKhar skya bo. [49]

These are the deeds Mila Happy Report performed, serving the Lama endowed with holiness, performing work according to the Lama's orders, with difficulties without measure.

> The Lama, though revered, would not listen to his request for the holy Dharma;
> The Lady could not prevail upon him to admit Mila to the Doctrine;
> She said: rNgog will bestow all the profound Siddha Dharma (*sgrubs zab mo'i chos kun gnang*);
> I bow down to his success in learning the Dharma. (11)

This is the exposition:

Mila Happy Report, in this way, through penance and difficulty, succeeded with the Lady as his benefactress. Since Marpa did not wish to bestow even a word of Dharma, the Lady out of kindness now recommended a course of action. Since the Dharma was not being bestowed at all, he was sick at heart. She gave him a portion of goods and he went before the Dharma Rock-cave of rNgog to request the Dharma in great earnest.

Folio 211:

She secretly provided Mila with a bit of food and provisions along with a hair from the head of glorious Nāropa. She said: "Hurry so as to ask for the Dharma; Marpa has been unwilling from the start to bestow it. Both Lamas can do it. Since Marpa has been putting off giving you the teachings, go to him." So Mila Happy Report went before the Lama and asked to be allowed to obtain the Dharma from Lama rNgog. He went quickly and supplicated.

Lama Marpa said: "O my good man, you are unhappy because I have not bestowed the Dharma. The Great Pandit Nāropa granted me the profound essence of many oral instructions, so you had better stay here with me!"

Once more, Mila went away in a hurry. He then quickly returned before the Lama and made respectful supplication, but the teachings were not granted. He made prostrations. Lama Marpa said to the Lady: "Lady, Lady, you gave Happy Report some advice on your own. Your words were unsuccessful." Then he struck Mila, kicked him, scolded him, and sent him away. The Lama was angry.

"O Mother, did you provide him with a portion of provisions?"

"I did not lend any provisions."

"O no? You *did* send them, so that Happy Report could go asking for Dharma from another person. It is not permitted to grant him any provisions." Then Marpa chased her away. He took back all the provisions that the Lady had given. He flung a cushion (*phyi sgan sngas*) and went out.

Happy Report set up his pack and went before rNgog chos kyi rdo rje. He met the Lama. With faith, he reverently bowed. He inquired about his health. rNgog said: "My Lama Marpa Lotsawa had a special type of salute.

Folio 212:

As for you, where do you come from?"

Mila responded: "I myself come from Lama Marpa Lho Brag Pa."

Lama rNgog said: "Well, then you must be the one from his Presence who is named Mila Happy Report."

"Yes, I am the one named Happy Report. I have been sent to you by the Lady with this letter, this hair of glorious Nāropa, and this offering of a bit of food. Please consider bestowing the Dharma that comes down to us from Marpa and the lineage."

Lama rNgog replied: "If such is the command of the Lady, so be it: I must certainly teach you so as to manifest the Doctrine. But before teaching you … I have an enemy. Cast hail upon him and then I will teach you Dharma."

In this way, Happy Report was accepted and granted the oral instructions. An assembly of Dol was gathered. Lama rNgog carried a sheep in order to repay the destroyer-spirits. In the middle of the field the destructive hail was unleashed. The hail fell.[50] It was a severe hailstorm. Many houses of that land were destroyed. All the harvest, too, was wrecked. All the people suffered devastation. Then, he went home. The corpses of the birds killed by the hail were all gathered together right in front of him. A basket was full of them. As measureless sorrow arose in him, he pondered: "In order to obtain the Dharma—on account of what I have done—in order to attain complete Buddhahood in one life, I have to accumulate evil deeds like this!" So he thought and wept. Lama rNgog said: "Did you unleash the hail? Did it arrive?"

"A very severe hailstorm was cast upon them; many houses of the town were destroyed; the whole harvest was leveled; all the people came to grief. On land and in the sky over the place, all sentient beings were killed.

Folio 213:

I came to the Lama in order to attain Buddhahood. As a result of this, I have accumulated hellish deeds!" He emptied his robe (*chu ba*), placing the corpses of the birds killed by magic before the Lama. Weeping, he sat down. The wife of Lama rNgog said again and again, "Do not weep, Mila." Lama rNgog said: "Do not weep, my son; you need not weep. All these sins will not pursue you; the profound Doctrine for attaining Buddhahood in one lifetime and in one body outshines sin. I now must give the teachings." He took an oath (*snying bzhes* [?]).

Then at that time, the permission given prior to the empowerment of the Lady Nairātmyā was granted. From the distorted path of a great sinner, he undertook the meaningful path of skillful means, receiving the transmission of the doctrine of the noble ones. The immeasurably profound doctrine having been bestowed many times (*mang du*), and with provisions provided by the Lama and his wife, he was enclosed in a cavern and the opening was sealed with clay. There he dwelt for one year in pursuit of spiritual attainment; realization did not arise—merely a slight experience occurred.[51]

Under these circumstances, Mila Happy Report met Lama rNgog and requested the profound doctrine.

> Master rNgog and his disciple went together before Marpa-
> Since his defiled deeds had been exhausted, he was now
> A worthy vessel in which to pour spiritual teachings;
> He became a master of all the Dharma teachings;
> I bow down and praise the prophecy[52] (*lung du stan*) about
> the Saint. (12)

This is the exposition:

Then Lama rNgog said to Mila Happy-Report when he had finished his practice: "Now that the house of the Lama, 'Turquoise Roof' (i.e., sKu mKhar dGu Thog), is finished I am going to bring offerings to Marpa. You, too, should come along." He set forth measureless goods both worldly and religious as offerings, and Master and disciple went to the gathering.

Folio 214:

Then, Lama Mila went on ahead, met and saluted the Lady, and inquired about her health. She was very delighted, and grasped Mila's hands. He placed her feet in homage on his head. He also went before the Lama, greeted him and inquired about his health. The Lama, very delighted, asked: "Have you received the teachings?" Mila told him the instructions he had received in detail. "Very well," he replied. Then Lama rNgog arrived. He offered many generous gifts. All the masters and students were approaching Marpa at that time.

The Lama said to Lama rNgog: "Did you bestow the Dharma on Mila?" He replied: "I gave him the teachings." Marpa said: "Very well, very good. As of last year, I had not granted Mila the teachings. I was not kind to him. In his mental continuum were immeasurable sin and defilement. In order to cleanse these, I used tilling the soil, erecting the fort, etc., as a form of service."

"In general Mila, you possess a worthy vessel that is, however, impure. The vessel has to be worthy to receive the oral instructions. Your previous sins are now completely cleansed by these preliminary practices. It will now be sufficient to bestow on you the oral instructions of the main practices.[53] Stay with me so that I may bestow on you that which is needed." Before the disciples, the Lama said, "Now this time of one year is very serious. He is to withdraw into solitude, not seeing anyone, for the period of six months. He will withdraw from all other persons." He bestowed all the doctrine on Mila the way one pours into a flask; thus he was granted the initiation and the oral instructions on awakening Bodhicitta [*sems skyed*; *bodhicittotpada*]. The necessary teachings were entirely complete as soon as he had requested them. "Now all you need is practice and experience of results.

Folio 215:

In general, to reach attainment one needs three years of practice for experience to appear." Mila said: "In that case, I should perform such practices in my own country where there are many solitary places where great perfected ones have dwelt. Now it would be suitable to show me how to remove obstacles and obtain spiritual progress in my mind."

The Lama said: "This is suitable. In addition, I will bestow the instructions for removing obstacles and granting spiritual progress. I am one of the foremost disciples of Nāropa; I studied with thirteen learned Lamas for twenty years; all was received, nothing was held back. All was taken into the center of my heart." Mila obtained these oral instructions.

Then Mila went to Lama rNgog Chos kyi rdo rje; he had mastered the true Dharma view against mere opinion and theory, but he did not possess more than Mila. They made a comparison of the profound oral instructions of the Dharma concerning the right time for the ejection of consciousness (*'pho ba'i gnas skabs na*)[54] showing that rNgog was worthy and profound, but only to a lesser extent. He was not superior to Mila.[55] Comparing meditation experiences, there was no one more excellent than Mila. Among Lord Marpa's principal sons, such as Mila (*der mid la'i thugs dgongs la*) and rNgog chos kyi rdo rje, the inner circle became very famous. They lacked none of the precepts. Their aim and purpose was unsurpassed, entirely because of the doctrine that Marpa so carefully bestowed. To Lord Marpa Lho Brag pa be limitless honor! On that occasion, immeasurable delight and happiness arose.

These things were done by the Saint Mila, relying on the great Lord Marpa Lho Brag pa when he became the receptacle of the oral instructions, having exhausted all obscurations;[56] having in his heart all the doctrine of the hearing lineage, he arrived at the goal.

Folio 216:

The Saint Mila possessed the essence of the oral instructions;
Having obtained the entire Dharma,
He remembered his mother and sister;
He went before the Guru to ask permission to return to his homeland.
I bow down to the Saint's obtaining permission to go. (13)

This is the exposition:

When Mila Happy Report had perfectly received all the teachings and oral instructions, he knew all the essentials about dispelling obstacles and obtaining spiritual progress, and so forth. After three years of practice, as the Dharma began to flower, he wished to be permitted to go in person to his own land and to the holy places (*gnas chen rnams*); for a long time he had not been to his homeland.

Out of compassion, he wanted to see his mother, sister, and so forth. He went before the Lama. "O precious Guru, relying on your strong and enduring compassion, I who had accumulated all manner of evil have been made a pure vessel for receiving the entire Dharma-instructions just as fluid is poured into a vessel. I know all the essentials of removing obstacles and of acquiring spiritual progress. Since the flower of the Dharma has begun to blossom, so as to attain the height of realization, I now request permission to return to my own country, a holy place. I will practice until *siddhi* is attained. Please be kind to me so that I may come to meet the Father-Mother Guru on a particular occasion in the future."

The Lama said: "How is it that you are speaking this way? (*bu khyod rang ji ltar zer ba bzhin*) All the instructions are completed. You have been taught the essentials of removing obstacles to make spiritual progress, and so forth. All sinful karma has been purified. You must do as I did for so long a time. You must mediate until (*bar du*) in general, you have attained *siddhi* as the flowering of my teachings. In particular, by practicing for three years in solitude you will attain what was at first unobtainable. You must come to meet me on certain occasions.[57] Now, go in haste to your homeland." Thus Mila decided to return to his homeland and thus he received permission.

Folio 217:

These are the facts about Mila Happy Report who, having fully acquired the entire Dharma of the oral instructions, asked for permission to visit his homeland, in order to become an attainer (*thob po*) of *siddhi*.

> Thus, when he received permission
> On the point of departure,
> He asked a blessing of his spiritual parents,
> Bowing down to them;
> Seven times he devoutly placed his head at the feet of the
>   Lady;
> I bow down to the Saint overcome with faith. (14)

This is the explication:

Then, Lord Mila Happy Report properly obtained permission from his guru in order to return to his homeland. His parent gurus provided him with the Dharma and requisites for the journey; as he was about to set forth up country, Mila went to his Parent Gurus with a small gift.

Lama Marpa Lho Brag pa said: "You, O Mila Happy Report, are

someone with great force in the accumulation of karma; you are one who has a great dose of courage. All the instructions of my Guru are entirely given to you; take up, then the paternal line of the bKa' brgyud pas; undertake the task of a teacher of the Practice Lineage."

He was thus commissioned as a Master of Dharma by mind-to-mind transmission (*thugs la thugs sprod*). Then Mila Happy Report reverently bowed to both mother and father gurus; he shed tears as he grasped the feet of each of them. He then placed the crown of his head to the feet of the gurus. He received from the mouth of the guru the blessing of his mind, not to be separate from him in all things [all circumstances] and all times.

The Lama directed: "O Mila Happy-Report, from time to time, you are to come to meet me." Then the Lady accompanied him a short distance.

Folio 218:

"Now, Happy Report, I had a prophetic dream: it is suitable for you to uphold the foundation of the bKa' brgyud teachings; it is suitable to raise up the victory banner of the Practice Lineage teachings. It is suitable to use the power to work all manner of wonders (*zil gnon*) and miracles (*rdzu 'phrul*), and so on. It is suitable to accomplish extensively the salvific aims of sentient beings; it is suitable to perform great deeds of penance and asceticism, until these things happen. These things you must know; now, make haste and go; seek to be happy."[58]

To her, Happy Report said: "I bow down many times to the Lady. I make you my guide in all things and for all time. I make you father and mother, for you have protected this body, I am obligated to you who are my greatest benefactress, since the time I was born until I die." Seven times he grasped the feet of the Lady and venerated her. He requested her secret water,[59] since she was a non-human wisdom *ḍākinī*. Whether they had been together or apart, her body had provided much kindness.[60] He therefore asked her to be inseparable from him, in her compassion, at all times and in all things.

Having embraced the Lady, he was very much overcome and wept. Since they had been together a long time, they had much to remember; tears fell abundantly from the Lady's eyes. "O my son, Happy Report, we are inseparable in all things and for all time even should you be far away."

Having done these things, Mila Happy Report began his journey to his homeland. He saluted reverently both the guru and the lady, who had kindly bestowed the precepts and made a prophecy.

Then he went up to Gung Thang and arrived at the village of rTsa;
His mother having died, he found the field untilled, hard and infertile,

Folio 219:

And the house caved in;
His sister had been evicted from her own land
Immense sorrow of soul arose.
I bow down to the Saint in whom renunciation arose. (15)

This is the exposition:

Having left the presence of his guru, the Lord Mila Happy Report went up to his own town on the high road where he had an easy and well-favored journey. Then he arrived in his homeland. His mother was dead. The house was wrecked. His sister had been evicted. Then he went to the door of his home and there arose a sentiment of grief. A house without a master—no wonder it decayed! A mother who has died—no wonder, with no one to care for her! A sister has been evicted from her land—no wonder, without a guardian! He wept much from the core of his being, out of grief for his mother, sister, and property. But as he did this, he reflected that these are the ways of incarnate existence in the world, and no wonder! An immense desire for renunciation was born in him. He sang this song:[61]

I bow down to the Gurus of the lineage;
Alas, alas without any essence
Without any substance at all, in general,
This is the nature of cyclic existence!

Eternally insubstantial! [*rtags shing rtags shing*]
Insubstantial, ever changing, ever becoming:
All three: mother, sister, property—
All three of them are insubstantial,
At this time, they are insubstantial;
Thus, why don't I seek for the essence of yoga! (*rnal 'byor snying po cis mi tshol*)

In this way, Mila Happy Report looked upon the desolation of his land, his mother, sister, etc. And he came to know the meaning of the insubstantiality of all things.

His sister

Folio 220:

Peta heard that the saint had arrived;
They both met at White Rock Hermitage Cave;
Having been embraced by his sister,
They wept and fainted because of sorrow (*gdung pas*);
I bow down to the meeting of the Saint and his sister. (16)[62]

This is the exposition:

Then Mila Happy Report went down to his town. He sat in meditation for a few days at the start of the higher ground of the valley of rTsa. Several days passed. One evening in a dream, he saw a field being plowed by a ploughman, who could not finish it. At that time the dream was an outward manifestation of the inner signs of spiritual growth. "I thought it was not appropriate to leave the plowing incomplete; thus I sang this song":

On the primordial ground—
Like the origin itself—
A pair of two great oxen are yoked[63]
Setting in place the plow of Insight and Skillful Means.
For one who is a ploughman of the mind, who knows how to plough,

Who is fierce and has done the plowing assiduously—
Though the soil is firm and compact, he succeeds.

He then went to the White Rock Horse Tooth Cave hermitage. "At this place I intend to attain the flower of *siddhi* by practicing in solitude for three years in accordance with the instructions of my Guru. I will neither think about nor speak about these three: food, clothing, and drink. I will practice all alone in penitence and austerity."

At first, the psychosomatic veins of all bodies obstruct interior energies like water swirling over a dam; the whole body shakes and many obstructions in the veins work against the currents of energy. It is like the waters swirling over a dam. In order to liberate oneself, the recollected consciousness mediates on the inner *vajra* in the *avadhūtī* (central psychosomatic channel).[64] By meditation, one visualizes the "diamond" as abiding in the *avadhūtī,* the consciousness is liberated, binding the obstruction of the channels with the "noose" of *vajra.*

Folio 221:

In this state (*gags*) of mind, one can confront immeasurable grief, fear, terror, etc., when such obstruct the mind; thus the mind is liberated by meditation and possesses peace, bliss, wisdom, and joy. When fear and terror appear as obstacles, one meditates on gods and goddesses. One is liberated from fearful destinies[65] by following the meditation instructions of fearlessness. Other obstacles of various types can occur to anyone. Thus, each one is liberated by meditation uniting consciousness and essence. Being a liberated person and a defiled person cannot occur simultaneously.

In the peaceful state of this meditation, he abode without eating or drinking, exploring the mind by means of penance and austerity.

His sister Peta, having been evicted, was wandering towards sNye nam. She heard that Lord Mila Happy Report had arrived nearby. She brought nine handfuls of grain and a quantity of cooked food. She met some people on the way. She said: "I heard that my brother Happy Report is nearby. Did you see him?" They replied: "A few say they have not seen him. Some people say he is meditating in the mountains at White Rock; perhaps he is!" She went on seeking him towards the mountains. She looked up and there was a cave on a rock; the entrance was closed off. There was a man inside. Peta thought: "He must be my brother." She knocked at the entry and spoke with a weak voice. Mila Happy Report said: "Who is there?" Peta asked him for some sort of signal or word. She thought, "The voice is like my brother's." Weeping, she recognized her own elder brother, Happy Report.

Lord Mila Happy Report

Folio 222:

thought: "My sister Peta has arrived, she is not dead!" He went to the entryway and rolled away the stone. They met. Both of them embraced and wept for a long time. The sister gave an oral account of her many sorrows since they had parted, while they both wept for grief. "My dear brother, at first our mother and I were very afflicted. There was no household any more. There was no food. Our mother became rather sick. Even though I strenuously sought to take care of her, it was useless and she died of starvation. I wandered from the town in torment towards sNye nam. Then I heard that my brother had returned, and I went to meet you right away, at first I did not recognize you."

Lord Mila Happy Report said: "Yes, it is I. Even though I dwell without meeting with many people, I do get familiar with them individually. Thus, I certainly heard what happened. Our afflicted mother surely deserves our compassion, and I thought I would not meet you again. Now we, brother and sister, have the joy of meeting again." He then caressed his sister's hand. "Please accept the food I offer to you, my sister. In fact, all the food I have for you is only a bit of powdered nettles. What may I give you?"

His sister said: "It is true, then, that my brother is without anything at all. For this reason, I would like to offer this cooked food and nine handfuls of grain." He crumbled some powdered nettles for her and each offered the other some food for the soup pot; both brother and sister shared it. Lord Mila Happy Report said: "I have occupied this place for six months. I have not been fully fed for that long."

Folio 223:

Peta said: "O my brother, what difficulties you are enduring!"

That evening, he lay down in the White Rock cave. The next morning she gave him the nine handfuls of grain. "I will go to the village below the fields to seek alms of butter and food. If I receive a suitable offering, I will give it to you."

Thus a month or two passed by and his sister came, leaving behind many offerings. When the portion of powdered nettles and so forth was used up, he again encountered considerable difficulties. Thinking that it might be useful to gather butter on the pasture lands where his aunt was, he went there. He set out for where his aunt was milking a yak and asked for alms. The aunt said: "You good-for-nothing! Shameless! So it is indeed true—you have finally turned up. So you need something! You did the deed of magic—so what happened to us?" Thus she abused him exceedingly. She pulled out a tent pole and chased him with it. He fled. Because of his great austerities, he tripped and fell on a basket used for collecting dung; she caught up with him and thoroughly pummeled him. Still blazing with anger, she turned around. The Saint had this thought about her: "Since even going forth for alms is unprofitable, it is better to die."

He went back to White Rock and continued his practice of physical austerity. Then, after a little while, Peta received some excellent dry food for having done such work as irrigation, weaving, and carrying daily loads. She offered what she had, including a small pot of fermented drink. "I have searched continuously and found only this. Other peoples' Dharma practice benefits self and

Folio 224:

others, but my brother's Dharma practice makes trouble for himself and for us! It is not good! It would now better to give up this Dharma practice." Mila Happy Report replied: "One needs to be able to give up body and life to practice Dharma. My Dharma practice is not mistaken. Just wait and see!" He did not heed her advice.

Seeing her brother Mila Happy Report without clothes, possessing only the torn sheepskin blanket of a dead beggar, Peta thought: "I will make my brother something to wear." She wandered off to the town. At that occasion, a Bon po named Dar po had assembled the offerings and ritual objects for removing evil influences. Peta gathered these things, including the colored yarn[66] in a skein, making a ball of thread and two pieces of cloth from the discarded ritual objects. She brought along some of the leftovers from the feast, and went before Milarepa. She suggested that he wear the two pieces of cloth that she had assembled, offering them with the leftover food. Mila Happy Report said: "I am satisfied with my garments. This is a waste of time that is harmful to one's practice. Neither skin nor bone needs a covering, so why should you go to any trouble for my sake? Is it that your mind is troubled because I go without?" He then cut the two pieces into unrelated shapes for his loins and wrapped it around his waist. He made use of the things she collected for food. He said: "So you think you are more of a *yogin* than I?" Having put up with these difficulties, he shut the door and resumed meditation.

After a while, at a certain time, one day a little understanding regarding the illusory body and the mystic heat arose. At night, he had a small experience of the appearance of light in a dream.

Folio 225:

In short, some food in the belly gives rise to spiritual experience![67] Then Mila Happy Report was content and energetic, thanks to the small amount of beer offered him by Peta. Another time she came to offer some provisions and other things; he asked her for some more beer, because it delighted him. He acted happy and clear-headed, and sang this song:

Not able, o Peta to bear the sorrow of life,
I went to White Rock Peak, high in the sky;
The hermitage in the middle of the Sky-Cave;
Above, the purple cloud of the south floats by,
Below, the vulture hawk breaks the fowler's net,
In the middle, beasts of prey disport themselves;
This is my place of solitude!
I, the *yogin* Mila Happy Report, say so![68]
Happy, delighted in mind, delighted in the body,
Happy destiny! I am without encumbrances,
Happy, full of fortitude, free from fear—
Happy, possessing the non-dual view of things,
Happy, I am Mila the *yogin*, a body made of mind![69]
Sister Peta, you are my patron and comfort;
Why aren't you in haste to practice meditation in solitude?

Peta said: "How can you be joyful when there is unhappiness in the family? We have nothing to eat! We are completely without property! Your happiness has no value for me! Being obliged to go out gathering alms is in itself a good reason to be unhappy!" Happy-Report replied: "We may dedicate our hearts to the Three Jewels! Though endless misfortunes come to us, we shall be without reproach. Now be off!" Then Peta went down toward the town to seek alms.

Then the Saint abode in meditation continuously clarifying the mind on the spot where he met his sister, practicing his usual austerities.

A group of hunters came along.

Folio 226:

They asked if Peta were carrying any portions of food, or if there were any books to carry off. Since there was nothing they beat up Lord Mila. Mila explained the Buddhist doctrine on the cause and effect of karma to these hunters. "This is how great evils come about. One should not act like this—there is future merit to be lost or gained." They replied: "What can be done to gain this so-called great merit?"

Mila Happy Report said to them: "A great meditator like me is not inclined to steal even a blade of grass. If you think like that, you will attain great merit." They replied: "Fine. We will think as you do." Lord Mila Happy Report just sat there, hungry and mute (*ltogs kug tu*). They moved him around, lifting him high in a tree. From that spot, they suspended him over a precipice. They treated him roughly! But they did not acquire the guilt of an evil deed. He told them about accumulating merit, and so forth.

They said: "Well then, if we do this, to whom is the sin attributed, and what is this so-called great merit?" He replied: "It is great merit indeed to offer supplications to the Three Jewels." They said, "Then we want to pray some more!" Each of them poured dust into the mouth of Lord Mila Happy Report, which was gaping wide open, and each made a request. Then they did this a second and a third time. As they did this, they supplicated. In brief, this was how these hunters caused the Saint difficulties. But, fearing him, for a long time they provided service to Peta, giving her portions of grain and excellent food, as offerings.

Mila said: "Having resided here for three years, I have been provided for by you and have been offered what little water and supplies I needed. Now you, Peta, may always have my provisions and there is no longer any need to gather alms. You have remained here until you had no flesh on your body and have become exhausted.

Folio 227:

I will not remain in this place. I will go up to a hermitage in the mountains. You yourself should abide here and take care (*bsos gcig*) of yourself on whatever you get. In the future we, brother and sister, will meet again and converse in detail." Then Peta said: "Up until now, I have had no closer relation than you, my brother."

Then he went up through the town.

These things occurred when Mila Happy Report went back to his hometown. Immeasurable compassion arose in him by means of his having taken up the practice of austerity and asceticism.

In this life he meditated in equanimity,
And practiced austerities in the six meditation caves,
Including Ling ra, and others;
All alone, he planted the victory banner of spiritual practice;
I bow down to the Saint, perfected in his asceticism. (17)

This is the explication.

Then Mila Happy Report meditated and practiced this type of austerity at the following places, caves, and hermitages (and at others as well): Red Rock Linga Cave, sMin rgyud grib ma Cave, rKyang dpal nam mkha'i Cave, Rag ma byang chub Cave, etc.

First, at the Red Rock Linga Cave, where he went to meditate, he had only nettles for provisions and nothing else (*men gcig dang med*). At that time, he purified the illusory body (*sgyu lus*) in the daytime, and at night he worked on the clear-light meditation. At that time, no matter what occurred in his practice of austerities (physical yoga, *haṭha* yoga),

Folio 228:

he kept to a diet of nettles. Even his body took on the green color of nettles.[70]

After a long time, Peta came, bringing along a half peck of parched barley and butter packed in skins. She saw the renunciate's body, colored all over like the green of nettles, and she thought: "My brother is without anything to eat—this is the reason for his condition. That is why he is this color—he looks like a dead man." So she thought, and she wept many tears. Then she thought to boil some cold water for soup. But when Mila Happy Report picked up the pot, he could not hold it in his hand—it slipped away and broke and a disk of dried food shaped like the pot came out. The disk rolled around and down the mountain. Many people heard that this had happened. Some heard about it and wept (*'chi ma shor*), and for some, faith arose.[71] Peta went to the village for him. He dwelt alone by himself, meditating.

Men of sNye nam who had gathered the feathers of many eagles came to his cave. Having seen the green color of the body of Saint

Mila, the feather gatherers said: "It's an elf [i.e., a nonhuman]!" Light rays pass through him! (*'o zer nas*). Mila said to them: "I am not an elf!" "So what is your name?" "I am the son of Shes rab rgyal mtshan of rTsa, Mid la Happy Report." Thus the feather-gatherers came to know the facts. They also offered him some excellent provisions. They also started to use nettles for food and exerted themselves in meditation. A small experience of the illusory body arose; at night, they finally saw the streaks of the clear light.

Then a few women disciples from Gung Thang heard that a son of Shes rab rgyal mtshan of rTsa, called Happy Report,

Folio 229:

had achieved spiritual attainment; they offered him three years' worth of barley. Extraordinary faith arose in them when the group of ladies went to meet Mila, when he was dwelling at Ling ra. The ladies said to him: "We ourselves want to know about what Mila the son of Shes rab rgyal mtshan does." Mila told them: "Yes, I am he; because I ate a lot of nettles, my former color has thus changed to green." They bowed to him. All of them offered some of the articles they had on hand. They asked him if he now would no longer eat nettles. They wanted to offer other provisions. In reply, Lord Mila Happy Report sang this song:

> I bow down to the Lord Gurus,
> I Mila, am of the nettle clan
> And nettles belong to Mila's clan;
> Nettles and Mila cannot be distinguished!
> You, too, Lady Patrons, are of the clan of faith;
> Faith, too, is of the Ladies' clan;
> Faith and patroness cannot be distinguished!
> Mind, too, is of the clan of luminosity;
> Light belongs to the clan of Mind;
> Light and Mind—these two—cannot be distinguished.

He discoursed on the nature of duality to these Patronesses[72] and other matters, and they felt much remorse. They brought forth many useful things, offering provisions to Mila.

Thus Mila Happy Report went hither and thither to both Ling ra and sMin brgyud grib ma Caves, exploring the path of yoga practice and so experienced something of the clear light and illusory body. Then he went to rKyang dpal nam mkha' Cave.

Folio 230:

He went up to that place and also down to Brag dkar, there to explore the practice of the mystic veins and inner currents by means of his austerities. He combined the currents in the central channel, but that night when he stopped the breath process, nothing happened.[73]

One evening, four ladies came to him, massaging his body, and using their skills to help his practice. They told him: "You must use this technique." They taught him the posture called "the hearth" consisting of tying himself up at six points and then they disappeared.[74] On that occasion, Mila Happy Report meditated in accord with this device and that evening was able to produce warmth wearing only cotton. Thus he needed only a simple lower garment of cotton, and is famous as Mid-la the Ras-pa (one who wears cotton cloth).

Since that time, he used each of several cushions for two or three months as he meditated without moving. The result was that many virtues[75] arose. While he was performing energy current and subtle channel practice, he had a visit from Marpa Lotsawa[76] during his meditation period. Then he continued to meditate, earnestly equipoised and concentrated. Then he attained full accomplishment and the power to fly in space arose. At that time, from the rising to the setting of the sun, he flew toward the sun at White Rock Horse Tooth Cave;[77] at sunrise, when the sun warms the hillside, he flew from Horse Tooth to White Rock. In that town there was someone named Gung po mgon po dpal. He and his son saw Mila flying overhead while they plowed their field. The son said: "A person is not able to fly!" The father said: "Lead the ox away quickly. He looks like Milarepa, a mad man (*smyon pa*).[78] He flies because he is following the sun." He had no faith in him.

Then upon an occasion a truly accomplished perfected *yogin* arrived in that region from Sa smad and

Folio 231:

met Milarepa, who asked him: "Where are you from?" The *yogin* (*sen ta ba*) was from around Lho Brag. He asked him spiritual questions. He had heard that Lama Marpa of Lho Brag was dead. Saint Mila Happy Report offered up prayers to him. Sobbing sorrowfully, he made many exclamations of misery. Then he had the intention of going to see the Lama Parents and make supplications. His mind was deeply recollected, however, and he became detached from his emotional reaction.

These are the things that Saint Milarepa did while pursuing the practice of asceticism, steadying the inner currents in the psychosomatic channels, and immense virtue arose.

> Once he went towards sNye nam;
> A patron arranged or his provisions;
> But not abiding with him, he afterwards went
> Into the La phyis snow mountains;
> I bow down to the Saint meditating in the snow ranges. (18)

This is the explication:

Then when the Saint-Victor Milarepa had heard that his Guru Marpa Lho Brag pa had died,[79] he abandoned his practice to go to Lho Brag. He went to Tsar ma of sNye nam. A patroness named rNgog dor mo met him and became full of faith toward him. She approached him and paid him homage, asking: "Are you the Saint-Victor Milarepa?" The patrons supplicated him to remain there. They offered to bring him provisions. The Saint, taking only nine handfuls of grain, went off toward La Phyis. That morning, clouds began to gather at the place. For eighteen days it snowed without interruption.

Folio 232:

Mountains and valleys were completely covered with the snow. No one could travel. In that great snowfall, not even the animals could go outside. The patrons could not bring him provisions for seven months. All the people of sNye nam said that he, the perfect *yogin*, had been killed by the snow. Both male and female patrons wept sorrowfully.

During that time, he thought to himself: "I myself am alive; no one can get here because the road is cut off. If I go out, I might die. It seems that I am to die here in La phyis. Perhaps I should perform the ejection of consciousness (*'pho ba*)." A woman dressed in leaves came along and said: "Do not perform the ejection of consciousness. Please eat *samādhi!*[80] Day and night, do nothing but the meditations of generation and completion (*skyed rdzogs*); we, the Dharma master *ḍākinīs* will bless you. You are not in danger of death. We are taking care of you!" Therefore, he let go of his worries and did not perform the ejection of consciousness. Day and night he meditated in a state of contemplative absorption (*samādhi*). He recounted: "Now and then, there was a sensation of cold; of snow blindness; of deafness in my ear, etc. Many states of difficulty arose. At times, I was free of these difficulties. A feeling of lightness occurred, at times without apparent cause. I was stirred by the rush of inner energies and was stunned. Little by little, the clear light dawned and increased." In those seven months, in short, hardly having food enough to fill the end of a spoon, meditating in a state of *samādhi*, taking his contemplation as food, his body was not overcome by death. Innumerable evident signs of virtue also came from within. At that time, immortality

Folio 233:

was achieved, the *siddhi* of Life-Immortal (*tshe'i dngos grub bgyi ba*). At that time in his practice, though sentient beings are impermanent, he manifested the opposite quality.[81] This apparent body is not dominated by death when this *siddhi* is accomplished. He thus had the *siddhi* of never needing food. The great mass of sentient beings does not understand the accumulation of such merit. Whether with food or without food, because he had achieved this *siddhi*, he was without any hunger (*kres pa*).[82] Unerringly, the supreme accomplishment is thus achieved.

Exclusively showing forth the doctrine for his disciples, he achieved the *dharmakāya*, which is described as not changing; unmovable; fully accomplished. In short, he entirely attained both ordinary and supreme accomplishments.[83]

These things the Saint did when he went to the La phyis snow mountains, obtaining Accomplishment (*siddhi*) through the practice of austerities.

> Thinking that the Saint was dead for seven months,
> A few people, having made offerings, set out to see him;
> The Lord was not dead, so they reverently invited him to
> their town;
> I bow down to the Saint of wonders! (19)

Then, the Saint Victor Milarepa, having gone to the La phyis snow ranges, abode for seven months where it was cloudy without any light. At that time he entirely achieved supreme and ordinary accomplishment. Several of the patrons of sNye nam, among the first of whom was rNgog dor mo, thinking that the Saint had died, went to search for the corpse with the intention of cremating it. They recited the noble Seven Day cycle of prayers.[84] They made many offerings, and set off carrying a shovel, a fine blanket, and a conch. At that time, the Saint went to a place one day's journey from his cave and stayed there a week. Meanwhile, the people of the search party reached the place where the Saint had been staying.

Folio 234:

The people sought for him. They blew the conch. They made loud noises. Thus the Saint heard the sound of human voices and of the conch. From his cave-rock with snow on top he saw the people coming. They blew the conch. Making the path clear of snow, they searched. Mila thought: "They are looking for me." Sitting on top of the snow, he offered a prayer; as he prayed, there was a lovely sound, which was heard by the search party. They were very happy to find him. "It is evident that I am not dead." Because of a huge steep snow-drift, they couldn't get to him. The search party could not free him. The Saint held his breath and flew to the search party, going to where they were. Then he even loaded them on himself and flew over the snow mountains. Then he arrived at his cave. The Saint still had the sack of nine measures of parched barley, and with it a side of meat that he had not eaten. He gave it to the search party. Patroness Dor mo grasped the Saint and wept: "Our Saint is not dead! How has it happened that our Saint is not dead?" The Saint said: "The reason I did not die is that I wear the clothing of mystic heat (*gtum-mo*); I eat the food of contemplative absorption; I meditate on Guru-yoga and practice the generation and completion stages of meditation. One has the help of deities and *ḍākinīs*, thus I did not die." Great wonder arose in the chief patron and in all the members of the search party. They performed many prostrations, placing his feet on their heads. They were indeed very happy that the Lord was not dead. "Now we invite you to our town."

Folio 235:

They asked him to leave that place by all means. The Saint granted their wish with delight, and accompanied them to their town. At that time, his fame and renown spread beyond the boundary of sNye nam. All became his reverent devotees. All the people the valley came to meet him. Upon a certain occasion, with limitless faith and devotion around, all the people made vast offerings to the Saint; some offered gold, some turquoise, also copper, and silk garments, various cotton items, etc. The Saint was surrounded by delightful objects, so that only his head could be seen! He had too many things! In particular, the patron-couple rNgog offered thick woolen clothing for his body, a horse for riding, a turquoise for fastening around the head, as gifts of devotion, and they grasped the feet of the Saint. These Patrons said:

"We are meeting a Siddha like you because of the accumulation of great merit; we want to be inseparable from you all the time. Please grant this, in your compassion." Tears poured from their eyes. The whole group of people wept and prayed in the same way. On that occasion, the Saint did not take the wealth offered to him, but returned it to all the people, the male and female patrons. This was his "custom." Then he said: "Now I offer this song about what happened to me previously in the snow:

At the end of the year of the Tiger,
At the start of the year of the Hare[85]
As a *yogin*, I went off to the snow mountains of La phyis
Yes, I went to the La phyis snow ranges;
Both sky and earth danced (*'bros pa*)
They shoved the air by the great power of a windstorm,
In the south, a purple cloud moved like a host arrayed;
Both the sun and moon were taken captive
The deep snow came down for nine days and nine nights—
In all, it came down for eighteen days and nights

Folio 236:

That was how the snow was
A the time of the new year—both snow and wind were great,
But there were three things struggling on the snow mountain peak—
For the cotton cloth on the *yogin*'s body was the third—
And the winner in the fight was the cotton garment!
Either the cotton cloth is warm, or else,
The snow mountain is warm! Or else—
The air is very mild!
Happy in equanimity is the realm of the *yogin*'s body!
How are you, o patrons?
Indeed, the *yogin*'s fame is seen and heard
Everywhere!"

Having said this to the patrons and patronesses, he explained the doctrine of self-and-others. He left that place; he did not stay there. Deeply touched by his deeds, all the people experienced great wonderment toward him. His light and fame spread in all directions: "A great Siddha has arisen among us!"

These things were done by the Saint Mila Happy Report the *yogin* when he attained immeasurable virtue, having gone to the La phyis snow ranges. O Holy Saint, meeting with patrons and patronesses, preaching all the doctrine in song, we reverently bow to you!

Then the Lord went to meditate in the forest
Of the Land of Senge, towards Mon (Bhutan);
Having attained virtue, he sang all his songs[86] to a circle of
disciples;
Holy Saint, we reverently bow to you! (20)

This is the explication:

When the Saint-Victor Milarepa went to meditate in the forest of Senge Ling in the land of Mon, where there was a very pleasant grove with fruit trees. Many flowers grew there. It was a place of many monkeys and langurs. A place of solitude, without any people! Local gods and spirits

Folio 237:

gathered there. Very powerful and fierce beings arrived and sat down at that place. At the root of a great tree-trunk, he abode within a cave the size of two men, with his copper pot. Without paying attention to day or night, he meditated next to the tree on the ground, equipoised in contemplation.[87] Thus he abode at that time. He went without food except an occasional bit of the fruit. Contemplative absorption (*samādhi*) was like a food offering to him. The evident signs of virtue arose strongly in him. At that time, the patrons and patronesses of sNye nam spoke, sending two men to the Saint with an invitation. The two men sought the fruit grove in the land of Senge. For a long time, they could not find him. Finally, they encountered him where he dwelt, near the tree trunk. They bowed and inquired about his health. "My state of health is very good. How are you?" The Saint continued:

"In this holy place, various flowers grow
Here there are the cries of sweet-sounding bird song.
A grove where monkeys and langurs play—
Thus I reside alone in a wilderness place,
Happy."

Thus he sang, offering many songs. The two envoys said to him: "We two disciples implore you by all means to accept our invitation." The Saint said: "I will not go back with you." Suddenly, he got up and went away. The two men followed after him. But he climbed through the cave, which was so narrow that barely one man could fit in it, and got away. The envoys called to him: "Here you have no servants, no furniture, and so forth. How can you be happy?"

Folio 238:

They tried to get him to go with them for the sake of the disciples. The Saint sang,

Here water and wood is near to me—
But a so-called servant is a false need;
My need for food and companions is rather small;
If you have *gtum mo* in the body, you have heat aflame!
So clothing, too, is a false need,
My need for woolen cloth is also small;
Illusions appear at the root of mind—
Thus, even relatives and friends are a false need.
Having cares and worries is also unnecessary—
A meditator leaves the mind alone, in its "natural state"
One's need for the thoughts that rise up is also small—
Delusions!—who needs them?
The true nature of reality arises in the mind of itself
So-called grammar and logic are also false—

The need for literacy and knowledge is rather small,
If one finds the treasure of the precious Mind;
Even food and wealth are seen as false;
And as for this "enjoyment"—the need is small,
If we bring about the boundless goal of beings!
So-called patrons—who needs them?
And my need for your invitation is small, too!

Thus he sang, for he did not wish to go. The two men made entreaties and offerings to him, but he just sat where he was. The Saint said nothing whatever. Suddenly, he got up and went away. The envoys went after him. Water, rocks, trees, all three, were so tangled and dense that a person could not get through. But, having held his breath, Mila Happy Report flew away. The two went home unsuccessful. All the patrons and patronesses of the town let out sobs and made lamentations.

These things the Saint did as he meditated in the forest of Senge Ling, acquiring the signs of limitless virtue, when he refused the invitation of patrons and patronesses.

Then, upon an occasion,
He went to sNye nam brod bur.

Folio 239:

His aunt and sister heard about the fame of the Saint;
Both ladies went to meet him, to invite him;
I bow down to the Saint when he sang a song
Upon meeting them. (21)

This is the explication:

The Saint Milarepa did this: after a while, he went to sNye nam brod bur where he meditated assiduously. bKra shis rtsengs and Legs se became his patrons. After that, the Saint abode below that place, without any difficulties. At that time, both his aunt and sister heard that his fame and reputation had become great and they went to the place where the Saint dwelt. The aunt and the sister went there carrying many things, which they held in their hands along with things loaded on a white yak and on a hornless yak (*yo wo*)—flour, butter, etc. They went to meet him with various requests, entrusting themselves to the disciple named Se ras pa. The Saint said to Se ras pa: "Now my aunt is coming to Mila Happy Report, but you should let her know that I have no need of her visit. Tell her I am not dying of hunger and can do without the offerings she is carrying. I cannot meet with her."[88] He then said to Se ras pa: "Tell Peta to come up." So he did. Peta said: "Dear aunt, wait here and sit upon that cloth. I will now go to ask him for a hearing." The aunt agreed, and sat down. Se ras pa asked the other disciples to keep her company. Then he said to Mila Happy Report: "You must give an audience to your aunt!" But he shook his head and would not grant it. Then Peta went to meet him and paid homage, receiving his blessing. "O my brother, are you well?

Folio 240:

I hope you are content?" He replied: "Welcome, Peta. I now have enough food and clothing without begging." Then Peta asked for an audience for the aunt. "We are brother and sister, and we now have only our aunt as a relative. At the very least, you should hear her out." The Saint said:

> Our aunt has the body of a relative,
> But has the hostility of an enemy;
> In the body of a human being, but
> The mind of a demon.

"What did she do when I was destitute? At any rate, now I will not see her. If she comes to see me I will go away." He started to load up his bag. Seeing him make preparations to depart, his sister Peta was frustrated and began to cry. "O Saint, please hear me! Please at least consider a brief meeting with your aunt." The Saint said: "Peta, you are very kind, and you are both father and mother to me; I have to listen to you. If she is to meet with me, set up a curtain between me and her. That way she can meet me." Peta told this to the aunt. "My brother is in strict meditation. There is a curtain between us and him. There will, however, be an audience. Please come in." The aunt went to see him and asked about his health. The Saint composed this song:

I bow down to the Lord Guru!
In rTsa-valley of the five towns in Gung Thang,
There were these three: mother and two children;
Becoming the enemies of their relatives, we were scattered
Like a heap of beans with a stick.
Then I wandered in unfamiliar lands,
Where there was no "aunt";
In the White Rock Peak solitude,
Urged on by both hunger and thirst,
I went to my aunt, who called me a disgraceful beggar;
She pulled out a tent pole and chased me—
With hatred aflame in her body, she pursued;
Without strength in my body,

Folio 241:

I fell in a ditch.
Remember that you struck me until I was swollen?
Meeting me now, aren't you ashamed?

Out of shame, his aunt was unable to reply. She fell down and wept saying: "Truly, truly." Peta was pleased at this. Then the Saint said: "A bad rebirth occurs from the accumulation of the karma of hatred and attachment. First our aunt does great malice to me. Now she does this out of great attachment to me. This gives rise to birth in lower realms. Don't be attached to me![89] Instead, generate reverent faith and respect. Don't produce anger and malice, instead purify yourself." He pushed aside the curtain and showed his face and blessed her. At that, his aunt repented of her formed deeds and confessed them. At last, she performed acts of faith, reverence, and even great devotion. When this had ripened in her, she received initiation; with all her heart she offered all her wealth and possessions to the Saint. She placed his feet upon her head. Wanting to return to her abode, she also asked the Saint to come there with her, but this he did not accept.

These things the Saint did when he arrived at sNye nam brod from Senge Ling. He met his sister and, afterwards, his aunt was converted.

> After that, he dwelt in Chu dbar and in Brin;
> Innumerable gods, demons, and Tse ring ma[90]
> Created numerous threats, marvels, and omens;
> I bow down to the Guru who then seized and destroyed
> them. (22)

This is the explication:

Then the Saint-Victor Milarepa dwelt for a long time in meditation at Chu dbar and Brin, when it was the water-male dragon year,[91] in the first month of summer, in the part of the month when the moon is waxing, on the eighth day just at pre-dawn (3 to 4 a.m.):

Folio 242:

The Eighteen Great Demons, along with a retinue filling the whole sky with deities and demons of all kinds, made the sound of thunder and earthquake, and so forth, manifesting marvelous omens. From the group of them, there were five demons emanating ugly and fierce forms. There were the five great flesh-eating goddesses manifesting various ugly forms, such as that of a laughing skeleton-woman who raised up Mount Sumeru and banged it on her lap. There were mountain-haunting demons in female form; a wolf-face appeared cleverly from the vulva where blood streamed in a steady flow. A mouth appeared in the sky, sucking up the great ocean. Yama in the form of a *yakṣī* appeared with a fang the size of a huge spike; she played the sun and the moon like cymbals. A *yakṣī* in the form of a woman appeared; her color was like something charred; her body as tall as Mount Sumeru, she caused the planets to fall from the sky. Then there was an especially fascinating and charming Lady Goddess unequalled in external appearance. She tried to seduce the Saint forcefully, greeting him alluringly. There were other illusory *yakṣas*, some multiform, some formless, some many-armed, and *rakṣasas* of the rugged mountains who scattered rocks and soil in the four directions. He was entirely surrounded. A fire gathered together in the sky, and so forth, so that there were many fearsome and dangerous omens and signs, making threats and external manifestations toward the Saint. They then tried to make mischief with his meditation practice, so he then offered the deities and *ḍākinīs* this song:

> To the Precious Guru possessing the Three Jewels
> Named all-famous Marpa, and all the Siddhas
> I make a prayer, longing to possess bliss!
> I beseech your compassion from the Dharmadhātu[92]

Folio 243:

> Alone, in Chu dbar of Brin,
> I a cotton-clad *yogin* of Tibet
> Spend this one life in deep meditation. . . .

Thus, and more, he sang.[93] The gods and demons thought that he had become slightly afraid as he sang. They thought they had great power to make obstacles. The gods and demons unanimously assembled and said to him: "You have presented us with an offering of song, you made an offering at the right time to us gods and demons. Aren't you Milarepa?"—and so forth. Mila Happy Report replied with words of prophecy, these being the thoughts of the Lord: "Again, the essence of mind is to be unborn, unobstructed, indestructible, and free from illusion, and so it is! This is the array of Yama, 100 million strong." There was a rain of sharp weapons that also came at him, but he did not move and it did not destroy him, for his mind was without fear of death or birth. He was free from grasping and attachment, especially to the body, for it is the karmic result of grasping and attachment in terms of agglomerated flesh and blood.[94] "O gods and demons, if you want it, you can have it! I have no attachment to this! Indeed, the self is both cause and effect and, for those who understand, illusion comes from ignorance." Entering a state of fearlessness and confidence, he presented this song:

> In the town named Brin[95] of Ding ri,
> There are many merchants making profits;
> Both India and Tibet are nearby,
> And on the high snow mountains dwells the Fierce Lady of
> Long-Life ...

And so forth, he sang. He pacified the hatred and malice in the mental continua of all the assembly of *yakṣas* and *yakṣīs,* subjecting them to religious discipline. Unanimously, these non-humans supplicated the Saint and said: "Listen, o Cotton-Clad *Yogin*! You have accumulated the merit of a human body;

Folio 244:

you are indeed fortunate to be an accomplished *yogin*!"—and so forth, but it had no effect on his mind.

Then, one evening, on the tenth day of the first of the three months of summer, five ladies,[96] lovely, wonderful, and luminous, came before the Saint, saluted, and circumambulated many times.

They said: "These are the curds of a wild ox," which they served him on a ladle of sapphire.[97] They bowed reverently. The first one, who was clever, asked:

> The red-faced *rakṣasa* of Tibet—
> Like the snowy valley and the mountains
> Which are close together—
> And a *yakṣa* to whom belongs this snow mountain ...

She thus offered a song, with reverence and devotion, saluting with her body. He taught them about the secret-mantra of the Vajrayāna, and they practiced meditation to lead to conversion and liberation. These things the Saint did when dwelling in Chu dbar of Brin. Scorned amidst innumerable gods and demons including the Tse ring mas, who tried to make obstacles, the Saint overpowered them and afterwards converted them. This is the meaning.

> Then the Lord went to the valley of the Land of sNye nam, to liberate
> A Bon po of sNye nam who voyaged in the intermediate state;
> Geshe Dar bLo became faithful and devoted;
> I bow down to the taming of the virtuous assembly[98] of the Samgha. (23)

This is the explication:

Then Saint Milarepa went to sNye nam. There was a Bon po of sNye nam named gShen[99] Khro rgyal who had power and wealth. He believed in, made offerings to, and propitiated the Saint, lifting his foot to his head many times. Then the Bon po was about to die. He made out his last will and instructed his eldest son: "For myself, I need no other roots of virtue than Milarepa. For my benefit, I ask you to give offerings to the Saint and ask his loving kindness for me." The son himself did as he had been requested.

Folio 245:

Then, after three or four days, they wrote down the name of the dead man and made repeated supplications to call his consciousness into the written name; then the name-sign on the piece of paper began to shake. Then there was a sound and light, and he dissolved into the heart of the Saint. The family of the Bon po was delighted, and had faith in him. On that occasion great devotion arose.[100]

Peta was at rTsa, weeping very much. There, on that occasion, the Saint did not weep. He asked: "What is the meaning of this?" Peta said: "This is what has occurred to the Mila clan of Khu kun. We are sinful, you and I, and our parents. Where have they both gone after death?" And so she wept. The Saint said: "Our afflicted parents died because the power of Yama took them away. From the start until now I have used all three: body, speech, and mind for virtuous deeds. Since kindness to parents includes all sentient beings,[101] I have already brought about their salvation, since I am in manifestation, and they both are not (in fact, they are silent). So do not weep, I mentally performed the transfer of roots of virtue to our parents."

Then it came about that the great fame and reputation of the Saint Mila Happy Report became widely known. Attendants and provisions gathered like a cloud and at that time he became very popular.

In that place there was a teacher of grammar and debate named Dar blo. He was an Abhidharmist,[102] and he knew many *piṭakas*. He was learned in verse. He and Mila were comparable in merit. One day, Teacher Dar blo thought to engage Mila in debate: "This so-called Milarepa the *yogin* is illiterate. He is getting all the offerings for the dead and is becoming the object of the people's faith—this is how he eats. People are even comparing my fame and merit to his. Today I must tell the people about him and then subdue and expel him from this town."

Folio 246:

He went up one day to meet with the Saint. There, Ras chung pa rDo rJe grags pa and others, including some of the cotton clad *yogins*, were in the presence of the two of them. rDo rJe grags pa said to the Saint: "The Debate-Teacher Dar blo is burdened with a measureless heap of sinful karma from previous lives as a master of studies. Today he has come to meet you." He offered a sign of reverence, and returned the bow submissively. The associates of the scholar also requested the same sign of respect. The Saint did not comply and remained seated, as if asleep.[103] The Teacher Dar blo went up to him; he had a butter offering in his hand. He bowed and inquired about his health. The Saint did not accept his bow or his offering. He lifted up his feet a little bit. Then the Teacher Dar blo said: "You are said to be a great Siddha, mighty in yoga (*yogeśvara*). We should both engage in debate on our opinions of the Doctrine." Mila got up and said: "Fine. Then let us debate." They both began a little dispute on their respective opinions. The Teacher Dar blo was unable to defeat Mila Happy Report: the Saint vanquished him. Dar blo said: "You are a destroyer of Buddha's teachings; you are in the wrong toward the Three Jewels; you are not a Dharma practitioner. From the start, you are full of imposture. You wrongly eat the goods of the deceased and the offerings of the faithful." He abused him in various ways and kicked at his head. He then threw dust and dirt in his mouth. The Saint did nothing whatever at the time; he just let him do it. Then, after a while, Dar blo's rage calmed down and he put his

Folio 247:

robe back on. These things provoked Ras chung pa to say: "We should do to this evil doer as he did to our Lama! Strike him!" As he was about to strike Teacher Dar blo, the Saint said: "Don't hit! Don't hit! Just wipe my mouth clean of this dirt." He then cleaned the dirt from his head by shaking it around. This being done, Ras chung pa cleaned the dirt from his mouth. The Saint said: "O Ras chung pa, your meditation discipline is diminishing. Let us both join in song together." He offered this song to Dar blo:

I bow down to the lord Gurus;
Excellent is the peace of Dharma, separated from passion;
Excellent to go for refuge to the Doctrine of the Holy Path;
O Master Dar blo, listen!
You are respected as one who is knowledgeable in this
 world—
We are both excellent in hearing, analysis, and meditation;
We are now meeting so as to converse,
but in you, hatred is like a fire
Ignited in the mind;
The Five Paths are aflame with the Three Afflictions;
We two men are trapped by the din of jealousy,
And thus this place is like a hell realm—
Which is a shame for the Three Refuges!
You yourself do not know the nature of mind,
And what you know of the Holy Doctrine

Is of no profit to you!
For you are not pacified in mind—
You, a so-called great scholar, are not accomplished;
Since you are not striking the head of "Self"
What good is it to strike Mila Happy Report's head?
You are not casting dirt upon delusion—
So what good is it to cast dirt on me?
Your mental motivation is not pure—
So what good are your monastic vows?
You lack diligence in these three: body, speech, and mind,
So you have put on the three robes of the monk to no avail;
You have not abandoned these three: Lust, Hate, and
  Delusion—

Folio 248:

So what good is it to make distinctions
Among different sects and practices?
I am the *yogin* Milarepa;
Previously, there was nothing I hadn't done;
And even now, having criticized you, I feel a little sad;
There is nothing I haven't meditated upon
But here is something new—
A meditation on dirt in my mouth;
There was nothing I hadn't "kicked" before—
But now you've kicked me with your foot!
Although you are a master of the Holy Doctrine,
The allies pride and misery increase
In one who is a receptacle of fully ripened,
Amassed evil karma;
Negative accumulations are gathered in the mind,
And not just in the body—so that
For a hundred aeons one is not set free,
But if one undertakes right contemplation,

Then good fruit may ripen, so it is said;
If you only have intellectual Dharma,
It creates evil deeds;
If you are a true listener,[104] you will achieve tranquility
But if you are "clever" in doctrinal distinctions,
Then hatred and selfishness increase.

Dar blo was then ashamed for the faults he had committed. Pondering, he went away. "That which the father Mila says is so; nothing is false of what he said. I myself have accumulated great sins. Now I will confess these sins," he thought. Then he went back to where the Saint was, and when he met him, the Saint manifested five likenesses, all the same. Several sat inside, some were outside. Some were in the entry way. Some going up, some going down. The teacher Dar blo pondered this. The Saint manifested many likenesses at the same time. Dar blo wondered: "To which one should I make my confession?" But the Saint knew his thoughts and Mila Happy Report said: "There is a Paṇḍita[105] inside; go there. Go up there and start a debate." Dar blo asked him what he looks like.

Folio 249:

Mila said: "He has knowledge and intelligence. If you can defeat him, you won't have to confess to me and your sins will certainly be wiped off." So he went inside. The venerable Paṇḍita who appeared was carrying a column of bronze. He said: "We can both debate with this *tantrika* and put him on our lap (to humble him). He who is the victor will be established as the Teacher over the one defeated." They both engaged in debate. Whatever he did, Dar blo did not win the debate. Then the Paṇḍita made extensive offerings and dissolved into Mila Happy Report. Then the other manifestations dissolved into one. Finally, Mila dissolved into himself! This is what Master Dar Blo thought: "This Guru has acquired the power to command illusory manifestations. He has attained perfection. Formerly, for a little while, because of my karmic accumulations, I was imagining wrong things about him. But now perfect faith and reverence have arisen." He said to the Saint, "I now offer my confession of sins with regret and repentance." He then requested teachings and he followed Mila's advice. The Saint became compassionate, bestowed the doctrine, and advised him to meditate. With good meditation experience, the state of perfection dawned.

Then, at that time, among the monks of sNye nam, Gung thang, and elsewhere, hatred arose against the Saint. There was a small *vihāra* named rDzing bu where the monks said to the Saint: "You are someone who adheres to false views." They struck the cotton-clad *yogins* with rocks and heaped immense abuse on them. One day, the Saint went there and said: "Today I want to go to the *vihāra* at rDzing bu." The Master and three disciples, these four, went. There were many good dogs of that *vihāra*.

Folio 250:

None of these dogs bothered the Saint and his disciples. They licked them and were happy. Then a monk arrived. The Saint and his disciples were recognized. The monk said: "O deceitful Mila—master with disciples—why have you come to our place? To beat us up?" Just then, ten monks arrived. They all cruelly beat and dragged off the Saint and his disciples, but no harm came to the Saint, not even one thing. Then they said: "Even when beaten nothing happens to these rogues. We'll tie them up one by one with iron, put them on the pinnacle of the monastery, and leave them there." They took them all and handcuffed them and when they were all tied up, they went back outside. The monks left them all, master and disciples, well tied up. Then the Saint said: "*Phaṭ!*" All of them who had been bound, master and disciples, were set free. Their captors, the monks, were now tied up! Then several other monks showed up and said: "This rogue knows a lot!" The rest of the monks came and said: "Tie this rogue up well!" "Throw him off a cliff! Come on!" Each monk went and brought a rope. They tied the Saint up tightly. Fifteen monks tried to drag him down the hill, but they couldn't move the Saint. They tried everything, but nothing happened; they could not harm him. In that place, on that occasion, the Saint performed a great deed with his power. He pulled outside all the people and objects that were stored inside. He brought the animals that were corralled outside, inside! In short, in this way he turned everything inside-out.[106] All became terrified and fearful. They made offerings to the Saint.

Folio 251:
The Saint offered this song:

I, the *yogin* Milarepa
Possess unobstructed might of non-ego
Yours is a monastery of impure beings
With non-devotion, wrong views, and slander;
How can you capture, tie up, strike, and beat others?
I can't accept this; I do not wish to do or to hear about such things,
Nor am I ashamed to use wildness (*spyod pa*) as skillful means;
If you stop doing evil, then offer faith and reverence,
But if you don't stop, I'll crush you to powder!

A rain of stones fell from space and the abbot and the leaders of that monastery, with all the monks, placed their heads beneath his feet; they became faithful and devoted. These things the Saint did as miracles and displays of magical power. He completely subdued those impious beings after they had captured him, and they became devoted. This is the explanation.

To awaken the spiritual understanding of the men and women of Brin,
He flew off a precipice;
And the patrons received a blessing from Tārā;
I bow down to the Saint, who bestows a blessing. (24)

This is the explication:

Then the Saint Victor Milarepa abode in Chu dbar of Brin with Ras chung rdo rje grags pa and patroness Legs se, a leader and a few other persons. The many patrons and patronesses of Brin came together at one time to make a request for the initiation of the five deities of Cakrasaṃvara. The Saint was overcome by compassion. He set up a *maṇḍala* of colored sand; the practitioners were first established in the empowerment of the Vase.[107] After they had perfected the preliminary empowerments, he then bestowed the higher empowerment of the Vase. "Now, since I am old, the vase

Folio 252:

itself will perform the rite." He at once recited the mantra: '*om na ma sarva tathā ga ta.*' Then it was not necessary to place the vase on top of the people individually. All of them marveled at what happened, the Yoginī Glorious Tārā[108] and the others as well. Many of the people muttered the mantra and acquired wisdom. For some people who did not even need to meditate, full comprehension arose. All became very cheerful and happy.

The Saint sang:

> I am of the Hearing Lineage, which I hand on intact;
> I unite the Supreme State inseparably with Bliss,
> And the initiation of the Five Wisdoms, with the Vase of Initiation working-by-itself;
> Thus I bestow the Buddha's wisdom
> Having acquired wisdom, a blissful light appears—
> True understanding arises in the initiation of the Victor,
> The experience arises to fulfill all wishes
> In the initiation rare, unlike any other!
> My system of initiation, that of Lama Mila,
> Is truly wonderful in essence and is needed by the devoted.

So he sang. Faith and devotion arose in all the people.

The next morning, Ras chung rdo rje grags pa drew an image of the Diamond Sow (*Vajravārāhī*) and Patroness Legs Se made one of Hevajra. In order to set them up, they asked for a consecration. They prepared the *pūjā*. Mila said to bring some barley as a substitute for flowers (*me tog nas khyer la shog*), and it was done as he ordered. The Saint told many stories. At that point the barley-flowers made a spitting sound: *Thu thu thu*. The Saint said: "From the time of my earliest childhood and upbringing I, Mila, have strewn flowers ritually. Now that I am old, I invite the head of the tutelary deity to strew the flowers." The image of Vajravārāhī nodded its head in front. At the same time, the image of Hevajra also shook. The barley-flowers that were in front began to pour

Folio 253:

forth the sound "*hram*" and the barley mingled with the image of the tutelary deities. This happened in front of them and they marveled; there was a great, marvelous light and they made obeisance. The Saint said:

> The invocation of the deity on canvas
> Is not needed for acquiring wisdom;
> The flowers of wisdom arise of themselves—
> O Ras chung pa! The consecration is permanent![109]

He sang this song and then went away. After a few days, he arrived at the home of Legs se and her husband, who went before the Saint and requested teaching on the mind. "Please give us both a teaching (*khrid*)[110] at the same time. One will guide the other after following your lead." The Saint said: "Yes, one can follow the other to guide one another. I accept your request."

Having situated the patron in meditation practice, the patroness performed reverential service. In the patron, the instruction did not give rise even to a brief experience of realization. But in the patroness, a state of good understanding and perfection arose. The Lama Saint bestowed the essential nature of mind (*ngo sprad pa*) on her[111] and the realization of wisdom arose in her. The patron said: "I also will carry provisions so that I will understand." His wife said: "You should also meditate!" Even for him, an understanding of wisdom and insight arose. On that occasion the patron went to get provisions and Legs se and the Saint ate the offerings. The Saint laughed and smiled. The patroness asked: "Why, o Saint, are you laughing and smiling?" The Saint said, "The patron is just now bringing a load [20 cups] of roast barley and other things for food and while going along he met a tiger on the road.

Folio 254:

The patron was not able to run away or even to strike back; he had to stand there! That's why I am laughing!" After a long time, the patron came with the offerings. He said, "I met a tiger today; I did not run away; I just stood there. By the compassion of my Guru, the tiger did not cause any harm." The patroness said to him: "We have really met a genuine Guru in this one!" Understanding arose in their minds. "Tigers and other fierce animals do no harm to us; we, an old man and an old woman, are both content."

At that time the Saint said:

> I am Milarepa the *yogin*;
> Having patrons is a great blessing;
> When I practice austerities, wandering among mountain
>   solitudes,
> My bodily necessities are set in order
> By you, male and female patrons;
> The right circumstances of causes and conditions are present
> And experience rises in the mind;
> No longer need one fear the sight of fearsome beasts
> Such as tigers and the rest.

To both patron and patroness, he is said to have given explanations of the fullness of wisdom (*yang dag pa ye shes kyi*); they both also firmly acquired realization of the fullness of wisdom.

On one occasion, to several patrons and patronesses of Brin, he gave an initiation of Vajrapāṇi Garuda and it happened that seven disciples flew in the air.

Again, upon a certain occasion several patrons and patroness of Brin performed a *gaṇacakra* (*tshogs kyi 'khor lo*).[112] At that *gaṇacakra*, the Saint said: "I am going to invite the eighty-four siddhas while you yourselves prepare the *gaṇacakra* and so forth." They asked him, "How much is needed?" He replied: "I am only teasing—this is sufficient." He then spoke the mantra:

Gu ru samaya hum//

at the same time, snapping his fingers and

Folio 255:

making a cracking sound. Then, in a little while, accompanied by a noise, the assembly of the eighty-four siddhas came to the *gaṇacakra*, the great Brahman Saraha and the rest! Then, [the participants] invited them to the *gaṇacakra*. After a little while there was a glow and a sound and the clamor of musical sound; the eighty-four great siddhas—every one of them—went away in silence. Then, at that time, in that place, understanding arose in several people. It also occurred that several were able to fly in the sky. So it was on that occasion. They were all blessed: the disciples, the patrons, and the patronesses. It happened that realization arose in many [of them.] Innumerable omens of a marvelous kind occurred.

The participants in the *gaṇacakra* asked for a dedication of merit. The Saint said: "I am not going to do it; I will send someone else. Do not disperse for a little while! Just sit!" Having said this, he went away. Then, after that, the Noble Tārā came; she was sitting on a throne. She gave the dedication of merit called *bsngo ba yon bshad*, and the rest. Then all the people were marveling and immense devotion arose. The Saint returned after a short while. "Did Saint (*rje btsun*) Tārā give the blessings and dedication of merit? Then that suffices!"

These things the Saint did, bestowing profound Dharma and initiatic power (*dbang*) on all of them, the faithful disciples, patrons, and patronesses. At that time he blessed them and immeasurable signs and wonders appeared.

> Then the Saint, Mila the *yogin*,
> Not abiding in that place, [went to]

Folio 256:

> Southern gTsang and the Three Provinces of Western Tibet,
> And to the North of gTsang;
> I bow down to his wanderings amount the mountain solitudes. (25)

This is the explication:

Then, the Saint-Victor Mid la ras pa,[113] at that time did not remain in any one place, but went wandering among the mountain solitudes without any direction. It was his intention (*dgongs pa*) to establish the doctrine of the Practice Lineage (*bsgrub brgyud*). In particular, whoever heard the name of the Saint, Mid la, was released from cyclic existence and became perfected in all virtues, it is said. So he thought: "Because my name and fame have spread in all directions, I am to wander like a vagabond in the mountain solitudes."

First, he went to the upper part of the three provinces of Western Tibet. He also went to the three Snow-Mountain Lakes. Of snow mountains, the king is Ti se; of lakes, the king is Ma pham; of mountains, the king is rTse rGya, and so forth. So he went to all of them. He established the teachings of the Practice Lineage; there his experience and understanding increased. He accomplished immeasurable good for many of the sentient beings of those places. Then he went down the road to Pu rangs (West Tibet), and bLo bo Gung thang, to many places thereabouts. He established the doctrine of the Practice Lineage while dwelling there for a short time. He accomplished immeasurable benefits for sentient beings. Then he went down to La stod in the south, to Lho byang, and to Ding ri, and to Bong Shong, to Shri ri, to Khrom, and so on, dwelling amid the holy places in the mountain solitudes of southern La stod. He established the doctrine of the Practice Lineage and accomplished immeasurable good for sentient beings. Then he went in the direction of G.yas ru byang, and then to rGyal thang[114] and to Shel lug and 'Gur klu rgyal gling po, mChog dkar gyi brag, and so on. Having also dwelt towards G.yas ru byang, he established the doctrine of the Practice Lineage.

Folio 257:

He accomplished immeasurable good for sentient beings in these places. First dwelling in Brag of the "Eighty" of rGyal thang, his understanding and realization increased more and more. When hawks flew up into the sky, he followed! The Saint also flew from the Rock of the Eighty in rGyal thang.[115] He left to go to Shel lcag ma; flying from Shel lcag he went to the Rock of the Eighty, manifesting innumerable wonders and he established the doctrine of the Practice Lineage. Then he dwelt in gLu rgyal gling po. A Nāga of gLing po offered things delightful to the body, chiefly a Mudrā (tantric consort). Mila engaged in practice with her to benefit and increase the arising of the clear light of wisdom of the four blisses.[116] He only ate crushed nettles as food.

On one occasion, the lady patrons of 'Gur klu rgyal prepared an offering. At that place also he established the doctrine of the practice-lineage, accomplishing the good of innumerable sentient beings.

Then he dwelt in the mountain solitudes of Bar tshigs and mChog dKar brag, and gTso bo stag gu. He instructed Lady Ko ne, and others for a long time. There too he established the doctrine of the Practice Lineage, accomplishing the good of innumerable sentient beings. Then he went to Cung gi yul po che la and Jo ro, and 'Bring 'tshams, and sTag tshang, and so forth, where he established the doctrine of the Practice Lineage and accomplished the good of innumerable sentient beings. He went wandering aimlessly in the mountain solitudes there and elsewhere; he did not remain in one place: there is no spot of ground which his feet did not travel. In these places he also performed austerities and established the doctrine of the Practice Lineage;

his realization and understanding increased[117] and he benefited innumerable sentient beings.

Folio 258:

He also possessed the effective means for benefiting beings.[118] In this way, the Saint dwelt in Zal mo (a district of Khams) in the land of Tibet, in this throne world beneath the umbrella of the sun.[119] No one was greater than he in establishing the doctrine of meditation (*sgrub tshugs*). Even now, there is no one like him. No one else could equal his (1) understanding and realization; (2) miracles; (3) meditative concentration (*zad par*); (4) his supremacy over Mārā; (5) supreme knowledge (*abhijñā*); (6) manifestation of forms and (7) transformation of circumstances; (8) meditation attainment; (9) virtues; and so forth.[120] No one was better than the Saint. No one has since arisen to be his equal. He accomplished benefits, some of which can be seen, others which cannot, for innumerable sentient beings. He could ripen and liberate them, especially incarnate beings with the body of a Buddha, such as was Lord Dwags po, sGampopa.

He obtained the unobstructed virtue of obtaining power over both mind and interior energies (*rlung*), like that of Ras chung rdo rje grags pa; he possessed faith and devotion like that of 'Bri sgom g.yang legs; he obtained the power of bliss and heat (*bde drod*) like Ras pa Zhi ba skyong; he was strong and patient in austerities and meditation like Rong chung pa ras pa; in benefiting sentient beings through perceiving wisdom and so on, he was like Lung skam ras pa, like sNi zhangs ras pa, like Se Ban ston chung, and other inner disciples like Patroness Legs se, Yoginī lCam me, or like Yoginī sGon me, and so forth. Thus there were many disciples accomplishing the immense benefit of sentient beings, their realization, perceiving wisdom directly having arisen in mind. Those who could do so increased their ability to help other beings. In this way, the Saint realized the voidness of the five heaps of the five poisons (*skandhas*). The demon of narrow views (*chung po'i bdud*) was conquered; all the desirable things were recognized as illusory, like dreams; the demon of the *devaputras* was defeated.

Folio 259:

Many beautiful women surrounded him, making sexual advances to test him, but he was not moved to lust. Thus he defeated the demon of delusion.

For those beings who believe themselves to be "eternal" (and thus lacking understanding), he showed the truth of impermanence by dying.[121]

The Teacher Lom thing nga of the North even gave him poison three times, but he didn't die. Thus he subdued Yama, he conquered the four demons of the [merely] relative meaning. Also, even from the absolute perspective, the five skandhas are not to be perceived as ordinary, but as a Buddha's body. Thus, the demonic delusion of the *skandhas* is overcome. All that arises, good or bad, is understood to arise in one's own nature as the Clear Light. Thus the Māras are subdued. In this way he fully realized inner attainment. The five poisons: desire, anger, ignorance, pride, jealousy, he realized to be the five wisdoms! Thus he overcame the miserable demon of delusion. He understood the meaning of ultimate reality as being without birth or death. He overcame the demon Yama. In this he also manifested the absolute truth. He completely vanquished the four demons of all space (*dbyings su bcom pa'i*) by his might in yoga. This great Victor among Siddhas suitably attained both the great and ordinary accomplishments (*siddhi*).

These things Lord Mila did: everywhere he established the doctrine of the Practice Lineage, wandering as a vagabond in the mountain solitudes. He benefited sentient beings immeasurably. This is the explication.

> Thus the Saint-Guru,
> Possessing the Six Perfections and Defeating the Four Māras,
> Having completed all his enlightened activity,
> Manifested the way to pass out of misery (*parinirvāṇa*);
> I bow down to the completion of the Saint's biography
> (*rnam thar*). (26)

This is the meaning:

Then, Milarepa, Lord of Yogins, having completely and perfectly accomplished all the work of benefiting beings, taught all his disciples as much as possible so that signs of accomplishment (*siddhi*) appeared. Having attained virtue, many of the disciples set out to benefit sentient beings.

Folio 260:

They introduced the good custom of asceticism; as great meditators, wandering the mountain solitudes, they became very eminent among the guru Siddhas of this Buddha field of both India and Tibet.

When the Saint was seventy-three years old, the age of a person worthy of veneration, amid some of the people and some followers and disciples, he said: "Whether I die or don't die makes no difference; except in order to teach impermanence to those disciples possessing the erroneous view of permanence. Especially for the purpose of delighting Teacher Byang 'bar, in this year, I am going to manifest the impermanence of this illusion body." In the presence of a circle of his disciples, the Saint was giving an initiation (*dbang can lags mod*). The disciples said: "For the benefit of others, take pity and do not die." The Saint said: "Formerly, the Blessed One, the Mighty Sage also died; he displayed the manner of passing away from suffering. From that, there arose causes that became more beneficial for sentient beings. In the same way, the Gurus of the bKa' brgyud also display the manner of passing away from misery, thus bringing about a greater good for the benefit of sentient beings. Just as I can accomplish the good of sentient beings by not passing away from misery, and have up until now done so, I am also able to accomplish the good of beings by passing away from sorrow." Thus he displayed the manner of dying to the misery of this world in an exoteric way, so it is said. "For the people, I am to appear in different aspects when I die." Then he sang this song:

I am the *yogin* Milarepa.
Having conquered the frost of Demon Yama,

I go to the further destiny;
At that time of death, many things will be seen;
For some, a heap, essentially an apparitional form [like a stūpa] will arise;
They will worship and make offerings to the Form of the corpse they clean;
For some, the apparition dies not (for mind dies not)
Having become a rainbow body.

Folio 261:

It departs this realm (*dhātu*);
Thus, both appearances seem true!

At that time, dwelling in the hermitage of Chu dbar, there were twelve *yogins* and *yoginīs* before him: 'Bri sgom g'yang legs, Yoginī lCam me, and the rest. Their appearance was like the Six Lords of Light.[122] Free of illness and other obstacles, they abode, making spiritual progress.

In the hollow of his bed linen, his rainbow-like bodily appearance departed this life. Ras pa Zhi ba skyong and patroness Legs se, and some of the rest saw the apparition (*snang ngor*).

In sNye nam, the Bon po Tsan dar 'bum, by the power of a passionate attachment, bestowed a fine turquoise on a beautiful woman as a bribe. He gave her a cup of curds into which poison had been mixed with butter and pan-roasted barley (*tsampa*). He said to her: "You are to bring this to him and by devious means get him to drink it. If Milarepa is an ordinary person, he will let you enter. If he is non-ordinary, it will serve as an example. Otherwise, give me back my turquoise." So off she went.

The curds offered to the Saint were cool. The Saint accepted the curds, even though he knew it was poisoned. He gave the cup back to the beautiful woman. "Because of this deed, you have obtained a turquoise. Because of this, the deed will completely fulfill the wishes of Bon Po Tsan dar. I am going to drink the curds. When it ripens fully, your connection toward this deed will not be too heavy; with my blessing ..." He then sent the beautiful lady away.

Then, after a while, he was ill. The disciples asked: "How is this sickness to be cured, if that is possible?" The Saint said: "It is not useful to cure it; at this time it is necessary that I go."[123]

"In the cave behind me, when I die, I have some money for the funeral, and some things that I give to you. You are to make offerings and perform worship, and so forth.

Folio 262:

Now you are to make reparation for infractions against your vows," he said.

Legs se said to him: "Since our Guru is without possessions, we need to take up a collection to make preparations for your funeral." She offered to do this, but he would not permit it.

Then, in the year of the monkey,[124] on the evening of the full moon day of the last of the three spring months, unattached to all passions, his consciousness mediated; then, it went to the realm of the Clear Light in space.

He said: "gShen chung pa, you have done me much good service. After I depart take my hat and my staff and bring them to Ras chung pa in a place called Lo ro."

Then, between nine and midnight, a butter lamp that burns for one night was lit and he gave Dharma teachings. In this way, he put his body in a yoga position; he poised his hand in a *mudrā* and said: "My sacred lamp is to be placed on my head." Thus they did as he said. He sat without moving all night. Then it was dawn. The attendants went to see if it was daybreak. He said: "Get up to check the evidence. Is it really morning?" "Now, take away the lamp. Now it doesn't matter to me whether I meditate or not. But I am doing this for the purpose of showing you a good example. I am an old man, so I am at the point of death. Even so, I meditate. If you don't meditate, you won't achieve Buddhahood. You *must* meditate." With that phrase, he died (*'pho ba*).

Then, in the midst of the atmosphere, there was a sound of music. A white ray of light emerged from the top of his head and remained, planted in the sky-realm. These and many other good omens occurred. Then there were tears in the eyes of the circle of disciples. They sat down before his remains and made offerings and prayers. Then behind his body,

Folio 263:

in the crevice, they opened the ground, where there were three categories of items: [1] Sacred objects: a mirror with a flame, a flaming silk, a rusty knife. That was all he had. As for his external possessions [2], there remained a pouch of flour with white patches, several cotton garments almost without any holes and a white undergarment (*'gan rka*) and [3] a ritual headdress with a mirror[125] and little *samaya* texts. Other than these, there were no other possessions or personal objects. Thus the disciples thought: "We need a support for our devotion." They made offerings to the corpse for a week into the intermediate state. Then the people of Brin and sNye nam, patrons and patronesses, met together. The people of Brin wanted to take the corpse to the district of Brin. Those from sNye nam wanted to take it to the sNye nam. Thus they did not agree! The leader of the folk of Brin named rGya gar bya ba said: "You are in the right, and so we are in the right. Now we both, Brin and sNye nam, can be seen from the mountain between us; therefore, we will cremate the corpse there." They decided in favor of his advice. Then all the patrons and disciples as a group announced this publicly. They met for three days. Then, at the time, the people of Brin, being covetous men, had intense devotion. At midnight they brought the corpse to Brin. They erected a shrine for the corpse. They tried to purify the corpse in a cremation fire, but amid the flames, it resisted being burnt.

Then, at the place of the assembly of all the disciples, they made offerings together and were very sad. Then also, some of them fainted, some wept, some beat their breasts, some disheveled their hair, etc. All of them became subdued. In the sky, there were many musical sounds descending.

Folio 264:

From the heart *cakra* of the corpse, flame arose of itself. Then, all the smoke came together to form a rainbow; all bowed their heads, and parasols, victory banners, and the eight auspicious objects and so forth appeared. In the sky, a sparkling light was all-pervading and appeared there along with heroes and heroines; also many assemblies of *ḍākinīs* gathered in the realm of the sky. A voice from the sky spoke:

The Precious Guru departed at this time;
Among all the people of his place on earth—
Some are fainting, some weeping—
Crying out in lamentation, beating the breast,
Disheveling the hair,
Making offerings very sincerely:
A self-arisen fire ignited from his heart,
The smoke became like a rainbow,
Bowing like a creeper;
Conches, a victory banner, and so forth,
Appear as signs with the eight auspicious omens—
With the sound of timbrel, conch, and cymbals,
The sound of ram's horn, reed pipe and sitara,
The musical sounds are heard with the appearance of
musicians—
A delightful celestial assembly of the *ḍākinīs*.
The Guru, powerful Lord of *ḍākinīs*—
Now his pure corpse departs to its place in the heavenly realm.

—and so forth, they sang, with many words and melodies. This was manifestly heard by all. All of those in that gathering became devoted with far more faith than ever before.

Then, for many days of the intermediate state, offerings were made at the sepulcher (*pur khang*). Afterwards, preparations for burial were made and the relics were arranged and placed in the tomb. Of the relics, not even a bit of the finger or toenails were left because they had been taken by the *ḍākinīs*.[126]

The aggregates composing the body passed away entirely without remainder (*sku phung po lhag med du mngon pa*) in the manner of a completely perfect Buddha. But the *nirmāṇakāya* still exists in as many manifestations as are necessary to help his disciples, and to accomplish the good of beings.[127] Also, in order to appear to certain disciples, an emanation went to Mang Khung.

Folio 265:

One emanation dwelt in the place of White Rock Ta po. So as to give Dharma teachings to certain disciples, he went to Mang Khung where dwelt Teacher Byang 'bar.[128] By the power of the former passions in his mind, he had offered poison to Milarepa, which the latter knew all along. He went there for the benefit of that Teacher, in order to display impermanence for those beings caught up in the idea of permanence: that is how it is to be understood. Indeed, that is how attainment is brought about: one attains it by one's own efforts, so it is said. He then displayed the way to die happily. "Whatever you think or do, I follow your thoughts—thus I manifest dying."

In brief, the Saint Victor Milarepa came forth from the narrow passage of asceticism and austerity, for disciples essentially both capable and not capable, showing how one naturally possesses the happiness of full realization; he established the doctrine of the Practice Lineage, accomplishing the aims of innumerable sentient beings and disciples; having set out to liberate all ripened sentient beings from contact, memory, hearing, and sight.[129] By contemplation, he completely passed beyond sorrow. This is the meaning!

These deeds of the Saint Victor Milarepa have been combined by rGyal thang pa bde chen rdo rje into a thoroughly wonderful, sublime biography, which expresses the faith clearly. It is now complete.

Beautiful! Corrected! Auspicious!

22

The Lives of Marpa and Milarepa by sGam po pa

[A.23; B.16. The Biographies of Lord (rje) Marpa and Saint (rje btsun) Mila]

[A.24] His son was the translator Marpa Lotsawa.[1]

As a youth, he delighted in being a troublemaker [to] everyone. His father thought: "This son of mine will kill someone, or he will surely get killed by someone. If [I] send him to study he may become a significant scholar." Having pondered this, he loaded up many goods and sent them [and Marpa] over to 'Brog mi Lotsawa.[2] [Marpa] offered a horse to 'Brog mi [A.25.1] in order to learn the Dharma. But 'Brog mi Lotsawa was very stingy with the Dharma, so he [Marpa] went to Nepal. While attending to the doctrine [or Buddha-Dharma] [propounded] by a Nepali named sPyi ther pa, he [learned] that all the Nepalis had to go to India to learn the doctrine. He thought: "Why shouldn't I go too?" and so, off he went.

He first met Lama Pendawa and also one named Karma tsa.[3] He stayed with him for three years. Then he went up to Gser Kha[4] in north Tibet. He offered three *srang* of gold to the Paṇḍita, who was [thereby] very pleased. He advised: "I have a Guru (bla-ma) named Nāropa; I will send you [there] to him." [A.26.1] He sent (*sprad pa*) him to Vikramaśīla, so [Marpa] said,[5] "I heard the doctrine from Nāropa, Maitrīpa, [B.17] and others. Nāropa's virtues were so great that, though I dwelt for six years in his presence, not once did I become weary. It sufficed merely to see him [meet him] to cause the accumulation of merit." Then, having meditated on the instructions of the Practice Lineage and the explanation-lineage, I went back to Tibet.[6]

On the way, while returning to Tibet, I gave a brief explanation of the doctrine. In dBus, Marpa mGo Yags[7] offered ten golden *srang* and asked for the doctrine from me. Then, while crossing some water at bsNubs[8] the instructions [notes taken on the teachings in India] were lost in the water. [However], it is also said that gNos Lotsawa, out of jealousy (*'phrag dog byas nas*) threw them into the water of the Ganges.

[Later], having returned [to India], I went to seek the Guru. Having gone to a forest hermitage, the Guru [Nāropa] was not to be found. Finally, when I did find [him], his speaking had ceased; having renounced everything, the Guru did not give teachings on the doctrine.[9] He merely bestowed a blessing on the ritual circle of *yogins.*[10]

[A.27]Marpa was a long-time disciple; [Nāropa] even bestowed his own skull cup [on him]. Having dwelt with him for two years, he again requested [teachings]. Then the Guru became tougher [with him] than before, so [he] said.

After he returned to Lho-Brag to dwell, Mes ston tshon po of the valley of the gTsang offered [Marpa] a field that required six *bre* [of seed] to be sown, covered with [items] of wealth, and asked for the doctrine.[11]

The Monk-Scholar gZhung pa was at that time studying the mantra-system of the rNying-ma-pa from the Monk-Scholar dGyer chung pa. Monk-Scholar dGyer chung pa heard an account of Lama Lho pa [Marpa]. They both left [the region of] rNgog to hear the doctrine [from Marpa], so it is said. The Master [rGyer chung pa?] and five disciples went to Lho Brag. They offered Marpa a horse. The Lama was amused [by this]: "If this horse of yours is a gift, it is too much; if it is an offering, it is rather small!" he said. He [thus] reminded them that attending instructions in the doctrine is a very great [matter]. [B.18]

Mes tshon po also sent a monk to ask [Marpa] to go to gTsang. Marpa decided to go up there. [However] gZhung thought to himself [A.28]: "I don't want to leave for gTsang; I have two parents [to care for?]. [However] instruction in the doctrine is also appropriate (*'phrod 'dug*) and [I] wish to remain with [Marpa]." Thus, he asked [Marpa] to come to gZhung; [Marpa] said: "Fine!" (*rung*). He went there and was offered seventy yak cows, a yak-hair tent, a dog, a white porcelain cup, and so forth.

Later, Mila became a servant (*mi las g.yog byas*) (i.e., disciple) [of Marpa]; it is said that he offered a herd of one hundred sheep, one hundred ten volumes of the scriptures, including the *Avataṃsaka*, and so forth.[12] The Lama [?] also offered the *Catupiṭha Tantra*, the *Mahāmāyā Tantra*, the [Vajra] *Pañjara Tantra*, and the *Hevajra Tantra* (*dgyes rdor*), and so on, were given besides, so it is said. All these great people having performed service [and thus honored the Guru], he granted their request for the doctrine.[13]

Then, one time when the disciples were gathered in a house, having blocked up the holes and windows, he "poured" consciousness into the corpse of a pigeon and caused it to fly away. Also, once when a yak had been sick and had died, the Lama said: "Is the yak [really] dead?" The disciples replied: "It is dead."[14] [A.29]

While dwelling wearing the mantle of one dressed in ragged skins the Lama, so it is said, crossed a wide field [?]. (*Tib: bla ma g.yangs shun hrul po cig/bsnams nas bzhugs tsa na/ yangs pa cig na skyal nas 'dug gsung/*)

His legacy (*phyag rjes*) was: a nine story fortress roofed and stone-walled, and the large number of sūtras that he compiled [or translated (*bzhengs*)].

Though abiding in the supreme view, he, the great translator, seemed not always to meditate. He remained undisturbed, always in samādhi. He realized the true continuum of reality (*Dharmatā*). In this way, he was like an incarnation [of a Bodhisattva, or of Vajradhara]. His son-disciples were also accomplished, and even better [than they] were their disciples,[15] in accordance with the prophecy (*lung ston*).

Among the sons was the translator Lama rNgog gZhung pa. From his youth, he had studied much. Then he met Lama Marpa. As an act of renunciation, three times he placed his head to [the Lama's] feet; the Lama bestowed all the oral instructions [on him]. [B.19] He (rNgog? Marpa?)[16]

looked upon the presence of the fifteen goddesses with Nairātmyā by means of the illusion body (*mayākāya*) in a dream, so it is said.[17]

[A.29.5–6. The Life of Milarepa]

Lama Mila was the spiritual son of both [Marpa and rNgog]. He was of the Mi la clan of Gung Thang; his name was Happy-Report (Thos pa dga'). The family consisted only of the father and son; there was a harmful dispute (*'khas*) [in the family]. [A.30]

He went to dBus to acquire magic power. After he had learned many magic techniques, he went back up [to Gung Thang]. Then, he attended instruction in the doctrine from a teacher in the gTsang po valley named Lha dga', who told him: "Now you are fortunate in [having found] the holy doctrine of the great perfection (*rdzogs pa chen po*), which is of all vehicles (*theg pa*) the supreme. It is the essence of all spiritual instructions; if you achieve it in the morning, you become a Buddha that morning. If you attain it in the evening, you are a Buddha that very evening."

Afterwards, they heard about the arrival (*byon pa*) of Lama Marpa.

The teacher [Lha dga'] said to him: "We assiduously meditate on this teaching, but there seems to be no progress [for both of us]. You should go to Marpa Lotsawa, who has just arrived; he possesses the oral instructions (*gdams pa*). Since I am now an old man, I am unable to go; if I had the ability, I would go," he said. Hearing the renown of Marpa, [Milarepa's] former good inclinations were awakened, and he went before Lama Marpa.

"[Since I am] without provisions, can you grant me both the doctrine and physical necessities?" he asked. [Marpa] replied: "Both cannot be given; which do you desire?" "I desire the doctrine." "Well then, go fetch water and so forth," said [Marpa]. Then he gave him the name "great magician" (*mThu chen*). He entered the inner group of his disciples. There are many stories about him [at this time]. [A.31]

He served Lama Marpa for five years. He requested the oral instructions of the Practice Lineage. Then he served rNgog for one year. He rendered assistance by making hail fall on rNgog's enemy. Though he was sued in court [?], there was no loss [on his part] or gain [on the side of his opponents]. Later on, faith in Lama Marpa arose [definitively].

Then Mila meditated in a cave with a lamp on top of his head. [B.20] At about midnight, he opened his eyes; he saw a white glow (*dkar yal le*). He thought: "A virtue has already arisen in me!" having forgotten about the butter lamp [on his head].[18]

He longed to return to his own land, but was not permitted by the Lama. Again and again he requested permission and [finally] the Lama granted it. Then, when he set out for Gung Thang, his father had been dead for many years. Grass was growing on the roof of the former family residence; all the doors were ruined [?]. He slept there, desolation having arisen in his heart. The next day, he offered the former house and field to a master of Mantrayāna [his former teacher].[19] Afterwards, he went to a hermitage above the village [A.32] where he practiced continuous meditation.

Being without provisions, he made nettles his food. The Lama [Mila] became green in color (*sngon por song*). His pot, cup, and ladle also became green! His sister and his aunt brought beer made from fifteen handfuls of barley; all three of them drank it, but there was too much [for them to finish].

One day, weeping, they said to him: "What an unfortunate condition this is, o brother!" He looked at his own body [for the first time in a long while]; the Lama was utterly without flesh; he was nothing but skin and bones. His leg was bluish-gray. Prior to [his sister's remark,] he did not realize that he looked [like that].

Then, at harvest time, he went to the mountains. In order to see the countryside, he went to the top of a mountain pass. The harvest had been reaped. The fields were full of domestic animals; a desire to leave arose [in him], so he went away. It happened that many people bestowed curds and butter on him. He remained there for two or three days; a feeling of renunciation arose, so he went to the upper mountains where he practiced meditation for a long time; in three years' time, he was able [to wear] only cotton cloth. [A.33]

He told his sister that it would not be necessary [for her] to make him clothes. She said, happily, "My dear brother has become a siddha."

One time, having exhausted his provisions, he went down to the village to beg for food and supplies. At the door of [a family group] performing a ritual ceremony, he sat among the gathered group of beggars. From the ranks [of the ritualists gathered inside the courtyard], a tantric practitioner proceeded to give an account of the doctrine to the group. [B.21] One of them said: "A *yogin* of the Mila [clan] went away to meditate; many years have elapsed; now he is considered a siddha."

One said: "How wonderful! One should see his face. If I go to seek him, where may he be found?"

One said: "He is right here today! How can it be, [if] he is meditating in the mountains?"

One said: "I know him."

Another said: "Which one is he?" [B. 21.2]

Grasping the Lama [Mila] he said: "This is the one!"

But they were not in agreement (*ma thun pas*) and [each] said: "I [want to] make him my [personal] object of veneration." At that occasion, he was not pleased. While those people were arguing, he fled at the same time to a mountain cave.

Toward evening, he went to Phar rang. He did not go to the village, but to the mountains of Gung Thang, to Mang yul. There he dwelt and practiced for a long time [A.34] at White Rock Horse Tooth Mountain.

One time, the [lamas] of a small temple [*g.nas chung cig*] of Gung Thang were envious of the great merit of the Lama. Intending to dishonor [Mila], they came to invite him [to their temple]: "You are a siddha with [many] virtuous qualities; we would like to venerate you." Having compelled him to enter [their] temple, [and after closing] the iron door, they invited him outside. So, the Lama went outside as well. They did not believe it, so they looked inside and he was [still] there! Seeing this, they knew he was a siddha, so all the monks asked for his forgiveness.

Then he dwelt in the mountains of both sNye nam and Mang yul.

At another time, an old man and an old woman without heirs venerated him, [giving him] six measures of barley flour, a skin of butter,[20] and a quarter carcass of meat. Carrying these away, he went to dwell in the snow mountains. All winter long it snowed. All the people of the town accused (*gyod brdal*) the old man and old woman [of contributing to the death of the Lama (?)]. The old man and old woman faced toward their Lama, shedding tears, unable to do anything else. Next spring, some of the snow melted. [They thought]: "Perhaps the Lama did not die, perhaps he is still there." Three men, taking provisions of barley and [B.22] donning snow boots, went to search. The snow had melted, so when they arrived at the mountain side the three men called out.

The Lama thought that no people at all would be there [A.35]; he thought [the sound] was that of a deer. But it became more and more like human speech. He made a smoke [fire]; they saw the smoke, and when they arrived where the smoke was, there, too, was the Lama. Of the three measures of barley flour, one still remained.[21] Half the butter was still there. He gave it to the three men. Having rested for about three days, they went to the town. On the trail, the three men, frozen by the ice, lay down near the Lama to warm themselves.[22]

When he came to the village with the [three] townsmen, the people greeted him and inquired about his health. At that time, the Lama composed and sang a song of life in the snow-ranges at Lapchi (*la phyi gangs*).

One time, the Lama and a group of disciples went to Nepal, because he had been invited. On the way, they met many merchants. Having seized the staff (*spa 'khar*) of the Lama, the Chief Merchant asked: "Who are you?" The Lama said: "Now you ask who I am, If you don't know, I am the *yogin* Mila[repa]. I compose [for you] this song of my staff."[23] [A.36]

Then, in order to view the land, he went to a mountain top. [He said,] "Now I am not going into towns; I am going to wander among the mountain peaks." His attendants said: "If you wander in the mountain tops you won't get anywhere [?] even in ten years."[24] He did not grant their request that he go to the villages.[25] Mila the *yogin* went off to the upper side of the mountains.

A man who was beloved[26] had died so they made a religious feast. Bringing along many people, they went searching for the eminent one (*spyan*), so as to invite him back to the village. All the people gathered and made him many offerings. A patron from the town offered him a horse of which he was very fond. The Lama said: "You should take back all these offerings of yours. I will not keep them." So each of them took the [offerings] back. With that, he also did not accept the patron's horse. [B.23] The patron said: "My father is dead!" and wept. The Lama said: "In that case, give me the hide that covers the horse,"[27] and he then departed for the [town of] bKra-shis tshe rings. He dwelt there at that time.

Monk-Scholar rNga sug pa, 'Bring Ston 'phags pa, and Jo sras mchod pa were the three great men of La Ston; they sought out the Lama. Having found him, they invited the Lama to their village. [A.37] [Milarepa] gave an account of how they venerated him. [After that] the Lama wished to move on, but the disciples would not allow him to go. Therefore, he swore an oath to return later on, and then set out.

[Systematically] cutting off the stream of breath at the mouth and the nose, the lower winds ascended to become the upper ones, going to the top of his head. A feeling of bliss arose in him as he meditated.[28] At about midnight, many women with hands folded in devotion [appeared] before the Lama. They said: "Even now, o Lama, you perform meditation without distraction." Accordingly, the Lama calmed his mind as he meditated. In a short while, the winds arrived at the "natural state" (*g.nas su tshud*).

Then, one particular evening, while setting out [to meditate], an obstacle arose, even as it had previously, but as he meditated he restored his strength. The obstacle had arisen because he had thought it not harmful to break his oath [to return to the circle of his disciples].

Then, between [the towns] of Brin and sNye nam, after the time when he was dwelling at Red Rock Mountain, he composed the songs about the soaring of a White Tailed Vulture (*thang dkar rgod po lding ba*), and so forth, so it is said.

Once, when the Lama was dwelling amidst a forest, a patron [A.38] came [to look at] him and then went away.[29] The Lama called him back. "Where do you now dwell?" he asked. [The man replied,] "I saw no [one I could call a] Lama! I dwell near a stūpa (*mchod rten*)."[30] Now at that time, the patron did not salute him; [rather] he stared at him and went away. The Lama called him and he [again] came back. "How is it that a little while ago you didn't salute me?" He replied: "The Lama was not on a seat (*gzims mal na*?)" [B.24].

A Rinpoche (sGampopa?) asked the Lama [Mila] at that time: "What did you do?" Mila said: "I did nothing whatsoever. [Just as] Atiśa was seen to be circumambulating on the pinnacle of the monastery of bSamye. Did he [really] perform this act? Even if he didn't do it, as a result of dependent causality, it appeared to others that way. Thus, the two bodies[31] appear to others according to their own requirements. There is, however[32] in fact, no 'doing' [at all]."

Another time, at bKra shis tshe ring of Brin, the circle of disciples accompanied the Lama when [Mila] fell down a great precipice. As he rolled down, the disciples wept, [as they watched] from the edge [of the cliff]. [A.39]. The Lama then came back up! The disciples said: "Even though you fell off so great a cliff, you did not die; you came back! How is that?" He replied: "If I were someone else, I would [have been] cut to pieces. I am [however] okay" (A.39.1–2 *gzhan cig yin na sha dum bu chad de 'gro ste/nga yang dga' rab byung gsung/*).

Another time, having become a crystal stūpa, he rose up in the sky, it is said.[33]

At one time, a man of Rong Kha bZhi of Nepal came to see Mila. Not taking faith, he said: "You, Mila the *yogin*! There is little significance to your great fame. There is a scholar named Bari Lotsawa; he bestows gold, parasols, trumpets, etc., on whomever comes to meet him." Saying this, he went away.[34]

In a few days, men of Rong Kha bZhi [went] to the Lama in the evening. Three times they saw the Lama mount a lion and three times he set out into the sky—three times! So people said. And by going there [for themselves] they, therefore [really] saw it. They developed very great faith in him. They made many acts of veneration and [service]. A man of Brag, along with the Lama's disciples, said [to them]: "Why are you now paying your respects [when before you didn't]?" [They replied]: "We see him in the sky every evening three times; thus we have faith in him."[35] [A.40]

A Rinpoche said: "That event [took place] the year before I went [?]."[36]

He explained the flesh-flavor of higher knowledge [?] (*mngon par shes pa'i sha ro bstan/*); what he vowed was great (*ma chung gang sdoms pas*); [B.25] he imbibed intelligence (*sngar ma 'thungs*)

A woman gave birth to a son when she was a maiden. He [?] went to the street where the house-festival (*mkhar ston*) was [in progress to celebrate the birth of the child] of [the young mother] mGur-mo. He said: "This is what I know" (*nga'i rig pa 'di yin*). The woman said: "What are the virtues that your Lama possesses?"

"He possesses good *samādhi*. He possesses the higher gnosis. He has freedom from thought-constructions."

She said: "Your Lama was one who knows the virtues. Have you known [them]? Have you seen? So that he may be delighted ..."[?] She [then] took out a goat's milk pail[37] from under her arm and made supplication at that time. "[Your] Lama comes here every evening three times; therefore, I have shown reverence to [you o] Lama." The woman was a *ḍākinī*, it is said.

Once, he was going along with his disciples in the Valley called lCags drang of Brin, when a great snowfall occurred. The Lama got away by flying, [but] the attendants said: "He did not arrive at all." [A.41] They went to the Rinpoche and asked him: "Didn't he fly away?"

He replied: "I will lift up my leg in a moment, and press the wind for a moment, and [I] will go [too]" [?]. But it did not happen, no more than [the length of] a bird's footprint.[38]

At the time, having dwelt there thirteen months, the Rinpoche went down there [?]. He dwelt at the house of Legs se, a female patron. The people asked the Lama: "Do you not want us to provide provisions?" He asked: "How much have you brought?" They said: "We brought six *bre.*" "That amount suffices." Thereafter, each month they gave a handful of rice, which was each time sufficient.

[The Rinpoche said]: "I wanted to ask him if previously he was hungry—'true or false'" [during this period of eating a handful of rice each month]. So he [the Rinpoche] went back [to where Mila was], returning from a place a single day's journey [away]. The Lama said: "Have you come back?" (Tibetan: *khyod log gam*). He then gave him some hot tea. [The Rinpoche] then asked [the same question again] and [Mila] replied: "While she [patroness Legs se] was not here (*med tsa na*) a *ḍākinī* provided me well with a bit of food, some beer, etc. I did not even eat much, just enough to touch the ring finger to my mouth. I [even] forgot about food for five days, or even six. [B.26] Some days I passed the entire day in meditation and I didn't eat."

The Lama also said: "Either on the high mountains or atop a fortress, I meditated for many days. [A.42] Even [my body] became light (*kyang yang bar 'dug*)."

Then someone named Dar ma brtan[39] went far from home.[40] His relatives were told that he was dead; they wept.

The Lama remarked: "What is the calamity?"

They replied: "Dar ma brtan has died," and so they mourned.

He said [to the disciples?]: "He did not die; he is on the way now." [The disciples asked Milarepa:] "Should we let them know this?"

Mila said: "Do so," and so they did. Thus they [the relatives] believed in him and stopped weeping. And then [Dar ma brtan] arrived.

[Mila] possessed immeasurable virtues. He did not move from *samādhi*.[41] He made no distinction between the state of meditative equipoise and the post-meditation period.[42] He realized the true continuum of Nature (*Dharmatā*).

His corporeal person was an emanation (*sprul pa'i gang zag yin*).[43]

Later, the funeral rites [for his corpse] were performed after his death at both Brin and [at Mount] Ti se, so it is said.

This account of how Lama Milarepa achieved his virtue and performed his deeds, in mere outline form, is now completed.

May I quickly achieve the state of Sugata!
Auspicious!

23

A Translation of the Biography of Vajradhara by rGyal thang pa

[This is the *rnam thar* of Vajradhara that we find at the start of the cycle of biographies by rGyal thang pa. The footnotes provide commentary that coordinates this tantric description of Buddhahood with the bKa' brgyud biographies.[1]]

Folio 1:

The Biographical Accounts of the Glorious Dwags po bKa' brgyud pa.[2] This is sGyur ban's book. Auspicious![3]

Folio 2:

Salutations to the glorious Guru![4] He [Vajradhara] is the master of all the Buddha-families, Chief of all the glorious ones, Master of the doctrine of the Secret Mantra, the teacher of the Mahāyāna. He is first of the Gurus of the bKa' brgyud; holder of the doctrines of the Practice Lineage.[5] He is the expounder of the commentary on the oral transmission. As it says in the root text:

1. Wondrous (e-ma)! A sage, a teacher, a master of the doctrine,
   Simultaneously ripening the streams of consciousness,
   Of all persons of sharp senses, he is manifest as the Lord
   Of the Secret Mantra:
   Praise be to Vajradhara (rDo rJe 'Chang), the excellent one
   who fully accomplishes the aims of sentient beings.

2. He is embodied in the perfect place, time, retinue, and so
   forth;

He possesses the state (*dngos*) of the five types of
knowledge[6]
And the seven factors,
Being united with the self-arisen consort.
Praise be to Vajradhara Saṃbhogakāya Buddha!

3. Victor possessing the eight sovereignties (*dbang phyug brgyad ldan*).

O Vajradhara,
The extraordinary Vajrayāna teachings are those, which, in
one lifetime, confer Buddhahood.
Praise[7] be to Vajradhara, who teaches the unsurpassable
doctrine.

4. He is on the thirteenth stage, which is the best among the paths (*mārga*) and stages (*bhūmi*),

Folio 3:

Vajradhara, the sixth of the perfect Buddhas, is the "holder of
the *vajra*";
He is completely extraordinary, reaching the state of
culmination.
Praise be to Vajradhara, Lord of the Buddha Families.[8]

This is what the root text says. Now, the explanation of the root text: The first point is that he was "a sage, a master of the doctrine, and so on," which means, should one wish to conjecture, "Just who is that Vajradhara, the Buddha of the sixth (*drug-pa*) Buddha Family? What kind of biographical account[9] does he have?" The answer, in the exoteric sense, is in the biography of the master of this doctrine, the Buddha Śākyamuni, the Teacher, the Blessed One, the Victor. At that time, the Buddha completely manifested the state of an Enlightened One in accordance with the visionary capacity of the pure disciples. At the same time the *saṃbhogakāya*, having a pure and excellent body, in a pure place, the Akaniṣṭha, the Palace of the doctrine, became enlightened.

By means of the teachings of the extraordinary doctrine of Vajrayāna, he came to the realization of the nature of reality as Vajradhara Buddha. In this way, the complete ripening of the mental continua of those disciples who are worthy vessels is accomplished. Also, in accordance with the visionary capacity of impure disciples, in this impure world of human beings, he manifested in the form of a sage in the emanation body (*nirmāṇakāya*) so that by whatever means, disciples can be formed.[10] By means of the vehicle of ordinary teachings (i.e., the "lesser vehicle") the mental continua of disciples (*śrāvaka*) who are worthy beings are ripened. In brief, the Buddha displays the form of a *nirmāṇakāya* and a *saṃbhogakāya*, in bodies both good and bad; at times both early and late, etc. He will arise in the sight of pure and impure disciples uncharacterized by (i.e., unrestricted to) a good or bad body, high or low levels, early or late times.[11]

Folio 4:

—at a single time, at a single place, in a single body, he is the Buddha! It is stated thus in the *Laṅkāvatāra Sutra*: "Having abandoned pure states (*śuddhāvāsa*), the Buddha was enlightened in the pleasant pure place called the Akaniṣṭha in the form of *saṃbhogakāya* Buddha. But here on earth, it was an emanation that became the Buddha."

The Master of the exoteric doctrine of Buddhism, this Lord of the Sages (*munīndra*), Buddha the teacher, belonging to the Buddha Family of those of acute intelligence,[12] is a person possessing good fortune and good previous actions (*karman*), who in a single life (i.e., his last earthly lifetime), in a single body, achieves the goal, and is able to ripen and liberate the streams of consciousness of pure disciples. The teacher, esoterically manifesting in union with the consort (*mudrā*) as Vajradhara *saṃbhogakāya* Buddha, master of the doctrine of the Secret Mantra teachings, benefits superior disciples.

Then, for those of dull intellect and for those of inferior destiny as their lot in numberless eons, and for the benefit of disciples desiring the goal, the Master manifested himself in the form of the *nirmāṇakāya* sage by providing disciples of little merit with the ordinary teachings of the doctrine. Though he used two forms, his nature is one and indistinguishable. As the *Abhisamayālaṃkāra* says:

> This Master manifested as the perfected *saṃbhogakāya* Sage, having the thirty-two marks of an excellent being and the eighty minor marks, in order to enjoy thoroughly the Mahāyāna.[13]

To those disciples who manifested worthy appearance, the Master of this teaching, the sage, the teacher of the extraordinary doctrine of the Mahāyāna manifested his own form as Vajradhara *saṃbhogakāya* Buddha.

> Form the Root Text: [repeat Verse 1]
> This is the explication of the meaning.
> [Now the second verse:]
> Being perfect in place, time, attendants, etc.

Folio 5:

In this way, the sage manifested as a Vajradhara *saṃbhogakāya* Buddha in accordance with the capacity of pure disciples. His deeds and biography appeared thus:

—The types of deeds of a Vajradhara *saṃbhogakāya* Buddha;
—The place that was the most perfect of places;
—In that place, the teacher was the most perfect of teachers;
—The doctrine of that teacher was the most perfect of doctrines.
—The teacher of the doctrine had attendants that comprised the most perfect of retinues.

All of these: retinue, doctrine, teacher, and place, occurred simultaneously; thus the time that was the most perfect of times was accomplished. In this way, his deeds fulfilled the five perfect circumstances.[14]

That place, which is not inferior to any other place, possesses perfect, excellent qualities, since it is above the five pure abodes[15] and the qualities of that place and the way it evolves (*chags tshad* = is formed) would be hard for anyone to measure, so excellent is that place [the Akaniṣṭha].

Thus said the teacher, Vajradhara *saṃbhogakāya* Buddha, who abides there, possessing the seven factors and the eight masteries (sovereignties), being a perfect teacher.[16]

The profound, extraordinary doctrine of the Vajrayāna that is taught by him is difficult to measure. It consists of practicing with the fruit, Buddhahood, as one's path; thus one practices the doctrine by which one may manifest Buddhahood, in one body, in one lifetime. This is the perfect Teaching!

An exquisite retinue of the pure ones, including Bodhisattva heroes and heroines, Vajragarbha[17] and others, manifests the path and stages.

In all three times: past, present, and future, the time is the perfect time in which the sound of the doctrine of the profound Secret Mantra is proclaimed continually and tirelessly.

Therefore, in terms of the perfect place, teacher, retinue, and time, such was Vajradhara *saṃbhogakāya*. The essence of the five bodies (*kāyas*) is the five types of knowledge. This means that the bodies are:

Folio 6:

The *dharmakāya* (the body of natural phenomena);
The *saṃbhogakāya* (the body of enjoyment);
The *nirmāṇakāya* (the emanation body);
The *svabhāvikakāya* (the self-arisen body); and
The *mahāsukhakāya* (the body of great pleasure).[18]

This is how the Buddha abides in his own form of the five bodies.
The mind consists of:

The knowledge of the sphere of phenomena (*dharmadhātu-jñāna*)
Mirror-like knowledge (*ādarśa-jñāna*)
Knowledge of sameness (*samatā-jñāna*)
Knowledge of distinctions (*pratyavekṣanā-jñāna*)

Knowledge about accomplishing what is to be done (*kṛtyānṣṭhāna-jñāna*)

Thus, the mind exists as the basis of the five types of knowledge.[19] It is written in the *Mañjuśrīnāmasaṃgīti:*

> A master truly possessing the five Buddha-Bodies; all-pervading Lord, master of the five types of knowledge; Master of the Five Buddhas, who possesses the crest-jewel.[20]

Now this is the meaning of his possessing the seven factors:[21]

1. One who possesses such a Buddha-body and who possesses knowledge (*ye shes*) is the first factor, thoroughly possessing the primary [thirty-two] and secondary [eighty] marks.
2. The second factor is the indivisible embrace of (wisdom and compassion called *yuganaddha*: the "pair-united").
3. Then there is the factor of the four blisses [comprising] the ultimate great bliss (*mahāsukha*).
4. Then there is the factor entailing the conclusion that the self is intrinsically unreal [Sanskrit: *niḥsvabhāva;* Tibetan: *rang bzhin bden med*].[22]
5. Then there is the factor of fully developed bodhicitta in relation to the two truths (*saṃvṛtti-satya* and *paramārtha-satya*).
6. Then there is the factor of absolutely not cutting off the continuity of compassion from the beginning (from the moment of its arising).
7. And there is the factor of not intending to rest, nor to abide in Nirvāṇa (but to aid suffering beings in Saṃsāra).

Through the state of possessing these seven factors, having joined the consort, in self-arisen union, enjoying great bliss from the beginning in the state of culmination. There is no other Bliss!

Thus, it is the *saṃbhogakāya* which possesses the seven factors.

From the tantra *De Kho na ñid yong su bstan pa'i* (*Tattva-nirdeśa-tantra*):[23]

"Fully possessing the major and minor marks; being united with great bliss; intrinsically without essence; full of *bodhicitta*; primordially not cutting off compassion; not intending to go beyond into Nirvāṇa;—a *saṃbhogakāya* is one possessing the seven factors."

Perfect enjoyment and great bliss, indivisible Union, intrinsically without essence, full of compassion, not ceasing from continuity, this indeed is a Buddha possessing the seven factors. It is thus accepted (as an argument) that Vajradhara Buddha wishes to enjoy (a special kind of delight in the company of) fully cultivated intelligent beings.[24]

Acting according to this system, following the doctrine of the Mahāyāna, is called the Factor of Enjoyment.[25]

Folio 7:

Therefore, the Factor of Union (*kha-sbyor*) is the state of being united with flawlessness; continuity of mind full of great bliss is therefore called the factor of great bliss; compassion that is immeasurable is therefore the factor of perfect compassion; possessing undivided continuity of action (*mdzad pa mnga' bas na rgyun mi 'chad pa'i yan lag*) is therefore the factor of undivided continuity; ceaselessly refraining from entering Nirvāṇa for the sake of beings is therefore the factor of ceaselessness.[26]

Thus, a Buddha possessing the seven factors is accepted as a *saṃbhogakāya* by Srī Vāgīśvarakīrti's system;[27] also, it is established by valid knowledge (*pramāṇa-buddhi*); thus, perfected Buddhas, ancient sages (*blo gros dang ldan*) and realized scholars (*mkhas grub*) have accepted this.

Such a Buddha, possessing the seven factors, joined with the self-arisen consort, enjoying great bliss, is therefore called *saṃbhogakāya*: perfect enjoyment body.

He is called "*vajra*" (*rdo rje*) since the adamantine Reality is held in his mind. In brief, according to our root text: "He possesses the seven factors, being united to the self-arisen consort: Praise be to Vajradhara, the Perfect *saṃbhogakāya*."

Next, the Victor Vajradhara is the possessor of the eight masteries. This is what it means:

The sage, Vajradhara *saṃbhogakāya* Buddha, possessor of the body of seven factors (Skt. *saptānga;* Tib. *yan lag bdun*) and the eight masteries: mastery of body, of speech, of mind, of miracles, of ubiquity, of place, of wishing, and of obtaining the desirable. He is the one who is a possessor of these eight masteries (*dbang phyug brgyad po*).[28]

1. The first mastery (of body): He is powerful in this body to master all phenomena, including the forms of Saṃsāra and Nirvāṇa. He is rich with the wealth of all desirable qualities combined in this body. Therefore, this is called the perfect mastery of the body.
2. The mastery of speech: He has mastered the power acquired through speech for combining all phenomena (*dharmāḥ*) with Saṃsāra and Nirvāṇa. (*'khor 'das dbang gis bsdus pa'i chos thams cad la gsung des dbang byed pas/*)[29] [Or: "Through his power of speech, he can expound the relationship between all phenomena and saṃsāra/nirvāṇa."]

Folio 8:

By his all-inclusive speech, he is rich with the wealth of all desirable qualities. Therefore, this is his mastery of speech.

1. The mastery of mind: Similarly, he has mastery because he is able to combine all the phenomena of Saṃsāra and Nirvāṇa in his mind. He is thus rich with the wealth of all desirable qualities collected in his mind. This is his mastery of the mind.
2. His mastery of miracles: By possessing the masteries of body, speech, and mind, he is rich with the wealth of the qualities of immeasurable miracles by his power to control (*dbang kha sgyur bas na dbang*) the immeasurable wonders of the body, speech, and mind. this is his mastery of miracles.

3. His mastery of ubiquity:[30] He has mastered the power that can fulfill the aims of all beings in Saṃsāra and Nirvāṇa. He is one who is not lacking any qualities (*phongs pa med par*) of Saṃsāra and Nirvāṇa. He lacks none of the qualities (*phongs pa med par*) of Saṃsāra and Nirvāṇa. Therefore, this is his mastery of ubiquity.[31]
4. Now, his Mastery of Place:[32] The Akaniṣṭha means the noble place, a place greater than all others, overcoming all others with its excellence and power, a place most excellent among places. It is rich with whatever qualities are possessed by all other places. Therefore this is his Mastery over Place.[33]
5. His mastery of Wishing: (Refers to his relationship with) the Mother of all the Buddhas of the Three Times; (who manifests in the tantras as:) *rDo rJe sNye Ma* (Diamond Ear of Corn; Skt.: *Vajra-vallarī* or *Mañjarī*); Nairātmyā; Vajravārāhī; Vajra Ḍākinī; Ratna Ḍākinī; Padma Ḍākinī; Karma Ḍākinī; Buddha Ḍākinī; etc.[34] The secret consort is included in the Mudrā-Family. Instantly, the inseparable pair enter Bliss and Voidness from the state of Mahāmudrā, having power to enter the balanced equipoise of sexual desire. Therefore, he is rich with the vast wealth of immeasurable wisdom and knowledge. This is his Mastery of Wishing.
6. The Mastery of Obtaining the Desirable: He is powerful with mastery over all qualities, possessing both supreme and ordinary *siddhis* (Accomplishments). He has abundant riches to the extent of gaining the Accomplishments (*siddhi*) sought after, whether superior or ordinary. This is his Mastery of Obtaining the Desirable.[35]

Folio 9:

Regarding this, it is said in the *Tārā-abhyudaya-tantra* of the highest-yoga-tantra, and in Ravigupta's *Viśuddha-cūḍā-maṇidhara*:

"Rich in the masteries of body, speech, and mind, miracles, ubiquity, place, etc., mastery is not difficult for him!"

In brief, the Buddha possesses the eight masteries "for the benefit of disciples who are worthy vessels, by the extraordinary secret teachings of the Vajrayāna, the Buddha perfectly bestows Buddhahood in one body, in one lifetime. Praise be to Vajradhara *saṃbhogakāya*, who has proclaimed the doctrine of incomparable (*anuttara*) meaning."

From the root text: "O Victor, Vajradhara, possessing the eight masteries; the extraordinary Vajrayāna teachings are those which, in one lifetime, in one body, bestow Buddhahood." [Verse 3]

This is the explication:

Now, the one holding the *vajra* is that being who is on the thirteenth, which is supreme among the paths and stages. This means that Vajradhara *saṃbhogakāya* is a Buddha of the seven factors. He has completely accomplished the course of the superior paths and stages, including:

The First Stage: Utterly Blissful
The Second Stage: Without Defilement
The Third Stage: Light-Creating
The Fourth Stage: Light Diffusing
The Fifth Stage: Difficult to Conquer
The Sixth Stage: Face-to-face (Skt. *abhimukhī*; Tib. *mngon du gyur pa*)
The Seventh Stage: Far-Gone
The Eighth Stage: Unshakable
The Ninth Stage: Good in Mind
The Tenth Stage: Cloud of the Doctrine[36]
The Eleventh Stage: Fully Illumined (also called the Incomparable Ray of Light; Tib. *dpe med* = incomparable, boundless)
The Twelfth Stage: Boundless, also called Great Wisdom
The Thirteenth Stage: Called the Stage of the Holder of the Ritual Scepter (*vajra*)[37]

This, in brief, is the explanation of the Stages (of a Bodhisattva and of a Buddha).

Now, the path for all: there is the mundane path and the supramundane path, for there are two paths. The first path consists of the path of accumulation joined to the path of preparation. Then, there is the supramundane path, which consists of the path of seeing, the path of meditation, and the path of no-more-to-be-learned. In sum, there are five paths of the Secret-Mantra Vajrayāna.[38]

Vajradhara, the Buddha of the sixth family, has realized as such [i.e., as the five paths] the perfect fulfillment of the culmination of all virtues of the paths and stages of the Secret-Mantra Vajrayāna.

Folio 10:

He is the master of all the families of the Buddhas: the body, speech, and mind, virtues, and activities. And *vajra* means inseparable voidness and wisdom/skillful salvific means. Therefore, *vajra* means maintaining the adamantine reality (*dharmatā*) in the mental continuum.[39] This is called *vajra.* This means that for all disciples who are suitable receptacles for the Secret Mantra Vajrayāna there are three entryways: faith, devotion, and praise.

This is the meaning of praise (*bstod*). Again, from the root text: "On the most excellent of the Paths and Stages, the Thirteenth, is the Holder of the Vajra, so as to display perfectly one who has reached the full culmination: Vajradhara, the Sixth Buddha; Praise be to Vajradhara, Lord of the Buddha Families!" [Verse 4]

In brief, Vajradhara *saṃbhogakāya* is the Lord of all the Buddha Families, master of all that is glorious; possessing in himself the seven factors and endowed with the eight masteries; this is Vajradhara Buddha, so it is said. This is the explication.

Now this is the second meaning of Vajradhara Buddha: The inner (esoteric) explanation is as follows: Vajradhara Buddha is all those who hold in their mental continua the realization of *dharmakāya* as voidness, being the highest truth of nature (*dharmatā*). Thus it is stated in the *Vajraśekhara Tantra*:[40] "The Buddha was asked, 'You spoke of Vajradhara. What does that mean?' He replied: 'Whoever is firm in *bodhicitta* and in the wisdom of all the Buddhas, that is the Victor, Vajradhara, the Lord of all the Tathāgatas'."[41] This means that whatever (*gang yin*) altruistic attitude (*bodhicitta*) exists is the wisdom of the Buddhas. Vajradhara Buddha is what the enlightened attitude is. This is what the Buddha's wisdom is in the *Vajraśekhara Tantra*; knowing reality *is* wisdom, and it is the realization of the *dharmakāya* as well. He has completely abandoned the extremes of eternalism and nihilism. Such wisdom is immortal in itself. So does that mean that a *yogin* who meditates also realizes the meaning of the wisdom of *dharmakāya*? If one were to contemplate in that way, would he become like Vajradhara? Of course, we accept this for someone who has the wisdom of Vajradhara! As the same tantra states: "All yogis who realize the meaning of wisdom to be Vajradhara are thereby the unexcelled Vajradhara. So great is the number of Vajradharas."[42]

Folio 11:

In that case, is any *yogin* Vajradhara? From the perspective of the five grasping aggregates (*upadhāna-skandha*) such as form and the rest, he appears to be an ordinary person whose body shows signs of growing old, but it is not really appropriate to think of him as such. As the *Vajra-pañjara* says: "Therefore great is Vajradhara! Intending to benefit beings, he remains in an ordinary form," so it is said. Not only that, but all sentient beings possess the essence of Buddhahood, though it is not recognized, having been hidden by the defilement of temporary ignorance. Thus one is, without realizing it (*ma rtogs*), from the beginning, a Buddha wandering in Saṃsāra. As the *Hevajra-Tantra* says: "There is not even one sentient being in existence who is not a Buddha. It is certain that in the family of the Buddha, the Blessed One, there are *yogins* possessing the form of ordinary living beings possessing contemplative tranquility, neither proud nor contemptible."[43] And in the same tantra: "Sentient beings are Buddhas, even though covered temporarily by defilement. As soon as they are purified, they quickly become Buddhas."[44]

If this is so, what sort of Buddhas are sentient beings? The *Tattva-nirdeśa-tantra* states: "Because there are pure and impure disciples, Buddha appeared as *saṃbhogakāya* and *nirmāṇakāya;* they are one reality; distinctions arise because minds are diverse. In meaning, all the Buddhas are one." Evidently, Buddha manifests as *saṃbhogakāya* and *nirmāṇakāya* in accordance with the capacity of pure and impure disciples. Actually, the ultimate meaning of all Buddhas is one reality. In brief, all phenomena whatever (*skyed tshad*) of Cyclic Existence and Liberation are pervaded by voidness and are Vajradhara Buddha alone. This is from the viewpoint of the *Vajraśekhara Tantra*: "What is held when one holds the *vajra*? The interior is essentially solidity without hollowness, not burnable (*sreg med*), not cuttable, not to be destroyed, not to be crushed; thus, he proclaims Voidness to be Adamantine (*vajra*)." Also, Vajrapāṇi (*phyag na rdo rje*)[45] is the gatherer of all the doctrines of the Secret Mantra Vehicle. The perfections (*pāramitā*) (i.e., the *Prajñāpāramitā-sūtras*) and the doctrine of the Scriptures (*sūtra*) were gathered by Ānanda. Actually, these two are one in nature (*ngo bo*)

Folio 12:

but only appear to be separate according to the capacity of disciples, though not fully recognized by them. The scripture entitled the *Śitavanika-sūtra*[46] states: "To the learned monk (*bahuśrota*), to one who grasps the Secret Mantra, and to Ānanda I bow and offer praise."

These three types are, in the absolute sense, one: The Buddha, a Teacher demonstrating doctrine, and the doctrine, which is being demonstrated, and the gathering before which the doctrine is disclosed. From the *Hevajra Tantra*: "I am the teacher, and I am the doctrine, I am the disciple endowed with good qualities."[47] In short, the essence of voidness is called *vajra.*

Thus, Vajradhara Buddha is whoever is called holder-of-the-scepter because he can hold voidness in his mental continuum. This is the inner meaning well explained. In this way, a being is indeed purified of defilement by means of the path, by the doctrinal system of the Secret Mantra Vajrayāna. The nature of Vajradhara is manifested by all beings whatever who are purified as the fruit of Wisdom; this is accepted. Now, from the *Hevajra Tantra*: "All beings arise from me; the three worlds arise from me; I pervade all that exists; this world consists of nothing else" (HVT I. viii, 41). This is what it truly means! In brief, he, the Buddha, is called Vajradhara; this is the meaning of all these quotations. Do not accept that anyone else lacks that quality: if one realizes the meaning of self, one can achieve Buddhahood in the primordial (*rang ngor*) form of Vajradhara. The one who holds the succession of the bKa' brgyud-pa[48] should realize the primordial nature of oneself; Buddhas do not exist extrinsically (*zur du*). In this way, the inner explanation of Vajradhara is completely finished. Having made known the nature of *vajra*, I ask you to learn, to practice, and to experience! (*nyams len la 'tad par zhu*). All fortunate beings have power to become connected with the doctrine; Buddha is not apart from the self; by this means alone one may achieve Buddhahood. All holy doctrines are in one's own mind! You must put this into practice; it will be well! All Cyclic Existence and Liberation are one's primordial nature. Thus, if one gives up hatred and attachment, one will be liberated.

Folio 13:

If the mind neither accepts nor rejects virtue and non-virtue, there is neither cyclic existence nor ultimate extinction; there is no other cause and effect apart from oneself (*de kas dge sdig 'dor len gyis*)! One's own mind is the bKa' brgyud lama.[49] If one makes a request with devotion, a blessing will enter. All the six classes of sentient beings are one's own appearance. The benefit of all these sentient beings arises through kindness and compassion. All the visible things that exist in Cyclic Existence and Liberation are oneself. All are made by oneself. Wishing to achieve Buddhahood, or wandering in Cyclic Existence, depends on one's own creations; if one does not see self and others as one, a person cannot have merit in his continuum of being. One should not follow along the way of non-virtue; the virtue and non-virtue of oneself and others are one and the same. [From the *Avadāna-Śataka*:][50] "The actions of sentient beings are inexhaustible for one hundred eons; when the time arrives, (*karmas*) fully accumulated, become ripened as a result." The meaning of cause and result is one in essence; this is the meaning of both skillful salvific means and wisdom; this meaning *is mahāmudrā*.[51] This meaning is ultimate Vajradhara. This completes the exposition on the Buddha Vajradhara. Thus!

If the biography of Vajradhara *saṃbhogakāya* (Buddha) were to be written in a lengthy presentation, it would be immeasurable. Since one may be afraid of a great accumulation of words, an easily understandable compilation has herein been composed. This presentation of Vajradhara *saṃbhogakāya* Buddha, both clear and illuminating of the faith, is respectfully compiled, rich with the wealth of the learned thoughts culled from scriptures and logic [or the precepts of the Saints and the learning of the sages].[52]

It was made upon the admonition of slob dpon 'Od zer mgon pa, who has great faith in the assembly of bKa' brgyud teachers, abiding firmly in meditative absorption (*ting 'zin bstam na sgom la nges gnas shing*).

It was composed by rGyal thang pa, who resides in a hermitage,[53] meditating in the snow, because of his reverent devotion for the Buddha. Exemplifying those virtues which have been accumulated as merit in the three times, may I myself and all disciples and all sentient beings achieve the excellent state of Vajradhara. Thus! Auspicious! Bliss // Corrected /

24

Milarepa's Oral Teachings from the *gDams ngag mdzod*

24.1. Folio 109.6. *The Clarification of the Three Cycles*, and So Forth, Related to the Oral Transmission, by the Great Saint Milaraspa. [*Rje btsun chen po mi la ras pa mdzad pa'i snyan brgyud gsal ba skor gsum sogs* (*Zur mang snyan brgyud*)] from the *gDams ngag mdzod* vol. V., ff. 109–120.

This Clarification of Reality is by Saint Milarepa.

I prostrate to the Holy Masters!

I submit to the lotus feet of the Precious Master with the cloud-gathering of my body, speech, and mind. I prostrate in all the three times to the Zur mang Oral Transmission.

Having obtained the kindness of the holy Master, I prostrate to the Dharmadhātu, which is the non-dualistic supreme path.

Folio 110.1:

I prostrate to the Torch of Intuitive Wisdom, which illuminates the darkness of ignorance. I also prostrate to that Shining Appearance which has completely severed and dispelled the continuum of cyclic existence. Master Tilopa bestowed it on Nāropa, who bestowed it on Marpa, who bestowed it on Mila. For a long time [Mila] he circumambulated at the feet of [Marpa], and listened to him with faith. Marpa was attentive and compassionately granted [the teachings]. Willingly and forcefully, Milarepa practiced according to the instructions. Through meditation, the virtues arose: the yogic heat blazed up in his body and

Thos pa dga' [Milarepa] only wore cotton cloth; the Clear Light dawned in his mind; he obtained many transmissions. In Tibet, there are no transmissions equal to these. Now let us examine particular features:

When one undertakes spiritual practice in a place of great solitude, the stages are:

1. The natural, primordial state.
2. The path.
3. The arising of fruition.

First of all, consideration of the body:

The body is the abode of Dharma, consisting of the five kinds of awakening, the channels, bodhicitta, impure substances, and conceptuality. There are three essential points related to bodily posture:

1. Body
2. Place
3. Time

Folio 110.5:

If one does not know how to direct the four types of breath (winds), it is hard for the virtues to arise.

{Comment by Lodro Tharchin:[1] In the *Nāro chos drug*, the breath is understood to refer to *rlung, prāṇa*. If not properly, i.e., yogically, directed and channeled, these winds are just ordinary mundane life-fluxes.}

Now start by making the body straight and well-poised. Meditate [gathering the winds] like "Knots in a Fibula" and "Bent like a Hook" [use your vital energy to inhale elemental winds]:

{Comment: This "fibula" is a kind of cloth or thread button made up of loosely interwoven knotted threads. In meditation, it means to keep all the elemental winds gathered together and entwined, not extended or scattered. Bent like a hook does not refer to the shape of the upper part of the *avadhūtī*, but to the primary wind of the body which, through the power of inhalation, draws in all the elemental winds, which seem to be the particular energies associated with each of the five elements. The Hook is thus the primary wind itself.}

Then you interlace the legs like weaving [in *padmāsana*] [before] doing "Shooting like an Arrow upwards." The four types or aspects of the respiratory cycle are:

1. inhaling
2. filling/abiding
3. revolving the breath within the body
4. swift exhalation, like an arrow

Then there is the practice known as "Gradually Milking the Sky-Cow."

{Comment: The usual full or half-lotus position is indicated. Not only does one hold one's breath during respiratory cycles, but one also "revolves" the wind deep in the abdomen. Method: Hold the breath for 21 cycles of the following maneuver: slap the right knee, left knee and forehead each once, then snap the fingers once. At the same time, move the abdominal muscles to stir up the air held in the lungs, down to the lower abdomen. Then exhale quickly and vigorously through the nostrils.[2] Called: *rlung bum chen.*

"Milking the Sky Cow" refers to the meditation on the red and white drops. At the crown of the head there is a white droplet with the letter Haṃ. At the navel, there is a reddish droplet with Raṃ or E; gradually the meditator causes the two to unite, filling the body with great bliss.}

Then contemplate the four cakras and then the empty cylinder of the central channel. This emptiness inside is the best of voidnesses!

{Comment: The four cakras: here they are at the *uṣṇīṣa* (swelling at the top of the head), throat, heart, and navel. Please note that in the Vajrayoginī system, the subsidiary *nāḍīs* are visualized like spokes extending from the wheels (cakras); here the *nāḍīs* are intertwined in the cakras. Voidness here presupposes the early Buddhist and Mahāyāna analysis of voidness (of self, of phenomena, interdependence, impermanence, etc.). In tantra, the practical aspect of voidness is emphasized in visualizing the deity's body as void and translucent. Also, our body is assimilated to the body of the yidam and the *avadhūtī* is visualized as also void and cylindrical. This visualization of an empty central channel is the best because it is the most practical for bringing about an existential encounter with the primordial voidness of all that appears to exist. Note that in the stage of generation you are working with a general approach to voidness; however, at that stage the disciple is also given the teaching on the voidness of the central channel, later to be intensively practiced and realized in the stage of completion. The voidness of the central channel is supreme because, as an object of meditation, the visualized void cylinder is more effective and precise than general meditation on emptiness.}

Now even among the many spiritual instructions, the best are those about the Channels and Winds. If you do the practice, the Virtues will arise (These are the essential points of Place).

Position and venerate the Master on your head. Cherish him like your own eyeballs.

Folio 111.1:

Now, for those so inclined, there is the way of messengers (i.e., consorts). When such men have recourse to a Wisdom-Lady, she has to perform the self-initiation and have faith. She has to be free from anger, possessing great compassion, with a lovely face, big eyes, a beautiful body adorned with youth. She has to be restrained and modest, like a sister or a maidservant. When one has recourse to the Wisdom Lady, having explained to her the essential points of the three paths, in a solitary place, the *yogin* closes the two doors. Thus relying on the Awareness Woman (*rig-ma*), there will be no obstacle. Abandoning specific features gradually, also one abandons the non-existence of virtuous qualities. So that wrong concepts do not arise in the mind, one first prays to the Master and the Three Jewels, making prostrations, training one's consciousness. This would correspond to the path of accumulation. Union is the path of application. In one moment, one obtains instantaneous knowledge. The path of seeing is this "knowing." Thus Vajradhara teaches an emanation of Vajradhara!

Folio 111.4:

Use Breath/Vital Force and effort (i.e., "functioning") at the time of holding the breath; keep the mind in non-conceptuality, visualize the full droplet in the form of the moon, contemplate the wisdom-endowed consort, meditate on yogic heat, like a fine candle-flame [at the navel]; or [on the drops] ascending and descending, uniting and melting. [All can be done] if you know how to keep mental constructs from spreading out towards their objects.

{Comment: *srog-rtsol* refers to the mental and physical energies of the body which are channeled into the *avadhūtī*. In fact, *srog* is the central channel and *rtsol* means the insertion of the "wind" energies so that they become "wisdom *prāṇas*." Keep the mind in a non-conceptual state at this time. Objects of meditation ideal to support this practice include a luminous droplet in the form of the full moon, the lovely and perfectly endowed wisdom consort, the flame of yogic heat sharply pointed at the top and rounded out at the bottom, or the father *tigle* (droplet) at the crown of the head and the warm mother *tigle* at the navel. The mother *tigle* ascends, unites with the father, melts and descends spreading blissful sensations at the throat, heart and navel cakras, producing *mahāsukha* (great bliss). Guided by the Master, these objects lend themselves to achieving perfect one-pointed meditative stabilization.}

Folio 111.5:

These are the essential points of Place.

But even if this is not clear, the mental constructs stop by themselves and virtue arises gradually. As for the special instruction on the path of means, with the exception of Heart Disciples—others, bad vessels, are not to be given these. Hide these instructions within the heart!

Relying on Action, one will see the object certainly; relying on Means, the virtues will certainly arise. Don't give these instructions to deceivers and flatterers.

Although from the beginning, Cause and Effect are non-dual,

Folio 112.1:

by the power of conceptualization, cause and effect appear [to be distinct]. Those persons who are without realization, if they take mere words as the meaning, deceive themselves and others. Though in reality it is like that, for them, it is not! Even though they see it, they really don't see it!

Thus, those who (immaturely) accept that everything is Buddha from the beginning will be like donkeys leaping upon lions; in the future, if they do this, they will die.

But for fortunate ones with [good] karma, this is ambrosia! For those without good fortune, changeable ones, this becomes a poison. Skillful and powerful tigers, hard to imitate … foxes and wolves from the cremation ground, it is difficult. But if they strive [?] even the water element can arise from the earth element. If they rub, even the fire element will emerge from wood. If a human being practices with effort, there is nothing that cannot be achieved. So cherish spiritual practice.

When the afflicted conceptualizations gradually stop, then the [sight of the] mountain of self-awareness wisdom becomes clear. It is hard to attain liberation practicing the ten perfections. It is hard to pass into *nirvāṇa* practicing the ten sins. When we do "cultivating and abandoning," it is hard for non-conceptuality to arise.[3] Thus it is for all those who have bodies.

Folio 112.5:

This essential goal (Buddhahood) abides primordially;
Thus sentient beings [merely create] the cause [of the manifestation] of Buddhahood;
In fact, the Result was implanted in the Cause.
Abiding there, having been there [primordially], it [cannot be said to be] implanted now;
Now the implanting is done by the conceptual mind, [only insofar as concepts can tend toward the goal];
Only thus does the conceptual mind implant causes and conditions tending toward the goal.

{Comment: The whole notion of "planting" is conjured up by the word set: *'debs, btab, thebs.* Of course, in the view of Vajrayāna Buddhism, no one plants or purifies, no one creates, and no one acts to bring about perfection in the ultimate sense.

In the relative sense, however, there are practices that clean off the adventitious defilements that obscure the primordial, innate, ultimately pure Buddha-nature. These practices, such as working with the drops, winds, and channels to arrive at an experiential knowledge of the essentially void nature of all phenomena, are themselves participants in the nature of conceptuality. So there is a paradox: we are liberated from concept-making by making concepts. In fact, a plethora of spiritual practices are made possible by using the conceptual mind. The problematic nature of concept-production contains within itself mechanisms that can be employed to subvert concept-production. When one attains the stabile breakthrough that recognizes conceptuality and conceptualization for what they are, all the concepts, methods, and mental constructs fall apart of themselves, from moment to moment. This is what Tilopa is trying to teach Nāropa in the *Mahāmudropadeśa.* Here, in the path of method, we are invited to act on our own minds by working with what's there in order to realize the essential nature directly and experientially, in contrast to methods that rely on the use of discursive meditation, debate, or study. For Milarepa, method is identified with the practices of the stage of perfection (the six yogas) that work with winds, drops, and channels as a means by which the disciple learns directly about the essentially open ("void") nature of phenomena.}

Folio 112.6:

It's like fire killing fire; it's like taking a mirage for water, so don't practice the view, practice the method. [Otherwise it is as if] one would like to see the unseen country, without taking the path to arrive in that country. So cultivate all the features of the path.

This is suitable for those who act so as to realize an actual result, precisely when relying on method, at the time of causation

{Comment: When practice is the cause and realization is the result.}

it is neither void (for what benefit comes from voidness?) nor non-void. If you were to ask who has it, it is possessed by a perfect Buddha. It arises in the awareness (*rig pa*) of a *yogin*.

> Though common for a realized one, it is special for ordinary people. 113.1

It arises through reliance on method; it abides continuously in one who has supreme qualities (*yon tan*) of bliss and void. For such a person, there is no difference between meditative equipoise and subsequent arising. [Whereas] the person of middling capacity realizes subsequent arising as void and the one of small capacity sees subsequent arising as illusory.

This is *The Clarification of Reality* by rJe btsun Milarepa. It was transmitted through sNyi ba Rinpoche; given to Lhopa Rinpoche, who gave it to me [Dus gsum mkhyen pa].

24.2. Folio 113.4. This Is the "Clarification of Ignorance" by rJe btsun Milarepa

I prostrate to the Realized Masters.

Having obtained the kindness of the Holy Master, having collected the necessary items, in a place suitable for practice, with articles for attaining success, accumulation of merit, *bodhi*[*citta*] and mystical attainment, the goods needed to sustain one's life: it is very important to have the four conditions [favorable factors related to yogic practice].

The person who is a renouncer of worldly deeds generates himself quickly as the deity, like a fish jumping rapidly from clear pure water.

Now there are two types of path:

—one which brings about ripening
—one which leads to liberation

On the *path of ripening*:
There are three types of path and initiation.

Once one has been ripened, one takes up the path of liberation:

1. Generation and
2. Completion, each of which has 2 [sub]categories:
   1a. One which generates
   1b. One which has been generated
   2a. One with elaborations
   2b. One which is spontaneously arisen (*sahaja*).

Now, concerning (2a) the one with elaborations, one relies on

consciousness,
droplet,
winds, and
in the body, channels and winds.

In that [path], it is suitable to produce the non-conceptual state, which abides in and is produced in the body.

Folio 114.1:

Though they abide in the body, they are not produced by the body. As, for example, in the case of a ship or a house. [The ship is in the water but is not made by the water, and so on.]

This is the path of definitive meaning, with its result:

The Holy Master's kindness being obtained …

Now I'm not saying that only the path of method is true, but [I do say] that the features of whatever Realization may occur are beyond the power of speech.

One who is on the path of liberation by means of the path of desire has to practice with strong effort, applying himself to the union of *kumbhaka*[4] (114.2). Through exertion, the vital energy will definitely enter the "place" [the *avadhūti*].

Folio 114.2:

The elements will dissolve into one another. Yogic heat [*caṇḍalī*] blazes up forcefully and the *bodhicitta* blazes up definitively. Within,

In my opinion, that is wrong. It is the moon, but not the moon of the fifteenth day!

> It is knowledge, but not yet non-conceptuality!
> It's the shape, but not the body.
> It's just another thing to be exemplified.
> Rely, therefore, on the Path of Method!

As for those who have exhausted the path of accumulation, there is the actual and imaginary [practice with consort]. When you use the imaginary one, have in your mind whatever you like. When you are enjoying being together, think of whatever you like. This is where mind functions as object. Now when you actually rely on a genuine partner, the qualifications of such a consort are explained in all the tantras. Now in my own opinion, as a *yogin*, whatever suits your mind is a qualified consort. If you share a lot of Accumulation [of Merit], if her actions are lovely, if she performs secret actions free from hurry. Now go to a solitary place together and perform actions without fear/shame. Even one's own mother, daughter or sister may become a special basis and the virtues will arise without faults [?]. But if it has to do with instructions lacking the virtuous qualities, don't even think about that!

In all the tantras it is said that quotations such as "relying on mother or sister" are Buddha-word subject to non-literal interpretation. But some people think these quotations are [literally] true. So, without practicing in accordance with the Meaning, they do it [that way] with individuals. Don't even sit on the same seat as a *yogin* who [does this] without knowing the way of union; his actions, like those of ordinary beings, bring no benefit and are faulty. Therefore, one should rely on this instruction of one who is skilled in the way of union. These practices are only for the few and not the practice for everybody. Otherwise, Secret Mantra practices, instead of being the path of method become just confusion without control. They don't produce the virtues and become instead the path of blame. So practice in secrecy.

Folio 116.7: This profound instruction of Secret Mantra, in my opinion, is superior from the point of view of the path of method rather than (*'khags*) from the perspective of the view.

> Just as water in the ear is brought out by more water 117.1
> Just as poison inside can be eliminated by a medicine made of poison,
> Just as a little child fights with a child, or a stain cleans up a stain,
> So, if you want to cure diseases there are innumerable branches of medicine …
> So cherish this Path of Method.

Other people say [erroneously] these words:

"By the virtues occurring through meditation on generation or completion stages, from the unproduced *dharmakāya*, one arises as the two form bodies and thus benefits sentient beings."

In my opinion, this is not correct. Is it appropriate that the pure form bodies should arise from an impure *dharmakāya*? In reply to that, they will say: "In such a case, what is real?" Asking that, implies the following:

"By the power of previous merit, in Bodhisattvas abiding on the *bhūmis* and in sentient beings with pure thoughts, and by the power of great compassion, that is the way things appear."

But it is not so in reality. For example, what a magician creates is not what he becomes. For this meaning is difficult to understand, but it is the non-dual view: *Mahāmudrā*, in accordance with its real intent which is one's own consciousness of the Clear Light, is the goal and meaning of non-conceptuality. It has been exemplified in words and letters and was taught by the Buddha. We possess [that clear consciousness], but it is not [yet] realized. It is in front of your gaze, but you are blind [to it]. By means of the path of method one trains without being dependent on anything else, so as to [produce] the body-with-signs (the form bodies). One has to scorch to purify! The afflictions gradually cease and non-conceptuality arises as a by-product (i.e., spontaneously). This is the [Attainment] Stage of the Yogic Path. I am stingy in handing this out to others. It is given only to suitable disciples. The expansive [view] of those with experience, if practiced, brings satisfaction. But when written in words and letters, it is not something that all can grasp. Here there is no distinction between broad or narrow activities. [By doing this] one repays the kindness of one's Master. One is to stay alone in an isolated place and one is to realize one's own mind for oneself.

Folio 118.1: One reflects on death, but as for fear of the three lower rebirths, one relies on the stages of transmission of one's Master [*guru parampara*]. From another perspective, there is:

1. the *yogin*'s body.
2. the Dharma to be practiced.
3. the body wherein experience arises.

It is well to keep these three in extreme secrecy. They are explained here for those who have faith. Please repay my kindness!

This is the experience of Milarepa, written down and titled *The Clarification of Ignorance*. It is finished. It was transmitted through sNyi ba Rinpoche.

24.3. Folio 118.3. By Milarepa: "The Purification of the Stains of Mental Elaboration [*prapañca*]."

I prostrate to the Holy One.

This is how to become a suitable vessel:

First, initiation.

There are two ways of understanding initiation:

1. Its bestowal primordially, which naturally abides.
2. Its bestowal as a condition [leading to realization].

Second, the way to put initiation into practice:

This is the path of method; realization arises from practicing this.

This is how I understand "initiation."

Sacred bonds (*samaya*) are also recognized to be of two types.

1. primordial and great "guarding" (custody, watchfulness)
2. ordinary "household" watchfulness against infractions.

Folio 118.4 [Text here may be corrupt]: Guarding, keeping custody of one's sacred bonds ...

Now the actual result of primordial custody [is Buddhahood]!

Of the view there are also two aspects:

1. the verbal way to posit the view
2. the way the view comes about as experience

This is the way to posit the view [in the practice of method]:

Channels, winds, and cakras are important. If the key points of "Vitality and Effort" are not penetrated, that which is not suitable may occur. This is why the path of method is exceptional.

This is the way to posit the view verbally:

Beings who are not as ignorant as I am, up to fully awakened Buddhas, are like a mute or a young girl in this.... They can use exemplification, but they cannot explain its essential identity.

There are also two types of meditation:

1. meditation with an object [the deity]
2. meditation without an object [voidness]

The first is what the *yogin* does meditating on the body-with-signs [i.e., the yidam in *saṃbhogakāya* form] as object; the second is meditation on voidness, the essential nature of phenomena. Both faults and virtues indeed arise from that state [voidness] appropriately/suitably.

There are innumerable ways to remedy [obstacles, defects, faults].

{Comment: The guru knows these remedies, how, when, and where to apply them. He has supramundane knowledge and the wisdom of an enlightened Buddha.}

The armor of voidness is of great importance.

{Comment: Voidness meditation shields us from conceptualization; *rely* on voidness, rather than on the fear generated by confusions deriving from conceptualizations.}

Unless you gain certainty [on the teaching of voidness], how could you possibly attain experiential realization?

{Comment: *nyams rtogs*, experiential realization, can be understood in two ways:

1. *nyams*:
   a. realization of the deities through habitual pure vision.
   b. seeing the (void) nature of all phenomena.
2. *rtogs*: means direct understanding.}

Having first obtained the kindness of a holy guru

{Comment: the *snyan brgyud* teachings are precisely dependent on an intimate spiritual connection between guru and disciple and require receiving the empowerments, transmission and personal practice instructions.}

one stays in a solitary place.

{Comment: Far away from noise and the confusion of cities, etc.}

When the "place" has been penetrated by vitality and exertion

{Comment: The place is the "*u-ma*," the central channel. *srog-rtsol* has a dual referent:

1. Placing the Guru's instructions/kindness into the central channel
2. Placing all the winds in the central channel. The winds are of two kinds, pure and impure. When they are all gathered into the central channel, they become "wisdom winds."}

heat and cold are blended within; then certainty will arise, and conceptuality will gradually cease. The supreme goal cannot be harmed by the mist of external appearance. In that suchness of pure meaning, there is no duality between object of meditation and meditator.

The action is taught to be of two types:

1. those which can be done [materially]
2. that which cannot be "done."

On the level of those which can be done, one acts like a mute or a madman; as for that which cannot be "done": Suchness is the supreme activity.

As for results, there are two types:

1. *dharmakāya* and
2. *rūpakāya*

The identity of the *dharmakāya* is like the sky without sides, surface, or bottom. It cannot be posited as a "this." In this ultimate state there is nothing to attain, nothing to abandon or hopes and fears. It is like showing the moon with a finger: by relying on words we can only give examples. If the actual meaning has not been realized, how can it be explained as being "something"? If it were an existent thing, it would be suitable for it to be understood once explained. But although an eloquent person may teach about the meaning, his hearers, who depend only on his words, are in need of commiseration!

That which is beyond both existence and non-existence and void of nihilism and permanence can merely be exemplified when words are used.

Now, how can it be suitable that the form bodies (*rūpakāya*) arise from anything which [itself] has conceptual features? Though the Buddha said that the form bodies arise from the *dharmakāya*, in intentional meaning (*dgongs pa*), some conclude that this is the definitive meaning, but in my opinion this is not correct. Well then, one may ask how does it arise? What appears to arise as the two form bodies manifests to sentient beings having pure vision in accordance with the power of previous aspirations; they thus arise individually and [seem to] exist.

Folio 120.1:

Because it is appearance, it is not Suchness.

Now, if this were to be taught to ordinary persons, they would be frightened. Buddha never ceases to benefit sentient beings, and the Dharma, how can it vanish?

This "Purification of the Stains of Mental Elaboration" was taught directly to disciples. It was proclaimed in words; now you practice it. I am not skillful in expressing the experience of spiritual practice in words: please make extensive words concise.

Herein whatever is easy to understand verbally has been taught by Milarepa.

24.4. *Mahāmudrā* in Relation to Tantra and in Relation to *Śamatha-vipaśyanā* Practice

[Milarepa's teaching[6] on Mahāmudrā from the *gDams ngag mdzod*, vol. V, pp. 66–67 and 120–121.]

"The root text on making clear the gnosis of *mahāmudrā*."

Homage to the Realized Masters!

(The succession of the Masters of the lineage is as follows:)

To the great Master Tilopa, to Nāropa, to Marpa of Lho Brag ...

I, a *yogin* from Gung Thang, developed faith and devotion in the saint of Lho Brag, who bestowed his compassion on me while I served him for a long time.

I meditated diligently and forcefully in accordance with the instructions I received from him, and I received his blessing.

Yogic heat blazed up in my body and I was warm, though dressed only in cotton cloth.

The Clear Light dawned in my mind.

I received many tantric transmissions to which other [transmissions] cannot be compared, so pay attention to these specific aspects.

When one practices, there are three aspects:

1. The natural, primordial state.
2. The path.
3. The arising of fruition.

Now, in this teaching, understand that the essence of mind is the natural state and this is *mahāmudrā*.

Now there are three features of *mahāmudrā*:

1. Ground Mahāmudrā
2. Path Mahāmudrā
3. Fruition Mahāmudrā

The first topic: The mode of abiding of phenomena in their natural state.

"The intentions of the Buddhas" and the "nature of the mind of sentient beings" are not established as shape or color, or margins or center; these are free from partiality and extremes. They neither engage in existence nor non-existence; they do not err, nor are they free from error; they do not arise from any cause, nor do they change in relation to conditions. They are not contrived by a skillful (i.e., knowing) Buddha, nor corrupted by dull sentient beings; nor do they improve through Realization nor worsen by error. This is Ground Mahāmudrā.

[The second topic:] This is Path Mahāmudrā.

One engages in one's practice of Dharma in the experience of the Ground. When settled, one does so without observations; while abiding, one remains without agitation; while going along, one does so without grasping. When something appears, it appears as Dharmatā; when released, it is self-released.

This is Path Mahāmudrā.

[The third topic:] Fruition Mahāmudrā.

It is without anything to be liberated and without anything that liberates. It is without expectations (hope/fear).

Since it has gone beyond mind, it is said to be non-grasping, non-exhausting of mind and of phenomena. It is also inexpressible. That is Fruition Mahāmudrā.

One practices these three as one: ground, path, fruition.

The "Clarification of *Mahāmudrā*" instruction by rJe btsun Mila the *yogin*.

Notes

Preface

1. The biography is part of *mTshan ldan bla ma rnams kyi rnam thar bzghugs* found in *bKa' brgyud pa'i bla ma gsung sna tshogs phyogs sgrig* (vol. 7).
2. W. Y. Evans-Wentz, ed., *Tibet's Great Yogi Milarepa: A Biography from the Tibetan*, 2nd ed. (London: Oxford University Press, 1969).
3. Garma C. C. Chang, *The Hundred Thousand Songs of Milarepa: The Life-Story and Teaching of the Greatest Poet-Saint Ever to Appear in the History of Buddhism* (New Hyde Park, NY: University Books, 1962).
4. Evans-Wentz, *Tibet's Great Yogi Milarepa*, vii–viii.
5. Francis Tiso, "A Study of the Buddhist Saint in Relation to the Biographical Tradition of Milarepa" (PhD diss., Columbia University, 1989).
6. What we have today of Milarepa's "oral instructions" consists of texts edited by disciples—especially by Ras chung pa—in the form of outlines and prose notes, some of which reveal more of the historical Milarepa than the literary works redacted by the great gTsang Smyon Heruka that have become so popular.
7. George N. Roerich, trans., *Blue Annals* (Delhi: Motilal Banarsidass, 1979), 432.
8. Victoria Kennick Urubshurow, "Symbolic Processes on the Buddhist Path: Spiritual Development in the Biographical Tradition of Milarepa" (PhD diss., University of Chicago, 1984), 385–86. Some of the ages and dates are approximations derived from events presented in various sources.

Chapter 1

1. The term *bka'* merits some attention. It is the "oral"—that is, spoken—transmission or even the "aural" (heard) transmission. Above all, it

is understood as a "word of power" delivered and disclosed by the guru that opens the experience of enlightenment to the disciple. Tucci points out that *bka'* is in reference to the superior character of the lama's instructions: *bla ma'i gdams ngag*. Giuseppe Tucci, *The Religions of Tibet*, trans. Geoffrey Samuel (Berkeley: University of California Press, 1988), 22. For the term *dkar brgyud*, see E. Gene Smith, *Among Tibetan Texts* (Boston: Wisdom Publications, 2001), 40.

2. Other lineages that fused with the four major orders (the traditional term is *chos lugs chen po bzhi*) include the gCod pa, the Shangs pa bKa' brgyud, and Pha Dam pa Sangs rgya's Zhi byed teaching. 'Jam mgon Kong sprul, the genius behind the nineteenth-century *ris-med* (unbiased) movement in Eastern Tibet classified the orders as rNyingma, bKa' gdams (including the dGe lugs pa), Sa skya (or *lam 'bras*), Marpa bKa' brgyud, Shangs pa bKa' brgyud, Zhi byed and gCod, Dus 'khor (Jonang and Zhalu), and U rgyan bsnyan sgrub. See Smith, *Among Tibetan Texts*, chaps. 3, 4, and 17. Non-Buddhist Vajrayāna practices were transmitted by the Bon po, who maintained cordial relations with individual rNyingma practitioners.
3. Abhayadatta, *Buddha's Lions: The Lives of the Eighty-Four Siddhas*, trans. James B. Robinson, Tibetan Translation Series (Berkeley: Dharma Publishing, 1979).
4. Published materials on these figures include David Templeman, trans. and ed., *The Seven Instruction Lineages* (Dharamsala: LTWA, 1983); Fabrizio Torricelli, *The Life of the Mahasiddha Tilopa by Mar-pa Chos-kyi bLo-gros*, trans. Acharya Sangye T. Naga, ed. Vyvyan Cayley (Dharamsala: LTWA, 1995); Herbert V. Guenther, trans., *The Life and Teaching of Naropa* (London: Oxford University Press, 1963); Nalanda Translation Committee, *The Life of Marpa the Translator: Seeing Accomplishes All* (Boulder: Prajñā Press, 1982).
5. E. Gene Smith, *Among Tibetan Texts*, 41.
6. Ibid., 43.
7. Rgod-tshang-ras-pa Sna-tshogs-rang-grol, *The Life of the Saint of gTsang*, ed. Lokesh Chandra, with a preface by E. Gene Smith (New Delhi: Sharada Rani, 1969), 2. See also Smith, *Among Tibetan Texts*, chap. 5.
8. Cf. the Hebrew rabbinic *chavurah*, the table fellowship of a rabbi and his disciples; the life patterns of Cistercian medieval granges; and the

intimate spiritual sharing typical of early Egyptian desert monasticism recounted in John Cassian's *Conferences*.

9. See Nalanda Translation Committee, *The Life of Marpa the Translator*, 49–50; and John Locke, *Buddhist Monasteries of Nepal* (Kathmandu: Sahayogi, 1985).
10. Tsang Nyön Heruka, *The Life of Marpa the Translator: Seeing Accomplishes All*, trans. Nalanda Translation Committee under the direction of Chögyam Trungpa, 1st ed. (Boulder: Prajñā Press, 1982); David N. Gellner, *Monk, Householder, and Tantric Priest: Newar Buddhism and Its Hierarchy of Ritual* (New York: Cambridge University Press, 1992).
11. gTsang smyon Heruka, *The Life of Milarepa*, trans. Lobsang P. Lhalungpa (Boston: Shambhala, 1984), 57–58.
12. Toni Huber has photographed the buildings at Lho brag, including the tower built by Milarepa.
13. These caves of Milarepa have been photographed by Toni Huber.
14. George Roerich, *Blue Annals*, 2 vols. (Calcutta: Royal Asiatic Society of Bengal, 1949–53), 474–80.
15. Keith Dowman, *The Power-Places of Central Tibet* (Delhi: Timeless Books, 1996), 19.
16. Sakya Pandita Kunga Gyaltshen, *A Clear Differentiation of the Three Codes*, trans. Jared Douglas Rhoton (Albany: State University of New York Press, 2002). Sa Paṇ is critical of the *Ras chung snyan rgyud* and lay religious movements in general. See Alex McKay, ed., *The History of Tibet*, vol. 2 (London: Routledge Curzon, 2003), 399.
17. Giuseppe Tucci, *Deb T'er Dmar Po Gsar Ma: Tibetan Chronicles by bSod nams grags pa*, vol. 1 (Roma: IsMEO, 1971), chaps. 5 and 6. Elliot Sperling recounts the rivalry between 'Bri gung and Sa skya from the 1240s to the 1290s in "Some Notes on the Early 'Bri gung pa Sgom-pa." McKay, *The History of Tibet*, 375.
18. Smith, *Among Tibetan Texts*, 43. He translates a song lamenting the civil war of 1434, 50–51.
19. See McKay, *The History of Tibet*, Turrell Wylie, chap. 60 and Georges Dreyfus, chap. 61.
20. Smith, *Among Tibetan Texts*, 59–61.
21. David Jackson, *A History of Tibetan Painting* (Wien: Verlag der Österreichischen Akademie der Wissenschaften, 1996), 73–74, cites an

episode of such behavior in the court of Mustang in which gTsang smyon's intent was to reform poor liturgical practice among the court lamas. Gene Smith relates the circumstances of gTsang smyon's break with monastic life in *Among Tibetan Texts*, 64.

22. Janet Gyatso, "The Literary Transmission of the Traditions of Thang-stong rGyal-po: A Study of Visionary Buddhism in Tibet" (PhD diss., University of California, Berkeley, 1981).
23. 'Brug-pa Kun-legs, *Vie et chants de 'Brug-Pa Kun-Legs le yogin*, Traduit du tibétain et annoté par R. A. (Rolf Alfred) Stein (Paris: G.-P. Maisonneuve et Larose, 1972).
24. See various *chos 'byung* accounts of gTsang smyon's disciples, such as the '*Brug pa chos 'byung* and the *Lho rong chos 'byung*.
25. In earlier studies of Tibetan history, this conflict has been described in terms of "red hats" versus "yellow hats," which reflects the evolution of Tibetan historiography for the period after the great Fifth Dalai Lama, oversimplifying the complex relationships among the various orders both before and after the reform movement inaugurated by rJe Tsong Khapa.
26. Giuseppe Tucci, *Deb T'er Dmar Po Gsar Ma*, contains a number of contemporary accounts: unrest in Yar lung in the 1430s, 219; unrest in gTsang in the 1460s and 1470s, 222–23; war between gTsang and Yar lung in the 1480s, 224–26. See especially 226 for the state of affairs during the period in which gTsang smyon was writing the *Mila rnam thar mgur 'bum*.
27. Preface to the *Life of the Saint of gTsang*, 3; cf. Smith, *Among Tibetan Texts*, 60.
28. The murderer is described as a Bon po in the *Ras chung snyan rgyud*, folio 124, line 2 (catalog number 73-902914). Catalog number 84-900297 does not identify the murderer. rGyal thang pa identifies him as Bon po Tsan dar 'bum on folio 261. gTsang smyon calls him dge bshes rtsag phu pa, pg. 813, *Standard Edition*, 1989.
29. *Cakrasaṁvara Tantra Ḍākinī Oral Lineage Instructions.*
30. *Index to the Ras chung Oral Teachings*, 12–13 vols. in manuscript, written with gold ink toward the end of gTsang smyon's life. See Smith, Preface to the *Life of the Saint of gTsang*, 4n7.
31. See Smith, *Among Tibetan Texts*, 61.

32. Fabrizio Torricelli, "Padma dkar po's Arrangement of the *bDe-mchog snyan-brgyud*" (unpublished manuscript); Fabrizio Torricelli, "The Tibetan Text of the *Karnatantravajrapada*," *East and West* 48, nos. 3–4 (1998): 385–423.
33. The history of the various branches of the bKa' brgyud order is given in detail in the introduction (by E. Gene Smith) to the *Dkar Brgyud Gser 'Phreng: A Golden Rosary of Lives of Eminent Gurus,* comp. Mon Rtse Pa Kun Dga' Dpal ldan, ed. Kun Dga' 'Brug Dpal (Leh: Sonam W. Tashigang, BPO Nemo, 1970), 1–8. See also Smith, *Among Tibetan Texts*, chap. 3.
34. Lokesh Chandra, ed., *Tibetan Chronicle of Padma-dkar-po*, foreword by E. Gene Smith (New Delhi: International Academy of Indian Culture, 1968); J. MacKenzie, *The Life of Gampopa* (Ithaca: Snow Lion, 1995).
35. Smith, *Among Tibetan Texts*, 81–86. See also Torricelli, op. cit.
36. Pad ma dkar po, *Tibetan Chronicle of Padma-dkar po* (New Delhi: International Academy of Indian Culture, 1968), 82–83.
37. Ibid., 1, 4, 5.
38. The first major recognized *sprul sku* was Karma Pakshi, the incarnation of Dus gsum mkhyen pa, the first Karmapa, who was a disciple of sGampopa. See Geoffrey Samuel, *Civilized Shamans* (Washington: Smithsonian Institute Press, 1993), 479, 599n3.
39. See Jackson, *A History of Tibetan Painting*, 73–74.
40. Personal oral communication at a public lecture, Columbia University, 1986.
41. And such chronicles as Tucci, *Deb T'er*, cf. 226.
42. The circle of disciples around gTsang smyon knew the work of rGyal thang pa. For example, Lha btsun rinchen rnam rgyal made use of rGyal thang's material to produce an expanded biography of rGod tshang mGon po rdo rje (1189–1258). See Smith, *Among Tibetan Texts*, 75–76.
43. For example, 'Bri gung Til has an entire section of its territory dedicated to hermitages that are still used by advanced *yogin*-monks.
44. Interview at Bouddha, Kathmandu, Nepal, April 2, 1997.
45. See Toni Huber in McKay, *The History of Tibet*, chap. 56.
46. See *Jamgon Kongtrul's Retreat Manual*, trans. and ed. Ngawang Zangpo (Ithaca: Snow Lion, 1994).

Chapter 2

1. Hayden White, "The Value of Narrativity in the Representation of Reality," in *On Narrative*, ed. W. J. T. Michell (Chicago: University of Chicago Press, 1981), 1.
2. R. A. Stein, *Vie et chants de 'Brug-Pa Kun-Legs le yogin* (Paris: Maisonneuve et Larose), 101–2. "Quant à la mienne (de biographie), elle est écrite cahin-caha, en prenant par le nez, en prenant par les poils. Elle n'est pas écrite pour que les évéments apparaissent sous un jour admirable. Chaque fois que je me suis notoirement (couverte de honte), j'ai écrit ce dont je me souvenais (consciencieusement). D'ailleurs, dans les biographies des lamas, arrangées en fort bon ordre, c'est comme dans un carnet de créancier où il est écrit: telle année, tel mois et tel jour, j'ai reçu tel gage, aussi dois-je encaisser tant de charges d'orge ou de poix. C'est vraiment terriblement mesquin." Obviously he is criticizing biographies that sound like account books of "offerings received"!
3. See the root verses 1–26, 190–94; *rnam thar*, that is, biography, appears in verse 26. rGyal thang pa bDe Chen rDo rJe, *Dkar brgyud gSer 'phreng* (Palampur, Tashijhong: Sungrab Nyamso Gyunphel Parkhang, Tibetan Craft Community, 1973). The *Life of Milarepa* is found on folios 189–265.
4. Frank E. Reynolds and Donald Capps, eds., *The Biographical Process: Studies in the History and Psychology of Religion* (The Hague: Mouton, 1976).
5. For example, the Buddha himself is said to recount the life of the Buddha Vipassi in the *Dīgha Nikāya*, ii, 1–54. T. W. and C. A. F. Rhys Davids, trans., *Dialogues of the Buddha*, part 2 (London: Henry Frowde, 1910), XXIB, *Mahāpadāna Suttanta*, 4–41.
6. Stanley J. Tambiah, *The Buddhist Saints of the Forest and the Cult of Amulets* (Cambridge: Cambridge University Press, 1984), 21–24. See also K. R. Norman, trans., *The Elders' Verses: I Theragāthā; II Therīgāthā* (London: Pali Text Society, 1969, 1971), passim.
7. Philip B. Yampolsky, trans., *The Platform Sutra of the Sixth Patriarch* (New York: Columbia University Press, 1967), 125n1: "Prior to the *Platform Sutra* we have no instance in which a work which was merely the record of the career and sermons of a certain master is given the name Sutra. Strictly speaking, of course, it is not one. Thus

Ch'i-sung took pains to justify its classification as such: '[Hui-neng] … was a Bodhisattva monk, and his preaching of the *Platform Sutra* is basically no different from the Buddha's preaching of the sutras.'"

8. LM, colophon, 201–3, which treats the life as a source of spiritual power precisely because the saint depicted attains complete enlightenment and is thus equal to the Buddha himself.
9. BA, 448. The life of Milarepa is told to the child rDo rje khro bo (Se ston Jo khro), who proceeds to meditate in a cave in imitation of the *rJe bTsun*. Compare the life of St. Teresa of Jesus, who as a child imitated the Desert Fathers and who once ran away from home in search of martyrdom at the hands of the Moors in Kieran Kavanaugh, O.C.D., and Otilio Rodriguez, O.C.D., trans., *The Collected Works of St. Teresa of Avila*, vol. 1 (Washington, DC: Institute of Carmelite Studies, 1976), chap. 1, 4–5, 33–34. On conversion, see Victoria Kennick Urubshurow, "Symbolic Process on the Buddhist Path," 232–34.
10. *Songs*, 100.
11. Compare the attitude of early Christian Gnosticism, which held that only those persons who possessed a "pneumatic" soul had the capacity to respond to the Gnostic teachings. See Kurt Rudolph, *Gnosis: The Nature and History of Gnosticism*, trans. Robert McL. Wilson (San Francisco: Harper and Row, 1983), 90–91.
12. Jo Nang Tāranātha, *The Seven Instruction Lineages*, trans. David Templeman (Dharmsala: LTWA, 1983), 25.
13. LM, op. cit., 197.
14. *Songs*, 98–99. It is possible to attain a brief glimpse of the highest illumination early in one's practice, but one must continue to deepen the experience and stabilize realization until literally every moment of one's continuum of existence is suggested with the energy of enlightened consciousness. Marpa explained to Milarepa that such realization is not the result of teachings alone: "In my lineage an enlightening energy is transmitted which has no similarity to that of others." LM, 48.
15. LM, 200.
16. Ibid., 12. This false identity has contributed to confusion about the actual identity of the author/redactor of the *mila rnam thar*. gTsang smyon Heruka was not a disciple of Ras chung pa. He lived in the late fifteenth century and was a holder of the *mkha' 'gro ma'i snyan*

brgyud transmitted by Milarepa to Ras chung pa and Bodhi Radza. See rGod-tShang Ras pa sNa Tshongs Rang Grol, *The Life of the Saint of gTsang*, ed. Lokesh Chandra, with a preface by E. Gene Smith (New Delhi: Sharada Rani, 1969), 3–4.

17. Urubshurow, "Symbolic Process," passim.
18. H. H. the XIV Dalai Lama, first Panchen Lama, Jamyang Khyentse Rinpoche, and Kalu Rinpoche, *Four Essential Buddhist Texts* (Dharamsala: LTWA, 1982), 59–85. Glenn H. Mullin, trans. and ed., *Tsongkhapa's Six Yogas of Naropa* (Ithaca: Snow Lion, 1996). See Urubshurow, "Symbolic Process," 19 and 20, where she emphasizes the oral explanation of the contents of *rnam thars* by qualified teachers. There are hints of profound teachings in the *rnam thrs*, and we even find examples in the *Songs* of what amount to a summary of the "stages of the path," but detailed instruction on practice are not found in these works. The *rnam thar* of Milarepa by sGampopa is another example that makes quite clear the fact that the *rnam thar* is a sort of an outline (folio a.42.4: *dzad spyod zur tsam rnam par bshad pa'o//* "in mere outline form") used by a teacher who will, in appropriate circumstances, enlarge upon the practices mentioned for the benefit of the specific disciples who sit before him. Janice Willis, "The Search for Padma-can: A Study in the Interpretation of Tibetan Sacred Biography," *Journal of Religious Studies XIII*, no. 1 (Spring 1985), 57, actually makes the assertion that "Siddha biographies in terms of content, are comparable to and complement, the Tantras and their commentaries. As such, one of the main functions of the *rnam-thar* is the actual imparting of tantric practice instructions." But the example she gives is so veiled by symbolic allusions that only the oral instructions of a guru would enable the disciple to know what is actually going on, much less to obtain "detailed practice instructions ... to put the teachings particular to a certain Siddha into practice."
19. Such instructions are found in manuals of oral instructions such as are found in Jamgon Kongtrul the Great's compilation of the *gdams ngag mdzod*. G. Mullin has translated some similar instructions from the works of rJe Tsong Khapa. Even these instructions require detailed "how to" instructions from the living master, because some of the procedures to be followed are not self-evident.

20. Robin Kornman, "Hidden Literary Criticism in Tibetan Biographies" (paper delivered to the Modern Language Association in New York, December 29, 1985), 1–2.
21. In Willis, op. cit., 57–58, the three are described as corresponding to (1) outer: the biography including details of birth, conversion, education, teachers, and external activities; (2) inner: giving the meditative practices and initiations; and (3) secret: describes visions and related experiences of the "hierophant." But a bKa' brgyud pa *tulku*, Dugu Choegyal Gyamtso, in his foreword to Keith Dowman and Sonam Paljor, trans., *The Divine Madman: The Sublime Life and Songs of Drukpa Kunley* (Clearlake, CA: Dawn Horse, 1980), 21–22, places visions and *sampannakrama* realizations under "internal" (*nang*) biography and considers the "secret" biography to reveal a lama's life "in terms of his perfect activity, and there is no distinction made between external events and the inner life … it is called 'secret' because without having realized the Lama's state of mind, we cannot understand it." In terms of our own categorization of the saint, the latter distinction makes more sense: outer recognition, inner contemplative experience, and finally a category "secret," that is uniquely Buddhist.
22. See R. A. Stein, *Vie et Chants*, 150, and R. A. Stein, *Recherches sur l'Epopée et le Barde au Tibet* (Paris: Presses Universitaires de France, 1959), 489.
23. *Songs*, chap. 25.
24. For rNgog, see LM, 64–70 and our version of rGyal thang pa's account, folios 211–15.
25. E. Lamotte, *Histoire du Bouddhisme Indien* (Louvain-La-Neuve: Institut Orientaliste, 1976), 765–75, but not restricted to the sources mentioned by Tambiah (note 6) and by Lamotte.
26. Edward Conze, trans. *The Perfection of Wisdom in Eight Thousand Lines and Its Verse Summary* (San Francisco: Four Seasons Foundation, 1973), chap. 30, 277–90.
27. LM, 59.
28. Amalia Pezzali, "Śāntideva, un mistico buddhista," *Studia Missionalia* 35 (1986): 323.
29. James B. Robinson, trans., *Buddha's Lions: The Lives of the Eighty-Four Siddhas* (Berkeley: Dharma Publishing, 1979), which is the

Caturaśiti-siddhi-pravṛtti by Abhayadatta; translated into Tibetan as *Grub thob brgyad cu rtsa bzhi'i lo rgyus* by sMon grub Shes rab.

30. See Daniel Richard Gold, "The Lord as Guru in North Indian Religion: Hindi *Sant* Tradition and Universals of Religious Perception." (PhD diss., University of Chicago, 1982), especially chap. 4, "The Indian Master in Greater Religious Contexts," and the charts on 355–56.
31. Templeman, op. cit., 82–97. The siddha is said to have built a *stūpa* on a hilltop at his guru's command but with the illegitimate aid of another, thereby earning a reprimand from the guru. Ibid., 87–88. The *yoginī* Dīnakarā, his disciple, has a biography that seems to *anticipate* the Hindi life of Mirabai! Ibid., 98–100.
32. Giuseppe Calia, *Sahaja Yoga: Il metodo della realizzazione spirituale secondo la via di Dādū* (Roma: Ubaldini Editore, 1985).
33. Distinctions among such literary forms as the *avadāna* (tales of one's own realization), the *jātaka* (tales of the previous lives of a Bodhisattva), and the *vimukti* (Tibetan: *rnam thar*) have not as yet proven to be a productive line inquiry. They all fit under the literary genre of sacred biography/hagiography.
34. See Derwas J. Chitty, trans., *The Letters of St. Antony the Great* (Fairacres, Oxford: SLG Press, 1975), vii.
35. Charles Van Tuyl, "An Analysis of Chapter Twenty Eight of the Hundred Thousand Songs of Milarepa, a Buddhist Poet and Saint of Tibet" (PhD diss., Indiana University, 1972).

Chapter 3

1. N. Perrin, *What Is Redaction Criticism?* (Philadelphia: Fortress Press, 1969), 1ff.
2. Geoffrey Samuel, "Shamanic Power and Popular Religion," in *Tantra and Popular Religion in Tibet*, ed. Geoffrey Samuel, Hamish Gregor, and Elisabeth Stutchbury (New Delhi: Aditya Prakashan, 1994), 62.
3. Perrin, *op. cit.,* pp. 15–16.

Chapter 4

1. See a brief list of sources for Marpa and Milarepa in Dan Martin's review of *The Life of Marpa the Translator*, translated by the Nālandā

Translation Committee under the direction of Chogyam Trungpa, in *Journal of the Tibet Society* 3 (1984): 83–92.

2. As we are reminded by Helmut Heimer in "Life and Activities of Atiśa Dīpamkaraśrījñāna," *Journal of the Asiatic Society*, 27, no. 4 (1985): 3–5.
3. Compare BA, 399–404, for the use of the Marpa account, and 432–35 for the Mila account.
4. For example, *'mur* is frequently given for *mgur*. (Notebook, March 5, 1997).
5. *Bde mchog snyan brgyud Biographies: Reproduction of a Collection of Rare Manuscripts from the Stag-sna Monastery in Ladakh* (Darjeeling: Kargyud Sungrab Nyamso Khang, 1983).
6. Conversation with Drikung Kyabgon Chetsang Rinpoche at Dehra Dun, India, April 14, 1997.
7. Conversation with Cyrus Stearns in Kathmandu, April 25, 1997. Stearns expressed doubt that the *Black Treasury* was really written or even redacted by the Third Karmapa, mainly because such an important work would have been listed in his collected works, but is not.
8. Microfilm o/21, Ms. Tibetan. A.11 (R) = 215 exp. Francis Younghusband led Indo-British forces into Tibet in 1904 to force a trade agreement and diplomatic relations on the Tibetan government. This was one of the last military actions of the "Great Game" of colonial rivalry in Central Asia between Russia and Great Britain.
9. Reproduced from a rare manuscript from the library of Hemis Monastery (Ladakh) by the Sixth Khams-sprul don brgyud Nyi ma (Tashijhong, Palampur, Himachal Pradesh: Sungrab Nyamso Gyunphel Parkhang Tibetan Craft Community, 1973), folios 189–265.
10. See BA, 686–87; 695. The problematic character of the identity (and even the spelling of the name) of rGyal thang pa is discussed by Peter Alan Roberts in his dissertation: "The Biographies of Ras-chung-pa: The Evolution of a Tibetan Hagiography" (PhD diss., University of Oxford, 2000), 75–86. After much valuable analysis, Roberts concludes, "Nevertheless, in spite of having to rely solely on internal evidence, none of which is completely decisive, the strongest probability is that rGya ldang pa [*sic*] was a pupil of rGod tshang pa, and that the text was written in the mid-thirteenth century." Ibid., 86.

11. Oral communication, 1986.
12. Famous Christian saints such as Francis, Clare, and Nicolas were depicted in the same way; also the *Via Crucis* has some features in common with this devotional pattern, including the ritual bow (or genuflection) at each "station" or episode along the way. The work in the LA County Museum is published inter alia in Marilyn M. Rhie and Robert A. F. Thurman, *Wisdom and Compassion: The Sacred Art of Tibet* (New York: Harry Abrams, 1991), 79, 239.
13. Peter Alan Roberts, op. cit., 90: "Though dGam-po-pa, Bla-ma Zhang and Don-mo Ri-pa/rDo-rje mDzes-'od made references to songs, and quoted a few lines, rGya-ldang-pa [*sic*] is the first to provide us with songs by Mi-la Ras-pa and Ras-chung-pa, and will therefore be particularly relevant in tracing the history of these songs."
14. Ibid., 92.
15. George N. Roerich, trans., op. cit., 1.
16. Ibid., ii.
17. These are the folios in the text used by Roerich. In Lokesh Chandra's edition, the pages are 373–81. See 'Gos Lotsawa Gzhon nu dpal (1392–1481). *Blue Annals* (New Delhi: International Academy of Indian Culture, 1974).
18. The archaic spelling of Milarepa's name, which also turns up in the BA, 427ff.
19. BA, 432.
20. The Zi ba 'od account was probably a literary (i.e., written) source already in existence before the BA were compiled. Note that in gTsang smyon's *mila mgur 'bum,* there are sung autobiographies on 160–61, 207–8, 266–68, 279–81, 283, 333–34, 474–75, 533–34, 536–37, 537–38, 544–45 (Garma Chang translation).
21. Herbert V. Guenther, *The Life and Teaching of Nāropa* (London: Oxford University Press, 1963), xii. See Smith's critique in his foreword to *Smanrtsis shesrig spendzod,* vol. 11 (the *Bde mchog mkha' 'gro snyan rgyud,* Leh, Ladhak, S. W. Tashigangpa, 1971), 5–7.
22. Mircea Eliade, *A History of Religious Ideas,* vol. 3, trans. Willard R. Trask (Chicago: University of Chicago Press, 1985), 282.
23. The Nālandā Translation Committee also discussed this material correctly in their introduction to the *Life of Marpa the Translator,* xiv–xxiv.

24. E. Gene Smith, preface to the *Life of the Saint of gTsang*, 1–2. Smith's numerous and frequently anonymous prefaces to the publications edited by Chandra and others are a treasure trove to the Tibetologist in search of fundamental data on a wide variety of texts. They are now available in an anthology: E. Gene Smith, *Among Tibetan Texts* (Boston: Wisdom Publications, 2001).
25. The title in English: *The Ḍākinī Hearing-Lineage Teachings on the Tantric Cycle of Cakrasaṁvara.*
26. See the *Bde mchog snyan rgyud Biographies: Reproduction of a Collection of Rare Manuscripts from the sTag-sna Monastery in Ladakh* (Darjeeling: Kargyud Sungrab Nyamso Khang, 1983), folios 123–89.
27. LM, 9–11.
28. Urubshurow, op. cit., 16ff.; cf. *Life of the Saint of gTsang*, folio 135; see complete account in folios 137–64.
29. *Bde mchog snyan brgyud Biographies* (Darjeeling: Kargyud Sungrab Nyamso Khang, 1983), folios 133–89. And *Bde mchog mkha' 'gro snyan rgyud*, vol. 1 (New Delhi: 1973), folios 97–125.
30. Milarepa was known as an inspired bard, according to the *mgur 'bum:* "But if you are really [Milarepa], you should be able to preach the Dharma through songs. As we all know, the Jetsun Milarepa is a yogi who has completely opened the nadis of the Throat Center, and is thus capable of preaching any Dharma without the slightest hesitation or difficulty" (*Songs*, 538). These are the attributes of the entranced bard who sings the epic, itself a sacred recitation.
31. R. A. Stein, "Introduction to the Gesar Epic," in *The Epic of Gesar*, vol. 1 (Thimphu, Bhutan: Kunsang Tobgyel, 1979), 2–4.
32. Albert B. Lord, *The Singer of Tales* (Cambridge, MA: Harvard University Press, 1960), 4–5.
33. Ibid., 101.
34. "The bard cannot recite 'cold' without being in trance or inspired." His hat is "necessary" for the trance. See Stein, *Recherches sur l'épopée et le barde au Tibet*, 322, 333; cf. 342–47.
35. R. A. Stein, *Recherches sur l'Épopée et le Bard au Tibet*, 318–19. In fact, the process is comparable to other types of performance trance in Tibet, such as that of diviners. Ibid., 335–36.
36. Ibid., 323, 328–29, 332, 330–31.

37. Ibid., 320.
38. Ibid., 511–13. Based on the theme of conflict with the paternal uncle, Stein suggests that the life of Milarepa was an influence on the plot of the epic, but in the light of the complex literary history of the biography, it is possible that the epic may have shaped the retelling of the life of the saint.
39. The nudity of Milarepa alludes not only to his detachment from worldly concepts of "shame" but also to his links to the warrior/sorcerer. The association of bards with pilgrimage offers a connection with Mila's determination to meditate in numerous caves and holy places. "En remontant à Mi la ras pa, nous devons constater que non seulement ces poètes ont les même attitudes et accoutrements que le jeune Gesar et le barde, leur style même est identique à celui de l'epopée (métaphores et prosodie)." Ibid., 493.
40. Mila is presented as a songster from his youth; his yogic attainment completes the initiatic trials of a sacred bard so that he no longer sings *glu* but rises to the dharmic themes appropriate to the *mgur.*
41. See Stein, *Recherches sur l'Épopée et le Bard au Tibet*, 498, 500, 506.
42. Ibid., 490–91.
43. Mila and Gesar even have names in common. Mila is called *bzad pa rdo rje* ("laughing Vajra") by Marpa; Gesar is called *padma bzad pa* ("laughing lotus") or *bzad pa rtsal* ("skillful laughter"). They are both called *thos pa dga'* ("happy report"). See ibid., 505. *Thos pa dga'* also means *evangelion*, the Gospel word usually translated as "good news." Is it possible that the Nestorians were able to transmit this concept to China and Central Asia to the extent that it could enter the vocabulary of the epic? If Gesar (Caesar), why not Gospel? See P. Y. Saeki, *The Nestorian Documents and Relics in China* (Tokyo: Toho Bunkwa Gakuin, 1951), 274 (*A wan chū li yung = evangelium*) and 314 ("The Nestorian Hymn in Adoration of the Transfiguration" from CE 720).
44. Stein, *Introduction to the Gesar Epic*, 4–5. Abnormalities and faults in epic heroes are discussed in Alf Hiltebeitel, *The Ritual of Battle: Kṛṣṇa in the Mahābhārata* (Ithaca: Cornell University Press, 1976), 44ff.
45. Stein, *Épopée et Barde*, 560–62; these battles can be a kind of playful sport in the epic.

46. Ibid., 351 and 508. The *sādhana* of Gesar is identical in structure to any other divinity's *sādhana;* it amounts to a type of "arising stage yoga," *utpattikrama* (*skyed rim*) (336–37). There is a definite tendency toward a kind of syncretism. "Gesar became a *dgra-lha* (warrior god) and received a cultus, inaugurated by the Third Karmapa, Rang 'Byung rdo rje (1284–1339)." Ibid., 523. This Karmapa was noted for his interest in rNying ma pa teachings.

    Gesar himself is regarded, esoterically, as an incarnation of Vajradhara. In a certain sense, the "possession" of the lineage holder (who is being held and by whom?) by Vajradhara constitutes the holiness of the tantric saint (siddha). This can be affirmed, keeping in mind the view of Buddhist dogmatics that would deny the validity of an analogy making Buddhahood an external deity that "seizes" upon a believer to sanctify him or her.
47. Tucci, *The Religions of Tibet*, 13–14.
48. *Songs*, 395.
49. LM, 141–43; RTH, folios 239–41.
50. This idea is discussed in relation to the interplay of oral and written sources in Lama Kunga Rimpoche and Brian Cutillo, trans., *Drinking the Mountain Stream: Further Stories and Songs of Milarepa* (Novato, CA: Lotsawa, 1976), 33–34.
51. Conversations in Dharamsala, India, April 20, 1997.

Chapter 5

1. Our references to the Chinese edition (1980) of the *rnam thar* and *mgur 'bum* mention this as the *Standard Edition*; it is based on the sDe dge edition.
2. He is mentioned by gTsang smyon Heruka in the *mila rnam thar* (see LM, 144), in *Songs*, 330, and in the BA, 435.
3. Fabrizio Torricelli, "Padma dkar-po's Arrangement of the bDe-mchog snyan-brgyud" (unpublished manuscript, 1997), courtesy of the author.
4. For a discussion of the Mad Yogin as an expert in tantric art, see David Jackson, *A History of Tibetan Painting*, 73–74. The use of illustrations (thangka showing episodes around a large central figure) of the *mila rnam thar* as propaganda by the Mad Yogin is presented in the same work, 371–73.

5. This is affirmed by the greatest living exponent of this tradition, Khenpo Tsultrim Gyatso of the Marpa Institute for Translators, Boudha, Nepal, and by many of the *sngags pa/rnal 'byor pa* practitioners I interviewed in the Tibetan exile communities and in the still-extant communities of Dol po.
6. See Jamgon Kongtrul (Kong-sprul Blo gros mtha' yas, 1813–99), *Jamgon Kongtrul's Retreat Manual*, trans. with introduction by Ngawang Zangpo (Ithaca: Snow Lion, 1994).
7. Cf. *gdams ngag mdzod* vol. 5, folios 66–67 and 120–21; also an obvious example on folios 109.7–110.2.
8. Folios 359.7–360.
9. A recent study of the Ras chung pa biographical tradition is also a support to the arguments advanced here. See Peter Alan Roberts, "The Biographies of Ras-chung-pa: The Evolution of a Tibetan Hagiography" (PhD diss., Oxford University, 2000).
10. On the other hand, when Milarepa is giving teachings that were originally traditional, his "own voice" is suppressed and he transmits the Indian Buddhist tantric tradition in its own terminology, according to the standard Tibetan translation language. Sometimes he speaks didactic prose in his own style, deviating from the received tradition as in his frank comments on the practice of karmamudrā.
11. My translation is based on Marie-Jose Lamothe, trans., *Milarepa: Les Cent Mille Chants* (Paris: Librairie Artheme Fayard, 1986), 112–13; the *Standard Edition*, 265ff.; *Songs*, 88–89; and the parallel text in the *Bu chen bcu gnyis* manuscript from Newark, folios 100–101.
12. See the *Standard Edition* of the Tibetan text, 133–35 and 137–38; compare Lhalungpa's translation, 103–04, 105–07. The *bka' brgyud mgur mtsho* has been translated as *The Rain of Wisdom: The Vajra Songs of the Kagyu Gurus* (Boulder: Shambhala, 1980).
13. These two lines are found only in the Rumtek edition of the *bKa' brgyud pa mgur mtsho*, otherwise the texts are identical and demonstrate the importance of the *Bu chen* text for the living tradition.
14. Lhalungpa, 113–14; *Standard Edition*, 145–6; *Bu chen*, 17R–18.
15. Note that, in my discussion of the death pericopes, I established the confines of narrative units of text. I have also illustrated editorial/redactional techniques on traditional materials in the songs.

16. For the purposes of this chapter, I will focus in on the indications given in the texts available to me.
17. Oral instructions from Lodro Tharchin, Rinpoche, Tibetan Parliament in Exile, July 1997.

Chapter 6

1. *Bu chen*, 25R-26F, comparable to Garma Chang, 279–81.
2. *gdams ngag mdzod*, vol. 5. *rje btsun chen po mi la ras pa mdzad paí snyan brgyud gsal ba skor gsum sogs* (folios 109–20), folios 114–16.
3. Ibid.

Chapter 7

1. Francis Tiso, "The Religion of Milarepa Before His Conversion," in *The Notion of Religion in Comparative Research: Selected Proceedings of the XVI IAHR Congress (1990)*, ed. U. Bianchi (Roma: L'Erma di Bretschneider, 1994), 608–12.
2. For example, the ninth chapter of the Mad Yogin's account of the life of Milarepa has the structure of a folk pageant, probably based on popular ritual at the site of the death and cremation of the saint.
3. rGyal thang pa, *rDo rje 'chang rnam thar*, folio 194.
4. Ibid.
5. *Vimalakīrtinirdeśa,* 400, Lamotte translation.

Chapter 8

1. Lhalungpa, *The Life of Milarepa*, xviii.
2. This is one of the principal reasons why I have used the Wylie transliteration extensively in this work: to emphasize the themes insistently represented by the terms *bKa'* and *brgyud.*
3. A good discussion of this problem in its social context may be found in N. J. Girardot, "Max Müller's *Sacred Books* and the Nineteenth-Century Production of the Comparative Science of Religions," *History of Religions* 41 (2002): 213–50.
4. For example, the Society for Tantric Studies; recent meeting: "Tantra: Constructions and Deployment of Power" at Flagstaff, Arizona,

October 11–13, 2002, http://www.uncg.edu/rel/flagstaff/, and the "Daoism and the Contemporary World" conference at Boston University, June 5–6, 2003, organized by the Department of Religion and the Fairbanks Center at Harvard University.

5. A by-no-means unique but exemplary work of this kind is Robert R. Desjarlais, *Body and Emotion: The Aesthetics of Illness and Healing in the Nepal Himalayas* (Delhi: Motilal Banarsidass, 1994). More controversial work in cultural anthropology has been offered by Sarah Caldwell, *O Terrifying Mother! Sexuality, Violence, and Worship of the Goddess Kālī* (New Delhi: Oxford University Press, 1999), and Jeffrey Kripal, *Roads of Excess and Palaces of Wisdom: Eroticism and Reflexivity in the Study of Mysticism* (Chicago: University of Chicago Press, 2001).
6. Paul E. Murphy, *Triadic Mysticism: The Mystical Theology of the Śaivism of Kashmir* (Delhi: Motilal Banarsidass, 1986); cf. work of José Pereira, ed., with introduction and notes, *Hindu Theology: Themes, Texts and Structures* (Delhi: Motilal Banarsidass Publishers, 1991), 357–88; R. Gnoli, *Abhinavagupta: Essenza dei Tantra (Tantrāsara)* (Torino: Boringheri, 1979); R. Gnoli, "Introduzione," e Attilia Sironi, traduzione e commento, *Vijñānabhairava: La Conoscenza del Tremendo* (Milano: Adelphi Edizioni, 1989).
7. In other words, early Buddhism (as transmitted in the Pali Canon and related traditions), great vehicle Buddhism, and Vajrayāna, as taught in the Later Diffusion Tibetan orders.

Chapter 9

1. Alex Wayman, *An Historical Introduction to the Buddhist Tantras.* For a seminar volume on Buddhist Tantra to be published by the Central Institute of Higher Tibetan Studies, Sarnath, India, Typescript, 1.
2. See Michael Saso, "Kuden: The Oral Hermeneutics of Tendai Tantric Buddhism," *Japanese Journal of Religious Studies* 14 (1987); 2–3, 235–46.
3. Giovanni Verardi, "*Homa" and Other Fire Rituals in Gandhara* (Naples: Istituto Universitario Orientale, 1994). See also the recent work of Christian K. Wedemeyer, "Tropes, Typologies, and

Turnarounds: A Brief Genealogy of the Historiography of Tantric Buddhism," *History of Religions* 10 (2001): 223–59.

4. See Eva M. Dargyay, *The Rise of Esoteric Buddhism in Tibet* (New York: Samuel Weiser, 1978).
5. Later in the sense that they are canonically known as written texts associated with specific gurus.
6. See Ronald Davidson on this tantra in McKay, *The History of Tibet*, 9 and chap. 48.
7. A discussion of *anuttarayogatantra* as a term not to be found in Sanskrit classifications of the Buddhist tantras may be found in Elizabeth English, *Vajrayoginī: Her Visualizations, Rituals, and Forms* (Boston: Wisdom Publications, 2002), 5–6.
8. Alexis Sanderson has influenced the thinking of a generation of scholars on the rapport between Śaiva and Buddha tantric systems. See English, *Vajrayoginī*, 163, 396n60, 466n395, 480n446; McKay *The History of Tibet*, 5 (and, 30–31n9); David Gordon White, *The Kiss of the Yoginī* (Chicago: University of Chicago Press, 2003), 1, 8, 21, 153, 158, 163, 194, 196, 213, 234.
9. See David Snellgrove, *Indo-Tibetan Buddhism: Indian Buddhists and Their Tibetan Successors*, 2 vols. (Boston: Shambhala Publications, 1987). These authors are also named in catalogs of the *bsTan 'gyur.*
10. See *The Life and Teaching of Naropa*, trans. Herbert V. Guenther (London: Oxford University Press, 1963).
11. See K. R. Sundararajan and Bithika Mukerji, *Hindu Spirituality: Postclassical and Modern* (New York: Crossroad, 1997), 181–82.
12. English, *Vajrayoginī*, 195f.
13. Don Messerschmidt, *Muktinath: Himalayan Pilgrimage, a Cultural and Historical Guide* (Kathmandu: Sahayogi, 1992), 16–17.
14. *Dorje Chang Tungma*, translation from the Karma Kagyupa Tibetan Buddhist center "Kilmainham Well House," Ireland.

Chapter 10

1. *gDams ngag mdzod* Volume V., folio 112.5. See Part Three.
2. Wayman, *Historical Introduction to the Buddhist Tantras*, passim.

3. Tsong Kha pa, *Tantra in Tibet: The Great Exposition of Secret Mantra*, vol. 1, with an introduction by H. H. the XIV Dalai Lama, trans. and ed. Jeffrey Hopkins (London: George Allen and Unwin, 1977).
4. See my article, "The Bodhisattva as a Buddhist Saint," in *Premier Colloque E. Lamotte* (Louvain-la-Neuve: Institut Orientaliste, 1993), 141–48.
5. At times there have been debates on the possibility of a being so degenerate that it will never attain liberation, but this view has never prevailed widely.
6. Thrangu Rinpoche, *Buddha Nature* (Ithaca: Snow Lion, 1994), 27
7. Ibid.
8. Ibid. Cf. the exemplary account in Kurtis R. Schaeffer, *Himalayan Hermitess: The Life of a Tibetan Buddhist Nun* (New York: Oxford University Press, 2004), part II, chap. Four.
9. See Thomas Tillemans, *Materials for the Study of Āryadeva, Dharmapāla and Caṇḍrakīrti,* in *Arbeitskreis für Tibetische und Buddhistische Studien*, vol. 1 (Wien: Universität Wien, 1990), 59.
10. *yaḥ pratītyasamutpādam prapañca upasamam sivam // Mūlamadhyamakakārikā,* 19; cf. 52, 56.
11. *Mahāvastu*, The Buddha's First Sermon. See Franklin Edgerton, *Buddhist Hybrid Sanskrit Reader* (Delhi: Motilal Banarsidass, 1972), 17–18; verse 5 from the *Lalitavistara* on *pratītyasamutpāda,* ibid., 24.
12. Francis Tiso and Fabrizio Torricelli, "The Tibetan Text of Tilopa's *Mahāmudropadeśa*," *East and West* 41, nos. 1–4, verse 5.

Chapter 11

1. David Templeman, trans. and ed., *The Origin of the Tārā Tantra by Jo nang Tāranātha* (Dharamsala: LTWA, 1981).

Chapter 12

1. Author of the Milarepa *rnam thar* that we have translated and discussed in this work. For discussion of his name, date, location, and lineage, see Peter Alan Roberts, *The Biographies of Ras-chung-pa: The Evolution of a Tibetan Hagiography* (PhD diss., Faculty of Oriental Studies, University of Oxford, 2000), 75–86. He opts for the spelling "rGya ldang pa."

2. rGyal thang pa, *rdo rje 'chang rnam thar*, folios 10–11.
3. Vāgīśvarakīrti, *Saptāṅga* (*Yan lag bdun*), in the *Tibetan Derge Tanjur*, vol. 44, folios 379a.3–405 a.3.

Chapter 13

1. See Part Three.
2. See E. Gene Smith, *Among Tibetan Texts*, chap. 3. A late example is *Biographies of Eminent Gurus in the Transmission Lineage of Teachings of the 'Ba' Ra Dkar-brgyud-pa Sect*, vol. 1 (Dehradun: Ngawang Gyaltsen and Ngawang Lungtok, 1970), folios 1–33.
3. Judith Hanson and Mervin Hanson, "Freedom and Contingency: The Concatenating Buddha: A Shangs pa rnam thar of Vajradhara," in *Soundings in Tibetan Civilization*, ed. B. N. Aziz and M. Kapstein (New Delhi: Manohar, 1985).
4. Ibid., 298.
5. L. P. Lhalungpa, *The Life of Milarepa* (Boulder: Shambhala, 1984), 207n18.
6. Reproduced from a rare manuscript from the library of the Hemis Monastery by the 8thj Khams-sprul don brgyud nyi ma; rGyal thang pa bDe Chen rDo rJe, *Dkar brgyud gSer 'phreng* (Palampur, Tashijhong: Sungrab Nyamso Gyunphel Parkhang, Tibetan Craft Community, 1973), folio 10.
7. For example, in Glen H. Mullin's translation of the songs of the Seventh Dalai Lama, *Songs of Spiritual Change* (Ithaca: Snow Lion, 1982), we find occasional mention of the "seven kisses," which in fact is our set of seven features: cf. 121, 131, 196.
8. F. D. Lessing and A. Wayman, *Introduction to the Buddhist Tantric Systems* (New York: Samuel Weiser, 1968, 1980), 267.
9. Ibid., 325.
10. This text may be found in the Derge Tanjur (sDe-dGe bsTan' 'Gyur), vol. 44, folios 379a.3–405a.3; cf. Coné edition, vol. 172 [Pi], 191a 1.205a.4.
11. Lessing and Wayman, *Introduction to the Buddhist Tantric Systems*, 325. This text may be found in the Derge Tanjur (sDe-dGe bsTan' 'Gyur), vol. 44, folios 379a.3–405a.3; cf. Coné ed., vol. 172 [Pi], ff. 191a 1.205a.4. *Blue Annals*, 206, 227, 380–82, 384, 402, 736, 758, 851, 869.

Pham thing pa originated a tantric practice centered on a particular form of Vajrayoginī who appeared to him during a meditation retreat at this native place (Pharping) in the Kathmandu Valley, about 18 kilometers southeast of Swayambhunath; the lineage of this practice is continued by the Sa sKya pa order. (Information kindly provided by Hubert Decleer and confirmed by Tibetan informants in the valley.)

12. In tale number 34, gTsang sMyon joins the story of the conversion of a group of three logicians to the story of the scholars Lo ston dge 'dun 'bum and Ra ston Dar ma blo gros. The latter dies filled with hateful thoughts and is reborn as a fearful demon (see *The Hundred Thousand Songs of Milarepa*, trans. Garma C. C. Chang, 395). The rGyal thang pa version may be found on folios 246–49; Dar blo is converted.

Chapter 14

1. English, *Vajrayoginī*, 27.
2. Already, 'Bri gung pa (1143–1217) was teaching: "Other spiritual teachings regard the main practice as being profound; We regard the preliminary practice as being profound." Quoted by H. H. Dudjom Rinpoche in *Extracting the Essence of Realization* (Darjeeling, India: Ogyan Kunsang Choekhorling, n.d.).
3. See Judith Hanson, *The Torch of Certainty by Jamgon Kongtrul* (Boulder, CO: Shambhala, 1977). The *sādhana* used in the Karma bKa' brgyud is by Lord Sharmapa Wangchuk Dorje, from his commentary on *sahaja-mahāmudrā* titled *The Chariot That Carries Us along the Noble Way.* There are numerous introductions to the special preliminary practices (Tibetan: *sngon-'gro*) depending on the milieu in which practice is taking place. Kristin Pizzi (personal communication, June 2002) makes the claim that these practices are a Tibetan construction after the "Second Diffusion," certainly an important topic requiring further research.
4. Discourse of H. H. Gyalwa Drukchen at Plouray, Brittany, July 23, 1994, in the context of Cakrasaṁvara teachings.
5. Cited by H. H. Gyalwa Drukchen in the context of transmitting Cakrasaṁvara teachings.
6. English, *Vajrayoginī*, 6, citing the Tohoku catalog, numbers 360–441; these are also called *yoginītantras.*
7. Tiso and Torricelli, *Mahāmudropadeśa.*

Chapter 15

1. Inter alia, Judith Hanson, *The Torch of Certainty of Jamgon Kongtrul* (Boston: Shambhala, 1977); Jane Tromge, *Ngondro Commentary: Instructions for the Concise Preliminary Practices of the New Treasures of Dudjom* (Junction City, CA: Padma Publishing, 1995); Ven. Tulku Thondup and Brian Beresford, *The Dzogchen Innermost Essence Preliminary Practice of Jig me ling pa* (Dharamsala: LTWA, 1982); Namkhai Norbu, *The Stairway to Liberation: Instructions on Ngondro* (Tsegyalgar: Dzogchen Community, 1990); Sermey Geshe Lobsang Tharchin, *A Commentary on Guru Yoga and Offering of the Mandala* (Ithaca: Snow Lion, 1987).
2. Jamgon Kongtrul is a nineteenth-century traditionalist, making use of a variety of written and oral sources to recover practices that were in danger of disappearance. See also the reformist voice of Tsele Natsok Rangdröl (born in 1608) in *Empowerment* (Kathmandu: Rangjung Yeshe Publications, 1993).
3. Sarah Harding, trans. and intro, *Creation and Completion: Essential Points of Tantric Meditation by Jamgon Kongtrul* (Boston: Wisdom Publications, 1996), 7.
4. Ibid., 8.
5. Ibid., 10.
6. Ibid., 10–11.
7. Ibid., 11.
8. Ibid., 17.
9. Cf. ibid., 14.
10. See Lessing and Wayman, *Introduction to the Buddhist Tantric Systems*, which has extensive material on the classes of tantras. The entire system is made manifest in the chapels of the great stūpa at Gyantse. See G. Tucci, *Gyantse and Its Monasteries*, Śatapiṭaka Series, vol. 351 (New Delhi: Aditya Prakashan, 1989); E. Lo Bue and F. Ricca, *Gyantse Revisited* (Firenze: Casa Editrice Le Lettere, 1990).
11. Ngawang Zangpo, ed. and trans., *Jamgon Kongtrul's Retreat Manual* (Ithaca: Snow Lion, 1994), 21f.
12. Milarepa also mentions the protector Mahākāla in one of his *gdams ngag mdzod* teachings; Mahākāla is the deity of the daily evening pujā in bKa' brgyud pa monasteries. Other yidams mentioned in the *rnam thar* include Cakrasaṁvara, Hevajra, and Vajravārāhī.

Chapter 16

1. Teachings given in France, July 1994.
2. This is a controversial point discussed in the works of Sakya Pandita. See *A Clear Differentiation of the Three Codes* (Albany: State University of New York Press, 2002), 22, 162 verse 504, and 195n100.

Chapter 17

1. Given at Plouray, France, in July 1994; repeated at Arcidosso, Italy, December 1996.
2. His Holiness consistently calls this deity Cakrasaṁbhāva, which corresponds to his interpretation of the meaning of this name, as explained in chapter 17.
3. The identical proverb was quoted to me in a private conversation on spiritual practice with the Ven. Shrivatsa Goswami, pūjari of the Rādhāramaṇa Mandir in Vṛndāvana, a master of the Śrī Caitanya Vaiṣṇāva tradition.
4. Milarepa's own teachings on the Vase Initiation in relation to meditation experience in Cakrasaṁvara is given in the *gdams ṅgag mdzod*, vol. 5, folios 263–84; he relates this tantra to the six yogas in folios 285–317 and in 317–25.
5. In other words, love, heroism, revulsion, anger, mirth, fear, grief, wonder, and tranquility.
6. Cf. Kazi Dawa-Samdup, ed. with notes by G. Tucci, *Shrīcakrasambhāra Tantra: A Buddhist Tantra*, Tantrik Texts under the general editorship of Arthur Avalon, vol. 7 (New Delhi: Aditya Prakashan, 1987), 17–25.

Chapter 18

1. *Blue Annals*, 455–56.
2. BA, 456. See also the discussion of the relationship between heat yoga and dream yoga in Glenn Mullin, *Tsongkhapa's Six Yogas of Nāropa* (Ithaca: Snow Lion, 1996), 77: "The degree of proficiency required in the six yogas emanates from the foundation, the inner heat doctrine, and what the meditator has achieved by means of it in terms of the

yogic ability to induce the elemental dissolutions and consciously experience the stages of that dissolution, from the vision of the mirage up to the emergence of the clear light."

3. Tamil Siddha tradition also recognizes this and reports on the apparently spontaneous character of the attainment, as we discovered during fieldwork in Tamil Nadu in February 2003. Once the preliminary work has been done under the guru's guidance, the transformation of the cells of the yogin's body proceeds in rapid succession. See also *The Clarification of Ignorance*, folio 114.2
4. BA, 457. Further discussion in *Mahamudra Teachings of the Supreme Siddhas*, 141n108.
5. Ibid.
6. BA, 458–59.
7. It can be done with a real or imaginary consort. See *The Clarification of Ignorance*, folio 116.
8. See *The Clarification of Ignorance*, folio 114.1.
9. Glenn Mullin, *Readings on the Six Yogas of Naropa* (Ithaca: Snow Lion, 1997), 14.
10. Ibid.
11. "A profound teaching explaining how to determine the path of the mind, using instructions on the intermediate state."
12. Ibid., 16.

Chapter 19

1. Cf. *Life of Marpa,* 150: "Meat and alcohol enlarge the nadis, the prana and the bindus."
2. A very rewarding article on the "beer of enlightenment" is by John A. Ardussi, "Brewing and Drinking the Beer of Enlightenment in Tibetan Buddhism: The Dohā Tradition in Tibet," *JAOS* (1977): 115–24.
3. In the *Dīghanikāya*, xxvii, 10ff., in the *Aggaññasuttanta.* In the ADK, see chap. 3, 98a/b.
4. Alex Wayman, "Buddhist Genesis and the Tantric Tradition," in *The Buddhist Tantras: Light on Indo-Tibetan Esotericism* (New York: Samuel Weiser, 1973), 28.
5. Ibid., 29.

6. The Asaṅgan concept of reversal is discussed in Alex Wayman, *Analysis of the Śravakabhūmi Manuscript*, which includes Romanized texts and English translations of Asaṅga's views on food, "*Bhojane matrajñata*" (leaves 226–54) and of his *Paramārtha-gathas* and commentary (leaves 275–98) (PhD diss., University of California, Berkeley, 1959). Cf. G. Tucci, *The Religions of Tibet*, 93–94.
7. Cf. Geshe Khelsang Gyatso, *Clear Light of Bliss: Mahamudra in Vajrayana Buddhism* (London: Wisdom Publications, 1982), 212.
8. By not dying, Milarepa manifested his transcendence of the basic fact of impermanence, because he has gone beyond Cyclic Existence. See the *rnam thar* of rDorje 'chang, folio 11.
9. Lessing and Wayman, *Introduction to the Buddhist Tantric Systems*, 220–21n13; Wayman, *Yoga of the Guhyasamājatantra* (Delhi: Motilal Banarsidass, 1977), 289–93, et passim; Tiso and Torricelli, *Mahāmudropadeśa*, xxxi.
10. Even though this text, a *gter ma*, came to light after rGyal thang pa's biography of Milarepa, there had been similar texts in circulation, probably from the time of Guru Padmasambhava and the very early translation of the *Sarvadurgatipariśodhana Tantra*. In the *gdams ngag mdzod*, vol. 5, 344–61, there is a teaching on the bardo attributed to Milarepa that corresponds in many details to the *Bardo Thodol* tradition.
11. Some Mahāyāna texts condemn "eating ecstasy," precisely as an obstacle to progress in attaining perfect enlightenment. See especially the *Laṅkāvatāra Sūtra* and texts dependent on it. However, in the *Vimalakīrtinirdeśa* (21, Thurman translation), "He [Vimalakīrti] seemed to take food and drink, but he nourished himself always with the flavor of ecstasy" (*dhyāna-rasa asvādana*). The peril is to end up becoming denser, like the primordial beings who ate the sweet earth, a form of nectar or "amṛta" and fell into the habit of gluttony.
12. See commentary on *srog tsol* on folio 111.4 in "Clarification of the Three Cycles," in chapter 24.
13. See *Ratnagotravibhaga*, trans. Jikido Takasaki (Roma: IsMEO, 1966), 219–20.
14. See "Texts in Translation" later in this book.
15. Cf. Wayman, *Yoga of the Guhyasamājatantra*, 172–200.

16. The term great seal refers to the intuition in this system that all phenomena are characterized by nothing other than voidness; to realize this is to attain enlightenment.
17. See Tiso and Toricelli, *Mahāmudropadeśa.*
18. *Ratnagotravibhaga*, śloka 46.

Chapter 20

1. From the "Buddhist Genesis," the *Aggañña Suttanta*, in the *Dīgha Nikāya*, part 3, translated by T. W. and C. A. F. Rhys Davids (Oxford: Pali Text Society, 1991), 77–94. A more recent version would be Maurice Walshe, trans., *The Long Discourses of the Buddha: A Translation of the Dīgha Nikāya* (Boston: Wisdom Publications, 1995), 407–15.
2. Mullin, *Readings on the Six Yogas of Nāropa*, 35–41.

Chapter 21

1. The title *rje btsun* is the Tibetan equivalent of Sanskrit *bhaṭṭa* (lord, learned Brahman) or *bhaṭṭāraka* (great lord, venerable one). The term is used of gods, learned Buddhist monks, and a class of Śaiva monks (see discussion in Giuseppe Tucci, "Buddhist Notes: *A propos* Avalokiteśvara," in *Mélanges Chinoises et Bouddhiques,* 9éme vol. [1948–51], 184). It is the title used of Nāropa, Marpa, and other saints. In *Tsang Nyon Heruka. The Life of Marpa the Translator: Seeing Accomplishes All*, translated from the Tibetan by the Nālanda Translation Committee under the direction of Chogyam Trungpa (Boulder: Prajna Press, 1982), 22, corresponding to the Tibetan text folio 247.3, Marpa addresses the entire *dharma* circle of Śāntibhadra with this title. It became a traditional name for Milarepa. It suggests saint as much as the title siddha does (*'grub thob*). Cf. *mnga' bdag* (Lord) as the title of Maitrīpa (*Life of Marpa*, folio 24), which would be a synonym for *rJe.* Translating *rje btsun* as saint shows that one has attained mastery over inner practice and is worthy of veneration.
2. Mid la is a common variant spelling of his family name.
3. Roots of goodness, see MPPŚ, 1969ff.
4. *rigs ngan* or *rang bzhin phal pa'i*: an essentially ordinary family.

5. Prophecies "from Vajradhara" may take the form of a warning; see R. A. Stein, *Vie et Chants*, 223–24.
6. *Rjes bzung*; Sanskrit: *anugraha*.
7. He had died and his consciousness *skandha* was in the dimension between death and rebirth.
8. Cf. folio 244 where *Dgu chen* becomes *dge 'dun*.
9. But see folio 251; later, see folio 255, where it seems that the patrons were blessed by Tārā, or perhaps by Milarepa in the form of Tārā.
10. Or "I bow down to the Saint's wandering freely amid the mountain solitudes."
11. In other words, *mya ngan 'da' tshul (b)stan*, the term for the death of a holy lama.
12. Or "to the complete biography of the Saint."
13. In the *Uttaratantraśāstra* of Maitreya, there are three types of *sprul sku* (*nirmāṇakāya*): (1) *Bzo* (*śilpa*) the artistic; (2) *Skye ba* (*jāti*), birth; and (3) *Mchog gi* (*uttama/vara*), the excellent or superior.
14. The prose sections of the biography serve as a "commentary" on each of the verses of the biographical poem.
15. The *Vimalakīrtinirdeśa* states, "It is always permissible for Bodhisattvas to create an oasis of a pure land in the midst of an impure land" (400, Lamotte translation).
16. BA, 436, says that he was *ācārya* 'Jam dpal bshes gNyen (Mañjuśrīmitra). This is probably the rDzogs pa chen po master who was a disciple of dGa' rab rdo rje. See Chögyal Namkhai Norbu and Adriano Clemente, *The Supreme Source: The Fundamental Tantra of the Dzogchen Semde* (Ithaca: Snow Lion, 1999), 26, 31–35.
17. A womb within which, so to say, the realization of Nāgārjuna might manifest; this is a circumlocution for the "perfection of wisdom" or "Yum Chen mo"—the "great mother" of all Buddhas.
18. In other words, his life was characterized by poverty.
19. *Stobs* is not found on Folio 19. The author (or transcriber) seems to have been relying on his *memory* of the verses.
20. This passage is a useful description of economic conditions in Tibet around the year 1050; note that already the people depend on commerce to supplement agricultural income and that the ancient habit of nomadic life is in direct continuity with the life of the wandering

peddler. Also, we note that villages had to be clustered near one another in newly pioneered regions so that if the fire went out in one house, it would be easy to rekindle the fire from a neighbor's hearth. Mila's father tried to make a new life for the family as a pioneer on new land, but his efforts were not entirely successful and there was fear that his family would fall apart in spite of his efforts. Only his wife's dream saved the marriage. The pioneering of new land suggests that the population in long-settled regions was growing or that the fertility of the bottom lands was wearing out—or both—and younger men were searching for more fertile land higher in the hills.

21. Peter Aufschnaiter, "Lands and Places of Milarepa," *East and West* 26 (1970): 175–89, gives valuable on-site information.
22. Francis Tiso, "The Religion of Milarepa before his Conversion," in *The Notion of Religion in Comparative Research: Selected Proceedings of the XVI IAHR Congress* 1990, ed. U. Bianchi (Roma: L'Erma di Bretschneider, 1994), 607–15.
23. There are three versions of her name on a single page of the manuscript!
24. The fifth Tibetan month (under the sign of Gemini), as explained in the Kagyu Samye Ling Tibetan Calendar, 1998–99.
25. *Dka' thub dang dka' spyad dpag tu med pa.* This is the first time in the text that this phrase appears; it will characterize the entire life of Milarepa, for it means hardship and difficulty as much as austerity and penance.
26. See R. A. Stein, *Tibetan Civilization*, trans. J. E. Stapleton Driver (Stanford: Stanford University Press, 1972), 48, for the royal mythology of a rope leading up into heaven. The rope (*dmu*) is to be ascended at the king's death; heaven is the home of his maternal line.
27. This would have been 1043 or 1055. The death is said to have been in a monkey year in this *rnam thar*, seventy-three years later, which would have been either 1116 or 1126.
28. (Possibly corrupt passage: *mar ri sa srang bcu tham pa 'gor ba yod pa de / mar khal lnga ru song ba la sogs pa'i ltas bzang po dpag tu med pa dang bcas te bde bar 'khrungs so.*)
29. Verse 7 should be quoted here.
30. The heartland of Tibetan civilization.
31. *mgo ni zho thum bzin btang 'dug* (unclear).

32. Already, on folio 197, she had been prepared to abandon her husband and the town of rTsa, even before Mila's birth.
33. Dan Martin, "The Early Education of Milarepa," *Journal of the Tibet Society*, vol. 2 (1982): 53–76, especially, 54–62.
34. See ITB, 399–407, esp. 406, for rapport between Bon po and rNying ma pa practitioners; Dan Martin, "The Early Education of Milarepa," 58–59.
35. See Dan Martin, "The Early Education of Milarepa," 58–60, for a thorough investigation of current knowledge on these teachers and their methods. See also Namkhai Norbu, *Drung, Deu and Bön* (Dharamsala: LTWA, 1995), chap. 15.
36. For information on weather-making magic in Tibet, see René de Nebesky-Wojkowitz, *Oracles and Demons of Tibet* (The Hague: Mouton, 1956), 465–66, 467–80, 485.
37. The attainment or realization of Buddhahood cannot be the result of "causes and conditions" the way ordinary deluded thinking sees everyday reality. Practices are designed to cut through the deluded thinking that stands between ordinary thoughts and the enlightened mind. Attaining this state continuously in a single lifetime is the highest aspiration of tantric Buddhism.
38. Presumably because his own level of realization was not sufficient.
39. See Dan Martin, "The Early Education of Milarepa," 61–62, for a translation of Rang 'Byung rDo rJe's interpretation of this encounter in greater detail. *rDzogs chen* is discussed in Samten G. Karmay, "A Discussion on the Doctrinal Position of rDzogs Chen from the 10th to the 13th Centuries," *Journal Asiatique* 263 (1975): 147–56; John Myrdhin Reynolds, *Self-Liberation through Seeing with Naked Awareness* (Ithaca: Snow Lion, 2000); Brian C. Beresford, ed., *The Dzog Chen Preliminary Practice of the Innermost Essence, the Long chen Nying thig Ngon dro*, with original Tibetan root text composed by the Knowledge-Bearer Jig me Ling pa (1729–98), trans. Tulku Thondup (Dharamsala: LTWA, 1982); Namkhai Norbu and Kennard Lipman, trans., *Mañjuśrīmitra: Primordial Experience: An Introduction to rDzogs-Chen Meditation* (Boulder: Shambhala, 1987).
40. Ladakhi usage: *skye ru ma 'dod.*
41. See Thurman, *Vimalakīrtinirdeśa*, 46. Wisdom *and* skill in liberative technique is necessary.

42. Tibetan text: *lo tstsha [ba],* which means "the translator."
43. Note that this suggests one purpose of a *rnam thar*, which is to reawaken roots of virtue and vows from former lives that conduce toward the auspicious encounter of guru and disciple. Placing the feet of a guru on one's head is a type of guru devotion. In fact, the whole passage suggests the climate of guru-yoga, for Mila directs his devotion not only to Marpa but also to 'Bre ston.
44. The ability to recognize the guru as Buddha in all circumstances of the daily life of a disciple is an essential aspect of guru-yoga and as such an essential indication of the likelihood of success on the part of the disciple. See the Lamotte translation of *Vimalakīrti,* 142–43: Śāriputra is told that the correct way to meditate is not to be absorbed in recollection nor to manifest body and mind in the trifold-dimension of time. Rather, without abandoning the recollection of cessation, *nirodha-samāpatti,* he is to manifest ordinary attitudes, and though not renouncing spiritual attainments already obtained, to manifest all the features of an ordinary person, *pṛthagjana.* sGampopa's biography of Marpa says, "Although the great translator seemed always to abide without meditating, he remained undisturbed, always in *samādhi.* He realized the true continuum of reality (*dharmatā*)" (cf. BA, p. 404).
45. See Thurman, *Vimalakīrti,* 50: "Reverend Śāriputra, did you come here for the sake of Dharma? Or did you come here for the sake of a chair?"
46. See BA, 418–15, for another sorcerer disciple of Marpa.
47. *mi la*: a possible pun?
48. *nya ris chu shags su?*
49. In other words, Sras-mkhar-dgu-thog.
50. Or "He put the hail producing magical substance (an amulet) in the middle of a field."
51. But at least *some* experience occurred, unlike under 'Bre ston. The biography clearly indicates that there are gradations of efficacy in the teachings available, depending on the skillful liberative techniques of the guru, the special power of particular lineages, and the capabilities and merits of the disciple.
52. Marpa's prophecy of Mila's eventual attainment of Buddhahood. A song sung by Nāropa to Marpa at Phullahari (See *Life of Marpa*, 89):

byang phyogs mun pa'i smag rum na// gangs la ñi ma shar ba bzhin // thos pa dga' zhes bya ba yi// mi la khyod la phyag 'tshal lo//. Oral comment by Tibetan teacher Geshe Lobsang Jamspal (during collaborative work on the translation in 1986): "The realization of Marpa and Mila is considered to have been the same, but because of Marpa's outer, apparently worldly activities, many disciples would lose faith in him. But Mila would not engage in worldly activities, so his practice would be more effective than Marpa's in training disciples."

53. Judith Hanson, *The Torch of Certainty*, trans. Jamgon Kongtrul (Boulder: Shambhala, 1977), explains the "Four Special Foundations" practice in detail, but there is some doubt that this form of "special preliminaries" may not yet have been devised in the days of Marpa and Mila. Private communication from Kristin Pizzi, August 25, 2002.
54. Chandra Das, *Tibetan-English Dictionary*, 751, gives temporal state and opportunity for *gnas skabs* (Sanskrit: *avasara, avasthā*); Lokesh Chandra, *Tibetan-Sanskrit Dictionary*, gives *adhikāra, daśā, mātra*; and other Sanskrit equivalents.
55. They were both "saints," but their abilities as gurus differed in degree and extent. This applies both to knowledge of Doctrine and to ability to guide disciples.
56. Definition of an Arhat, corresponding to the irreversible Bodhisattva (cf. *Abhidharmasamuccaya* of Asaṅga, etc.). *Tibetan: las sgrib thams cad zad nas.*
57. But this does not occur.
58. bDag med ma's speech to Milarepa is a good illustration of one of the purposes of a *rnam thar*. It also expresses something of the vision and spirituality of the bKa' brgyud pa. The lineage of spiritual practice of the Indian mahāsiddhas is to continue in Tibet; this lineage is destined to spread. It is a missionary enterprise involving the use of signs, miracles, and wonders in the context of Buddhist tantric practice. It is a tradition in continuity with Mahāyāna, seeking to benefit all beings. It does not avoid difficulties but seeks to make skillful use of obstacles as a part of the spiritual path.
59. Urine (*gsang chu*)? Suggests context of the "secret" *abhiṣekha*. See also Janice D. Willis, "The Search for Padmacan: A Study in the Interpretation of Tibetan Sacred Biography," *Journal of Religious Studies*

13 (1985): 66–69. Willis speaks of *sgrub chu* as nectar/water hidden in sacred caves, but the context is esoteric initiation into a *rdzogs rim* practice involving a "woman" (= Padma can = one characterized by having a lotus). The water in the *rnam thar* she is studying turned to *sin dhu ra* (red color), suggesting menstrual blood (see ibid., fn. 23).

60. Meaning that she fed him while he was with Marpa and also took care of him when he was with rNgog.

61. The word *mgur* is missing from the verse here but not in the opening section of the *rnam thar* (folio 192).

62. Note that by now the pattern of verses is well-established as a devotional exercise in which the author invites the reader to visualize the scene and perform a prostration before it. Compare, for example, the public practice of following the Via Crucis.

63. *Zung 'jug, yuganaddha;* to force the *citta* into the *avadhūtī.*

64. See the notion of *vajra* as interior voidness, which is uncuttable, unburnable, indestructible, and so on in the account of Vajradhara, folios 11–12. The following comment on the channeling of inner energy is from a teaching given by Tai Situ Rinpoche, a Karma bKa' brgyud pa master: "According to the profound method, you must use the 'inner' body in an adequate way, in accord with the physical body. This refers to such exercises as the Six Yogas of Nāropa, in which first one purifies the negative currents to make the veins functional, since some of them have not functioned for a great length of time, others function in an incorrect way; this is like a kind of cure for the veins, in which the 'inner' body is made functional and in which one needs to learn to perceive everything adequately and to cause the flows to go in positive rather than negative directions." (Italian text translated by the author; text provided by the kindness of Franco and Kristin Pizzi.)

65. See Tadeusz Skorupski, *The Sarvadurgatipariśodhana Tantra: Elimination of All Evil Destinies* (Delhi: Motilal Banarsidass, 1983), an entire tantra devoted to this goal.

66. See Nebesky-Wojkowitz, *Oracles and Demons of Tibet,* 459–61, use of thread crosses, and so on.

67. See *Life of Marpa,* 150: "Meat and liquor expand *nāḍī, prāṇa,* and *bindu.*"

68. The self-referential style is typical of the Tibetan epic.

69. Having a body made of mind is one of the characteristics of the primordial beings in the "Buddhist Genesis" account, *Dīgha Nikāya: Aggañña Sutta.*
70. The white cotton garment, long hair, green color, and a hand held to the ear became the key features of Milarepa's iconography.
71. Lobsang Jamspal says that this relic still exists at Tashilungpo (cf. Lhalungpa, *Life of Milarepa,* 217n6).
72. The tendency to distinguish the grasper and the grasped, yours and mine, and so on.
73. He made an error and the *prāṇa* went into the wrong *nāḍīs.* This is another example (cf. when in the sGampopa version he erred in imagining the glow from his butter lamp to be "illumination") of the saint's mistakes in contemplative practice.
74. Translation of this technical passage concerning the practice of *gtummo* courtesy of Kristin Pizzi.
75. In other words, qualities of a realized yogin.
76. A mystical visit; see an expanded account in the gTsang smyon version, *Songs,* 3–4.
77. See Lhalungpa's translation of *The Life of Milarepa,* 129.
78. Hence he is not a holy man, he is just crazy. The reference, albeit hostile, to *smyon pa* in the thirteenth century indicates greater continuity between the early period of the bKa' brgyud pa and the time of gTsang smyon than one might think after reading the preface to the *Life of the Saint of gTsang* by E. Gene Smith. However, it could very well be simply an ordinary use of the term *smyon pa.*
79. Term for the death of a Buddha: *bde-bar gshegs pa* (cf. Sanskrit: *sugata*).
80. See Lamotte, trans., *Vimalakīrti,* 127–28. We may compare the attributes of Vimalakīrti to those of Mila Happy Report. "He [Vimalakīrti] seemed to take food and drink, but he nourished himself always with the flavor of ecstasy (*dhyāna rasa asvādana*)." Footnote 10 tells us that this consists of tasting the flavor or delights of ecstasy and is generally condemned in such texts as the as the *Laṅkāvatāra,* 212, 14; *Mahāyāna-sūtrālaṃkāra,* 160, 14; MPPŚ, 1027, 1045; ADK VIII, 144. See also, P. Demiéville, *Le Concile de Lhasa,* 62–70. Clearly, in the tantric context, the traditional objections are set aside as the full process of reversal is brought to completion.

81. By not dying, Milarepa manifested his transcendence of the iron law of impermanence because he has moved beyond samsāra. For this, see the *rnam thar* of Vajradhara, folio 11. See also, Robert Thurman, "Confrontation and Interior Realization," 246, sec. 5.
82. See Asaṅga on food and meditation in Wayman, *An Analysis of the Śrāvakabhūmi Manuscript*, chap. 5, "Asaṅga's Views on Food," 135ff.
83. See Lessing and Wayman, *Introduction to the Buddhist Tantric Systems*, 220–21n13, and Wayman, *Yoga of the Guhyasamājatantra*, 289–93, et passim, for the ordinary *siddhis* (i.e., mundane) and the supramundane *siddhi* of enlightenment.
84. Seven times seven, as in the *Bardo Thodol.*
85. Male Iron Tiger year/Female Iron Rabbit year = 1110–11.
86. This phrase is not in the set of verses at the start of the *rnam thar* but does correspond to what we find in the *Bu chen bcu gnyis* account of the songs in relation to the many disciples.
87. See N. Dutt, *Early Monastic Buddhism*, 157, for the *rukkhamūlikangam*; in the *Visuddhimagga*, and so on, the thirteen *dhutāṅgas*: "The Tree-Rootman's Practice." A clear instance, it would seem, of an early Buddhist practice embraced by Milarepa. Cf. Wayman, *Buddhist Insight,* 55, the "*dhūtaguṇas.*"
88. Here Milarepa is acting toward his aunt as Marpa had acted toward him. Through humiliation, he rapidly burns away the negative karma of his wrath-possessed aunt, preparing her for entry into the path of spirituality.
89. False, or wrongly motivated, devotion is as harmful as any other wrong attitude.
90. See Thurman, *Vimalakīrti*, 37: "The maidens of Māra are converted."
91. Consulting the chart in the *Bod rgya tshig mdzod chen po*, 3219; this would have been in 1112.
92. The invisible realm, which is "like space" and is the realm of Vajradhara, inseparable from the Dharmadhātu, the sphere, or "dimension" of all manifest realities.
93. The songs are not given in full, suggesting that the reciter is to present them from memory or, more precisely, to recreate them in bardic fashion.
94. Again, the food myth of human karmic degeneracy, which spiritual practice "reverses."

95. The town is north of Mount Everest, which is visible as one journeys along the valley.
96. The five goddesses of long life (*tse ring ma*).
97. See Chang translation, *Songs*, 313 and 316. Cf. also V. Urubshurow, "Symbolic Processes," 321.
98. In other words, the monks.
99. Gshen is one of the six Bon po clans, tracing its origins to Mi bo gshen rab (E. Gene Smith, personal communication).
100. Milarepa performs a rite for the dead, acting as a psychopomp. See M. Eliade, *Shamanism* (Princeton: Bollingen, Princeton University Press, 1964), 207ff., 414–21. See also Namkhai Norbu, *Drung, Deu, and Bön*, chap. 7 and Per Kvaerne, *Tibet: Bon Religion: A Death Ritual of the Tibetan Bonpos* (Leiden: E. J. Brill, 1985).
101. In the methods for generating compassion, one contemplates the love of parents for their children; then one recalls that all sentient beings have at one time or another been mothers to every other sentient being. We owe all of them the love we owe our mother in the present life; hence, we should show compassion to all living things.
102. Someone learned in the systematic works describing the phenomena of reality, such as the great *Abhidharmakośa* of Vasubandu.
103. Episode is found in the *Bu chen bcu gnyis* text.
104. Allusion to the title of Buddhist monks as those who listen to the word of the Buddha (i.e., *śravakas*).
105. A scholar learned in Sanskrit and scriptural debate. In reality, it is an emanation of Milarepa.
106. A typical *smyon pa*, or clown-like activity.
107. See Lessing and Wayman, *Introduction to the Buddhist Tantric Systems*, 312.
108. This could be the deity, but it could also be the "secret name" of one of the participants. (Informant: Pema Wangyal of Dolpo.)
109. These *thang kas* are believed still to exist at Pen che ling (i.e., Pan ches Ling at Swayambunath in the Kathmandu Valley). (Informant: Pema Wangyal and Hubert DeCleer; the thangkas are shown at great festival days.)
110. A *khrid* is a specific instruction on yogic practice given upon completion of the ritual of initiation and mantra recitations in retreat. The

experiences of patron and patroness are illuminated in Takpo, 132f, the guru, 143–45, the two basic paths as instantaneous and gradual. See also the Ninth Karmapa Wang Ch'ug Dor-je, *The Mahamudra: Eliminating the Darkness of Ignorance* (Dharamsala: LTWA, 1978), xiii–xiv. Introduction by Alexander Berzin.

111. R. A. Stein, *Vie et Chants,* 134.
112. Tantric ritual feast.
113. The text introduces this form of the saint's name, as if citing a preexisting source.
114. Author's region, in northwestern Yunnan. Cf. the seven limbs of the *sampuṭa* for "ubiquity," applicable to this aspect of the *Mila rnam thar,* as discussed in the Vajradhara *rnam thar.*
115. These details suggest that the author wanted to highlight features of his native territory. For this reason, I infer that 'rGyal thang pa' is the correct spelling of his name.
116. See Takpo, 440n23, Lhalungpa's comment on the Mudrā practice. Milarepa's own comments are in the *gdams ngag mdzod.*
117. See Thurman, *Vimalakīrti,* 39: "The more you teach and demonstrate virtuous qualities to others, the more you grow with respect to these virtuous qualities."
118. In other words, for setting in motion meaningful relations in the Dharma: *'brel ba.*
119. An allusion to the manifestation of the Cakravartin, the "World-Ruler" whose karma is equivalent to that of a Buddha.
120. An allusion to the list of seventeen virtuous qualities found in several early biographies of Milarepa, including that attributed to the Twelve Great Son-Disciples and that written by Ras chung pa. rGyal thang pa does not follow this scheme for his version of the biography, however.
121. Ironically, since he is said to resist poison three times, thus manifesting his victory over the delusion of death and illness. The Tibetan text is convoluted. In the following section, the final sickness and death of Milarepa is presented as a Bodhisattva's display of compassionate activity, in accord with the teaching of Vimalakīrti: "The sicknesses of the bodhisattvas arise from great compassion" (Thurman, *Vimalakīrti,* 43), and every deed of great compassion manifests liberation, even sickness, old age, death, and rebirth (ibid., 46): "Even his reincarnation is like a liberation."

122. Deities of the tantric maṇḍala. Cf. list in the *Bu chen bcu gnyis* version.
123. Thurman, *Vimalakīrti*, 47, is again our clue to the Mahāyāna doctrines underlying bKa 'brgyud pa spirituality in the *rnam thars*: "His liberative technique consists of not exhausting himself by trying to avoid all physical illness, and of applying himself to accomplish the benefit of living beings without interrupting the cycle of reincarnations."
124. If the "sheep year" of the birth account of rGyal thang pa is the water-female-sheep year (1043), then this is 1116; if the birth year is the wood-female-sheep year (1055), then this is 1128. The latter is more likely. Note that the age of seventy-three is given in the text, which also corresponds to the differences between 1043–1116 and 1055–1128. See Victoria K. Urubshurow, "Symbolic Processes," appendix 2, 385–86, for a discussion of Milarepa's chronology in the light of BA, 427–37, and the *rnam thar* by gTsang smyon Heruka. These sources give his age at death as eighty-three (1040–1123, an iron-male-dragon year to a water-female-hare year).
125. A Bard's hat, which is also a symbol of Vajradhara.
126. This very strong tradition is found in BA, 436. In the *rnam thar* by gTsang smyon, there is an elaborate, theatrical description of the scene of the cremation and the "spiriting away" of the relics, *Life of Milarepa*, Lhalungpa trans., 182–95.
127. An example of such Buddha activity may be in the *Śūramgamasamādhi Sūtra,* secs. 142–47, the fictional nirvāṇas of Mañjuśrī. Étienne Lamotte, trans., *La Concentration de la Marche Héroique* (Bruxelles: Institute Belge des Hautes Études Chinoises, 1965), 242–45. See also the *rnam thar* of Vajradhara, folio 11.
128. The one who had tried to poison him; see folio 260.
129. The chain of twelve links of *pratītyasamutpāda.*

Chapter 22

1. The text seems to begin in the middle of things. The name of the father was Marpa Wangchuk Oser (cf. folio 221.7 in the nineteenth-century xylograph).
2. See BA, 205–9, especially 208. Lobsang Jamspal says 'Brog mi, the disciple of Ātiśa, was one month's journey away from Marpa's home.
3. Or Lama Pendawa Karma-tsa, since Pendawa can also mean *pandita.*

4. A gold-mining area, according to Losang Jamspal.
5. At times the verb *gsung* means "it is said [that ...]," but it may also signify a personal reminiscence. In this case, it may be a personal reminiscence transmitted to sGampopa by Milarepa.
6. Practice Lineage (*bsgrub brgyud*): the actual practice of meditation and the rituals of the tantras. Explanation lineage (*bshad rgyud*): the tradition of commentary on the texts of the sutras and tantras. The former was especially transmitted to Milarepa, the latter to rNgog.
7. BA, 400–401: "At the time, a gold mine having been discovered at Nam-ra, a man known by the name of Marpa mGo yags of Tsam-lung showed partiality to him, because he belonged to the same family, and asked Mar-pa for initiation." This Mar-pa was of Byang-tsam-lung. Ibid., 403.
8. bsNubs is a place mentioned in ibid., 654, 659.
9. Nāropa was practicing sacred silence and had renounced even the act of teaching disciples. Har Dayal, *The Bodhisattva Doctrine in Buddhist Sanskrit Literature* (New York: Weiser, 1978), 276, where this is said to be a characteristic of the fourth *bhūmi*.
10. Sacred circle-feast (*tshogs 'khor*) among tantrikas. The text, A.26.6, has *tshogs dpon dang byin rlabs tsam g.nang*; B.17.4 has *tshogs dbon*.
11. Cf. Anāthapiṇḍada: the field covered with gold became the famous Jetavana, in the life of the Buddha. See LV 1.5; MV. i.4.13.
12. Was Milarepa that rich, or is this someone else? Is it he also who makes the offerings in the next paragraph? But see A.30.5, where Milarepa says he is without physical necessities.
13. The basis of a relationship between disciple and guru is a devoted, selfless service. This is the basis of guru-yoga. Guru yoga creates the psychological and spiritual climate wherein fruitful contemplative practice can be taught and practiced. One's capacity for selfless service is tested in guru yoga, which reveals the disciple's predisposition for the awakening and cultivation of bodhicitta.
14. See Glenn Mullin, *The Six Yogas of Naropa*, for a discussion of the Six "Yogas" of Nāropa, including the practice of the transference of the consciousness principle. The passage on the yak here is highly compressed. See *The Life of Marpa*, 155: "At another time, a yak had died near the site of a feast where many people had gathered. When

the workers were preparing to take the corpse away, Marpa said, 'My share of the work will be to carry away the corpse of the yak.' He then transferred his consciousness into the yak and brought the yak's corpse up to the courtyard. Then Marpa stood up and said: 'The essence of the dakini's body, speech, and mind / is the horse of nadi, prana, and bodhicitta. / Urged by the whip of equal taste, / the old yak crosses the dangerous passage./'"

15. This was a prophecy of Nāropa. See *Life of Marpa*, 99: "All the future disciples of the lineage will be like the children of lions and garudas, and each generation will be better than the last." Cf. 181ff.
16. This is said of rNgog's son in BA, 406; check BA, 399–406.
17. See *Hevajra tantra*, 1, 126–27. Lessing and Wayman, *Introduction to the Buddhist Tantric Systems*, 257. *sgyu lus* = *māyā-kāya* = illusion body (Lokesh Chandra).
18. He was still only a beginner at this time and made the mistake of being deluded by the glow of the butter lamp; he was under the false impression that the light arose from the attainment of a mystical state.
19. Klu brgyad pa? See BA, 427. Cf. Lhalungpa translation of the *Life of Milarepa*, 204n4: the name may refer to an expert in the cult of the "eight nagas," that is, the eight perfect attributes that belong to the realm of *sambhogakāya* Buddha.
20. *mar tshud bu cig* = a skin of butter, that is, butter preserved in a bladder skin, as is done in many parts of the world. Quarter carcasses of sheep can be seen in the vicinity of the great Bouddhanath stūpa just outside Kathmandu. They are dried (literally freeze-dried) in the winter and carried by the Himalayan nomads for provisions.
21. But in A.34.3, it specifies *phye bre drug* = six measures of barley flour.
22. *gtum mo*? Cf. the first of the "Six Yogas."
23. Unfortunately, the text does not give us the songs of the staff and of life in the snow ranges, but these are found in their early form in the *Bu Chen bcu gnyis* text and in developed form in the compilation of gTsang-smyon Heruka and also in the *rnam thar* by rGyal thang pa. This biography was probably an outline from which the raconteur would elaborate, depending on the occasion.
24. (A) *lo bdun*, (B) *bcu na* "get anywhere" = *rtol na* (to reach, to pierce).

25. A.36.2 has *rgyu byas bsam gzhad*, which is probably a scribal error. We have accepted B.22.5–6: */rgyu byas pas ma g.nang.*
26. *mi gces pa cig shi nas.* Cf. Chandra Das, 389, col. 2: *nged kyi mi gces pa*, or "a man dear to us."
27. Here it would be useful to examine customs surrounding a death. The presence of the lama as psychopomp in Tibet is of great significance. See, for example, the so-called Tibetan Book of the Dead (*Bardo Thodol*). Milarepa uses the occasion to show a profound spiritual truth: that holiness cannot be bought. Offerings to a lama must indicate a true willingness to abandon egoism; offerings made to "bribe" a lama or a deity into acting as a psychopomp imperil the cultivation of a right attitude.
28. See *Four Essential Buddhist Texts* (LTWA), 64: *The Great Seal of Voidness,* transmitted to the First Panchen Lama by Kha drub Sang gya ye she: "In the practice of the completion stage (*rdzogs rim; sampanna-krama*) of the highest yoga tantra, the various energy-winds (*rlung; vayu; prāṇa*) of the body are channeled into the central energy channel for the purpose of realizing voidness with the resulting blissful fine consciousness." The way to control the breath and body is given on pages 71–74, including the accompanying visualizations.
29. *yon bdag cig tsar byungs nas log nas song/ tsar* means "near him." This phrase seems to be in Western Tibetan dialect, according to Lobsang Jamspal.
30. Mila's strange appearance made an appropriate salutation seem unnecessary to the prospective patron, who was expecting to see something more worthy of veneration, someone who looked more like a "lama." These phrases seem to presume accompanying gestures of salutation (or their absence!).
31. Probably the two *rūpakāyas.* This passage deserves extensive comment. The following points should be noted here: (1) a historical reference to Atiśa within a half century of his death; (2) Mila's use of the Madhyamaka doctrine of the Two Truths, *saṃvṛttisatya* and *paramārthasatya*; (3) Mila's use of the doctrine of dependent co-arising (*pratītyasamutpāda*) to explain the fact that, whether it happened or not, Atiśa's miraculous circumambulation was believed to have

happened and therefore there were causes and conditions that required such a belief to arise. The spiritual capacities of individual disciples seem to determine apparent causality. Is this a comment on the historical versus religious value of miracles in a *rnam thar*? In any case, what appears to a Western scholar as the subordination of historicism to the religious intent of the hagiographical account is already understood within the theoretical frame of reference of the account itself! That is precisely why we have presented the *rnam thar* of Vajradhara, in which the tantric understanding of the *trikāya* theory is lucidly expounded. The *rūpakāya* manifestations arise codependently with the capacities and needs of various categories of disciples. Cf. also the characteristics of the seventh *bhūmi, Dūrangamā*, for discussion of skillful salvific means (*upāya*) in H. Dayal, *The Bodhisattva Doctrine in Buddhist Sanskrit Literature* (Delhi: Motilal Banarsidass, 1975), 289ff.

32. In the sense of the absolute truth, *paramārthasatya.*
33. This may be the basis for the story (having the flavor of a miracle play) in the final chapter of gTsang smyon's version of the carrying off of the relics of Milarepa by the *ḍākinīs* in a crystal stūpa. See Lhalungpa's translation, 186–94.
34. Bari Lotsawa was a contemporary of Milarepa. See BA, 73, 186, 211, 293, 405, 407, 469, 472, 556, 1024, 1048. Some of his works, including secret magic texts, have been published. Peta, Mila's sister, was impressed with his worldly fame and success. See Lhalungpa, 135.
35. The basis for public cult is the evident manifestation of siddhi. See Mila's comments on Atiśa's levitation and circumambulation.
36. Who is this Rinpoche? Could it be sGampopa, who arrived late in the career of Milarepa? If we translate the passage as "The Rinpoche said . . ." it perhaps becomes a personal reminiscence of the author, taken down by disciples.
37. See G. Tucci, *Santi e Briganti nel Tibet Ignoto*, 1937 edition, for a photo of one of these "pails" made of yak's horn.
38. This does not mean "invisible like a bird's footprint in the air." Rather, it means that the Rinpoche was not Milarepa's equal; he could not even fly the length of a bird's footprint (Geshe Lobsang Jamspal, oral comment, 1986, at Columbia University, New York)!

39. See BA, 166. He was an expert on the "Five Treatises of Maitreya," if he is the same person. The date is hard to determine, but it is possible that toward the end of Mila's life, this Dar ma brtan was middle aged.
40. A and B are at considerable variance: A.42.1 *yang da ras ba ltan bya ba cig byes su song ba* / B.26.1 *yang dar ma brtan bya ba cig byes su yod ba 'am/*.
41. Acalā, the eighth *bhūmi* of the *Daśabhūmikasūtra*. This is the stage at which one is "irreversible" (*avaivartika*).
42. For a discussion of this, with practical methodology, see Lhalungpa's translation of Takpo Tashi Namgyal, *Mahamudra: The Quintessence of Mind and Meditation* (Boston: Shambhala, 1986), 279–92.
43. See Dayal, *Bodhisattva Doctrine in Buddhist Sanskrit Literature*, 277. The ninth *bhūmi*, especially in the *Śatasāhasrikā-prajñāpāramitā*.

Chapter 23

1. Reproduced from a rare manuscript from the library of Hemis Monastery (Ladakh) by the Eighth Khams sprul Don brgyud nyi ma. From the Preface by E. Gene Smith,

> Among the precious Dkar-brgyud-pa and Rnying-ma-pa prints and manuscripts preserved in the Hemis Monastery near Leh in Ladakh is a beautifully illustrated manuscript of a group of Dkar-brgyud-pa hagiographies, a *Dkar brgyud gser 'phreng*, by one Rgyal-thang pa Bde-chen-rdo-rje. No biography of this master is immediately available, but it is known that he was a disciple of Rgod-tsang-pa Mgon-po-rdo-rje (1189–1258), the last guru whose biography appears in this collection. This Dkar-brgyud *gser 'phreng* must therefore belong to the thirteenth century and is thus one of the oldest surviving examples of the genre. On the last Folio we find a list of the successive gurus in the transmission up to the teacher at whose behest the present manuscript was presumably made: Rgyal-thang-pa Bde-chen-rdo rje; Chos-rje Thogs med pa; Slob-dpon Shes rab 'byung gnas; Dka' bcu pa Sangs rgyas bkra shis; Mkhas grub Chos kyi rgyal mtshan; Bdag Swa sti dhwa tsha (i.e., Legs pa rgyal mtshan of Zur). The style

of the miniatures and the script suggest that this manuscript belongs to the late 15th or early 16th century.

2. This is the only version of the text that has come to light, to my knowledge and that of my Tibetan informants, Losang Jamspal and Pema Wangyal, whose assistance is gratefully acknowledged. Since many of the '*bKa' brgyud gser 'phreng* begin with a similar text (*rDo rJe 'Chang rnam thar*), we can make corrections in our text on the basis of these similar works in the absence of a number of manuscripts and xylographs that might make a critical edition possible. According to Losang Jamspal, the script is *'bru yig*, "seed-shaped letters," because the round parts look like seed grain. It is a type of *dbu med* (headless cursive script). This *'bru yig* is said to be popular in Khams. Pema Wangyal suggests that it is not sufficiently pointed on the top and bottom of the letters to be called *'bru yig*. He is of the opinion that the style is Himalayan, from the region of sNye nam.
3. In small handwriting below the title, an addition to the text, which we give here only for historical purposes and to assist a future investigation of manuscript provenance. Note also that in the left margin of each obverse folio is the word Vajra (transliterated as *vazra*), an abbreviation for Vajradhara, whose *rnam thar* this is. In the same way, the biography of Mila ras pa has Mi la in the left margin.
4. Ungrammatical Sanskrit: *Śri guru namo.*
5. LM, 207n18, on the definition of Vajradhara.
6. LM, 206: "In tantra … the Five Defilements are to be transformed into the Five Transcendent Awarenesses through the meditation process. A yogin such as Milarepa can and does achieve enlightenment by exploiting the hidden potentialities of the human body and mind." Wayman comments (392, *Hist. Relig.*): "In Mahāyāna Buddhism, Enlightenment consists of the four or five knowledges or wisdoms, the four being the 'mirror-like' (because devoid of discursive thought), the 'sameness' (of all the *dharmas*), the 'discriminative' (of the individual and general characteristics of all the *dharmas*), and the 'procedure of duty' (for the happiness and welfare of sentient beings) kinds of knowledge; and the fifth, the 'pure *dharmadhātu* knowledge' which is both the object of the other four and their basis." This material is

discussed in Asaṅga's *Mahāyānasūtrālamkāra* (see S. Lévi, trans., chap. 9, 67–74, 88–90, for the Four Knowledges). The idea is to reverse the thrust of the "aggregate of perception" (*vijñāna-skandha*) so as to give rise to the Five Knowledges; tantric Buddhism optimistically embraces this Mahāyanā idea and takes it to extreme conclusions, especially in the *yogatantras*. See folio 6. See also, LM, 209n5.

7. For "praise" of Buddhas and Bodhisattvas, see E. Lamotte, trans., MPPŚ (1976), Tome IV, 1976ff.
8. The *buddha-gotras* or *kulas*. Tibetan gives *rigs kyi bdag po*. See ITB, 204ff. for Vajrasattva as the Sixth Buddha of the *maṇḍala*. "Vajrasattva (Adamantine Being) is an epithet of absolute power such as pertains to Vajrapāṇi (vajra-in-hand) at the summit of his successful career when he is effectively identified with Vajradhara (Vajra-holder), a title of the sixth Buddha favored generally in the tradition associated with the Eighty-Four Great Adepts" (205). See also ITB, 221 and fn. 167. Effectively, by visualizing Vajradhara, one automatically encompasses the other five; he is all-in-one. In possessing the state of the Five Types of Knowledge (see verse 2), he also possesses the absolute state of all the Five Buddha Families. In the *Vimalakīrtinirdeśa*, chap. 8, we find descriptions that in later tantric Buddhism were developed into visualizations of the Five Buddha Families and that also give some of the characteristics of the eighty-four mahāsiddhas. See, especially, in the Thurman translation, 64–66, and the poem, 67–72, where there are many items comparable to details in Tibetan *rnam thars*.
9. A biography of an "archetype" seems strange. With Vajradhara, we are speaking of a universal Buddha, as Roerich points out in a note on pages 356–57 in BA: "Here the word Buddha does not mean the Buddhas who dwell in a particular sphere and preach individually to a group of disciples … (here a universal Buddha is meant)."

   Notice how the *Origin of the Tārā Tantra* begins with a mythic biography of the goddess, in which she begins her path as the Princess "Moon of Wisdom." See David Templeman, trans., *The Origin of the Tārā Tantra* by Jo-nang Tāranātha (Dharamsala: LTWA, 1981), 11–15, which is similar to the Buddhist "genesis myth," for which see Alex Wayman, "Buddhist Genesis and the Tantric Tradition," in *The*

Buddhist Tantras (New York: Samuel Weiser, 1973). In some of the bKa' brgyud *gser 'phreng* cycles, there is also a biography of Vajrapāṇi. See, for example, *The Rwa Lung Dka' Brgyud Gser 'Phreng*, vol. 1 (Palampur: Sungrab Nyamso Gyunphel Parkhang Tibetan Craft Community, 1975), 29–35.

10. Formed. In the sense of "spiritual formation," the term used commonly in religious orders to describe the process by which persons are trained and by which they internalize their spiritual training.
11. In their translation of the *rnam thar* of Vajradhara from the *Shangs pa gser 'phreng* by rMog lcogs pa, the Hansons, Deshung Rinpoche, and Lobsang Lhalungpa call these conditions the "five certainties" and state that "the Sambhogakāya fulfills others' aims through the 'five certainties.'" They give the same quote from the *Laṅkāvatāra Sūtra* as we give in the next sentence. Most importantly, we find the basic idea already in Asaṅga's *Mahāyānasūtrālaṁkāra*, ix, 60–66; see also Lessing and Wayman, *Introduction to the Buddhist Tantric Systems*, 156.
12. Judith Hanson, in notes for a draft translation of the *Shangs-pa rnam thar* of Vajradhara that she kindly shared with the author, translates *yongs sgoms blo ldan rnams* as "fully cultivated intelligent ones"—a special class of beings. See at the end of folio 6. See also Alex Wayman, "Twilight Language and a Tantric Song," in *The Buddhist Tantras*, 129, citation of the commentary on the *Guhyasamājatantra* by Caṇḍrakīrti (the *Pradīpoddyotana*): *viśiṣṭaruci-sattvānām*, which he translates as "for sentient beings having superior zeal," which refers to those for whom the twilight language of the Tantras and the tantric *dohās* was intended. Of course, *ruci* may refer to desire from the point of view of sensuality, but in combination with *viśiṣṭa*, it should be taken in the sense of a term of praise and admiration, hence "zeal."
13. See Conze translation VIII, 3, 98: The Enjoyment Body: "The body of the Sage which possesses the thirty two marks and the eighty minor characteristics is considered as his Enjoyment Body, because it enjoys the happiness of the [dharma of the] Great Vehicle."
14. Judith Hanson translates *phun sum tshogs pa lnga* as "the five certainties" to indicate that of these five situations, each has an invariable element; later, the Shangs pa text goes on to speak of five noncertainties. This certainty / noncertainty dyad reflects one of the Sanskrit

equivalents of *phun sum tshogs pa: praṇihita* = imposed, ascertained, fixed, and so on (Lokesh Chandra, *Tibetan-Sanskrit Dictionary*, 1535).

See also, the Fourteenth Dalai Lama, *Opening the Eye of New Awareness*, trans. Donald S. Lopez Jr. and Jeffrey Hopkins (London: Wisdom Publications, 1985), 100–101.

The five "perfections" are discussed in Lessing and Wayman, *Introduction to the Buddhist Tantric Systems*, 156n7, in accordance with the *Thob yig gsal ba'i me long*, vol. 2, 72a–74ff., as perfection of body (including possession of the seven members of the *saṁpuṭa* and the characteristics and minor marks), merit, retinue, place, and affiliation.

The five perfect circumstances of sambhogakāya probably originate in the work of Asaṅga, we find five characteristics of a sambhogakāya in the *Mahāyānasūtrālaṁkāra*, ix, 60–66, 86–88, in S. Lévi's translation. The Asaṅgan tradition is succinctly presented in the *Awakening of Faith* attributed to Aśvaghoṣa (Hakeda trans., 69–70).

15. The *Abhidharmakośa* discusses the *rūpadhātus* in terms of deities abiding in seventeen celestial realms, according to the type of *dhyāna* they enjoy (ADK, chap. 3, verses 71ff.). There are four *dhyānas*; the Akaniṣṭha is in the fourth *dhyāna*, where it is the highest of eight classes. From the point of view of the "five pure abodes" (*śuddhāvāsakāyika*), it is the fifth and highest class (see Edgerton *BHS Dict.*, 1). In the *Mahāpārinirvāṇasūtra*, 41.1–18, 34–36. Franklin Edgerton, ed., *Buddhist Hybrid Sanskrit Reader* (Delhi: Motilal Banarsidass, 1972); we have an account of the death of the Buddha in which is demonstrated his ascent in contemplative absorption from the first *dhyāna* to the cessation of ideation in the *arūpyadhātu*, followed by a descent to the first *dhyāna*. This descent is followed smoothly by reascent to the fourth *dhyāna*, still within the *rūpadhātu*, from which the Buddha enters Nirvāṇa, and *not* from the cessation of ideation in the *arūpyadhātu*. Subsequent development identified the highest level of the fourth *dhyāna* with the Akaniṣṭha heaven (that in which none is the youngest, or, simply, the highest, the greatest), and it was understood that at this level of his contemplative absorption, the Buddha attained the highest state.
16. LM, 204n4, calls these the eight perfect attributes, which belong exclusively to the realm of a *sambhogakāya* Buddha:

1. Attribute of formal manifestation in infinite varieties.
2. Attribute of intentional communication with others.
3. Attribute of total awareness.
4. Attribute of the power to transform into any intended form.
5. Attribute of all-encompassing mind which embraces all universes.
6. Attribute of perceiving and partaking in the sensations of the body caused by spiritual enlightenment.
7. Attribute of bringing about the fulfillment of the wishes and aspirations of all sentient beings.
8. Attribute of the power to maintain any intended form for a great length of time.

These are not the "eight masteries" of the Theravāda tradition (*abhibhāyatana*), for which see P. V. Mahāthera, *Buddhist Meditation in Theory and Practice*, 2nd ed. (Kuala Lumpur: Buddhist Missionary Society, 1975), 481f. These are also found in Wayman, *Buddhist Insight*, 90f.; in the ADK, viii, 211–13; and in the *Mahāyānasūtrālaṁkāra*, vii, 9, 58.

In the *Mahāyānasūtrālaṁkāra*, we find the four sovereignties (*vasitā*), which may also provide a source: (1) sovereignty over the field, by which a Buddha field is purified; (2) of nondifferentiation; (3) of complete knowledge of all particulars; and (4) of action in the application of the *abhijñās*. See chap. 11, 46, S. Lévi trans., with chart on p. 28.

17. Cf. *Laṅkāvatārasūtra: A Mahayana Text*, translated from the Sanskrit by Daisetz Teitaro Suzuki (Boulder: Prajna Press, 1978), chap. 2, XL, 88, "Vajragarbha, the Bodhisattva-Mahāsattva"; see also HVT, Vajragarbha is Hevajra's interlocutor in chapter 1, i, vii, x; chapter 2, ii, iii, iv; cf. *Daśabhūmikasūtra*, "le discours sur la 6e bhūmi" in S. Lévi, *Vijñaptimātratāsiddhi*, vol. 1 (Paris: Librarie Ancienne Honoré Champion, 1932), 43; George Elder, "The Saṁpuṭa Tantra," chap. 1, 161ff.
18. See HVT, introduction, 37–38, with the addition of a fourth *kāya*, known by three possible names: self-existent body (*Svabhāvika-kāya*), the innate body (*Sahaja-kāya*), or the body of great bliss (*mahāsukha-kāya*). This would go with the fourfold understanding of

the *cakras* inherited from the mahāsiddhas but might be thought deficient in relation to the Five Buddha families (see Lessing and Wayman, *Introduction to the Buddhist Tantric Systems*, 296).

Buddha-kāya theory is the theme of a song of Marpa (see *Life of Marpa*, 59). The *dharmakāya* is presented as the "sky" emanating clouds of Buddha-emanations: "The sky of *dharmakāya* is thick with rain clouds of wisdom. The continuous rain of emanations spreads over all beings ... The *dharmakāya* like the sky is the Buddha, great Vajradhara. The thick rain clouds of wisdom are the two rūpakāyas."

Deshung Rinpoche, in notes given to the Hansons, explained that each of the three "*kāyas*" acts as a sort of support (Tibetan: *rten*) for Buddha activity of various kinds; Buddha activities and qualities are considered to be impermanent, changing, and without essence, but they do have a basis. The *dharmakāya* is the basis for the *saṃbhogakāya*, and the *saṃbhogakāya* is the basis for the *nirmāṇakāya*. The *nirmāṇakāya* is the basis for the "Twelve Deeds" of the Buddha, and so forth.

sGampopa gives extensive descriptions of the *saṃbhogakāya* in his *Jewel Ornament of Liberation*. He says that "as soon as we live on a high spiritual level, we can meet with the *saṃbhogakāya* as a spiritual friend (*kalyanamitra*)" (33) and that of the two "form *kāyas*" (*nirmāṇa* and *saṃbhoga*): "*Saṃbhogakāya* is for those who require teaching, but are already purified (of the grossest ignorance)" (264). The *saṃbhogakāya* operates on the level of verbal communication and has eight characteristics, which sGampopa derives from the *Mahāyānasūtrālaṁkāra* (IX, 61): (1) surroundings in which it is enjoyed are the Bodhisattvas living on the *bhūmis*; (2) fields where it is enjoyed are the pure Buddha realms; (3) the body by whom it is enjoyed is Vairocana and the other Buddhas (the Five Buddhas as symbols of the various aspects of transcending awareness: Vairocana, Ratnasaṃbhava, Amitābha, Amoghasiddhi, and Akṣobya); (4) the marks accompanying the enjoyment are the thirty-two major and eighty minor characteristics of a Buddha (see MPPŚ, 271ff., and *Abhisamayālaṁkāra*, VIII, 12); (5) the doctrine through which it is enjoyed is the Mahāyāna teaching exclusively; (6) the activity resulting from its enjoyment is the instruction by the sons of the Victorious One;

(7) its spontaneity is its own effortlessness. It is as if the king of jewels (the wish-fulfilling gem) were present; (8) without a nature of its own means that though it appears in different forms, it does not possess different qualities like colors, which can only be known discursively (265, Guenther translation).

Other presentations of *kāya* theory may be found in the MPPŚ, 1906ff.; in Asaṅga *Mahāyāna-saṁgraha* (dharma-k.: 268–314; saṃbhoga-k.: 317–23; nirmāṇa-k.: 340–43; svabhāvika-k.: 329, 331–38); chap. 10 presents the *tri-kāya* as the fruit of gnosis—*phala-jñāna*—which we have presented in this translation as being of five kinds. Also, the *Mahāyāna-sūtrālaṁkāra* IX, 60ff.

Marpa's song goes on to speak of the *svabhāvika-k.* as the other three "free from origin" and of the *mahāsukha-k.* as all four "beyond conditions" (*Life of Marpa*, 60). Further theoretical comment may be found in Lessing and Wayman, *Introduction to the Buddhist Tantric Systems*, 49–53, where *Svabhāva-k.* is identified with *Tathāgatagarbha* in certain *Sūtras*, a view rejected by the dGe lugs pa School, especially in their debate with the Jo nang pa branch of the bKa' brgyud pa. Fivefold models for Buddha-kāya theory may be said to be based on the idea that rGyal thang pa expresses in the next passage to the effect that each of the five kinds of knowledge corresponds to a Buddha Family, which also corresponds to a Buddha-kāya: this set of three fives should be thought of as the fruition of the reversal of the five *skandhas* with their corresponding defilements, each of which represents a potentiality, which, by means of tantric practice, can produce complete Buddhahood. See, for example, A. Wayman, *The Yoga of the Guhyasamājatantra*, 254, 247, 231 (*skandhas* and *Tathāgatas*), 132.

19. See HVT (*pañca jñāna*) Wisdom as Fivefold: 29n58, 59n129, *śloka* I.viii, 6–7, II. iv.46. Wayman (in Lessing and Wayman, *Introduction to the Buddhist Tantric Systems*, section on the Yoga Tantra, 222n17 and 232n28) says that there are two traditions on *pañcajñāna*: (1) The *Vairocanatantra* gives *samatā* as the first (cf. *Avataṃsakasūtra*), (2) *Anuttaratantra*, for which the *dharmadhātu* is the basis and *ādarśa-jñāna*, is the first.
20. See A. Wayman, trans. and ed., *Chanting the Names of Mañjuśrī* (Boston: Shambhala, 1985), 79, chap. 6, v. 18: "Buddha with five-body

nature; pervading lord with five-wisdom nature; crowned with five Buddhas; bearing unhindered the five eyes." Wayman also gives a chart of the five Buddhas, five families, five bodies, five wisdoms, and five eyes. Comparison of the texts in Sanskrit and Tibetan follows:

From our text:

sangs rgyas sku lnga'i bdag nyid can//
khyab bdag ye shes lnga yi bdag//
sangs rgyas mnga' bdag cod pan can//

Wayman's edition:

sangs rgyas sku lnga'i bdag nyid can//
khyab bdag ye shes lnga yi bdag//
sangs rgyas lnga bdag cod pan can/ (spyan lnga chags pa med pa 'chang//)

Wayman's edition of the Sanskrit:

pañcakāyātmanko buddho pañcajñānātmako vibhuḥ/
pañcabuddhātmamakutaḥ pañca-cakṣur asaṅgadhṛk//

21. Judith Hanson calls these "seven aspects of supreme union" in her work on a Shangs pa *rnam thar* of rDo rJe 'Chang: "[Buddha] possesses the 'seven aspects' [of supreme union], the *kha-sbyor-bdun*: 1. perfect enjoyment (*saṃbhoga*); 2. union (*kha sbyor*); 3. great bliss; 4. no self-nature; 5. great compassion which completely fills [space]; 6. unendingness; 7. unimpededness."

Note that our text refers to these as the *yan lag bdun*, for which Lokesh Chandra, p. 2136, gives only *saptāṅga*. For *kha sbyor*, he gives *dasanocchista* (a kiss; a sigh) or *sambhukta* (enjoyed; eaten), for which the former is more likely the accurate term, suggesting the bliss of union and Saṃbhoga-kāya, that is, body in a state of enjoyment. However, the notion of a "kiss" is found in the songs of the Seventh Dalai Lama, for which see Glenn Mullin, trans., *Songs of Spiritual Change*, 197 ("The Seven Kisses: Seven qualities of the stage of Vajradhara, the state of Buddhahood attained through tantric practice," 121, and 131).

In BA, 445, we find a transmission of this teaching in the account of Mar-ston Tshul Khrims: "From Ras pa dBang nge he obtained numerous precepts of Ras chung pa, including the *yan lag bdun ldan* and others." BA also mentions this *yan lag bdun ldan* (*Saptāṅga,* Tg. rGyud, no. 1888) on page 763 in a discussion of the *Kāla-cakra.* This *yan lag bdun* should not be confused with the seven limbs of enlightenment (*Mahāyānasūtrālaṁkāra* XI.12; MPPŚ, 1200ff., vol. 3, etc.), nor with the seven limbs of religious service.

In Lessing and Wayman, *Introduction to the Buddhist Tantric Systems,* the five perfections of a complete Buddha have as "perfection of body" possession of the seven members of the *saṃpuṭa,* decorated with the Characteristics and Minor Marks (see 156–57n7). The seven members of the *saṃpuṭa* are as stated by the ācārya Vāgīśvarakīrti (in his *Saptāṅga,* Toh. 1888, Derge Tanjur Rgyud): (1) Saṁbhoga-k., (2) *saṃpuṭa,* (3) great beatitude (*mahāsukha*), (4) no intrinsic nature (*niḥsvabhāva*), (5) state of being filled with compassion, (6) noninterruption, and (7) no cessation (see 266–68). That this completes the process of initiations and is the fruition of the *sampannakrama* is suggested on page 327.

A pretantric basis for this set of sevens might be found in the *Mahāyānasūtrālaṁkāra,* xix, 59–60 (280–81), in the two verses on the grandeur of the great vehicle, which were given seven "grandeurs": (1) an immeasurable extent of ideals and sūtras; (2) initiatives for self and others; (3) cognition of the voidness of self and of phenomena; (4) enormous perseverance and energy; (5) application of skillful means, remaining in transmigration in the absence of defilements; (6) great success in attaining the powers, assurances, and ideas of the Buddhas; and (7) repeated exhibition of the deeds of Buddhas, including the attainment of enlightenment and the great decease.

22. For a presentation of the classic *Prajñāpāramitā* doctrine of *niḥsvabhāva,* from chap. 79 of the *Large Sūtra on Perfect Wisdom,* trans. and ed. E. Conze (Berkeley: University of California Press, 1984), 628–31: "The Exposition of the Non-Existence of Own-Being." This point of view is criticized in the *Sandhinirmocanasūtra*; for comments on this, see J. Takasaki, *A Study on the Ratnagotravibhāga* (Roma: IsMEO, 1966), 57–58; *Sandhinirmocana,* ed. and trans. E. Lamotte (1935), chap. 7, 30–31. Takasaki helpfully observes (p. 59) that the *Ratnagotravibhāga* seems to have its own theory, independent of the

Prajñāpāramitā and the *Cittamātra* traditions: "The *Ratna.* never uses the expression of *Cittamātra*. . . . In other words, the emphasis lies on the identification of *gotra* or *garbha* with the *dharmakāya* and any difference of the *garbha* or the *sattvadhātu* from the *dharmakāya* is rather neglected." This same perspective in our bKa brgyud pa texts can be found in such passages as "The essential nature of the *tri-kāya* consists of the pure voidness (*dharmadhātu*) detached from all discrimination." From chap. 8 of the *Guhyasamājatantra*: "Dharmas which are unborn possess a distinctive nature; It has been described as awareness arising through perfect non-discrimination." In the Shangs pa *rnam thar* of Vajradhara, the *dharmakāya* is the support (*rten*) for all dharmas in Saṃsarā and Nirvāṇa.

23. We have not been able to locate this text.
24. Translation suggested in consultation with Judith Hanson. See Snellgrove, *Four Lamas of Dolpo*, glossary 340; *tshad* suggests "wanting." The Tibetan here is *bdag 'dod tshad mas yongs sgoms blo ldan rnams dang 'dod.* Thus, *bdag 'dod tshad mas* might indicate a desire to enjoy oneself.... Another suggestion is that *bdag 'dod* refers to the nondependent reality of the *Tathāgatagarbha.*
25. Note that we are dealing with a systematization of tantric doctrine and practice; see Part Two on the system of Śri Vāgīśvarakīrti (or *ngag gi dbang phyug grags pa*; see BA, 206).
26. See Part Two on the seven limbs of Vajradhara.
27. This tantric master, either identical with Pham thing pa (BA, 227) or his younger brother (ibid., 384), in any case, was connected with Nepal (Ibid., 227) and was the Gate-Keeper Paṇḍita at the Southern Gate of Vikramaśīla (Ibid., 206). He was a Guhyasamāja expert (Ibid., 384) and taught the father-tantras (Ibid., 869) and yogic breathing (ibid.). The relevant work is his *Saptāṅga.* Pham thing pa is associated with the Vajrayoginī lineage and we note that her image is on folio 2 of this manuscript, being an important bKa brgyud pa *yidam.* Pham thing pa had a vision of Vajrayoginī at the village of Pharping in a special form that was subsequently transmitted as a practice within the Sakya pa Order and among certain Newari vajrācāryas.
28. The eight perfect attributes in LM, 204n4.

29. This mastery is of special importance for Milarepa, who was a master of spontaneous tantric songs. See John Ardussi, "Brewing and Drinking the Beer of Enlightenment in Tibetan Buddhism: The *Dohā* Tradition in Tibet," *JAOS* (1977): 116: "An ability that, by implication, possessed the nature of a magical attainment, resulting from their high level of yogic realization and from the great merit they had accumulated during their previous lives. Having gained control over their 'subtle physiology,' the *cakras* or mystical centers symbolically located along the axis of their bodies, and the winds or forces which move along the mystical 'veins'. They are able to concentrate this force in the center located at their neck, usually identified with the saṃbhogakāya or 'Enjoyment Body' of the Buddha. The process is a meditative one, and the practitioner at this level is regarded as partaking of Buddhahood and becomes able to produce songs of the Absolute Truth spontaneously." The present translation represents an exposition of this process of "partaking of Buddhahood" deriving from the systematic thought of the bKa' brgyud pa.
30. Could this mean that he benefits beings in every state of existence? *kun 'gro'i* = all destinies? Lhalungpa has, for this fifth among the eight perfect attributes, "an All-encompassing mind which embraces all universes," Lhalungpa in LM, 204. It is also possible that *kun 'gro'i* means all-pervading. See also on *gati* the excellent elucidation of M. Kedem in P. Denwood and A. Piatigorsky, eds. *Buddhist Studies Ancient and Modern* (London: Curzon, 1983), 53–57. See especially his discussion of refuges and "resorts," of limit and nonlimit, of the "final '*gati*'" (ibid., 56), and the father-mother "*gati*" related to Vajradhara (ibid., 57).
31. Probably "all-pervading." Ubiquitous activity is given by Deshung Rinpoche as the topic of "secret" *rnam thars*: "A Buddha functions on three levels: the outer (*phyi*) level, e.g., Sākyamuni's performance of the prescribed "Twelve Deeds"; the inner (*nang*) level: e.g., Vajradhara or Heruka's spiritual accomplishments through the *bhūmis*; the secret (*gsang-ba*) level: his influence as a perfect Buddha as seen by other Buddhas throughout the universe" (notes taken by Hansons, August 1978).
32. LM, 208: "Attribute of perceiving and partaking in the sensations of the body caused by spiritual enlightenment."

33. LM, 208n3: *mNgon dga'* and *'Og min* are names for the Pure Land of Buddha *mNgon dga'*: perfect joy, the Buddha realm of Akṣobya, ("the Unshakable One"). "When an initiate visualizes the Five Buddha Realms in his meditation, *mNgon dga'* is thought of as situated in the east. The term '*Og min* means literally 'not being under', hence the highest Buddha realm of saṃbhogakāya. Sometimes '*Og min* as an adjective qualifies the noun *mNgon-dga'* so as to present a descriptive term, '*Og min mNgon dga'* the Highest Joyful Realm." Going back to the context, on page 10, we find that this is in the setting of the opening of the *rnam thar* in which Ras Chung pa receives a celestial vision that inspires him to request the biography of Milarepa (see LM, 10). A celestial disciple of the Buddha, hearing that the *Life of Milarepa* is even more marvelous than those of the lineage predecessors, conjectures that such an advanced Bodhisattva must now dwell in *mNgon dga'* or *'Og min.* Indeed, this passage tells us a great deal about the importance of a *rnam thar* in Tibetan Buddhism.
34. Some of these correspond to the *yoginīs* of the *maṇḍala* of Hevajra. See Snellgrove, HVT, vol. 1, 74, 128. The Inner Circle includes *Vajrā, Gaurī, Vājrayoginī, Vajraḍākinī,* and *Nairātmyā,* and the Outer Circle includes *Gaurī II, Caurī, Vetalī, Ghasmarī, Pukkasī, Savarī, Candālī,* and *Dombinī.* See HVT vol. 1, viii, 10.
35. In other words, he transforms Saṃsāric desires into *siddhis.* But Lhalungpa gives "attribute of the power to maintain any intended form for a great length of time." He does not give his source and this list does not appear in the text translated by the Hansons.
36. See *Mahāyānasaṃgraha* V, 196ff., Lamotte trans., for the ten *bhūmis* as cause and fruit. Tabulation of the Ten Stages in various texts is given by Har Dayal, 273ff.
37. What is the source for the *bhūmis* higher than ten? Wayman observes, in *The Buddhist Tantras,* 87n8, that the stage of Buddha is the eleventh stage. Evidently, this eleventh stage has been divided into three. For some of the theoretical issues that have contributed to this, see S. B. Dasgupta, *An Introduction to Tantric Buddhism,* 184–86, et seq. "Nirvana as Mahasukha in the Buddhist Tantras," in the *Jewel Ornament of Liberation,* 113, after a pairing of the Ten Bodhisattva Stages with ten perfections, sGampopa goes on to discuss three additional

developments on a very high level of the evolution of the enlightened attitude (*bodhicitta*): "When the formation of an enlightened attitude is accompanied by the 'grove of the Dharma' it is like an echo to which those who are to be educated and want liberation delight to listen; when by a path which may be followed in one direction only it is like the current of a river, always helpful to sentient beings; and when by the Dharmakāya it is like a cloud on which the good of sentient beings depends, because it illustrates the stages of the Buddha's life from his stay in the Tuṣita heaven onwards. These three types belong to the Buddha level of spirituality" (113–14). But sGampopa also elucidates thirteen spiritual levels attained through the five paths (239): "the two levels of the beginner and of devoted interest and behaviour, the ten belonging to the Bodhisattvas and that of a Buddha." He identifies the Buddha level with the stage of the path of fulfillment (251). sGampopa's chap. 20, "Perfect Buddhahood," is a possible source for the bKa' brgyud thinking on the three Buddha-bodies. But how did the idea of "stages" higher than ten or eleven evolve? The fact that BA (361) says that the "fourteenth stage" is that of a *jñāna-kāya* suggests that it is the tantric development of *kāya* theory that led to the creation of a system of higher stages descriptive of complete Buddhahood. In Lessing and Wayman, *Introduction to the Buddhist Tantric Systems*, 296, we find a discussion of the "fruitional bodies," which include *dharma*, *saṃbhoga*, *nirmāṇa*, and *mahāsukha-kāya*; the "bodies … constitute achievements of the Steps of Completion" (Sanskrit: *sampannakrama;* Tibetan: *rdzogs rim*). Further complexity is discussed in footnote 2, 312–13, indicating a variety of systems for accommodating the anuttarayogatantra practices to the maturation of complete Buddhahood.

38. "These represent the stages of development of any practitioner of Buddhism who progresses from one to another gradually. They are the paths of accumulation, application, insight, mediation, and mastery" (*Vimalakīrtinirdeśa,* Thurman trans., 151). A chart of the paths in Hīnayāna and Mahāyāna is given on page 178, *Tantra in Tibet* by Tsong Khapa. The paths are also discussed in the tradition of Mādhyamika in MPPŚ, 1736ff.

In Lessing and Wayman, we find a discussion of the five paths. There are two basic paths; *pāramitā* and *mantra.* The *pāramitā* given by *mKhas grub rje* seems closer to what our text refers to as "the Secret Mantra Vajrayāna": (1) of equipment (*saṃbhāra-mārga*), (2) of training (*prayoga-m.*), (3) of vision (*darśana-m.*), (4) of intense contemplation (*bhāvāna-m.*), (5) beyond training (*aśaikṣa-m.*): *Introduction to the Buddhist Tantric Systems,* 16, 18, 21, 42, 45. Mantra has common (*sadharaṇa-m.*), 321, and uncommon (*asadharaṇa-m.*), 271. Another way of looking at the mantra-path is from the point of view of the two "stages" in tantric practice, that is, of creation and of completion. See page 267 for the result of the "tantra of effect," which is given as the *aśaikṣa-yuganaddha.* There is also a division of the mantra-path from the point of view of action, page 230; Bodhisattva, page 70; Entrance, page 151; Equipment, pages 16, 21; initiation, page 271; liberation, pages 184, 331, which is the path leading to realization, page 45; maturation (*vipāka-m.*), page 331; passion, page 169; and purification, page 231. In *The Jewel Ornament of Liberation* by sGampopa, we find the paths discussed as follows (112–13): The preparatory path (Sanskrit: *saṃbhāra-mārga;* Tibetan: *tshogs lam*), which corresponds to the "formation of an enlightened attitude ... accompanied by an earnest desire, ... general intention, ... and ... strong inclination ... three varieties on the novice's level ... When the formation of an enlightened attitude is accompanied by an earnest application, it is like fire, consuming the veils which hide the three kinds of omniscience. This is the Path of Application (Skt. *prayoga-mārga;* Tib. *sbyor lam*)." This is followed by a pairing of the ten Bodhisattva Stages with a system of ten perfections (going beyond the usual six with beneficial expediency, aspiration, strength, and transcending awareness born from wisdom). "They have their operational field in the Path of Insight (Skt. *darśana-mārga;* Tib. *mthong lam*) and the Path of Concentrated Attention (Skt. *bhāvanā-mārga;* Tib. *sgom lam*)."

39. In other words, in the central channel.
40. The *Vajra-sikara-mahā-guhyayoga-tantra* (*gsang ba rnal 'byor chen po'i rgyud rdo rje rtse mo;* Kg. rgyud 'bum 480), referred to in the BA, 227, 354, 355, 534. ITB, 460, gives a discussion of this work and the alternative spelling *Vajraśekhara.* See 460n142 (K. Eastman, "The

Eighteen Tantras of the *Vajraśekhara / Māyājāla*," in *Trans. International Conference of Orientalists in Japan*, 26, 95–96). This Tantra is said to be the yoga tantra explanatory tantra for the *Tattvasaṃgraha*.

41. In other words, the basis of *bodhicitta* is the wisdom of the Buddhas.
42. This section is the very heart of the introduction, for it gives the theoretical basis for what a "saint" is: the saint is identified with Vajradhara through his realization of the primordial wisdom of *dharmakāya*. The number of Vajradharas is as numerous as the number of truly realized *yogins*. The cycle of biographies to follow in the *gser 'phreng* will illustrate the diversity of the displays of this truth in the actual lives of the lineage masters.
43. Another translation from Snellgrove, HVT, vol. 2, xi, 8: "It is certain that in the family of the Blessed One, there are beings who make use of the conventional form, but who are [really] yogins neither cultivating pride nor meriting contempt."
44. Cf. Snellgrove, from HVT, vol. 2, iv, 69: "The Lord said: All beings are Buddhas, but this is obscured by accidental defilement. When this is removed, they are Buddhas at once, of this there is no doubt." See also Lessing and Wayman, *Introduction to the Buddhist Tantric Systems*, 267, in discussing "tantra of ground": "Nāropa maintains that this is the 'jewel-like person,' who is chief among the candidates for the high goal of the *Anuttara* [tantra]. Śāntipā and Abhayākara maintain that it is the True Nature of Mind (*citta-dharmatā*) intrinsically pure but possessed of adventitious defilements." Footnote 15: "This explanation involves a sense of the word tantra virtually equivalent to the old Buddhist terms *samtāna*, 'stream of consciousness.'" See also rGyal thang pa's use of *rgyud* in his version of Milarepa's songs, folio 243.7–244.1; 238.1–4.
45. See ITB, vol. 2, 134–41. See also *Vajrapāṇitantra*, said to contain seven definitions of *vajra*; it is part of the cycle of Krīya Tantras. (Cf. notes from Namkhai Norbu Rinpoche, July 21, 1996).
46. Śitavana is the place where the Vajrayāna *Sūtras* were revealed.
47. Snellgrove, HVT, vol. 1, 92, and George Elder's translation of the *Saṃpuṭa Tantra*, 190.
48. *Songs*, 266: "As one light is kindled from another, the teaching has been transmitted down from dharmakāya, the great Dorje Chang," and so on.

49. *Songs*, 199n12: "A tantric yogi should know that all manifestations are representations of Absolute Truth, and that the 'real Guru'—the embodiment of the Absolute—is his own mind. Thus, to meditate on one's own mind is to realize the identity of the manifestations and the gurus." See also ibid., 378–79: "My guru is my own mind."
50. See M. Léon Freer, ed., *Avadāna-Śataka* (Paris: Ernest Leroux, 1891), 6. This is a "stock phrase" appearing in over half of the *avadānas* in this collection.
51. For the Great-Seal is nothing less than ultimate reality. This is presented brilliantly in Takpo Tashi Namgyal's masterpiece, *Chakchen Dawai Ozer* (Moonbeams of Mahāmudrā).
52. *lung rigs man ngag thos bsam nor gyis phyug*. See Chandra Das, 1216.
53. This place is said by Losang Jamspal and by Khenpo Karthar Rinpoche to be about a day's journey away from Lhasa, near Reting; see folio 618–19, colophon. This Vulture Cave is said still to exist.

Chapter 24

1. The text of Milarepa is given with oral commentary by Lobsang Tarchin Rinpoche. Lobsang Tarchin Rinpoche is a member of the Tibetan Parliament in Exile in Dharamsala and a respected Karma bKa' brgyud pa incarnate lama. Acknowledging the difficulties that many yogins (Western and Eastern) experience when trying to put the teachings into practice, he generously granted me the following oral explanations on the practices and the terminology used by Milarepa and his lineage.
2. See *Tsong Kha pa's Six Yogas*, 262n44.
3. "Cultivating and abandoning" refers to the classic early Buddhist and Mahāyāna practices of renouncing evil deeds and all obstacles to spiritual progress while at the same time accumulating merit through virtuous activities. The obvious problem is that this tends to create a mind that is constantly judging according to preferences established according to criteria that tend to sustain the notion of a self, in the case of early Buddhism, that is making progress toward *nirvāṇa* or, in the case of the Mahāyāna that intends to attain perfect Buddhahood "for the benefit of all sentient beings."

4. Breath retention using the sphincter muscles and the lower abdomen.
5. During a tantric initiation.
6. Milarepa would normally have imparted teachings on mahāmudrā in the course of teaching on *Cakrasaṃvara*. Later, in sGampopa's adaptation of these teachings to the needs of his disciples, some were initiated into mahāmudrā on the basis of advanced teachings on śamatha and vipaśyanā meditation (calm abiding and insight). Several works in the lineage carry on this tradition descending from sGampopa, but it is evident from this oral instruction that Milarepa also taught in this way.

Glossary

amṛta (Sanskrit): The nectar of immortality; term used for the sacramental beverages used in some tantric ceremonies.

Aśoka: Emperor who united much of the Indian subcontinent in the third century BCE. He began to transform society in accordance with Buddhist moral principles. He left numerous edicts on granite pillars in different parts of the empire, guiding the people to practice justice, nonviolence, and religious tolerance.

Ā-tiglé: The typical Dzogchen visualization practice involving the Tibetan letter Ā in a sphere or "droplet" of the elemental colors. The whole visualization is located within the heart region of the meditator's body.

Bde mchog snyan brgyud: The cycle of yogic and ritual texts associated with the tantric deity Cakrasamvara, central to the practice of the bKa' brgyud pa order and its subdivisions.

Bhagavad Gīta: The "Song of the Blessed Lord," a portion of the great Sanskrit epic the *Mahābhārata*, in which the incarnate deity Krishna explains the meaning of life to his comrade in arms, Arjuna. One of the great sacred works of Hindu tradition, it sums up many themes of Upaniṣads, Yoga, and social theory.

Bhajans: Popular devotional songs in Hindi or Sanskrit widely used in temple worship and popular religious gatherings called *satsangs* or *samaj*.

Bhakti (Sanskrit): Divine devotional love.

Bhotia: Those Himalayan peoples who are related racially to the inhabitants of the Tibetan plateau. These would include Sherpas, Manangs, Mustangis, and Dolpo pas.

bKa' brgyud pa (sometimes written as *dkar brgyud*): The Lineage of the Oral Transmission; a group of Tibetan Buddhist schools founded in the eleventh century by Marpa the Translator and handed on by Milarepa to his disciples, especially Gampopa.

bKa' 'gyur (pronounced Kanjur): The principal part of the Tibetan Buddhist canon, containing the translations of the classic Dharma teachings of Buddha Sakyamuni from all three vehicles: Early Buddhism, the great vehicle, and the tantric vehicle.

Bon po: A non-Buddhist minority religious tradition of Tibet and the Himalayan region. Its history is controversial because of conflict with the Buddhism introduced into Tibet in the eighth century. Although it contains elements of shamanism and magic, it also has a sublime metaphysics and sophisticated meditation practices on a par with those of Tibetan Buddhism. In Dolpo, we observed a more refined painting style in the thangkas and wall paintings of the Bon pos than in those of the Buddhists.

Bu chen bcu gñis (The Twelve Great Son-Disciples): A group of *yogins* who had gathered around Milarepa in the final years of his life. One of them, Ngam rDzong ras pa, compiled a biography and a collection of his poetic teachings based on the reminiscences and writings of this group.

Catur-arya-satya (Sanskrit): The Four Truths that Pertain to the Noble Ones, which constitute the basic teaching of Sakyamuni Buddha in his First Sermon at Sarnath, India, in the fifth century BCE. The Four Truths are the following: suffering as a condition; the cause of suffering is desire; suffering can be annihilated; there is an Eightfold Path of conduct that leads to the annihilation of suffering. The full depths of this scheme are accessible only to those who have undertaken the path, hence it is not correct to speak of "Four Noble Truths"—"noble" here is not an adjective; it is a noun and refers exclusively to those who have at least had the first experience of liberation.

Chöd (Tibetan): The visualization practice revealed by the woman *yogini* Ma gcig Labdron in the eleventh century, which realizes voidness through a ritual of mental self-dismemberment and self-oblation. It is widely practiced in all schools but is a specialty of *ngag pas* and wandering *yogins* in the Himalayan regions.

ḍākinī (Sanskrit; Tibetan: *mkha' 'gro ma*): A female spiritual entity that inspires (but may also impede) the progress of a *yogin*, the *ḍākinī* is the third of the three roots of tantric Buddhism (along with the guru and the deity), giving special help in difficulties and integrating spiritual insight with life experience.

Dharmaḥ (singular) / dharmāḥ (plural): The singular refers to the Teachings of Buddha; the plural refers to the elements of nature itself, all phenomena.

Dzogchen (*rdzogs pa chen po*): Tibetan for the "great perfection"; a varied group of spiritual practices based on cultivating the natural state of awareness (*rig pa*); it is a specialty of the rNyingma school of Tibetan Buddhism, but is not restricted to that tradition. Dzogchen is also practiced by the non-Buddhist Bon po tradition.

gDams ngag mdzod (Tibetan title; English translation of the title: *A Treasury of Oral Instructions*): Title of a large, multivolume work compiled by Jamgon Kongtrul Lodro Thaye in the nineteenth century. It contains most of the esoteric instructions of the oldest schools of Tibetan Buddhism, including the oral teachings of Milarepa taken down by his closest disciples.

Gelugpa (Tibetan: *dge lugs pa*): The "reformed" (sometimes called "Yellow Hat") school of Tibetan Buddhism founded by rJe Tsong Khapa in the late fourteenth century.

gTer ma (Tibetan): Hidden texts or ritual objects. They were concealed by saints of the past, especially Guru Rinpoche (Padmasambhava) and his circle, so as to be rediscovered by their own rebirths at the appropriate time. The rediscoverers are called tertons, often designated by the sobriquet, ling-pa.

gtum mo (Tibetan): The yoga of inner heat. Milarepa and his heirs used this practice to resist the cold in their solitary mountain caves. It is also one of the key practices of the Six Yogas of Nāropa, by which the *yogin*'s body is perfected in anticipation of the completion of transformation into Buddha Vajradhara.

Kyirong/(La phyis) Lapchi: The region of southern Tibet just north of Nepal where Milarepa lived for many years and died in either 1123 or 1136.

mahāmudrā: The great seal, a doctrine of tantric Buddhism that asserts that the realized *yogin* can recognize in all phenomena the irreducible presence of the natural state of openness, or "voidness," such that there is no need for further meditation.

Mahāsukha: Great bliss, the experiential goal of tantric practices involving the ascent and channeling of the body's subtle energies, bringing about the divinization of the entire human person, even the material aspect.

maṇḍala: A sacred diagram representing the abode of a meditational deity in the Buddhist or Hindu tantras; this sort of image is usually highly symmetrical and abounds in colors, symbols, mystic syllables, and deity images. It can be painted or designed in colored sand.

Marpa the Translator: The eleventh-century Tibetan spiritual master who "tamed" the wild sorcerer Milarepa, applying the teaching of highest yoga tantra and *mahāmudrā* learned from Nāropa and other great Vajrayāna siddhas in India.

mgur (Tibetan): A sacred song, usually composed as an instruction from master to disciple and arising spontaneously in a particular teaching situation. These songs came to be organized liturgically and sung at tantric feasts.

Milarepa (circa 1050–1130): A southern Tibetan practitioner who took revenge on his childhood enemies by the use of black magic but later repented under the guidance of the great tantric master Marpa the Translator. He became one of Tibet's most beloved saints and poets, guiding disciples through the experience of solitary retreat in remote mountain caves.

Newars: The native tantric Buddhists of Nepal, guardians of the traditions in their numerous "bāhāls" or temples in the Kathmandu Valley.

Om mani padme hung: The mantra of Avalokiteśvara, the Bodhisattva of Compassion, recited millions of times by devout Himalayan Buddhists and often carved on stones and cliffsides.

Pūjā: General term for a ritual or prayer service in a temple; it is mainly a Hindu term (Sanskrit) but is often used in Himalayan Buddhism as well.

Rinpoche (Tibetan): It means "Precious One"; it is the usual title of recognized reincarnate lamas—that is, tulkus (*sprul bskus*).

rNyingma pa: The Old Translation School of Tibetan Buddhism, based on the eighth-century efforts of Guru Padmasambhava, Abbot Śāntarakṣita, and King Trisong Detsen (Khri srong lde btsan).

scholasticism: A form of intellectual discipline that strives to arrive at comprehensiveness and precision through definitions, distinctions, and categories. It is typical of late Medieval and Baroque theology in Western Europe and can be found in some of the Hindu traditions as well. The Buddhists have a long history of scholasticism going back to the Buddha himself. The *Abhidharma* portion of the Buddhist scriptures is a "scholastic" approach and the dge shes of the dGe lugs pa Order of Tibetan Buddhism are consummate scholastic dialecticians.

Six Yogas of Nāropa: Six distinct spiritual practices taught by Marpa's guru, the Indian saint Nāropa, derived from tantric practice cycles. These practices have much in common with advanced yoga (using energy currents, channels, and energy centers in the subtle body) and are based on a practitioner's proven ability to develop considerable stability of body and mind through meditation and ritual activity. They are usually listed as the yoga of inner heat, illusory subtle body, clear light, consciousness transference, forceful projection, and control over the intermediate state after death.

(s)ngags pa: Tibetan for a "mantra practitioner"; this is a highly respected title, granted only to those who have made long retreats in which they have perfected one or more tantric practices to the point of being able to help others on the way to spiritual liberation. They are frequently called upon as exorcists and healers.

Stūpa: Sacred Buddhist monument, usually containing sacred texts and relics of holy persons. The basic form is of a large hemisphere, often embellished with symbolic forms that represent the elements, the energy centers of the body, the honorific presence of Buddha-nature, and the levels of spiritual attainment.

Tanjur (Tibetan: *bstan 'gyur*): The Tibetan translation of the Buddhist scholastic treatises, tantric commentaries, liturgies, and vajra songs. It is the second major part of the Tibetan Buddhist canon, containing the teachings attributed to great Indian masters.

Tathāgatagarbha (Sanskrit): The germ/embryo of the Enlightened One. The teaching of one branch of Mahāyāna Buddhism that each sentient being possesses the germ of Buddha-nature, which is the basis on which sentient beings attain enlightenment.

Thang ka: A sacred painting on canvas, depicting some aspect of the Tibetan pantheon.

Theravāda: An early Buddhist school teaching the so-called doctrine of the Elders (companions of the Buddha); their beliefs are to be found in the still-extant Pali Canon, and their practices are maintained by Buddhist masters in Sri Lanka, Burma, and Thailand.

Trikāya: The triple body of Buddha—the *dharmakāya*, *sambhogakāya*, and *nirmāṇakāya*. The triadic structure of the Absolute in Mahāyāna Buddhism through which voidness is spontaneously present at the very root of all phenomena, on the level of subtle communication and enjoyment, and manifest in the world of ordinary sentient beings.

Tulku (Tibetan: *sprul sku*; Sanskrit: Nirmāṇakāya): Literally, an apparitional body. In ordinary usage, this term refers to those persons who have been recognized as the rebirths of masters of the past, one of the most characteristic features of Tibetan Buddhism.

ü-mé (*dbu med*): The Tibetan "headless" semicursive script.

Upaniṣads: Sacred texts compiled over many centuries and associated with the Vedic hymns; the earliest Upaniṣad may be 2,800 years old. They emphasize the search for the mystical and esoteric meanings of the Brahmanical rituals of ancient India.

Yab-yum (Tibetan): Father-Mother. The iconography of deities in sexual embrace.

Vajrācārya: The presiding master of a tantric ritual; the priest of a tantric Buddhist temple or monastic assembly.

Vajradhara: The archetypical tantric form of fully realized Buddhahood; the name means "Bearer of the Indestructible" and refers to the state of consciousness of the perfected Buddhist tantric *yogin*.

Vajrasattva: The peaceful Vajrayāna deity that is visualized to obtain purification of past moral defilements. The practice of Vajrasattva involves the use of the Hundred Syllable Mantra; as a preliminary practice to more advanced tantric yoga, this mantra is recited more than 100,000 times.

Vajrayāna: The Vehicle of the Indestructible (diamond or thunderbolt: the texts refer to both meanings of the word "vajra"); the Third Vehicle of historical Buddhism based on ritual and yogic practices designed to accelerate the realization of enlightenment. This is the form of Buddhism inherited from medieval India and practiced in Tibet and other countries of central and east Asia.

Vajrayoginī: An important Buddhist tantric deity in feminine form.

Selected Bibliography

A. Tibetan Sources

'Ba' ra dkar brgyud pa. *Bka' brgyud gser 'phreng chen mo. Rje btsun mi la ras pa'i rnam thar mdor bsdus zhig*, folios 203–73 (acc. no. 341. Library of Tibetan Works and Archives, Dharmasala). Dehradun: Ngawang Gyaltsen and Ngawang Lungtok, 1970.

Bde mchog snyan rgyud (*ras chung snyan rgyud*):

a. Byang chub bZang pa, ed. Ras chung pa. *The Short Biography of Milarepa*. Vol. 1, folios 97–125. I-Tib-73-90914. Reproduced from a rare manuscript in the library of Apho Rinpoche. New Delhi: 1973.

b. ———. *The Short Biography of Milarepa*, folios 133–89. I-Tib-84-900297. Darjeeling: Kargyud Sungrab Nyamso Khang, 1983.

c. ———. *Short Biographies of Milarepa*. Vol. 1, folios 91–93, 167–69. I-Tib-924556. Leh: Sonam W. Tashigang, 1971.

Bka' brgyud mgur mtsho, don gnyis brgyabs sab mo dgu. Chapter on the works of Milarepa, in which the text corresponds not to Gtsang smyon's version but to the *bu chen bcu gnyis* text. Block print from Rumtek Monastery. Sikkhim: n.d.

'Bri gung chos rje kun dga' rin chen. *The Miscellaneous Writings* (*bka' 'bum thor bu*). *Rje btsun mi la ras pa'i rnam thar dngos grub kyi snye ma*, folios 41–51. I-Tib-72-901803. Leh: S. W. Tashigangpa, 1972.

'Brug chen 'jam dbyangs chos kyi grags pa III. (1478–1523). *Ras chung snyan rgyud gsar ma. Mi la rnam thar*, folios 1–84. Kangra, HP: Khampa Gar Sungrab Nyamso Gyunphel Parkhang, Tibetan Craft Community, 1985.

'Brug pa'i chos 'byung: chos 'byung bstan pa'i padma rgyas pa'i nyin byed ces bya ba bzhugs so. Rje btsun mi la'i skor, folios 353–73. Publisher: Bod ljongs bod yig dpe rnying dpe skrun khang, 1992.

Bu chen bcu gnyis. Rje btsun chen po mid la ras pa'i rnam thar … mgur, 36.280 (IIB R-16), manuscript. Tibetan Book Collection of the Newark Museum, Newark, New Jersey.

Grub thob O-rgyan pa Rin chen dpal (1229/30-1309). *Bka' brgyud yid bzhin nor bu yi 'phreng ba* (*'bri gung bka' brgyud*), folios 174–245. *Mila rnam thar.* Leh: S. W. Tashigangpa, 1972.

gTsang smyon he ru ka. Mi la rnam thar (original block print). In *Mi la ras pa'i rnam thar: Texte Tibétain de la vie de Milarépa,* edited by J. W. De Jong. 'S-Gravenhage, Leiden: Mouton & Co., 1959.

gTsang smyon he ru ka (rus pa'i rgyan can byis btsams). *Rnal 'byor gyi dbang phyug chen po mi la ras pa'i rnam mgur.* mtsho sngon mi rigs dpe skrun khang, thengs gnyis pa dpar, 1989. [This is the text I am calling the *Standard Edition.*]

'Jam mgon kong sprul blo gros mtha' yas. *gDams ngag mdzod.* Vol. 5. *Mar pa bka'brgyud skor.* Delhi: N. Lungtok and N. Gyaltsan, 1972.

a. *Rje btsun mi la'i phyag rgya chen po ye shes gsal byed kyi rtsa ba,* folios 66–67.
b. *Rje btsun chen po mi la ras pa mdzad pa'i snyan brgyud gsal ba skor gsum sogs,* folios 109–20.
c. *Phyag rgya chen po ye shes gsal byed kyi ngo sprod,* folios 120–21.
d. *Gsang dbang dang 'brel ba steng sgo rnam par grol ba'i chos drug gi khrid yig,* folios 286–317.
e. *Bde mchog snyan brgyud kyi lam blo nas gcod pa bar do ngo sprod kyi gdams ngag zab mo,* folios 344–61.
f. *Bde mchog snyan brgyud kyi phyag rgya chen poye shes gsal byed,* folios 443–55.

'Jam mgon kong sprul blo gros mtha' yas (Karma Ngawang). *Yon tan rgya mtsho. L'Avvampare dello Splendido Fuoco di Saggezza: Guru-Yoga del Grande Getsun Milarepa e Rituale d'offerta.* Testo liturgico in tibetano, tradotto in Italiano da Margherita Blanchietti. Centro Milarepa, Pinerolo, Torino: 1984.

Kun dga' 'brug dpal, ed. *Dkar brgyud gser 'phreng. Mi la ras pa'i rnam thar* (Mon rtse pa kun dga' dpal ldan, compiler), folios 104–65. [The introduction to this work explains the three transmissions of the Cakrasamvara *Dakini* teachings to Sgam po pa, Ras chung pa, and Ngam rdzong ras pa.] I-Tib-912149. Smanrtsis Shesrig Spendzod Volume 3. Leh: Sonam W. Tashigang, BPO Nemo, 1970.

Lha btsun rin chen rnam rgyal, ed. *Rje btsun mi la ras pa'i rdo rje mgur drug sogs gsung rgyun thor bu.* [Rare block print edition of several songs of Milarepa.] Institute for Advanced Studies of World Religions, Stony Brook. n.d.

Mar pa lo tsā ba dang dar la 'byor don grub kyis mdzad / thub bstan phun tshogs kyis bsgrigs. *rtsa rlung 'phrul 'khor.* si khron mi rigs dpe skrun khang, 1992.

Mi la ras pa. *bde mchog snyan brgyud.* Royal Nepal National Archives.

a. *Rje btsun mi la'i tshe sgrub tshe ring mched lnga'i rjes gnang bzhugs so* (microfilm).

b. *Tshe khrid rin chen gter (ster) mdzod zab pa yang dag pa* (microfilm).

c. *Pra khrid lung bstan tilo'i gtad brgya* (microfilm).

d. *Mzhad pa rdo rje'i dbang bskur byin rlabs dang 'brel ba ye shes bcud sbyin* (microfilm).

Mi la ras pa. *Mar pa chos kyi blo gros rnam thar*, folios 63–96. *Mila ras pa rnam thar* by Ras chung pa, folios 97–125. In *Bde mchog mkha' 'gro snyan rgyud* (*ras chung snyan rgyud*). Yig-cha compiled by Byang chub bzang po, Vol. 1. I-Tib-73–902914. New Delhi: 1973.

Mtshan yongs su grags pa. *Rje btsun mi la ras pa'i rnam thar bzhugs so.* Vol. 2, folios 161–205, ms. acc. no. 2092. Library of Tibetan Works and Archives, Dharmasala.

Pad ma dkar po (1527–92). *mkha' 'gro snyan brgyud kyi yig rnying.* Vol. 2. I-Tib-82-902170. Darjeeling: Kargyud Sungrab Nyamso Khang, 1982.

a. *Rje mi la'i gtad rgya*, folios 521–25.

b. *Dpal mgon po'i las tshogs*, folios 527–46.

c. *Bde mchog snyan brgyud steng sgo rnam par grol ba'i chos drug.* Vol. 1, folios 493–560.

d. *Chos 'byung bstan pa'i padma rgyas pa'i nyin byed: Tibetan Chronicle of Padma dKar po. Mila rnam thar,* folios 236–56. New Delhi: International Academy of Indian Culture, 1968.

Rang byung rdo rje, the Third Karmapa (attributed). *Rnal 'byor gyi dbang phyug mi la bzhad pa rdo rje'i gsung mgur mdzod nag ma zhes pa 'rma pa* (2 vols.). Short title: *mdzod nag ma* (The black treasury). [This work is an expansion of the *Bu chen bcu gnyis* biography and songs.] I-Tib-79-901890. Dalhousie: Damchoe Sangpo, 1978.

rGod tshang ras pa sna tshogs rang grol. *Rje btsun ras chung pa'i rnam thar rnam mkhyen thar lam gsal bar ston pa'i me long ye shes kyi snang ba.* Mtsho sngon mi rigs dpe skrun khang, 1992.

rGod tshang ras pa sna tshogs rang grol. *The Life of the Saint of gTsang.* Lokesh Chandra, ed., with a preface by E. Gene Smith, Sata-Pitaka Series, vol. 79, Sharada Rani. New Delhi: 1969.

Rgyal dbang 'brug chen kun mkhyen Padma Karpo, ed. *Bde mchog snyan brgyud nor bu skor gsum.* Bhutanese ms. Tashijhong: 1985.

a. *Grol lam steng sgo rnam par grol ba'i chos drug,* folios 477–536.

b. *Bsam mi khyab don bzhi pa bzhugs so,* folios 551–60.

c. *Phyag rgya chen po'i ye shes gsal 'debs par byed man ngag.*

d. *Bdud dang bgegs phyir bzlog pa'i man ngag bla ma'i zhal gyi bdud rtsi,* folios 237–42.

e. *Bdud dang bgegs phyir bzlog pa'i man ngag gi 'grel pa,* folios 243–54.

f. *Rje mila'i gtad rgya,* folios 449–54.

g. *Til li'i pra khrid lung bstan gtad rgya,* folios 423–48.

Rgyal dbang 'brug chen kun mkhyen Padma Karpo IV, ed. *mkha' 'gro snyan brgyud kyi yig rnying: The Ancient Cycle of Practice Focusing upon the Cakrasamvara Tantra According to an Oral Transmission Received from Vajra-dakini by Ras chung rdo rje grags.* Vol. 1, folios 493–560. *Bde mchog snyan brgyud steng rnam par grol ba'i chos drug.* Vol. 2. *Rje mi la'i gtad rgya* (the "mind mandate" of Milarepa), folios 521–25. *Dpal mgnon po'i las tshogs*, folios 527–46. I-Tib-82-902170. Darjeeling: 1982.

Rgyal thang pa bde chen rdo rje. *Dkar brgyud gser 'phreng. Mi la ras pa'i rnam thar*, folios 189–265. I-Tib-73-904146. Tashijhong, Palampur, HP: Sungrab Nyamso Gyunphel Parkhang, 1973.

Rnal 'byor ba sangs rgyas dar po dang rgyal thang ba bde chen rdo rje brtsams. *rgod tshang ba mgon po rdo rje'i rnam thar.* mtsho sngon mi rigs dpe skrun khang, 1992.

Sangs rgyas 'bum, ed. and compiler. *Mi la ras pa'i rnam thar*, folios 167–208, from sPungs Thang blockprints from 1799 to 1803. Found in the *Rwa lung dkar brgyud gser 'phreng.* Vol. 1. I-Tib-76-900092. Palampur, Tashijhong: 1975.

Sgam po pa bsod nams rin chen (1079–1159). *The Collected Works (gSung-'bum) of sGam-po-pa bSod-nams Rin-chen. The Biographies of Lord Marpa and Saint Milarepa.* Vol. 1, folios 23–42. I-Tib-82-902155. sPyan snga bSod nams Lhun grub, ed. Darjeeling: Kargyud Sungrab Syamso Khang, 1982.

Zwa dmar mkha' spyod dbang po II. (1350–1405). *The Collected Writings of the Second Zwa dmar mkha' spyod dbang po.* Vol. 1. *Chos rje dpal ldan mi la ras chen gyi rnam par thar pa byin rlabs kyi sprin phung*, folios 188–317. I-Tib-78-903290. Gangtok: Gonpo Tseten, 1978.

B. Secondary Sources

Aris, Michael. (1975). "Autobiographies of Three Spiritual Masters of Kutary." *Contributions to Nepalese Studies* 2 (2): 45–87.

———. (1989). *Hidden Treasures and Secret Lives.* London: Kegan Paul International.

Asaṅga. (1973). *La Somme du Grand Véhicule d'Asaṅga (Mahāyānasamgraha).* Translated by Étienne Lamotte. Louvain-La-Neuve: Université de Louvain.

Aufschnaiter, Peter. (1976). "Lands and Places of Milarepa." *East and West* 26: 175–89.

Bacot, J. (1966). *Le Poete Tibêtain Milarêpa. Ses crimes, ses épreuves, son nirvana.* Paris: Éditions Bossard.

Beyer, Stephan. (1978). *The Cult of Tārā: Magic and Ritual in Tibet.* Berkeley: University of California Press.

Blondeau, Anne-Marie. (1980). "Analysis of the Biographies of Padmasambhava According to Tibetan Tradition: Classification of Sources." In *Tibetan Studies in Honour of Hugh Richardson,* edited by Aris and Aung San Suu Kyi, 45–52. Warminster: Aris and Phillips.

———. (1985). "*Mkhen-brce'i Dba'-po*: La biographie de Padmasambhava selon la tradition du Bsgrangs-Pa Bon, et ses sources." In *Orientalia Iosephi Tucci Memoriae Dicata,* vol. 1, edited by G. Gnoli and L. Lanciotti, 111–58. Rome: Istituto Italiano per il Medio ed Estremo Oriente.

Boord, Martin J. (1993). *The Cult of the Deity Vajrakila.* Buddhica Britannica Series Continua IV. Tring, UK: Institute of Buddhist Studies.

Broido, Michael. (1985). "Intention and Suggestion in the *Abhidharmakośa*: Sandhabhāṣa Revisited." *Journal of Indian Philosophy* 13 (4): 327–81.

Bru sgom rgyal ba g.yung drung. (1996). *The Stages of A-Khrid Meditation: Dzogchen Practice of the Bon Tradition.* Dharamsala: Library of Tibetan Works and Archives.

Cantwell, Cathy. (1995). "To Meditate upon Consciousness as Vajra: Ritual 'Killing and Liberation' in the rNying-ma-pa Tradition." In *Proceedings of the 7th Seminar of the International Association for Tibetan Studies (IATS),* edited by Ernst Steinkellner, Helmut Krasser, Michael Torsten Much, and Helmut Tauscher, 107–18. Graz, Austria.

Chang, Garma C. C. (1962). *The Hundred Thousand Songs of Milarepa.* New Hyde Park: University Books.

Chattopadhyaya, Debiprasad. (1970). *Taranatha's History of Buddhism in India.* Simla: Indian Institute of Advanced Study.

Chökyi Nyima Rinpoche. (1999). *The Bardo Guidebook.* Hong Kong: Rangjung Yeshe Publications.

Clarke, Graham E. (1980). "A Helambu History." *Journal of the Nepal Research Center* 4: 1–38.

Conze, Edward. (1973). *The Perfection of Wisdom in Eight Thousand Lines.* Bolinas: Four Seasons Foundation.

Crapanzano, Vincent. (1977). "The Life History in Anthropological Field Work." *Anthropology and Humanism Quarterly* 2: 3–7.

Crook, John, and James Low. (1997). *The Yogins of Ladakh: A Pilgrimage among the Hermits of the Buddhist Himalayas.* Delhi: Motilal Banarsidass.

Das, Sarat Chandra. (1983). *A Tibetan-English Dictionary.* Kyoto: Rinsen Book Company.

Daniélou, Alain. (1991). *Yoga: Mastering the Secrets of Matter and the Universe.* Rochester, VT: Inner Traditions International.

Davidson, Ronald M. (1981). "The Litany of the Names of Manjusri: Text and Translation of the *Mañjuśrīnāmasaṁgīti.*" In *Tantric and Taoist Studies in Honour of R. A. Stein,* edited by Michel Strickmann, 1–69. Brussels: Institut Belge des Hautes Études Chinoises.

———. (1990). "An Introduction to the Standards of Scriptural Authenticity in Indian Buddhism." In *Chinese Buddhist Apocrypha,* edited by Buswell, 291–325. Honolulu: University of Hawaii Press.

———. (1994). "The Eleventh-Century Renaissance in Central Tibet." Paper delivered at the University of Virginia, Charlottesville.

Davidson, Ronald, and Steven Goodman, eds. (1992). *Tibetan Buddhism: Reason and Revelation.* Albany: State University of New York Press.

Dayal, Har. (1975). *The Bodhisattva Doctrine in Buddhist Sanskrit Literature.* Delhi: Motilal Banarsidass.

Dehejia, Vidya. (1986). *Yogini Cult and Temples: A Tantric Tradition.* New Delhi: National Museum.

Demiéville, P. (1952). *Le Concile de Lhasa.* Vol. 7. Bibliothèque de l'Institut des Hautes Études Chinoises.

Deshung Rinpoche, Kunga Tenpay Nyima. (1995). *The Three Levels of Spiritual Perception: An Oral Commentary on the Three Visions (Nang Sum) of Ngorchen Konchog Lhundrub.* Translated by Jared Rhoton. Boston: Wisdom Publications.

Desjarlais, Robert R. (1994). *Body and Emotion: The Aesthetics of Illness and Healing in the Nepal Himalayas.* Delhi: Motilal Banarsidass.

Doboom Tulku, ed. (1995). *Buddhist Translations: Problems and Perspectives.* Delhi: Manohar.

Dor-je, Wang-ch'ug. (1978). *The Mahamudra Eliminating the Darkness of Ignorance.* Translated by Alexander Berzin. Dharamsala: Library of Tibetan Works and Archives.

Dowman, Keith. (1973). *The Legend of the Great Stupa and the Life Story of the Lotus Born Guru.* Berkeley: Tibetan Nyingma Meditation Center.

———. (1984). *Sky Dancer: The Secret Life and Songs of the Lady Yeshe Tsogyel.* London: Routledge and Kegan Paul.

———. (1988). *The Power Places of Central Tibet: The Pilgrim's Guide.* London: Routledge and Kegan Paul.

———, trans. (1994). *The Flight of the Garuda: Teachings of the Dzokchen Tradition of Tibetan Buddhism.* Boston: Wisdom Publications.

Drikung Kyabgon Chetsang Rinpoche. (1999). *The Practice of Mahamudra.* Ithaca: Snow Lion.

Dudjom Rimpoche. (1991). *The Nyingma School of Tibetan Buddhism: Its Fundamentals and History.* Translated by Gyurme Dorje and Matthew Kapstein. Boston: Wisdom Publications.

Eastman, Kenneth W. (1981). "The Eighteen Tantras of the Vajrasekhara/Mayajala." Unpublished paper presented to the twenty-sixth International Conference of Orientalists in Japan.

———. (1983). "Mahayoga Texts at Tun-huang." *Bulletin of the Institute of Buddhist Cultural Studies. Ryukoku University* 22: 42–60.

Édou, Jérôme. (1996). *Machig Labdrön and the Foundations of Chöd.* Ithaca: Snow Lion.

Ehrhard, Franz-Karl. (1990). "The Stupa of Bodhnath: A Preliminary Analysis of the Written Sources." *Ancient Nepal* 120: 1–9.

———. (1997). "A 'Hidden Land' in the Tibetan-Nepalese Borderlands." In *Maṇḍala and Landscape*, edited by A. K. MacDonald, 335–64. Delhi: DK Publishing.

Eimer, Helmut, and Pema Tsering. (1990). "Blockprints and Manuscripts of Mila ras pa's Mgur 'bum Accessible to Frank-Richard Hamm." *Frank-Richard Hamm Memorial Volume.* Bonn, Germany: Indica et Tibetica.

English, Elizabeth. (2002). *Vajrayogini: Her Visualizations, Rituals, and Forms.* Boston: Wisdom Publications.

Evans-Wentz, W. Y. (1928). *Tibet's Great Yogi Milarepa.* London: Oxford University Press.

Farrow, G. W., and I. Menon. (1992). *The Concealed Essence of the Hevajra Tantra.* Delhi: Motilal Banarsidass.

Ferrari, Alfonsa. (1958). *Mk'yen Brtse's Guide to the Holy Places of Central Tibet.* Edited by Luciano Petech. Rome: Istituto Italiano per il Medio ed Estremo Oriente.

Fremantle, Francesca, and Chögyam Trungpa. (1975). *The Tibetan Book of the Dead: The Great Liberation Through Hearing in the Bardo.* Boulder: Shambhala.

Germano, David F. (1992). "Poetic Thought, the Intelligent Universe, and the Mystery of the Self: The Tantric Synthesis of rDzogs Chen in Fourteenth Century Tibet." PhD diss., University of Wisconsin (UMI AAT 9231691).

———. (1994). "Architecture and Absence in the Secret Tantric History of the Great Perfection (*rdzogs chen*)." *Journal of the International Association of Buddhist Studies* 17 (2): 203–335.

Gianotti, Carla. (2001). *La Vita di Milarepa di gTsang smyon Heruka.* Torino: Unione Tipografico-Editrice Torinese.

Goodman, Steven D. (1983). "The kLong-chen sNying-thig: An Eighteenth Century Tibetan Revelation." PhD diss., University of Saskatchewan.

———. (1992). "Rig-'dzin 'Jigs-med gling-pa and the kLong-Chen sNying-thig." In *Tibetan Buddhism: Reason and Revelation,* edited by Ronald M. Davidson and Steven D. Goodman, 133–46. Albany: SUNY Press.

Goss, Robert Everet. (1993). "The Hermeneutics of Madness: A Literary and Hermeneutical Analysis of the *Mila'i rnam thar.*" Th.D. diss., Harvard University.

Granoff, Phyllis, and Koichi Shinohara, eds. (1988). *Monks and Magicians: Religious Biographies in Asia*. Oakville, Ontario: Mosaic.

———, eds. (1994). *Other Selves: Autobiography and Biography in Cross-Cultural Perspective*. Oakville, Ontario: Mosaic.

Grönbold, Gunter. (1996). *The Yoga of Six Limbs: An Introduction to the History of Sadangayoga*. Santa Fe: Spirit of the Sun Publications.

Gtsang smyon Heruka. (1984). *The Life of Milarepa*. Translated by Lobsang P. Lhalungpa. Boston: Shambhala.

———. (1993). *Les Cent Mille Chants de Milarepa*. Paris: Trad. par Marie-José Lamothe. Librairie Arthème Fayard.

———. (1995). *Milarepa: La Vie*. Trad. par M-J. Lamothe. Paris: Éd. du Seuil.

Guenther, Herbert V., trans. (1971). *The Jewel Ornament of Liberation by Sgam-po-pa*. Boston: Shambhala Publications.

———, trans. (1975–76). *Kindly Bent to Ease Us*. Vols. 1–3. Berkeley: Dharma Publishing.

———, trans. (1986). *The Life and Teaching of Nāropa*. Boston: Shambhala Publications. Originally published 1963.

Gyatrul Rinpoche. (1993). *Ancient Wisdom: Nyingma Teachings on Dream Yoga, Meditation, and Transformation*. Ithaca: Snow Lion.

———. (1998). *Natural Liberation: Padmasambhava's Teachings on the Six Bardos*. Boston: Wisdom Publications.

Gyatso, Geshe Kelsang. (1982). *Clear Light of Bliss: Mahamudra in Vajrayana Buddhism*. London: Wisdom Publications.

———. (1991). *Guide to Dakini Land: A Commentary to the Highest Yoga Tantra Practice of Vajrayogini*. London: Tharpa Publications.

Gyatso, Janet. (1981). "The Literary Traditions of Thang-stong rGyal-po: A Study of Visionary Buddhism in Tibet." PhD diss., University of California, Berkeley.

———. (1987). "Down with the Demoness: Reflections on a Feminine Ground in Tibet." *Tibet Journal* 12 (4): 34–46.

———. (1992a). "Autobiography in Tibetan Religious Literature: Reflections on Its Modes of Self-Presentation." In *Tibetan Studies: Proceedings of the 5th International Association of Buddhist Studies Seminar*, Vol. 2, edited by Shoren Ihara and Zuiho Yamaguchi, 465–78. Narita: Naritasan Institute for Buddhist Studies.

———. (1992b). "Genre, Authorship, and Transmission in Visionary Buddhism: The Literary Traditions of Thang-stong rGyal-po." *Tibetan Buddhism: Reason and Revelation*, edited by Ronald M. Davidson and Steven D. Goodman, 95–106. Albany: SUNY Press.

———, ed. (1992c). *In the Mirror of Memory: Reflections on Mindfulness and Remembrance in Indian and Tibetan Buddhism.* Albany: State University of New York Press.

———. (1996). "Drawn from the Tibetan Treasury: The gTer ma Literature." In *Tibetan Literature*, edited by José Cabezon and Roger Jackson, 147–69. Ithaca: Snow Lion.

———. (1998). *Apparitions of the Self: The Secret Autobiographies of a Tibetan Visionary.* Princeton: Princeton University Press.

Haarh, Erik. (1969). *The Yar-lun Dynasty.* Copenhagen: G. E. C. Gad's Forlag.

Hawley, John S., and Mark Juergensmeyer. (1988). *Songs of the Saints of India.* New York: Oxford University Press.

Hermann-Pfandt, Adelheid. (1990). *Dakinis: zur Stellung und Symbolik des Weiblichen im tantrischen Buddhismus.* Bonn: Indica et Tibetica.

Huber, Toni. (1997). "A Guide to the La-Phyi Mandala: History, Landscape and Ritual in South-Western Tibet." In *Mandala and Landscape*, edited by A. W. Macdonald, 234–86. New Delhi: DK Printworld.

———. (1999). *The Cult of Pure Crystal Mountain: Popular Pilgrimage and Visionary Landscape in Southeastern Tibet.* New York: Oxford University Press.

Jackson, David. (1980). "A Genealogy of the Kings of Lo (Mustang)." In *Tibetan Studies in Honor of Hugh Richardson*, edited by Aris and Aung San. Warminster: Aris and Phillips.

———. (1994). *Enlightenment by a Single Means: Tibetan Controversies on the "Self-Sufficient White Remedy" (dkar po gcig thub).* Wien: Verlag der Österreichischen Akademie der Wissenschaften.

Jackson, David, and Janice Jackson. (1996). *A History of Tibetan Painting.* Wien: Verlag der Österreichischen Akademie der Wissenschaften.

Jamgon Kongtrul Lodro Thaye. (1977). *The Torch of Certainty.* Translated by Judith Hanson. Boston: Shambhala.

———. (1992). *Le Lama Éternel: Commentaire de "L'Appel au Lama de Loin."* Vernègues: Claire Lumière.

———. (1994). *Jamgon Kongtrul's Retreat Manual.* Translated by Ngawang Zangpo. Ithaca: Snow Lion.

———. (1996). *Creation and Completion: Essential Points of Tantric Meditation.* Translated by Sarah Harding. Boston: Wisdom.

———. (1998). *The Light of Wisdom.* Vols. I and II. Root text by Padmasambhava. Hong Kong: Rangjung Yeshe Publications.

Jest, C. (1975). *Dolpo: Communautés de Langue Tibétaine du Nepal.* Paris: Éd du CNRS.

Jinpa, Thupten, and Jas Elsner. (2000). *Songs of Spiritual Experience: Tibetan Buddhist Poems of Insight and Awakening.* Boston: Shambhala.

de Jong, J. W. (1959). *Mi La Ras Pa'i Rnam Thar.* The Hague: Mouton.

Kapstein, Matthew. (1995). "From Kun-mkhyen Dol-po-pa to 'Ba-mda' Dge-legs: Three Jo-nang-pa Masters on the Interpretation of the Prajnaparamita." In *IATS*, edited by Ernst Steinkellner, Helmut Krasser, Michael Torsten Much, and Helmut Tauscher, 457–75. Graz, Austria.

Karmay, Samten G. (1972). *The Treasury of Good Sayings: A Tibetan History of Bon.* London: Oxford University Press.

———. (1975). "A Discussion of the Doctrinal Position of the rDzogs-chen from the 10th to the 13th Centuries." *Journal Asiatique* 263: 147–56.

———. (1980). "An Open Letter by Pho-brang Zhi-ba-'od to the Buddhists in Tibet." *Tibet Journal* 5 (3): 1–28.

———. (1988). *The Great Perfection (rDzogs-chen): A Philosophical and Meditative Teaching of Tibetan Buddhism.* Leiden: E. J. Brill.

———. (1998). *The Little Luminous Boy: The Oral Tradition from the Land of Zhangzhung Depicted on Two Tibetan Paintings.* Bangkok: Orchid Press.

Karthar Rinpoche. (1990). *The Profound Inner Meaning.* Woodstock: Karma Triyana Dharmachakra.

———. (1993). *The Ocean of True Meaning.* Woodstock: Karma Triyana Dharmachakra.

Khyentse, Dilgo. (1994). *The Wish-Fulfilling Jewel: The Practice of Guru Yoga According to the Longchen Nyingthig Tradition.* Boston: Shambhala Publications.

Kohn, Richard J. (2001). *Lord of the Dance: The Mani Rimdu Festival in Tibet and Nepal.* Albany: SUNY Press.

Kunga Rinpoche, and Brian Cutillo. (1986). *Miraculous Journey: New Stories and Songs by Milarepa.* Novato: Lotsawa.

———. (1995). *Drinking the Mountain Stream: Songs of Tibet's Beloved Saint Milarepa.* Boston: Wisdom.

Kunsang, Eric P., trans. (1994). *Advice from the Lotus-Born.* Hong Kong: Rangjung Yeshe Publications.

Kvaerne, Per. (1974). "On the Concept of Sahaja in Indian Buddhist Tantric Literature." *Temenos* 2: 88–135.

———. (1977). *An Anthology of Buddhist Tantric Songs: A Study of the Caryagiti.* 2nd ed. Bangkok: White Orchi.

———. (1983). "The 'Great Perfection' in the Traditions of the Bonpos." In *Early Ch'an in China and Tibet,* edited by Whalen Lai and Lewis R. Lancaster. Berkeley: Asian Humanities.

———. (1985). *Tibet: Bon Religion.* Iconography of Religions XII, 13. Leiden: E. J. Brill.

Lamotte, Étienne. (1966). "Vajrapani en Inde." In *Mélanges de sinologie offerts a Monsieur Paul Demiéville,* 113–59. Paris: Presses Universitaires de France.

Lati Rinbochay and Jeffery Hopkins. (1979). *Death, Intermediate State and Rebirth in Tibetan Buddhism.* Valois, New York: Gabriel/Snow Lion.

La Vallée Poussin, Louis de. (1923–31). *L'Abhịdharmakośa de Vasubandhu.* Rev. ed. 6 vols. Brussels: Institut Belge des Hautes Études Chinoises.

Lessing, F. D., and Alex Wayman. (1980). *Introduction to the Buddhist Tantric Systems by mKhas grub rje.* New York: Samuel Weiser.

Lewis, Todd T. (2000). *Popular Buddhist Texts from Nepal: Narratives and Rituals of Newar Buddhism.* Albany: SUNY Press.

Longchen Rabjam. (1989). *The Practice of Dzogchen.* Ithaca: Snow Lion.

———. (1998). *The Precious Treasury of the Way of Abiding.* Junction City, CA: Padma Publishing.

Lopez, Donald S., Jr., ed. (1995). *Curators of the Buddha: The Study of Buddhism under Colonialism.* Chicago: University of Chicago Press.

———, ed. (1997). *Religions of Tibet in Practice.* Princeton: Princeton University Press.

Macdonald, A. W., ed. (1997). *Mandala and Landscape.* Delhi: DK Printworld.

Manjusrimitra. (1986). *Primordial Experience.* Translated by Namkhai Norbu and Kennard Lipman. Boston: Shambhala Publications.

Mar-pa Chos kyi blo gros. (1995). *The Life of the Mahasiddha Tilopa.* Translated by Fabrizio Toricelli and Acharya Sangye T. Naga. Dharamsala: LTWA.

Martin, Dan. (1982). "The Early Education of Milarepa." *Journal of the Tibet Society* 2: 53–76.

———. (1992). "A Twelfth-Century Tibetan Classic of Mahamudra, the Path of Ultimate Profundity: The Great Seal Instructions of Zhang." *Journal of the International Association of Buddhist Studies* 15 (2): 243–319.

———. (n.d.). "Zhang Rinpoche and the Emergence of Sectarian Polity in Twelfth Century Tibet." Unpublished paper.

Mette, Adelheid. (1976). "Beobachtungen Zur Überlieferungsgeschichte Einiger Lieder Des *Mi La Ras Pa'i Mgur 'Bum.*" *Indo-Iranian Journal* 18: 255–72.

Mullin, Glenn H., trans. (1996). *Tsongkhapa's Six Yogas of Naropa.* Ithaca: Snow Lion.

———. (1997). *Readings on the Six Yogas of Naropa.* Ithaca: Snow Lion.

Nalanda Translation Committee. (1980). *The Rain of Wisdom.* Boulder: Shambhala Publications.

———. (1982). *The Life of Marpa the Translator.* Boulder: Prajna Press.

Namgyal, Takpo Tashi. (1986). *Mahamudra: The Quintessence of Mind and Meditation.* Translated by Lobsang P. Lhalungpa. Boston: Shambhala.

Nam-mkha'i snying-po. (1983). *Mother of Knowledge: The Enlightenment of Ye-shes mTsho-rgyal.* Translated by Tarthang Tulku. Berkeley: Dharma Publishing.

Nebesky-Wojkowitz, René de. (1993). *Oracles and Demons of Tibet: The Cult and Iconography of the Tibetan Protective Deities.* Kathmandu: Tiwari's Pilgrims Book House.

Ngag dbang skal ldan rgya mtsho. (1996). *Shel dKar Chos 'byung: History of the 'White Crystal': Religion and Politics of Southern La Stod.* Edited by Pasang Wangdu and Hildegard Diemberger. Wien: Verlag der Österreichischen Akademie der Wissenschaften.

Norbu, Namkhai. (1995). *Drung, Deu and Bön: Narrations, Symbolic Languages, and the Bön Tradition in Ancient Tibet.* Translated by Andrew Lukianowicz. Dharamsala: Library of Tibetan Works and Archives.

Orofino, Giacomella. (1994). *Sekoddesa: A Critical Edition of the Tibetan Translations.* Rome: Instituto Italiano per il Medio ed Estremo Oriente.

Ortner, Sherry B. (1978). *Sherpas through Their Rituals.* Cambridge: Cambridge University Press.

Petech, Luciano. (1939). *A Study on the Chronicles of Ladakh (Indian Tibet).* Calcutta: Calcutta Oriental Press, 1939.

———. (1973). *Aristocracy and Government in Tibet.* Rome: Istituto Italiano per il Medio ed Estremo Oriente.

———. (1990). *Central Tibet and the Mongols: The Yuan Sa-Skya Period of Tibetan History.* Rome: Istituto Italiano per il Medio ed Estremo Oriente.

Prats, Ramon. (1988). "'The Aspiration-Prayer of the Ground, Path and Goal.' An Inspired Piece on Rdzogs-chen by 'Jigs-med-glin-pa." In *Orientalia Iosephi Tucci Memoriae Dicata*, vol. 3, edited by G. Gnoli and L. Lanciotti, 1159–72. Rome: Istituto Italiano per il Medio ed Estremo Oriente.

———. (1995). "Toward a Comprehensive Classification of rNying-ma Literature." In *IATS*, edited by Ernst Steinkellner, Helmut Krasser, Michael Torsten Much, and Helmut Tauscher, 789–801. Graz, Austria.

Ray, Reginald A. (1994). *Buddhist Saints in India: A Study in Buddhist Values and Orientations.* New York: Oxford University Press.

Reynolds, John M. (2000). *Self-Liberation through Seeing with Naked Awareness.* Ithaca: Snow Lion.

Reynolds, Valrae, Amy Heller, and Janet Gyatso. (1986). *Catalogue of the Newark Museum: Tibetan Collection.* Vol. 3, Sculpture and Painting. Newark: Newark Museum.

Ricard, Matthieu. (1994). *The Life of Shabkar: The Autobiography of a Tibetan Yogin.* Albany: State University of New York Press.

Ricca, Franco, and Erberto Lo Bue. (1993). *The Great Stupa of Gyantse.* London: Serindia Publications.

Roberts, Peter Alan. (2000). "The Biographies of Ras-chung-pa: The Evolution of a Tibetan Hagiography." Doctoral diss., University of Oxford.

Robinson, James. (1979). *Buddha's Lions.* Berkeley: Dharma Publishing.

Roerich, George. (1949–53). *Blue Annals.* 2 vols. Calcutta: Royal Asiatic Society of Bengal.

Ruegg, David S. (1966). *The Life of Bu ston Rin po che.* Rome: Istituto Italiano per il Medio ed Estremo Orente.

———. (1969). *La théorie du Tathagatagarbha et du Gotra: Études sur la sotériologie et la gnoséologie du Bouddhisme.* Paris: École Francaise d'Extrême-Orient.

———. (1995). "The Preceptor-Donor (*yon mchod*) Relation in Thirteenth Century Tibetan Society and Polity, Its Inner Asian Precursors and Indian Models." In *IATS*, edited by Ernst Steinkellner, Helmut Krasser, Michael Torsten Much, and Helmut Tauscher, 857–72.

Samuel, Geoffrey. (1993). *Civilized Shamans: Buddhism in Tibetan Societies.* Washington, DC: Smithsonian Institution Press.

———. (1994). "Ge Sar of Ling: Shamanic Power and Popular Religion." In *Tantra and Popular Religion in Tibet,* edited by Geoffrey Samuel, Hamish Gregor, and Elisabeth Stutchbury, 53–77. New Delhi: Aditya Prakashan.

———. (1995). "The Vajrayana in the Context of Himalayan Folk Religion." In *IATS,* edited by Ernst Steinkellner, Helmut Krasser, Michael Torsten Much, and Helmut Tauscher, 843–50. Graz, Austria.

———. (1996). "Music and Shamanic Power in the Gesar Epic." In *Metaphor: A Musical Dimension,* edited by Jamie Kassler. Sydney: Currency Press.

Samuel, Geoffrey, Hamish Gregor, and Elisabeth Stutchbury, eds. (1994). *Tantra and Popular Religion in Tibet.* Delhi: Aditya Prakashan.

Sanderson, Alexis. (1988). "Saivism and the Tantric Traditions." In *The World's Religions,* edited by Peter Clarke and Stewart R. Sutherland et al., 660–704. London: Routledge and Kegan Paul.

———. (1994). "Vajrayana: Origin and Function." In *Buddhism into the Year 2000: International Conference Proceedings.* Bangkok and Los Angeles: Dhammakaya Foundation.

Sangpo, Khetsun, Rinbochay. (1982). *Tantric Practice in Nying-ma.* Ithaca: Snow Lion.

Scheidegger, Daniel A. (1988). *Tibetan Ritual Music: A General Survey with Special Reference to the Mindroling Tradition.* Switzerland: Opuscula Tibetana Fasc. 19. Tibet-Institut, Rikon.

Schmid, T. (1952). *The Cotton-Clad Mila: The Tibetan Poet-Saint's Life in Pictures.* Stockholm: Statens Etnografiska Museum.

sGam po pa. (1998). *The Jewel Ornament of Liberation: The Wish Fulfilling Gem of the Noble Teachings.* Translated by Khenpo Konchog Gyaltsen Rinpoche. Snow Ithaca: Lion.

Shakabpa, Tsepon. (1967). *A Political History of Tibet.* New Haven: Yale University Press.

Shantideva. (1979). *A Guide to the Bodhisattva's Way of Life.* Translated by Stephen Batchelor. Dharamsala: Library of Tibetan Works and Archives.

Sherab Dorje, trans. (1995). *Mahamudra Teachings of the Supreme Siddhas.* By the Eighth Situpa Ten pa'i Nyinchay. Ithaca: Snow Lion.

Simmer-Brown, Judith. (2001). *Dakini's Warm Breath: The Feminine Principle in Tibetan Buddhism.* Boston: Shambhala Publications.

Sindh, Pancham, trans. (1992). *The Hatha Yoga Pradipika.* New Delhi: Munshiram Manoharlal Publications.

Sivananda, Swami. (1994). *Kundalini Yoga.* Shivanandanagar: Divine Life Society.

Skorupski, Tadeusz. (1994). "The *Samputatantra,* Sanskrit and Tibetan Versions of Chapter One." With "An Overview of the *Samputatantra.*" In *The Buddhist Forum 4,* edited by Tadeusz Skorupski. School of Oriental and African Studies, University of London.

Slusser, Mary. (1982). *Nepal Mandala: A Cultural Study of the Kathmandu Valley.* 2 vols. Princeton: Princeton University Press.

Smith, E. Gene. (1970). *Introduction to Kongtrul's Encyclopedia of Indo-Tibetan Culture,* parts 1–3. Edited by Lokesh Chandra. New Dehli: International Academy of Indian Culture.

———. (2001) *Among Tibetan Texts: History and Literature of the Himalayan Plateau.* Boston: Wisdom Publications.

Snellgrove, David. (1959). *The Hevajra Tantra.* 2 vols. London: Oxford University Press.

———. (1987). *Indo-Tibetan Buddhism: Indian Buddhists and Their Tibetan Successors.* 2 vols. Boston: Shambhala Publications.

Snellgrove, David, and Hugh Richardson. (1986). *A Cultural History of Tibet.* Rev. ed. Boston: Shambhala Publications.

Sobisch, Jan-Ulrich. (1995). "Preliminary Remarks on the Three-Vow Theories (*sdom pa gsum*) of Tibetan Buddhism." In *IATS,* edited by Ernst Steinkellner, Helmut Krasser, Michael Torsten Much, and Helmut Tauscher, 891–902. Graz, Austria.

Stearns, Cyrus. (1999). *The Buddha from Dolpo: A Study of the Life and Thought of the Tibetan Master Dolpopa Sherab Gyaltsen.* Albany: SUNY Press.

Stein, Rolf A. (1959). *Recherches sur l'épopée et le barde au Tibet.* Paris: Presses Universitaires de France.

———. (1962). *La Civilisation Tibétaine.* Paris: Dunod Éditeur.

———. (1972). *Vie et chants de 'Brug-pa Kun-legs le yogin.* Paris: Maisonneuve et Larose.

———. (1981). "Saint et divin, un titre tibetain et chinois des rois tibetains." *Journal Asiatique* 269: 231–75.

Stewart, Jampa Mackenzie. (1995). *The Life of Gampopa.* Ithaca: Snow Lion.

Takasaki, Jikido. (1966). *A Study on the Ratnagotravibhaga (Uttaratantra).* Rome: Istituto Italiano per il Medio ed Estremo Oriente.

Tandar, Sangye, trans. (1995). *The Twelve Deeds: A Brief Life Story of Tonpa Shenrab, the Founder of the Bon Religion.* Dharamsala: Library of Tibetan Works and Archives.

Taranatha, Jo Nang. (1981). *The Origin of the Tara Tantra.* Dharamsala: Library of Tibetan Works and Archives.

———. (1983). *The Seven Instruction Lineages.* Translated and edited by David Templeman. Dharamsala: Library of Tibetan Works and Archives.

Templeman, David. (1995). "Buddhaguptanatha: A Late Indian Siddha in Tibet." In *IATS*, edited by Ernst Steinkellner, Helmut Krasser, Michael Torsten Much, and Helmut Tauscher, 955–65. Graz, Austria.

Tenpa'i Nyinchay, the Eighth Situpa. (1995). *Mahamudra Teachings of the Supreme Siddhas.* Translated by Sherab Dorje. Ithaca: Snow Lion.

Teresa of Avila. (1976). *The Collected Works of St. Teresa of Avila.* Translated by Kieran Kavanaugh and Otilio Rodriguez. Washington, DC: ICS.

Thondup, Tulku. (1984). *The Tantric Tradition of the Nyingmapa, the Origin of Buddhism in Tibet.* Marion: Buddhayana.

———. (1989). *Buddha Mind: An Anthology of Longchen Rabjam's Writings on Dzogpa Chenpo.* Ithaca: Snow Lion.

———. (1996). *Masters of Meditation and Miracles: The Longchen Nyingthig Lineage of Tibetan Buddhism.* Boston: Shambhala.

———. (1997). *Hidden Teachings of Tibet: An Explanation of the Terma Tradition of Tibetan Buddhism.* Boston: Wisdom.

Thurman, Robert A. F. (1976). *The Holy Teachings of Vimalakirti.* University Park, PA: Pennsylvania State University Press.

Tiso, Francis V. (1989). "A Study of the Buddhist Saint in Relation to the Biographical Tradition of Milarepa." PhD diss. (UMI 8919193), Columbia University, New York.

———. (1992). "The rDo Rje 'Chang rNam Thar in the Bka' Brgyud Gser 'Phreng Genre." In *Tibetan Studies: Proceedings of the 6th Seminar of the International Association for Tibetan Studies,* 884–88. Oslo, Norway: Institute for Comparative Research in Human Culture.

———. (1994). "The Religion of Milarepa before His Conversion." In *The Notion of Religion in Comparative Research: Selected Proceedings of the XVI IAHR Congress (1990),* edited by Ugo Bianchi. L' Erma di Bretschneider: Roma.

———. (1995). "Ultimate Reality and the Experience of Nirvana: Liberation in the Vajrayana." *Pro Dialogo* 90 (3): 300–11.

———. (1996a). "The Biographical Tradition of Mi la ras pa: Orality, Literacy and Iconography." *Tibet Journal* 21 (2).

———. (1996b). *Mil la ras pa: La Tradizione Biografica.* Unpublished manuscript, Isernia.

———. (1997). 'The Death of Mi la ras pa: Toward a *Redaktionsgeschichte* of the *Mi la rnam thar* Traditions." In *IATS,* edited by Ernst Steinkellner, Helmut Krasser, Michael Torsten Much, and Helmut Tauscher. Graz, Austria.

———. (1998). "In Search of the Voice of Milarepa: Songs and Teachings of Tibet's Great Yogin." In *8th Seminar of the International Association for Tibetan Studies,* July 25–31. Research Institute for Inner Asian Studies, Goodbody Hall, Bloomington.

Tiso, Francis V., and José Pereira. (1988). "The Evolution of Buddhist Systematics from the Buddha to Vasubandhu." *Philosophy East and West* 38 (2):172–86.

Tiso, Francis V., and Fabrizio Torricelli. (1991). The Tibetan Text of Tilopa's *Mahamudropadesa. East and West* (IsMEO) 41 (1–4): 205–29.

Torricelli, Fabrizio. (1995). "Two Anonymous Texts in the bsTan-'gyur." *East and West* 45 (1–4): 371–74.

———. (1998a). "A Thirteenth Century Tibetan Hymn to the Siddha Tilopa." *Tibet Journal* 23 (1).

———. (1998b). "The Tibetan Text of the *Karnatantravajrapada*." *East and West* 48 (3–4): 385–423.

Tsele Natsok Rangdröl. (1987). *The Mirror of Mindfulness: The Cycle of the Four Bardos.* Hong Kong: Rangjung Yeshe Publications.

———. (1989). *Lamp of Mahamudra.* Boston: Shambhala.

———. (1993). *Empowerment and the Path of Liberation.* Hong Kong: Rangjung Yeshe Publications.

Tsong-Kha-pa. (1977). *Tantra in Tibet: The Great Exposition of Secret Mantra.* Translated by Jeffrey Hopkins. London: George Allen and Unwin.

———. (1981). *The Yoga of Tibet: The Great Exposition of Secret Mantra.* Translated by Jeffrey Hopkins. London: George Allen and Unwin.

Tsultrim Gyamtso Rinpoche. (1994). *Comparison of Views and Four Songs of Milarepa.* Kathmandu: Karma Ling Summer University, Marpa Institute.

Tucci, Giuseppe. (1949). *Tibetan Painted Scrolls.* 3 vols. Rome: Libreria dello Stato.

———. (1956). *To Lhasa and Beyond.* Rome: Libreria dello Stato.

———. (1958). *Minor Buddhist Texts,* Part II. Rome: Istituto Italiano per il Medio ed Estremo Oriente.

———. (1972). *Il Libro Tibetano dei Morti (Bardo Tödöl).* Torino: UTET.

———. (1980). *The Religions of Tibet.* Translated by Geoffrey Samuel. Berkeley: University of California Press.

Urubshurow, Victoria Kennick. (1984). "Symbolic Processes on the Buddhist Path: Spiritual Development in the Biographical Tradition of Milarepa." PhD diss., University of Chicago.

Van Tuyl, Charles. (1972). "An Analysis of Chapter Twenty Eight of the Hundred Thousand Songs of Milarepa, a Buddhist Poet and Saint of Tibet." PhD diss., Indiana University.

Vasu, Rai Bahadur Srisa Chandra, trans. (1979). *The Siva Samhita*. New Delhi: Oriental Books Reprint Corp.

Vitali, Roberto. (1995). "Nomads of Byang and Mnga'-ris-smad: A Historical Overview of Their Interaction in Gro-shod, 'Brong-pa, Glo-bo and Gung-thang from the 11th to the 15th Century." In *IATS*, edited by Ernst Steinkellner, Helmut Krasser, Michael Torsten Much, and Helmut Tauscher, 1023–36. Graz, Austria.

———. (1996). *The Kingdoms of Gu.ge Pu.hrang: according to mNga'.ris rgyal.rabs by Gu.ge mkhan.chen Ngag.dbang grags.pa*. Dharamsala, India: Tho.ling.gtsug.lag.khang lo.gcig.stong 'khor.ba'i rjes.dran. mdzad sgo'i go.sgrig tshogs.chung.

Vostrikov, A. I. (1970). *Tibetan Historical Literature*. Translated by Harish Chandra Gupta. Calcutta: Indian Studies Past and Present.

Walshe, Maurice. (1987). *Thus Have I Heard: The Long Discourses of the Buddha: A Translation of the Digha Nikaya*. London: Wisdom Publications.

Wang Ch'ug Dor je, the Ninth Karmapa. (1978). *The Mahamudra Eliminating the Darkness of Ignorance*. Translated by Alexander Berzin. Dharamsala: Library of Tibetan Works and Archives.

Wayman, Alex. (1959). "The Twenty-One Praises of Tara: A Syncretism of Shaivism and Buddhism." *Journal of the Bihar Research Society* 45: 1–4.

———. (1961). *Analysis of the Sravakabhumi Manuscript*. University of California Publications in Classical Philology, vol. 17. Berkeley: University of California Press.

———. (1973). *The Buddhist Tantras: Light on Indo-Tibetan Esotericism*. New York: Samuel Weiser.

———. (1977). *Yoga of the Guhyasamaja Tantra: The Arcane Lore of Forty Verses. A Buddhist Tantra Commentary.* Delhi: Motilal Banarsidass.

———. (1997). "Asanga on Food." In *Untying the Knots in Buddhism: Selected Essays,* 335–67. Delhi: Motilal Banarsidass.

White, David G. (2000). *Tantra in Practice.* Princeton: University of Princeton Press.

Williams, Paul. (1989). *Mahayana Buddhism: The Doctrinal Foundations.* London: Routledge.

Willis, Janice D. (1987). "Dakini: Some Comments on Its Nature and Meaning." In *Feminine Ground: Essays on Women and Tibet,* edited by Janice D. Willis, 57–75. Ithaca: Snow Lion.

———. (1995). *Enlightened Beings: Life Stories from the Ganden Oral Tradition.* Boston: Wisdom Publications.

Wylie, Turrell V. (1962). *The Geography of Tibet According to the 'Dzam-gling-rgyas-bshad.* Rome: Istituto Italiano per il Medio ed Estremo Oriente.

———. (1963). "Mar-pa's Tower: Notes on Local Hegemonies in Tibet." *History of Religions* 3: 278–91.

———. (1977). "The First Mongol Conquest of Tibet Reinterpreted." *Harvard Journal of Asiatic Studies* 37: 103–33.

Young, Serinity. (1999). *Dreaming the Lotus: Buddhist Dream Narrative, Imagery, and Practice.* Boston: Wisdom Publications.

C. Recordings and Interviews

A visit to the *lha khang* of Gakar Gompa, Tarap-Dho, Dolpo with Lama Norbu Tsering, Lama Karma Angya, Lama Tsering Tashi, and Lama Kartse; Lama Khartse begins recitation of the *Mila rnam thar,* Nepal, May 29, 1997.

Courte Pratique de Chakrasamvara en union: Par sa Sainteté Gyalwang Drukpa, Centre Bouddhique Drukpa Kargyu, Plouray, France (n.d.).

Francis V. Tiso, Lecture on Milarepa and Spiritual Practice, Burlingame, CA, March 25, 2000.

H. E. Khandro Rinpoche, Mussorie, India, April 15, 1997.

H. E. Shenpen Dawa Rinpoche, *Nature of Mind Teachings*, Yeshe Melong Media and Archives, Orgyen Dorje Den, San Francisco, November 1995.

H. E. Trungram Gyaltrul Rinpoche (Sherpa lama who is believed to be an emanation of Milarepa), Kathmandu, Nepal, June 27, 1997.

H. H., the Fourteenth Dalai Lama, Dharamsala, India, July 23, 1997.

H. H. Drikung Kyabgon (Chetsang Rinpoche), Dehra Dun, India, April 14, 1997.

Karma Thinley Rinpoche, Kathmandu, Nepal, April 2, 1997.

Lama Khartse completes the fourth chapter of the *rnam thar* of Milarepa (May 29, 1997); Lama Ngawang Chöpel of Jampa Lhakhang recites the *Ras chung pa rnam thar*, Tarap-Dho, Dolpo, Nepal, May 30, 1997.

Lama Khartse recites four chapters of the *Milarepa rnam thar* at Gakar Gompa, Tarap-Dho, Dolpo, Nepal, May 29, 1997.

Lama Namgyal of Ri Bum Gompa, Tarap Dho, Dolpo, on the history of Buddhism in Dolpo; Zab tig and Chöd practice, Nepal, May 30, 1997.

Lama Norbu Tsering interviewed on his life and spiritual practices at Pokhara, Nepal, Tibetan Refugee Camp, February 22, 1997.

Lama Norbu Tsering sings selections from the *Mila rnam thar mgur 'bum* at Pokhara, Nepal (Tibetan Refugee Camp), February 19, 1997.

Lama Norbu Tsering sings the Guru Rinpoche Chen Den prayer from the "*Zab thig*" cycle, Pokhara, Nepal, June 8, 1997.

Lama Yeshe of Samye Ling, Scotland, lecturing on the fundamentals of Buddhist tantra in the Karma Kagyu tradition, Rome, Italy (n.d.).

Monks of Ngagyur Nyingma Institute and Palyul Namdroling Monastery, *Musical Highlights from Khen Lob Chö Sum*, 1997.

Monks Umdzé and Sonam Tsegyal sing the *Mila mgur 'bum* (selections) at Drikung Kagyu Institute, Dehra Dun, India, April 14, 1997.

Rituel du Bouddhisme Tantrique: Sangyé Menla, Éditions Marpa, Château de Plaige, La Boulaye, France (n.d.).

Tibetan folksongs sung by monks Tupden Khechok and Sangye Lama, Kathmandu, Nepal, June 15 and 17, 1997.

Tiso, Francis V. "A Catholic Priest Looks at Tibetan Buddhism and Inter-religious Dialogue." (A lecture). Dharamsala, India, July, 1997.

Ven. Khenpo Tsultrim Gyatso, Boudhanath, Nepal, April 2, 1997.

Index

B

C

D

E

H

I

J

K

M

P

Q

R

S

W

Y

Z

About the Author

Father Francis V. Tiso was Associate Director of the Secretariat for Ecumenical and Interreligious Affairs of the U.S. Conference of Catholic Bishops from 2004 to 2009, where he served as liaison to Islam, Hinduism, Buddhism, the Sikhs, and Traditional religions as well as the Reformed confessions. He served as Parochial Vicar of St. Thomas More Church in San Francisco and as Chaplain at San Francisco State University and the University of California Medical School. He was also Visiting Professor in the Archdiocesan School of Pastoral Leadership and Parochial Vicar in Eureka, California, and in Mill Valley, California.

Father Tiso holds a Master of Divinity degree from Harvard University and a doctorate from Columbia University and Union Theological Seminary where his specialization was Buddhist studies. He is a priest of the Diocese of Isernia-Venafro, Italy. He has led research expeditions in South Asia, Tibet, and the Far East and is the recipient of grants from the American Academy of Religion, the American Philosophical Society, the Palmers Fund in Switzerland, and the Institute of Noetic Sciences in Petaluma, California. He is a member of the Mind and Life Institute in Europe, sponsored by His Holiness the Dalai Lama.